METHUEN LIBRARY REPRINTS

SBN/416 32510 6/33

THE COMPLETE WORKS
OF
WALTER SAVAGE LANDOR

—

VOLUME XIII

WALTER SAVAGE LANDOR, AGE 29.
By George Dance, R.A

From a photograph by Emery Walker Ltd., from the original painting.

Poems I.

THE
COMPLETE WORKS
OF
WALTER SAVAGE
LANDOR

VOLUME XIII
POEMS

EDITED BY
STEPHEN WHEELER

I

BARNES & NOBLE, Inc.
New York
METHUEN & CO. Ltd
London

This edition, published in 1969

by Barnes & Noble, Inc., New York
and Methuen & Co., Ltd. London

is reproduced from the edition
published by Chapman & Hall, Ltd.
between 1927 and 1936

Manufactured in the United States of America

PREFACE

LANDOR's English poems are being printed, in this edition of his *Works*, for the most part as they were first published during his lifetime or after his death at Florence in September, 1864. In a few cases, for reasons which will be stated, a version later than the earliest is chosen as the text preferred; but whether one or the other method be adopted, variants are recorded either on the page where they occur or, if so extensive as to render that plan inconvenient, they will be found at the end of the volume. Whatever objections are felt to thus relying so much on first editions, that is what Swinburne recommended as the best way of dealing with Landor's work. To judge what might sometimes be lost by always adopting exactly the opposite course let the reader turn to a little poem in which Landor referred to Dante of Maiano and the more illustrious author of *La Divina Commedia*—"the diviner Alighieri" is the phrase as first printed. Barely a dozen years after Landor's death this was transformed into "the diviner Alfieri". Amazing as it was, the blunder has always escaped notice.

Poems have before now been attributed to the author of *Gebir* which were certainly not written by him. They will of course have no place in these volumes. There are a few others firmly believed by not inexpert critics to be his, but without positive proof that he wrote them. They must likewise be excluded unless, indeed, evidence more convincing than has hitherto been adduced is brought to light before the last volume of this edition is delivered from the press.

Most of the poems rejected on the grounds just indicated were found in periodicals, in books by other authors, or on printed leaflets. In one notable instance two of them, said to be copied from a manuscript, in Landor's handwriting, were published in an American magazine; and a facsimile reproduction of the manuscript was given as evidence that Landor was really the author. Any one capable of recognizing his style would have suspected a deception—innocent or deliberate; and the script of the fallacious illustration was not Landor's.

With regard to poems undoubtedly his but only preserved in his autograph manuscript, it has not been thought proper to ignore opinions he expressed in the preface to a book of poetry published in 1831. Only the wretchedest of poets, he declared, would wish all they ever wrote to be remembered. He strongly condemned the exhumation of mere garbage from the pens of Swift and Dryden. He hoped that much of what he had written in youth or with equal idleness afterward would never be raked together for publication. Such an inhibition need not be

PREFACE

enough to prevent some unpublished manuscripts being printed. It is here cited, however, as not unlikely to serve, with other and perhaps stronger deterrents, as a fairly valid excuse for any omissions detected in the forthcoming volumes.

Among heroic poems in Volume I are three which till now have been classed as "Hellenics". The substance and treatment of these compositions may warrant their transfer to a section which would otherwise afford too scanty means of judging Landor's success in writing heroic verse. "Hellenics" proper and what he styled heroic idylls will be in Volume II.

For footnotes and notes at the end of Volumes I–IV to which the initial [W] is attached the present writer who is editing Landor's English poems is responsible.

STEPHEN WHEELER.

CONTENTS OF VOLUME I

Section 1. HEROIC POEMS

Section 2. DRAMAS AND DRAMATIC SCENES

NOTES

HEROIC POEMS
GEBIR
A POEM IN SEVEN BOOKS

[Published in 1798; revised and so published 1803, reprinted 1831, 1846. A portion
ll. 60–254 of Book I, reprinted 1859. Latin version, "Gebirus", published 1803, reprinted
1847. See notes at end of volume. Text 1803.]

PRINCIPAL CHARACTERS

GEBIR . . . King of GADES	MYRTHYR . . Sister of DALICA
TAMAR . . . his Brother	NYMPH . . betrothed to TAMAR
CHAROBA . . . Queen of EGYPT	EGYPTIAN AMBASSADORS
DALICA . . . her Nurse	

ARGUMENT

GEBIR, his habitation and habits. Alarms of *Charoba*—imparted to *Dalica*—
Dalica's reply. The Queen's expostulation, and compliance—her interview with *Gebir*
Gebir returning, meets his brother *Tamar*—*Tamar* describes his wrestling with a
Nymph. *Her* victory, and promise. *His* regret and shame. *Gebir's* sympathy—his
determination to remain in *Egypt*, and to restore the city which *Sidad*, his ancestor,
had founded.

GEBIR
BOOK I

WHEN old Silenus call'd the Satyrs home,
Satyrs then tender-hooft and ruddy-horn'd,
With Bacchus and the Nymphs, he sometimes rose
Amidst the tale or pastoral, and shew'd
The light of purest wisdom; and the God
Scatter'd with wholesome fruit the pleasant plains.
　Ye woody vales of Cambria! and ye hills
That hide in heaven your summits and your fame!*
Your ancient songs, and breezes pure, invite
Me from my noon-tide rambles, and the force　　　　　10
Of high example influences my lay.
　I sing the fates of Gebir! how he dwelt
Among those mountain-caverns, which retain
His labours yet, vast halls, and flowing wells,

* In the first edition, it was improperly printed *name*. I believe, almost every hill
in that country has its descriptive name; and it often happens that the name alone is
remaining of its history, and the history is apparently that of some preternatural
personage. This explains the words "hide in heaven". [L. *footnote only in 1803.*]

Principal characters. *Only in 1803.*　Argument. *Only in 1803.*　ll. 1–11
om. 1831, 1846　A poem in "*Hellenics*" (see ii. 351) *begins in much the same way.*
1 Silenus [*A note in "*Gebirus*" refers to Virgil, Eclogue vi, 31.*]　8 fame] name
1798.　12 how he] He had *1831, 1846.*

Nor have forgotten their old master's name,*
Though sever'd from his people: how, incens'd
By meditating on primeval wrongs, †
He blew his battle-horn, at which uprose
Whole nations: how, ten thousand, mightiest men,
He call'd aloud; and soon Charoba saw   20
His dark helm hover o'er the land of Nile.
   What should the damsel do? should royal knees
Bend suppliant? or defenceless hands engage
Men of gigantic force, gigantic arms?
For, 'twas reported, that nor sword sufficed,
Nor shield immense,'nor coat of massive mail;
But, that upon their tow'ring heads they bore
Each a huge stone, refulgent as the stars.
This told she Dalica—then earnest cried
"If, on your bosom laying down my head,   30
I sobb'd away the sorrows of a child;
If I have always, and Heav'n knows I have,
Next to a mother's held a nurse's name,
Succour this one distress! recall those days;
Love me; though 'twere because you lov'd me then."
   But, whether confident in magic rites;
Or touch'd with sexual pride to stand implored,
Dalica smiled; then spake: "Away those fears.
Tho' stronger than the strongest of his kind,
He falls; on me devolve that charge; he falls.   40
Rather than fly him, stoop thou to allure,
Nay, journey to his tents: a city stood
Upon that coast, they say, by Sidad built,
Whose father Gad built Gades; on this ground
Perhaps he sees an ample room for war.
Persuade him to restore the walls himself,
In honor of his ancestors, persuade—

---

  * Tho' *Gibraltar* may not in strict etymology be derived from *Gebir,* nor even be
correlative, yet the fiction, as it does not violate probability, is just as pardonable
as the Teucro-latin names in Virgil. [L. *only in 1803. See notes at end of vol.*]
  † Primeval wrongs—in not possessing, as it appears his ancestors had, the throne
of Egypt. [L. *footnote only in 1803.*]

---

  16 how] here *1831, 1846.*   19 how] here *1831, 1846.*   mightiest men] of
most might *1798, 1831, 1846.*   22 damsel] virgin *1831, 1846.*   23 defenceless]
defenseless *1831.*   27 tow'ring] towering *1846.*   29 earnest cried] cried aloud
1831, 1846.   34 recall] recal *1798.*   37 touch'd] toucht *1831, 1846.*   43–44
Sidad . . . Gad [*see note at end of vol.*]   44 Gades] Gadir *1831, 1846.*   47 honor]
honour *1831, 1846.*

2

But wherefor this advice? young, unespoused,
Charoba want persuasions! and a queen!" *
  "O Dalica!" the shudd'ring maid exclaim'd,   50
"Could I encounter that fierce frightful man?
Could I speak? no, nor sigh!" "And canst thou reign?"
Cried Dalica; "yield empire or comply."
    Unfixt, though seeming fixt, her eyes down-cast,
The wonted buz and bustle of the court
From far, through sculptur'd galleries, met her ear;
Then lifting up her head, the evening sun
Pour'd a fresh splendor on her burnish'd throne,—
The fair Charoba, the young queen, complied.
    But Gebir, when he heard of her approach,   60
Laid by his orbed shield, his vizor-helm,
His buckler and his corslet he laid by,
And bade that none attend him: at his side
Two faithful dogs that urge the silent course,
Shaggy, deep-chested, crouched: the crocodile,
Crying, oft made them raise their flaccid ears,
And push their heads within their master's hand.
There was a bright'ning paleness in his face,
Such as Diana rising o'er the rocks
Shower'd on the lonely Latmian; on his brow   70
Sorrow there was, yet nought was there severe.
But when the royal damsel first he saw,
Faint, hanging on her handmaids, and her knees
Tott'ring, as from the motion of the car,
His eyes looked earnest on her; and those eyes
Shew'd, if they had not, that they might have lov'd,
For there was pity in them at that hour.
With gentle speech, and more, with gentle looks,
He sooth'd her; but, lest Pity go beyond,
And crost Ambition lose her lofty aim,   80
Bending, he kiss'd her garment, and retir'd.
He went: nor slumber'd in the sultry noon,

---

* Dalica, to discover the sentiments of the Queen, makes an indirect proposal of
an union with Gebir; to which she not only objects, but at first refuses to hold any
conference with him. [L. *footnote only in 1803.*]

---

48 wherefor] wherefore *1798, 1846.*   50 shudd'ring] shuddering *1831, 1846.*
55 buz] buzz *1846.*   58 splendor] splendour *1831, 1846.*   60 But . . . her] Gebir,
at Egypt's youthful queen's *1859.*   62 corslet] corset *1831–1859.*   67 *see
notes at end of vol.*   74 Tott'ring] Tottering *1831–1859.*   76 Shew'd] Show'd
1798.   *l.* 80 *not in 1798.*   81 kiss'd] kist *1831–1859.*

When viands rich, and generous wines persuade,
And slumber most refreshes; nor at night,
When heavy dews are laden with disease;
And blindness waits not there for lingering age.
Ere morning dawn'd behind him, he arrived
At those rich meadows where young Tamar fed
The royal flocks, entrusted to his care.
Now, said he to himself, will I repose   90
At least this burden on a brother's breast:
His brother stood before him: he, amaz'd,
Rear'd suddenly his head, and thus began.
"Is it thou, brother! Tamar, is it thou!
Why, standing on the valley's utmost verge,
Lookest thou on that dull and dreary shore
Where many a league Nile blackens all the sand.
And why that sadness? when I passed our sheep
The dew-drops were not shaken off the bar,
Therefor if one be wanting 'tis untold.*   100
     "Yes! one is wanting, nor is that untold,"
Said Tamar, "and this dull and dreary shore
Is neither dull nor dreary at all hours."
Whereon, the tear stole silent down his cheek.
Silent, but not by Gebir unobserv'd:
Wondering he gazed awhile, and pitying spake:—
"Let me approach thee: does the morning light
Scatter this wan suffusion o'er thy brow,
This faint blue lustre under both thine eyes?"
"O, brother, is this pity or reproach,"   110
Cried Tamar,—"cruel if it be reproach,
If pity—O how vain!"
                    "Whate'er it be
That grieves thee, I will pity; thou but speak,
And I can tell thee, Tamar, pang for pang."
     "Gebir! then more than brothers are we now!
Every thing—take my hand—will I confess.
I neither feed the flock, nor watch the fold;
How can I, lost in love? But, Gebir, why
That anger which has risen to your cheek?

83 viands rich ... generous] viands rich, and gen'rous *1798*; viands, couches, generous
1831–1859. *Edd. 1846, 1859 have comma after* wines. 86 lingering] ling'ring
1798. 88 where] were *text,* where *errata 1798.* 91 burden] burthen *1831–1859.*
97 many a league] beyond sight *1846, 1859.* 100 Therefor] Therefore *1798, 1846,
1859.* untold*] *for note only in 1803 see notes at end of vol.* 104 Whereon] Wheron
1831. 109 lustre] luster *1831.*

4

Can other men? Could you? What, no reply!   120
And still more anger, and still worse conceal'd!
Are these your promises; your pity this?"
 "Tamar, I well may pity what I feel—
Mark me aright—I feel for thee—proceed—
Relate me all." "Then will I all relate."
Said the young shepherd, gladden'd from his heart.
"'Twas evening, though not sun-set, and spring-tide*
Level with these green meadows, seem'd still higher;
'Twas pleasant: and I loosen'd from my neck
The pipe you gave me, and began to play.   130
O that I ne'er had learnt the tuneful art!
It always brings us enemies or love!
Well, I was playing—when above the waves
Some swimmer's head methought I saw ascend;
I, sitting still, survey'd it, with my pipe
Awkwardly held before my lips half-clos'd.
Gebir! it was a nymph! a nymph divine!
I cannot wait describing how she came,
How I was sitting, how she first assum'd
The sailor: of what happened, there remains   140
Enough to say, and too much to forget.
The sweet deceiver stept upon this bank
Before I was aware; for, with surprize
Moments fly rapid as with love itself.
Stooping to tune afresh the hoarsen'd reed,
I heard a rustling; and where that arose
My glance first lighted on her nimble feet.
Her feet resembled those long shells explored†
By him who to befriend his steeds' dim sight
Would blow the pungent powder in their eye.—   150
Her eyes too! O immortal Gods! her eyes
Resembled—what could they resemble—what
Ever resemble those! E'en her attire
Was not of wonted woof nor vulgar art:
Her mantle shew'd the yellow samphire-pod,
Her girdle, the dove-color'd wave serene.

121 still . . . still] stil . . . stil *1831–1859.* 124 proceed] procede *1831* 127 spring-tide*] the tide *1846, 1859. For footnote in 1803, 1831, see notes at end of vol.* 128 still] stil *1831;* yet *1846, 1859.* 134 methought] *mispr.* methough *1798.* 140 sailor] [*The Latin version has* simulans velut esset nauta. W.] 148† *for footnote see notes at end of vol.* 149 steeds'] steed's *1831–1859.* 150 their] the *1831–1859.* 153 E'en] Even *1846, 1859.* 156 dove-color'd] *see notes at end of vol.* -color'd] -colour'd *1831, 1846.*

"Shepherd," said she, "and will you wrestle now,
And with the sailor's hardier race engage*?"
I was rejoiced to hear it, and contrived
How to keep up contention;—could I fail   160
By pressing not too strongly, still to press.
"Whether a shepherd, as indeed you seem,
Or whether of the hardier race you boast,
I am not daunted, no: I will engage."
"But first," said she, "what wager will you lay?"
"A sheep," I answered, "add whate'er you will."
"I cannot," she replied, "make that return:
Our hided vessels, in their pitchy round,
Seldom, unless from rapine, hold a sheep.
But I have sinuous shells, of pearly hue   170
Within, and they that lustre have imbibed
In the sun's palace porch; where, when unyoked,
His chariot wheel stands midway in the wave.
Shake one, and it awakens; then apply
Its polished lips to your attentive ear,
And it remembers its august abodes,
And murmurs as the ocean murmurs there.
And I have others given me by the nymphs,
Of sweeter sound than any pipe you have.—
But we, by Neptune, for no pipe contend;   180
This time a sheep I win, a pipe the next."
Now came she forward, eager to engage;
But, first her dress, her bosom then, survey'd,
And heav'd it, doubting if she could deceive.
Her bosom seem'd, inclos'd in haze like heav'n,
To baffle touch; and rose forth undefined.
Above her knees she drew the robe succinct,
Above her breast, and just below her arms:
"This will preserve my breath, when tightly bound,
If struggle and equal strength should so constrain."   190
Thus, pulling hard to fasten it, she spoke,
And, rushing at me, closed. I thrill'd throughout
And seem'd to lessen and shrink up with cold.
Again, with violent impulse gushed my blood;
And hearing nought external, thus absorb'd,

158 *Tamar, tho' aware of her sex, affects, from the character she assumed, to consider
her as a sailor, that he might with more propriety accept her challenge. [L. *only in 1803.*]
161 still] yet *1831–1859*; press.] press? *1831–1859.*   170 hue] hue† *1859 with footnote for which see end of vol.*   173 chariot] charriot *1798.*   187 knees] knee
1846, 1859.   190 [*See footnote to l. 226 at end of vol.*]   191 spoke] spake *1831–1859.*

6

I heard it, rushing through each turbid vein,
Shake my unsteady swimming sight in air.
Yet with unyielding though uncertain arms,
I clung around her neck; the vest beneath
Rustled against our slippery limbs entwined: 200
Often mine, springing with eluded force,
Started aside, and trembled, till replaced.
And when I most succeeded, as I thought,
My bosom and my throat felt so comprest
That life was almost quivering on my lips,
Yet nothing was there painful! these are signs
Of secret arts, and not of human might,
What arts I cannot tell: I only know
My eyes grew dizzy, and my strength decay'd,
I was indeed o'ercome!—with what regret,   210
And more, with what confusion, when I reached
The fold, and yielding up the sheep, she cried,
"This pays a shepherd to a conquering maid."
She smil'd, and more of pleasure than disdain
Was in her dimpled chin, and liberal lip,
And eyes that languished, lengthening,—just like love.
She went away: I, on the wicker gate
Lean'd, and could follow with my eyes alone.
The sheep she carried easy as a cloak.
But when I heard its bleating, as I did,   220
And saw, she hastening on, its hinder feet
Struggle, and from her snowy shoulder slip,
(One shoulder its poor efforts had unveil'd,)
Then, all my passions mingling fell in tears!
Restless then ran I to the highest ground
To watch her; she was gone; gone down the tide;*
And the long moon-beam on the hard wet sand
Lay like a jaspar column half uprear'd."
   "But, Tamar! tell me, will she not return?"
"She will return: but not before the moon   230
Again is at the full; she promis'd this;
But when she promis'd I could not reply."
   "By all the Gods! I pity thee! go on—
Fear not my anger, look not on my shame;

  202 till] til *1831*.   203 succeeded] succeded *1831*.   216 languished] languisht
1846, 1859.   218 Lean'd] Leant *1831–1859*.   226 down the tide;*] down to the tide *1798*.
For footnote only in 1803 see end of vol.   228 jaspar] jasper *1798, 1831–1859*.   230 but]
yet *1831–1859*.   231 the] its *1798*.   232 But] Tho' *1831–1859*.   231, 232 promis'd]
promist *1846, 1859*.

For, when a lover only hears of love,
He finds his folly out, and is ashamed.
Away with watchful nights, and lonely days,
Contempt of earth, and aspect up to heaven,
With contemplation, with humility,—
A tatter'd cloak that pride wears when deform'd—   240
Away with all that hides me from myself,
Parts me from others, whispers I am wise—
From our own wisdom less is to be reaped
Than from the barest folly of our friend.
Tamar! thy pastures, large and rich, afford
Flowers to thy bees, and herbage to thy sheep,
But, battened on too much, the poorest croft
Of thy poor neighbour yields what thine denies."
    They hastened to the camp; and Gebir there
—Resolved his native country to forego—   250
Ordered, that from those ruins to their right
They forthwith raise a city: Tamar heard
With wonder, though in passing 'twas half-told,
His brother's love; and sigh'd upon his own.

END OF BOOK THE FIRST

243 reaped] reapt *1831–1859*.   250 forego] forgo *1831*.   251 Ordered, that]
And order'd [ordered *1831*] *1831–1859*. their] the *1831–1859*.

THE SECOND BOOK OF *GEBIR*

ARGUMENT

On the seventh morning the works are miraculously destroyed. *Gebir* exhorts his soldiers to deprecate the wrath of heaven. Proposes to *Tamar*, now the time draws near when the *Nymph* was again to meet him, that he himself should assume the brother's habit, and contend with her thus disguised. *Tamar* reluctant,—misinterprets the motive,—is satisfied,—complies. *Gebir* meets the *Nymph*—contends—conquers. Reasons suggested why the *Nymph* failed. Her astonishment—alarm—indignation—entreaty—reproach—and submission. Consoled—discovers to *Gebir* how the city is destroyed—prescribes a ceremony. He performs it. The earth opens—he descends.

GEBIR

BOOK II

THE Gadite men the royal charge obey.
Now fragments, weigh'd up from th' uneven streets,
Leave the ground black beneath; again the sun
Shines into what were porches, and on steps
Once warm with frequentation—clients, friends,

Argument only in 1803.

8

GEBIR: BOOK II

All morning, satchel'd idlers all mid-day,
Lying half-up, and languid, though at games.
  Some raise the painted pavement, some on wheels
Draw slow its laminous length, some intersperse
Salt waters thro' the sordid heaps, and seize   10
The flowers and figures starting fresh to view.
Others rub hard large masses, and essay
To polish into white what they misdeem
The growing green of many trackless years.*
Far off, at intervals, the ax resounds
With regular strong stroke, and nearer home
Dull falls the mallet with long labor fringed.
Here, arches are discover'd, there, huge beams
Resist the hatchet, but in fresher air
Soon drop away: there lies a marble, squar'd   20
And smoothen'd; some high pillar, for its base,
Chose it, which now lies ruin'd in the dust.
Clearing the soil at bottom, they espy
A crevice: they, intent on treasure, strive
Strenuous, and groan, to move it: one exclaims
"I hear the rusty metal grate: it moves!"
Now, overturning it, backward they start;
And stop again, and see a serpent pant,
See his throat thicken, and the crisped scales
Rise ruffled; while upon the middle fold   30
He keeps his wary head and blinking eye,
Curling more close, and crouching ere he strike.
Go mighty men, and ruin cities, go—
And be such treasure portions to your heirs.
  Six days they labor'd: on the seventh day
Returning, all their labors were destroyed.
'Twas not by mortal hand, or from their tents
'Twere visible; for these were now removed
Above, where neither noxious mist ascends,
Nor the way wearies ere the work begin.   40
There Gebir, pierced with sorrow, spake these words.

---

* "The growing green, &c." There was found the *Verde Antico* in this country.
[L. *not in 1798*; *The *Verde Antico* is of this country *1831*; **Verde Antico* is found
here *1846*.]

---

15 ax] axe *1846*. 17 labor] labour *1831, 1846*. 20 lies] spreads *1831, 1846*.
25 exclaims] exclames *1831*. 33 and ruin] invade far *1831, 1846*. 35 labor'd]
labour'd *1798, 1831, 1846*. 36 labors] labours *1798, 1831, 1846*.

"Ye men of Gades, armed with brazen shields;
And ye of near Tartessus, where the shore
Stoops to receive the tribute which all owe
To Bœtis, and his banks, for their attire;
Ye too whom Durius bore on level meads!
Inherent in your hearts is bravery;
For earth contains no nation where abounds
The generous horse and not the warlike man.
But neither soldier, now, nor steed, avails!   50
Nor steed nor soldier can oppose the Gods;
Nor is there aught above like Jove himself,
Nor weighs against his purpose, when once fixt,
Aught but, with supplicating knee, the Prayers.
Swifter than light are they; and every face
Though different, glows with beauty: at the throne
Of mercy, when clouds shut it from mankind,
They fall bare-bosom'd; and indignant Jove
Drops, at the soothing sweetness of their voice,
The thunder from his hand. Let us arise   60
On these high places, daily, beat our breast,
Prostrate ourselves, and deprecate his wrath."
    The people bow'd their bodies and obey'd.
Nine mornings, with white ashes on their heads,
Lamented they their toil each night o'erthrown.
And now the largest orbit of the year,*
Leaning o'er black Mocattam's rubied brow,†
Proceeded slow, majestic, and serene:
Now seem'd not further than the nearest cliff,
And crimson light struck soft the phosphor wave.   70
Then Gebir spake to Tamar in these words:—
"Tamar! I am thy elder, and thy king,
But am thy brother too, nor ever said,
'Give me thy secret, and become my slave;'
But haste thee not away: I will myself
Await the nymph, disguised in thy attire."

  * "The largest orbit of the year," what we call the *harvest-moon*. [L. *footnote only in 1803.*]
  † "Black Mocattam's rubied brow." ["Black . . . brow." *om. 1831, 1846.*]
Mocattam is itself of the plural number, and [is . . . and *om. 1831*] is a
ridge of mountains which forms [which forms *om. 1831*] the boundary of Egypt.
[Mocattam . . . Egypt *om. 1846.*]   "Rubied brow." [". . ." *om. 1831, 1846.*] The
summits in many places [in . . . places *om. 1846*] are of a deeply [deep *1831, 1846*]
red marble [marble *om. 1846*]. [L. *footnote not in 1798.*]

_____

  49 generous] warlike *1798.*   54 Prayers] *sc.* Λιταί, *Iliad*, ix. 502. [W.]   69 seem'd]
looked *1798.*

Then starting from attention, Tamar cried,
"Brother! in sacred truth it cannot be!
My life is your's, my love must be my own.
O surely he who seeks a second love   80
Never felt one; or 'tis not one I feel."
But Gebir with complacent smile replied,
"Go then, fond Tamar, go in happy hour.
But ere thou goest, ponder in thy breast,
And well bethink thee, lest thou part deceiv'd,
Will she disclose to thee the mysteries
Of our calamity? and unconstrain'd?
When even her love thy strength was to disclose.*
My heart, indeed, is full: but witness, heaven!
My people, not my passion, fills my heart." 90
 "Then let me kiss thy garment," said the youth,
"And heaven be with thee, and on me thy grace."
 Him then the monarch thus once more addressed,
"Be of good courage: hast thou yet forgot
What chaplets languished round thy unburnt hair,
In color like some tall smooth beech's leaves
Curl'd by autumnal suns?"—How flattery
Excites a pleasant, sooths a painful shame!
 "These," amid stifled blushes, Tamar said,
"Were of the flowering raspberry and vine: 100
But ah! the seasons will not wait for love,
Seek out some other now." They parted here:
And Gebir, bending through the woodlands, cull'd
The creeping vine and viscous raspberry,
Less green and less compliant than they were,
And twisted in those mossy tufts that grow
On brakes of roses, when the roses fade;
And as he pass'd along, the little hinds
That shook for bristly herds the foodful bough,
Wonder, stand still, gaze, and trip satisfied; 110
Pleas'd more if chesnut, out of prickly husk,†

* When she demanded a contest before she would acknowledge her love. [L. *footnote only in 1803.*]

 † "Pleas'd more if chesnut, &c." Pleased more at such an event than at the sight of the stranger. I am afraid I have, in more than one instance, mentioned plants which are not natives of Egypt. But they may have existed there in the time of powerful

---

78 cannot] can not *1846.* 83 Tamar] *misp.* Tamer *1798.* 84 goest] partest *1831, 1846.* 85 lest] *misp.* least *1798.* 88 was] had *1831, 1846.* 93 monarch] monarc *1831.* 96 beech's] beechis *1831.* 98 sooths] soothes *1831, 1846.* 100, 104 raspberry] rasberry *1831.* 108 pass'd along] passes on *1831, 1846.* 109 shook] shake *1831, 1846.*

Shot from the sandal, roll along the glade.
  And thus unnoticed went he, and untired
Stept up the acclivity; and as he stept,
And as the garlands nodded o'er his brow,
Sudden, from under a close alder, sprang
Th' expectant nymph, and seiz'd him unaware.
He stagger'd at the shock: his feet, not firm'd,
Slipt backward from the wither'd grass short-graz'd;
But, striking out one arm, though without aim,   120
Then grasping with his other, he inclos'd
The struggler; she gain'd not one step's retreat,
Urging with open hands against his throat
Intense; now holding in her breath constrain'd,
Now pushing with quick impulse and by starts,
Till the dust blackened upon every pore.
Nearer he drew her, and still nearer, clasp'd
Above the knees midway; and now one arm
Fell; and her other, lapsing o'er the neck
Of Gebir, swung against his back incurved,   130
The swoln veins glowing deep; and with a groan
On his broad shoulder fell her face reclined.
But ah she knew not whom that roseate face *
Cool'd with its breath ambrosial; for she stood
High on the bank, and often swept and broke
His chaplets mingled with her loosen'd hair.
  Whether, while Tamar tarried, came desire,
And she, grown languid, loosed the wings of love,
Which she before held proudly at her will;
And nought but Tamar in her soul, and nought   140
Where Tamar was that seem'd or fear'd deceit,
To fraud she yielded, what no force had gain'd—
Or whether Jove, in pity to mankind,
When from his crystal fount the visual orbs
He fill'd with piercing ether, and endued
With somewhat of omnipotence—ordain'd

kings, who would adorn their gardens and their groves with the most beautiful and rare exotics; and, in a poetical view, they may still more easily be allowed to flourish where every thing around them shoots up equally from fable. [L. *footnote only in 1803.*]
  * "But ah she knew not, &c." These four verses were not inserted in the first edition, nor were those three which follow soon after, beginning "And nought but Tamar in her soul". [L. *footnote only in 1803.*]

---

118 not firm'd] at once *1831*; at first *1846.*   121 inclos'd] enclos'd *1831*; enclosed *1846.*   127 still . . . clasp'd] yet . . . claspt *1831, 1846.*   *ll.* 133–136 *not in 1798.*   135 High] Higher *1846.*   *ll.* 140–142 *not in 1798.*

That never two fair forms, at once, torment
The human heart, and draw it different ways—
And thus, in prowess like a god, the chief
Subdued her strength, nor soften'd at her charms;   150
The nymph divine, the magic mistress, fail'd.
Recovering, still half resting on the turf,
She look'd up wildly, and could now descry
The kingly brow, arched lofty for command.
  "Traitor!" said she, undaunted—though amaze
Threw o'er her varying cheek the air of fear—
"Thinkest thou thus that with impunity
Thou hast forsooth deceiv'd me? dar'st thou deem
Those eyes not hateful that have seen me fall?
O heaven! soon may they close on my disgrace.   160
Merciless man; what! for one sheep estranged,
Hast thou thrown into dungeons, and of day
Amerst thy shepherd? Hast thou, while the iron
Pierced thro' his tender limbs into his soul,
By threats, by tortures, torn out that offence,
And heard him (O could I) avow his love?
Say, hast thou? cruel, hateful,—ah my fears!
I feel them true! speak, tell me, are they true?"
She, blending thus intreaty with reproach,
Bent forward, as tho' falling on her knee,   170
Whence she had hardly ris'n, and at this pause
Shed from her large dark eyes a shower of tears.
Th' Iberian King her sorrow thus consoled.
"Weep no more, heavenly damsel, weep no more,
Neither by force withheld, or choice estranged,
Thy Tamar lives, and only lives for thee.
Happy, thrice happy, you! 'Tis me alone
Whom heaven, and earth, and ocean, with one hate
Conspire on, and throughout each path pursue.
Whether in waves beneath or skies above   180
Thou hast thy habitation, 'tis from heaven,
From heaven alone, such power, such charms descend.
Then oh! discover whence that ruin comes
Each night upon our city; whence are heard
Those yells of rapture round our falling walls:

ll. 149–150 *not in 1798.*   152 still] stil *1831.*   154 lofty] loftly *1798.*   163
Amerst] Amerc'd *1798;* Amerced *1846.*   165 offence] offense *1831.*   169 intreaty]
entreaty *1831, 1846.*   171 ris'n] risen *1831, 1846.*   174 damsel] maiden *1846.*
175 withheld] witheld *1831.*   183 Then oh!] Wilt thou *1798;* Then O! *1846.*   185
falling] fallen *1831, 1846.*

In our affliction can the Gods delight,
Or meet oblation for the Nymphs are tears?"
He spake; and indignation sunk in woe.
Which she perceiving, pride refreshed her heart,
Hope wreath'd her mouth with smiles, and she exclaim'd—   190
"Neither the Gods afflict you, nor the Nymphs.
Return me him who won my heart; return
Him whom my bosom pants for, as the steeds
In the sun's chariot for the western wave,
The Gods will prosper thee, and Tamar prove
How Nymphs the torments that they cause assuage.
Promise me this! indeed I think thou hast;
But 'tis so pleasing, promise it once more."
"Once more I promise," cried the gladdened king,
"By my right-hand, and by myself, I swear,   200
And ocean's Gods, and heaven's Gods I adjure,
Thou shalt be Tamar's; Tamar shall be thine."
   Then she, regarding him, long fixt, replied,—
"I have thy promise: take thou my advice.
Gebir, this land of Egypt is a land
Of incantation; demons rule these waves;
These are against thee; these thy works destroy.
Where thou hast built thy palace, and hast left
The seven pillars to remain in front,
Sacrifice there; and all these rites observe.   210
Go, but go early, ere the gladsome Hours
Strew saffron in the path of rising Morn;
Ere the bee, buzzing o'er flowers fresh disclosed,
Examine where he may the best alight
Nor scatter off the bloom; ere cold-lipt herds
Crop the pale herbage round each other's bed;
Lead seven bulls, well pastur'd and well form'd,
Their necks unblemished and their horns unring'd,
And at each pillar sacrifice thou one.
Around each base rub thrice the black'ning blood,   220
And burn the curling shavings of the hoof;
And of the forehead locks thou also burn.
The yellow galls, with equal care preserv'd,
Pour at the seventh statue from the north."

188 sunk] sank *1831, 1846.*   194 chariot] charriot *1798.*   203 fixt] first
text, fixt *errata 1798.*   215 bloom;] bloom, *1831, 1846.*   216 pale] cold *text,* pale *errata
1798.*   218 necks unblemished . . .] neck unblemisht *1831, 1846.*   horns] horn *1846.*
220 black'ning] blackning *1798;* blackening 1846.

He listen'd; and on her his eyes intent*
Perceiv'd her not; and now she disappear'd:
So deep he ponder'd her important words.
    And now had morn aris'n, and he perform'd
Almost the whole enjoin'd him;—he had reach'd
The seventh statue, pour'd the yellow galls,   230
The forelock from his left he had releas'd,
And burnt the curling shavings of the hoof,
Moisten'd with myrrh; when suddenly a flame
Spired from the fragrant smoke, nor sooner spired
—Down sunk the brazen fabric at his feet.
He started back, gazed—nor could aught but gaze—
And cold dread stiffen'd up his hair flower-twined:
Then with a long and tacit step, one arm
Behind, and every finger wide outspread,
He look'd and totter'd on a black abyss.   240
He thought he sometimes heard a distant voice
Breathe through the cavern's mouth, and further on
Faint murmurs now, now hollow groans reply.
Therefor suspended he his crook above,
Dropt it, and heard it rolling step by step.
He enter'd; and a mingled sound arose
Like that—when shaken from some temple's roof
By zealous hand, they, and their fretted nest,—
Of birds that wintering watch in Memnon's tomb,
And tell the Halcyons when Spring first returns.   250

END OF BOOK THE SECOND

* It is not unknown that during the intensity of thought, the eye may be fixt
on an object and yet not see it: something more than merely the eye, tho' open and
direct, is requisite for sight—the application of mind and volition. [L. *footnote only
in 1803.*]

226 now she] she had *1831, 1846*   235 sunk] sank *1831, 1846.*   239 out-
spread] outspred *1831.*   244 Therefor] Therefore *1846.*   247 that] one *1831,
1846.*

THE THIRD BOOK OF *GEBIR*

ARGUMENT

Gebir hears his name repeated twice. *Aröar*, who had fought under his forefathers, approaches him. *Gebir* enquires with earnestness what power detains *them*. *Aröar* replies evasively—recapitulates the misery that would attend the disembodied Spirits having any intercourse with those on earth—then seriously addresses him, and promises, if he can endure the trial, that he shall gratify his wish. The *Gadite* kings appear—several are described. *Gebir* complains that he cannot see his father—turning to bid adieu, is clasped in his embrace. He briefly tells his son the cause of his suffering, which was the oath exacted of invading Egypt. He disappears—*Gebir* complains—reproved by *Aröar*, who reveals the laws by which these regions are governed—the flaming arch that separates the good from the wicked—once in every hundred years it suddenly starts back and discovers to each state its opposite—the contrast is exemplified in the abode of the ambitious and of the peaceful. *Aröar* teaches that those eternal fires which seem intended only for punishing the vicious, are calculated also to give verdure and pleasantness to the groves of the blest. *Gebir* asks a question on religion—the scene instantly vanishes—he rises, and visits his army.

GEBIR

BOOK III

O FOR the spirit of that matchless man*
Whom Nature led throughout her whole domain,
While he, embodied, breath'd etherial air!
   Though panting in the play-hour of my youth,
I drank of Avon, too, a dang'rous draught,
That rous'd within the fev'rish thirst of song—
Yet, never may I trespass o'er the stream
Of jealous Acheron, nor alive descend
The silent and unsearchable abodes
Of Erebus and Night, nor unchastized   10
Lead up long absent heroes into day.
When on the pausing theatre of earth
Eve's shadowy curtain falls, can any man†
Bring back the far-off intercepted hills,
Grasp the round rock-built turret, or arrest
The glittering spires that pierce the brow of Heav'n?
Rather, can any, with outstripping voice,
The parting Sun's gigantic strides recall?

---

*"That matchless man," Shakespear. [L. *footnote only in 1803.*]
 †"Can any man bring back the far-off intercepted hills," or can I hope to "lead up long-absent heroes into day," so as to exhibit their perfect character by a just description of their actions? [L. *footnote only in 1803.*]

Argument. *Only in 1803.*   5 dang'rous] dangerous *1831, 1846.*   6 fev'rish] feverish *1831, 1846.*   12 theatre] theater *1831.*   13 shadowy] shad'wy *1798.* any man] human hand *1798.*   16 glittering] glitt'ring *1798.*   18 recall] recal *1798.*

GEBIR: BOOK III

Twice heard was Gebir;* twice th' Iberian king
Thought it the strong vibration of the brain   20
That struck upon his ear; but now descried
A form, a man come nearer; as he came
His unshorn hair, grown soft in these abodes,
Waved back, and scatter'd thin and hoary light.
Living, men call'd him Aröar: but no more
In celebration, or recording verse,
His name is heard, no more by Arnon's side
The well-wall'd city, which he rear'd, remains.
Gebir was now undaunted, for the brave
When they no longer doubt, no longer fear,   30
And would have spoken, but the shade began.
    "Brave son of Hesperus! no mortal hand
Has led thee hither, nor without the Gods
Penetrate thy firm feet the vast profound.
Thou knowest not that here thy fathers lie,
The race of Sidad: their's was loud acclaim
When living; but their pleasure was in war:
Triumphs and hatred followed: I myself
Bore, men imagin'd, no inglorious part;
The Gods thought otherwise!† by whose decree   40
Depriv'd of life, and more, of death depriv'd,
I still hear shrieking, through the moonless night,
Their discontented and deserted shades.
Observe these horrid walls, this rueful waste!
Here some refresh the vigor of the mind
With contemplation and cold penitence:
Nor wonder, while thou hearest, that the soul
Thus purified, hereafter may ascend
Surmounting all obstruction, nor ascribe
The sentence to indulgence: each extreme   50
Has tortures for ambition; to dissolve
In everlasting languor, to resist
Its impulse, but in vain; to hear, frequent,
Nay, to take counsel from, and seek resource,

*"Twice heard was *Gebir*," i.e. the sound of Gebir's name. [L. *footnote only in 1803.*]

19 heard was] sounded *1831, 1846.*   24 thin and] a thin *1798.*   25 Aröar]
Aroar *1798, 1831, 1846, and so elsewhere.* [For Aroer, the city, see *Deuteronomy*, ii. 36
and Milton, *Par. Lost*, i. 407. W.]   36 Sidad] Sadad *text* Sidad *errata 1798.*   acclaim]
acclame *1831.*   40 otherwise!† *For footnote in 1798, 1803 see notes at end of vol.*
42 still] stil *1831.*   hear] here *text,* hear *errata 1798.*   44 rueful] ruful *1831.*
45 vigor] vigour *1831, 1846.*   52 languor] langour *1798*; languour *1831.*   *ll.* 53–56
to hear ... mankind *om. 1831, 1846.*   54 resource] resourse *1798.*

Be sooth'd by, or be scoft at by, (O Heaven!)
The vilest of mankind: to be enclosed
Within a limit, and that limit fire:
Sever'd from happiness, from eminence,
And flying, but hell bars us, from ourselves.
    Yet rather all these torments most endure   60
Than solitary pain, and sad remorse,
And tow'ring thoughts on their own breast o'erturn'd,
And piercing to the heart: such penitence,
Such contemplation, theirs! thy ancestors
Bear up against them, nor will they submit
To conquering Time th' asperities of Fate:
Yet, could they but revisit earth once more,
How gladly would they Poverty embrace,
How labour, even for their deadliest foe!
It little now avails them to have rais'd   70
Beyond the Syrian regions, and beyond
Phœnicia, trophies, tributes, colonies:
Follow thou me: mark what it all avails."
    Him Gebir followed, and a roar confused
Rose from a river, rolling in its bed,
Not rapid—that would rouse the wretched souls—
Nor calmly—that might lull them to repose.
But with dull weary lapses it still heaved
Billows of bale, heard low, but heard afar;
For when hell's iron portals let out Night,   80
Often men start, and shiver at the sound,
And lie so silent on the restless couch
They hear their own hearts beat. Now Gebir breath'd
Another air, another sky beheld.
Twilight broods here, lull'd by no nightingale,
Nor waken'd by the shrill lark dewy-winged,
But glowing with one sullen sunless heat.
Beneath his foot nor sprouted flower nor herb,
Nor chirp'd a grasshopper; above his head
Phlegethon form'd a fiery firmament: 90
Part were sulphurous clouds involving, part
Shining like solid ribs of moulten brass:
For the fierce element which else aspires

62 tow'ring] towering *1846*.   66 th' asperities] the asperities *1831, 1846.*
72 Phœnicia] Phenicia *1831, 1846. Between ll. 72–73 1798 has one line:*
      To have heard infants lisp the Gadite name:
75 its] it's *1798.*   78 still heaved] upheaved *1831, 1846.*   79 but] yet *1831, 1846.*   90
fiery] firy *1831.*   91 sulphurous] sulphureous *1798.*   92 moulten] molten *1831, 1846.*

Higher and higher, and lessens to the sky,
Below, Earth's adamantine arch rebuffed.*
  Gebir, though now such languor held his limbs,
Scarce aught admir'd he, yet he this admir'd;
And thus address'd him then the conscious guide.
"Beyond that river lie the happy fields.
From them fly gentle breezes, which, when drawn   100
Against yon crescent convex, but unite
Stronger with what they could not overcome.
Thus they that scatter freshness thro' the groves
And meadows of the fortunate, and fill
With liquid light the marble bowl of Earth,
And give her blooming health and sprightly force—
Their fire no more diluted, nor its darts
Blunted by passing through thick myrtle bowers,
Neither from odors rising half dissolved,
Point forward Phlegethon's eternal flame: 110
And this horizon is the spacious bow
Whence each ray reaches to the world above.
Fire rules the realms of pleasure and of pain.
Parent and element of elements,
Changing, and yet unchanged, pervading heaven
Purest, and then reviewing all the stars:
All croud around him in their orbits, all
In legions for that radiant robe contend†
Allotted them, unseam'd and undefiled:
Then, saturate with what their nature craves,   120
Unite the grateful symphony of guests,
Take short repose, and with slow pace return.
And not the glowing oceans of the sun
Fire fills alone, and draws there smaller streams,
And dashes them on crystal cliffs of hail,
And filters through black clouds and fleecy snows—
But penetrates each cold and blue abyss
Of trackless waves, and each white glimmering gem
That crowns the victim's immolated brow."
  The hero pausing, Gebir then besought   130

* "Earth's adamantine, &c." and repelled the flame, which had it been free would
have assumed its spiral form "and lessened to the sky". [L. *footnote only in 1803.*]

95 Below, Earth's] Below earths *1798.*   rebuffed] rebuft *1831, 1846.*   96 languor]
languour *1831.*   106 sprightly] spritely *1831.*   109 odors] odours *1831, 1846.*   112
above.] above." *1831, 1846.*   *ll.* 113–129 *om. 1831, 1846.*   118 contend †] *For footnote
only in 1803 see notes at end of vol.*   119 undefiled] undefil'd *1798.*

What region held his ancestors, what clouds,
What waters, or what Gods, from his embrace.
"Young man," said Aröar, "some indeed declare
That they the spirit, when it is itself,
Have wakened on; and with fixt eyes beheld
Fixt eyes; both stricken speechless, both would speak;
Both stretch'd their kindred arms and would embrace.
That spirit, which thus struggles in its flight
To some one dearest object, with a will
Omnipotent, ne'er, after this returns: 140
Neither can mortal see departed friends,
Or they see mortal: if indeed they could,
How care would furrow up their flow'ry fields,
What asps and adders bask in every beam!
Then oft might faithful fondness from the shades
See its beloved in another's arms,
And curse immoral laws, immodest vows,
Elysium, and the vanity of soul.
She who, evading Modesty, dares take
—With sacrilegious incest most accurst—   150
The lamp of marriage from a husband's tomb,
And beckon up another, to defile
A bed new-litter'd, a mere tavern-stall,
Biting her chain, bays body; and despair*
Awakes the furies of insatiate lust.
Others, if worse be any, float immerst
In prisons blackly green with ropy slime,
Where toughens the brown fungus, brittle-stalk'd:
Their grosser spirits with the putrid air
Amalgamate, and, in due time, ferment   160
Seed heretofore inert; hence crawls gay-wing'd
The gadfly, hence trails forth the fulsome snake.
Living, they never own'd that Nature's face
Was lovely, never with fond awe beheld
On her parental bosom, Truth repose!"
He paus'd; then sudden, as if rous'd, renew'd.
   "But come, if ardor urges thee, and force
Suffices—mark me, Gebir, I unfold

* "*Bays body*", looks up with unavailing desire to the corporeal state. The word is
the strongest I could find or imagine. [L. *footnote only in 1803.*]

---

ll. 133–165 *om. 1831, 1846.*   133 said . . . indeed] replied the hero, "some *1798.*
143 care] Care *1798.*   162 gadfly,] gadfly ? *text* gadfly *errata 1798.*   166 He . . . if] Aroar
then sudden, as tho' *1831, 1846.*   167 But . . . ardor] Come thou, if ardour *1831, 1846.*

No fable to allure thee—rise, behold
Thy ancestors!" and lo! with horrid gasp,   170
The panting flame above his head recoil'd,
And thunder thro' his heart and life-blood throb'd.
Such sound could human organs once conceive,
Cold, speechless, palsied, not the soothing voice
Of friendship, or almost of Deity,
Could raise the wretched mortal from the dust;
Beyond man's home condition they! with eyes
Intent, and voice desponding, and unheard
By Aröar, tho' he tarried at his side.
"They know me not," cried Gebir, "O my sires,   180
Ye know me not!—They answer not, nor hear.
How distant are they still! what sad extent
Of desolation must we overcome!
Aröar, what wretch that nearest us? what wretch
Is that with eyebrows white, and slanting brow?
Listen! him yonder, who, bound down supine,
Shrinks, yelling, from that sword there, engine-hung;
He too amongst my ancestors? I hate
The despot, but the dastard I despise.
Was he our countryman?"
                              "Alas, O King!   190
Iberia bore him, but the breed accurst
Inclement winds blew blighting from north-east."
"He was a warrior, then, nor fear'd the Gods?"
"Gebir, he fear'd the Demons, not the Gods;
Tho' them, indeed, his daily face adored,
And was no warrior, yet the thousand lives
Squander'd, as stones to exercise a sling!
And the tame cruelty, and cold caprice—
Oh madness of mankind! addrest, adored!
O Gebir! what are men, or where are Gods!   200
Behold the giant next him: how his feet
Plunge flound'ring mid the marshes, yellow-flower'd.
His restless head just reaching to the rocks,
His bosom tossing with black weeds besmear'd,
How writhes he 'twixt the continent and isle!
What tyrant with more insolence e'er claim'd

169 —rise,] . . on! *1831, 1846*.   177 Beyond . . . condition] [Humani non juris
erant *in the Latin version, which is not much plainer.* W.]   182 still] stil *1831*.
l. 184 *see notes at end of volume.* *ll.* 188–190 I . . . Alas, *om. 1831, 1846*: *after* ancestors?'
1831, 1846 have "O King!   188 amongst] among *1831, 1846*.   202 flound'ring]
floundering *1831, 1846*. 205 isle] ile *1831*.

Dominion? when, from th' heart of Usury
Rose more intense the pale-flamed thirst for gold?
And call'd, forsooth, *Deliverer!* False or fools!
Who prais'd the dull-ear'd miscreant, or who hoped   210
To soothe your folly and disgrace with praise.
   Hearest thou not the harp's gay simpering air,
And merriment afar! Then come, advance—
And now behold him! mark the wretch accurst,
Who sold his people to a rival king.
Self-yoked they stood, two ages unredeem'd."
"O horror! what pale visage rises there!
Speak Aröar—me, perhaps, mine eyes deceive,
Inured not, yet methinks they there descry
Such crimson haze as sometimes drowns the moon.   220
What is yon awful sight? why thus appears
That space between the purple and the crown?"
   "I will relate their stories when we reach
Our confines," said the guide; "for thou, O king,
Differing in both from all thy countrymen—
Seest not their stories, and hast seen their fates.
But while we tarry, lo again the flame
Riseth, and, murmuring hoarse, points straiter; haste!
'Tis urgent; we must on."
               "Then, O, adieu,"
Cried Gebir, and groan'd loud; at last a tear   230
Burst from his eyes, turn'd back, and he exclaim'd
"Am I deluded? O ye powers of hell!
Suffer me—O my fathers!—am I torne"—
He spake, and would have spoken more, but flames
Enwrapt him, round and round, intense; he turn'd—
And stood held breathless in a ghost's embrace.
"Gebir, my son, desert me not, I heard
Thy calling voice, nor fate witheld me more.
One moment yet remains: enough to know
Soon will my torments, soon will thine, expire.   240
O that I e'er exacted such a vow!
When dipping in the victim's blood thy hand,
First thou withdrew'st it, looking in my face
Wondering; but when the priest my will explain'd,

   207 th' heart] the heart *1831, 1846.*   *ll. 209–222 see notes at end of volume.*   217 visage] vissage *1798.*   228 straiter] straighter *1831, 1846.*   229 on] hence *1831, 1846.* 231 exclaim'd] exclamed: *1831,* exclaimed *1846.*   238 witheld] withheld *1846.*   243 withdrew'st] withdrewest *1798.*   244 explain'd] explaned *1831.*

Then swarest thou, repeating what he said,
How against Egypt thou wouldst raise that hand
And bruise the seed first risen from our line.
Therefor, in death what pangs have I endured!
Rackt on the fiery centre of the sun,
Twelve years I saw the ruin'd world roll round.   250
Shudder not; I have borne it; I deserved
My wretched fate; be better thine; farewell."
 "O stay, my father! stay one moment more.
Let me return thee that embrace—'tis past—
Aröar! how could I quit it unreturn'd!
And now the gulph divides us, and the waves
Of sulphur bellow through the blue abyss.
And is he gone for ever! and I come
In vain?" Then sternly said the guide, "In vain!
Sayst thou; what wouldst thou more? alas, O prince, 260
None come for pastime here! but is it nought
To turn thy feet from evil—is it nought
Of pleasure to that shade if they are turn'd?
For this thou camest hither: he who dares
To penetrate this darkness, nor regards
The dangers of the way, shall reascend
In glory, nor the gates of hell retard
That man, nor demon's nor man's art prevail.
Once in each hundred years, and only once,
Whether by some rotation of the world,   270
Or whether will'd so by some pow'r above,
This flaming arch starts back: each realm descries
Its opposite; and Bliss from her repose
Freshens, and feels her own security."
 "Security!" cried out the Gadite king,
"And feel they not compassion?"
       "Child of Earth,"
Calmly said Aröar at his guest's surprize,
"Some so disfigur'd by habitual crimes,
Others are so exalted, so refined,
So permëated by heaven, no trace remains 280
Graven on earth: here Justice is supreme;
Compassion can be but where passions are.

---

245 swarest] swearest *1798*. 248 Therefor] Therefore *1846*. 249 fiery
centre] firy center *1831*. 252 farewell] farewel *1798*. 256 gulph] gulf
1831, *1846*. 259 sternly] sternely *1798*. 268 That man] His steps *1831*,
1846. demon's] demons, *1798*. 280 heaven] Heav'n *1798*.

Here are discover'd those who tortured Law
To silence or to speech, as pleas'd themselves;
Here also those who boasted of their zeal,
And lov'd their country for the spoils it gave.
Hundreds, whose glitt'ring merchandize the lyre
Dazzled vain wretches, drunk with flattery,
And wafted them in softest airs to Heav'n,
Doom'd to be still deceiv'd, here still attune   290
The wonted strings and fondly woo applause;
The wish half granted, they retain their own,
But madden at the mockry of the shades.
While on the river's other side there grow
Deep olive groves: there, other ghosts abide:
Blest indeed they; but not supremely blest.
We cannot see beyond: we cannot see
Aught but our opposite, and here are fates
How opposite to our's! here some observ'd
Religious rites, some hospitality: 300
Strangers, who from the good old men retired,
Closed the gate gently, lest from generous use
Shutting and opening of it's own accord,
It shake unsettled slumbers off their couch:
Some stopt revenge athirst for slaughter, some
Sow'd the slow olive for a race unborn.
These had no wishes; therefor none are crown'd:
But their's are tufted banks, their's umbrage, their's
Enough of sun-shine to enjoy the shade,
And breeze enough to lull them to repose."   310
    Then Gebir cried, " Illustrious host, proceed.
Bring me among the wonders of a realm
Admired by all, but like a tale admired.
We take our children from their cradled sleep,
And on their fancy, from our own, impress
Etherial forms and adulating fates:
But, ere departing for such scenes ourselves,
We seize their hands, we hang upon their neck,
Our beds cling heavy round us with our tears,
Agony strives with agony. Just Gods!   320

287 merchandize] merchandise *1831, 1846.*   290 still . . . still] stil . . . stil *1831.*
292 The] Their *1798.*   their] they *in text,* their *in errata 1798.*   293 mockry]
mock'ry *1798;* mockery *1831, 1846.*   294 While on] Upon *1831, 1846.*   *ll.* 297–299
we . . . our's! *not in 1798.*   297 cannot *bis*] can not *1846.*   300 rites] rights *1831.*
307 therefor] therefore *1846.*   311 Then . . . "Illustrious] "Then," . . . "illustrious
1798.   proceed] procede *1831.*   312 realm] reign *1798.*

24

GEBIR: BOOK III

Wherefor should wretched mortals thus believe,
Or wherefor should they hesitate to die?"
   Thus while he question'd, all his strength dissolv'd
Within him, thunder shook his troubled brain;
He started; and the cavern's mouth survey'd
Near; and beyond, his people; he arose,
And bent towards them his bewilder'd way.

END OF BOOK THE THIRD

321 Wherefor] Wherefore *1846.*   322 wherefor] wherefore *1846.*   327 to-
wards] toward *1831–1846.*

THE FOURTH BOOK OF *GEBIR*

ARGUMENT

In what manner *Charoba* is affected by the report of *Gebir's* visit to the shades.
Collusion of *Love* and *Terror*. Retrospect. The various ways in which *Charoba* is
tormented. Universal alarm. Description of the species of patriotism that is generated
under monarchy. Violence against the *Gadites* meditated. *Dalica* recommends a
festival on their account. *Charoba* unsuspiciously consents—rejoices at the thought of
seeing *Gebir*—hesitates—argues with herself, and is satified—hears tymbrels and cymbals—suspects hostility—exclaims against *Gebir*—finds that the tumult proceeds from
the extravagant merriment of her own people. Description of an Egyptian holiday—
of an embassy—of the *Gadites* reposing in the evening. Reception of the Egyptian
elders at the Iberian tent.

GEBIR

BOOK IV

HE who could pity, he who could obey,
Flatter'd both female youth and princely pride,
The same ascending from amidst the shades
Show'd Pow'r in frightful attitude: the queen
Marks the surpassing prodigy, and strives
To shake off terror in her crowded court,

Argument. *Only in 1803.*   Before *l.* 1 edd. *1831, 1846 insert ten lines as follows:*
   THE king's lone road, his visit, his return,
   Were not unknown to Dalica, nor long
   The wondrous tale from royal ears delaid. [delay'd *1846*]
   When the young queen had heard who taught the rites
   Her mind was shaken, and what first she asked [askt *1846*]
   Was, whether the sea-maids were very fair,
   And was it true that even gods were moved
   By female charms beneath the waves profound,
   And joined [join'd *1846*] to them in marriage, and had sons . . .
   Who knows but Gebir sprang then from the Gods!
1 who . . . who] that . . . that *1831, 1846.*   3 amidst] amid *1831, 1846.*
4 Show'd] Shew'd *1831.* Pow'r] Power *1846.*   6 terror] terrour *1831.*

25

And wonders why she trembles; nor suspects
How Fear and Love assume each other's form,
By birth and secret compact how allied.
Vainly, (to conscious virgins I appeal,)   10
Vainly with crouching tigers, prowling wolves,
Rocks, precipices, waves, storms, thunderbolts,
All his immense inheritance, would Fear
The simplest heart, should Love refuse, assail;
Consent—the maiden's pillowed ear imbibes
Constancy, honor, truth, fidelity,
Beauty, and ardent lips, and longing arms;
Then fades in glimmering distance half the scene,
Then her heart quails and flutters and would fly.
'Tis her beloved! not to her! ye Pow'rs!   20
What doubting maid exacts the vow? behold
Above the myrtles his protesting hand.
Such ebbs of doubt and swells of jealousy *
Toss the fond bosom in its hour of sleep
And float around the eyelids and sink thro'.
    Lo! mirror of delight in cloudless days!
Lo! thy reflection: 'twas when I exclaim'd
—With kisses hurried as if each foresaw
Their end, and reckon'd on our broken bonds,
And could at such a price such loss endure—   30
"O what, to faithful lovers, met at morn,
What half so pleasant as imparted fears!"
How many a night serene, shall I behold
Those warm attractive orbits, close inshrined
In ether, over which Love's column rose
Marmoreal, trophied round with golden hair.
Within the valley of one lip, unseen,
Love slumber'd, one his unstrung bow impress'd.
Sweet wilderness of soul-entangling charms!
Led back by Memory, and each blissful maze   40
Retracing, me with magic power detain
Those dimpled cheeks, those temples, violet-tinged,
Those lips of nectar, and those eyes of heav'n!

* "Such ebbs of doubt, &c." These three verses were not in the first edition. [L. *footnote only in 1803*.]

---

8 Fear . . . assume] Love and Terror take *1798*.   15 Consent] Agree *1798*.
19 Then . . . fly] *not in 1798*.   *ll*. 23–5 *not in 1798*.   27 reflection] reflexion *1831*.
exclaim'd] exclamed *1831*.   *ll*. 33–4 *om. 1831, 1846*.   35 In . . . which]
Looking recumbent how *1831, 1846*.   37 Within] How in *1831, 1846*.   38 Love]
He *1831, 1846*.   43 heav'n] heaven *1846*.

Charoba, tho' indeed she never drank *
The liquid pearl, or twined the nodding crown;
Or, when she wanted cool and calm repose,
Dream'd of the crawling asp and grated tomb,
Was wretched up to royalty! the jibe
Struck her, most piercing where love pierc'd before,
From those whose freedom centers in their tongue,   50
Handmaids, and pages sleek, and courtiers aged.
Congratulations here, there prophecies,
Here children, not repining at neglect,
While tumult thus sweeps amplest room for play;
Every-where questions, answer'd ere begun,
Every-where groups, for every-where alarm.
Thus, winter gone; nor spring, tho' near, arriv'd,
Urged slanting onward by the bickering breeze
That issues from beneath Aurora's car,
Shudder the sombrous waves; at every beam   60
More vivid, more by every breath impell'd,
Higher and higher up the fretted rocks
Their turbulent refulgence they display.
Madness, which, like the spiral element,
The more it seizes on, the fiercer burns,
Hurried them blindly forward, and involved
In flame the senses, and in gloom the soul.
    Determin'd to protect the country's gods,
Still asking their protection, they adjure
Each other to stand forward, and insist   70
With zeal, and trample under foot the slow;
And disregardful of the Sympathies
Divine, those Sympathies whose delicate hand
Touching the very eyeball of the heart,
Awakens it, not wounds it nor inflames.—
Blind wretches! they with desperate embrace
Hang on the pillar till the temple fall.
Oft, the grave judge alarms religious wealth,
And rouses anger under gentle words.
Woe to the wiser few, who dare to cry   80
"People! these men are not your enemies:
Enquire their errand; and resist when wrong'd."

44 drank * *For footnote see notes at end of vol.*   47 Dream'd] Dreamt *1831, 1846.*
50 centers] centres *1846.*   51 Handmaids . . . aged] Handmaidens, pages, courtiers,
priests, buffoons *1831, 1846.*   54 thus . . . amplest] sweeps them ample *1831, 1846.*
56 groups] crowds *1831, 1846.*   61 impell'd] impel'd *1798.*   69 Still] And *1831,*
1846.   77 till] til *1831.*   ll. 78-9 *not in 1798.*   82 Enquire] Inquire *1846.*

Together, childhood, priesthood, womanhood,
The scribes, and elders of the land, exclaim
"Seek they not hidden treasure in the tombs?
Raising the ruins, levelling the dust,
Who can declare whose ashes they disturb!
Build they not fairer cities than our own,
Extravagant enormous apertures
For light, and portals larger, open courts,   90
Where all ascending all are unconfin'd,
And wider streets in purer air than ours?
Temples quite plain, with equal capitals,
They build, nor bearing gods like ours imbost.
O profanation! O our ancestors!"
   Though all the vulgar hate a foreign face,
It more offends weak eyes and homely age,
Dalica most; who thus her aim pursued.
"My promise, O Charoba, I perform.
Proclaim to gods and men a festival   100
Throughout the land, and bid the strangers eat:
Their anger thus we haply may disarm."
   "O Dalica, the grateful queen replied,
Nurse of my childhood, soother of my cares,
Preventer of my wishes, of my thoughts,
O pardon youth, O pardon royalty!
If hastily to Dalica I sued,
Fear might impel me, never could distrust.
Go then, for wisdom guides thee, take my name,
Issue what most imports and best beseems,   110
And sovranty shall sanction the decree."
   And now Charoba was alone, her heart
Grew lighter; she sat down, and she arose,
She felt voluptuous tenderness, but felt
That tenderness for Dalica; she prais'd
Her kind attention, warm solicitude,
Her wisdom—for what wisdom pleas'd like her's!
She was delighted: should she not behold
Gebir? she blush'd: but she had words to speak,
She form'd them and reform'd them, with regret   120
That there was somewhat lost with every change:
She could replace them—what would that avail—

84 exclaim] exclame *1831*.   86 levelling] leveling *1798*.   93 capitals] architraves *1831, 1846*.   96 foreign] forein *1831*.   100 Proclaim] Proclame *1831*.
103, 104 *1831, 1846 have* Dalica," *and* "Nurse.   108 impel] impell *1831, 1846*.
111 sovranty] Sov'reignty *1798*.   119 blush'd] blusht *1831, 1846*.

Moved from their order they have lost their charm.
While thus she strew'd her way with softest words,
Others grew up before her, but appear'd
A plenteous, rather than perplexing, choice.
She rubb'd her palms with pleasure, heav'd a sigh,
Grew calm again, and thus her thoughts revolv'd.
—"But he descended to the tombs! the thought
Thrills me, I must avow it, with affright.   130
And wherefor? shews he not the more belov'd
Of heaven, or how ascends he back to day.
Then, has he wrong'd me? Could he want a cause
Who has an army, and was bred to reign?
And yet no reasons against rights he urged.
He threaten'd not; proclaim'd not; I approach'd,
He hasten'd on; I spake, he listen'd; wept,
He pity'd me: he lov'd me, he obey'd;
He was a conqueror, still am I a queen."
        She thus indulged fond fancies, when the sound   140
Of tymbrels and of cymbals struck her ear,
And horns, and howlings of wild jubilee.
She fear'd; and listen'd, to confirm her fears;
One breath sufficed, and shook her refluent soul.
Smiting, with simulated smile constrain'd,*
Her beauteous bosom, "O perfidious man,
O cruel foe," she twice and thrice exclaim'd,
"O my companions equal-aged! my throne,
My people! O how wretched to presage
This day, how tenfold wretched to endure!"   150
        She ceas'd, and instantly the palace rang
With gratulation roaring into rage:
'Twas her own people. "Health to Gebir! health
To our compatriot subjects! to our queen
Health and unfaded youth ten thousand years!"
Then went the victims forward crown'd with flowers,
Crown'd were tame crocodiles, and boys white-robed
Guided their creaking crests across the stream.
In gilded barges went the female train,
And, hearing others ripple near, undrew   160
The veil of sea-green awning, if they found

127 rubb'd] rub'd *1831.*   131 wherefor? shews] wherefore? shows *1846.*
136 proclaim'd] proclamed *1831.*   139 still] stil *1831.*   141 tymbrels] timbrels *1831, 1846.*   145 constrain'd* *For footnote only in 1803 see notes at end of vol.*
147 exclaim'd] exclamed *1831.*   151 ceas'd] ceast *1831, 1846.*

Whom they desired, how pleasant was the breeze!
If not, the frightful water forced a sigh.
Sweet airs of music ruled the rowing palms;
Now rose they glistening and aslant reclined,
Now they descended, and with one consent
Plunging, seem'd swift each other to pursue,
And now to tremble wearied o'er the wave.
Beyond, and in the suburbs, might be seen
Crouds of all ages; here in triumph passed   170
Not without pomp, though raised with rude device,
The monarch and Charoba: there a throng
Shone out in sunny whiteness o'er the reeds:
Nor could luxuriant youth, or lapsing age
—Propt by the corner of the nearest street—
With aching eyes and tottering knees intent,
Loose leathery neck and wormlike lip outstretched,
Fix long the ken upon one form; so swift
Through the gay vestures fluttering on the bank,
And through the bright-eyed waters dancing round,   180
Wove they their wanton wiles, and disappear'd.
    Meanwhile, with pomp august and solemn, borne
On four white camels, tinkling plates of gold,
Heralds before, and Ethiop slaves behind,
Each with the signs of office in his hand,
Each on his brow the sacred stamp of years,
The four ambassadors of peace proceed.
Rich carpets bear they, corn and generous wine;
The Syrian olive's cheerful gifts they bear:
With stubborn goats that eye the mountain-tops   190
Askance, and riot with reluctant horn,
And steeds and stately camels in their train.
The king, who sat before his tent, descried
The dust rise redden'd from the setting sun:
Through all the plains below the Gadite men
Were resting from their labor: some surveyed
The spacious scite, ere yet obstructed, walls
Already, soon will roofs have, interposed.
Nor is the glory of no price, to take
The royal city in, as these presume.   200

170 crouds] crowds *1831, 1846.*   177 outstretched] outstretcht *1831, 1846.*
182 Meanwhile] Meantime *1831, 1846.*   185 signs] sign *1846.*   187 proceed] procede *1831.*
189 gifts] gift *1831, 1846.*   190 tops] top *1846.*   196 labor] labour *1831, 1846.*   197 scite]
site *1831, 1846.*   198 *comma after* have *om. 1831, 1846.*   *ll.* 199, 200 *om. 1831, 1846.*

Some ate their frugal viands on the steps,
Contented: some, remembering home, prefer
The cot's bare rafters o'er the high gilded dome,
And sing, for often sighs, too, end in song,
"In smiling meads how sweet the brooks repose,
To the rough ocean and red restless sands!"
But others trip along with hasty steps,
Whistling, and fix too soon on their abodes:
Haply and one among them with his spear
Measures the lintel, if so great its height   210
As will receive him with his helm unlower'd.
   But silence went throughout, e'en thoughts were hushed,
When to full view of navy and of camp
Now first expanded the bare-headed train.
Majestic, unpresuming, unappall'd,
Onward they marched; and neither to the right
Nor to the left, though there the city stood,
Turn'd they their sober eyes: and now they reach'd
Within a few steep paces of ascent
The lone pavilion of the Iberian king.   220
He saw them, he awaited them, he rose;
He hail'd them, "*Peace be with you.*" They replied
"King of the western world, be with you peace."*

END OF BOOK THE FOURTH

203 high gilded] gilded *1831, 1846.*   205 brooks] brook's *1798, 1831, 1846.*
206 sands!"] sands! *1831.*
  Between *ll.* 206–7 *1831, 1846 insert five lines:*

> Where are the woodland voices that increast
> Along the unseen path on festal days,
> When lay the dry and outcast arbutus
> On the fane-step, and the first privet-flowers
> Threw their white light upon the vernal shrine?"

207 But others . . . steps] Some heedless . . . step *1831, 1846.*   209 among] amongst
1798.   210 height] highth *1831, 1846.*   220 king] King *1798.*   223 peace."* *For
footnote only in 1803 see notes at end of vol.*

THE FIFTH BOOK OF *GEBIR*

ARGUMENT

DESCRIPTION of the city *Masar*—occupations of the inhabitants. *Dalica's* journey thither—accosted by a stranger—discovers her sister *Myrthyr*—explains to her the object of her journey—gives an account of *Charoba* from childhood—her sense and courage—enchanted by the spells of *Gebir*—reasons for thinking so—suspects that *Gebir* too is somewhat affected by the exercise of this art—how *Charoba* hates him—resolves his destruction. *Myrthyr* rejoices—takes *Dalica* home—points mysteriously to an incomplete woof. *Dalica* stands amazed. *Myrthyr* dips thrice in a poisonous dye, the garment she had shewn to *Dalica*, and delivers it as a present inevitably fatal to *Gebir*.

GEBIR

BOOK V

ONCE a fair city, courted then by kings,
Mistress of nations, throng'd by palaces,
Raising her head o'er destiny, her face
Glowing with pleasure, and with palms refreshed,
Now, pointed at by Wisdom or by Wealth,
Bereft of beauty, bare of ornaments,
Stood, in the wilderness of woe, Masar.
Ere far advancing, all appear'd a plain.
Treacherous and fearful mountains, far advanced.
Her glory so gone down, at human step   10
The fierce hyæna, frighted from the walls,
Bristled his rising back, his teeth unsheathed,
Drew the long growl and with slow foot retired.
Still were remaining some of ancient race,
And ancient arts were now their sole delight.
With Time's first sickle they had marked the hour
When at their incantation would the Moon
Start back, and shuddering shed blue blasted light.
The rifted rays they gather'd, and immersed
In potent portion of that wondrous wave   20
Which, hearing rescued Israel, stood erect,
And led her armies through his crystal gates.
     Hither—none shared her way, her counsel none—
Hied the Masarian Dalica: 'twas night,
And the still breeze fell languid on the waste.
She, tired with journey long, and ardent thoughts,
Stopt; and before the city she descried

Argument. *Only in 1803.*   6 ornaments] ornament *1846.*   7 Masar [*cf.*
Masr el-Kahira (Cairo). W.]   14 Still] Yet *1831, 1846.*   16 marked] markt *1831,*
1846.   19 immersed] immerst *1831, 1846.*

A female form emerge above the sands:
Intent she fix'd her eyes, and on herself
Relying, with fresh vigor bent her way;   30
Nor disappear'd the woman, but exclaim'd—
One hand retaining tight her folded vest—
"Stranger! who loathest life, there lies Masar.
Begone, nor tarry longer, or, ere morn,
The cormorant, in his solitary haunt
Of insulated rock or sounding cove,
Stands on thy bleached bones, and screams for prey.
My lips can scatter them a hundred leagues,
So shrivell'd in one breath, as all the sands
We tread on, could not in as many years.   40
Wretched who die nor raise their sepulchre!*
Therefor begone."
                    But, Dalica, unaw'd,—
Tho' in her wither'd but still firm right-hand
Held up with imprecations, hoarse and deep,
Glimmer'd her brazen sickle, and inclosed
Within its figur'd curve the fading moon—
Spake thus aloud. "By yon bright orb of Heaven,
In that most sacred moment when her beam
Guided first thither by the forked shaft,
Strikes thro' the crevice of Arishtah's tower—"   50
"Sayst thou?" astonished cried the sorceress,
"Woman of outer darkness, fiend of death,
From what inhuman cave, what dire abyss,
Hast thou invisible that spell o'erheard?
What potent hand hath touched thy quicken'd corse,
What song dissolved thy cearments; who unclosed
Those faded eyes, and fill'd them from the stars?
But if with inextinguished light of life
Thou breathest, soul and body unamerst,

* The Egyptians thought this the greatest calamity, from a belief that they should
come to life again, at the expiration of a certain term of years. [L. *footnote only in 1803.*]

29 fix'd] fixt *1831, 1846.*   30 vigor] vigour *1831, 1846.*   31 exclaim'd]
exclamed 1831.   38 a hundred leagues] o'er every sea *1846.*   Between *ll.* 38–9
ed. 1846 inserts one line:
                    Under the rising and the setting sun,
39 shrivell'd] shrivel'd *1798, 1831, 1846.*   40 as many] a hundred *1846.*   42
Therefor] Therefore *1846.*   43 still] stil *1831.*   45 inclosed] enclosed *1846.*
50 Arishtah's tower [*either* El Arish, an Egyptian town on the Syrian frontier, *or* the
modern Rosetta which, according to Bruce, was known by the name of Rashid. W.]
56 cearments] cerements *1831, 1846.*

Then, whence that invocation; who hath dared   60
Those hallow'd words, divulging, to profane?"
Then Dalica—
    "To heaven, not earth, addrest,
Prayers for protection cannot be profane."
 Here the pale sorceress turn'd her face aside,
Wildly, and mutter'd to herself, amazed,
"I dread her who, alone, at such an hour,
Can speak so strangely; who can thus combine
The words of reason with our gifted rites;
Yet will I speak once more—If thou hast seen
The city of Charoba, hast thou marked   70
The steps of Dalica?"
     "What then?"
        "The tongue
Of Dalica has then our rites divulged."
"Whose rites?"
    "Her sister's, mother's, and her own."
"Never."
   "How sayst thou never? one would think,
Presumptuous, thou wert Dalica."
       "I am,
Woman, and who art thou?" with close embrace,
Clung the Masarian round her neck, and cried
"Art thou, then, not my sister? ah I fear
The golden lamps and jewels of a court
Deprive thine eyes of strength and purity: 80
O Dalica, mine watch the waning moon,
For ever patient in our mother's art,
And rest on Heaven suspended, where the founts
Of Wisdom rise, where sound the wings of Power:
Studies intense of strong and stern delight!
And thou too, Dalica, so many years
Wean'd from the bosom of thy native land,
Returnest back, and seekest true repose.
O what more pleasant than the short-breath'd sigh,
When laying down your burden at the gate,   90
And dizzy with long wandering, you embrace
The cool and quiet of a homespun bed."

62 Then Dalica—] Dalica cried, *1831, 1846.* 63 cannot] can not *1846* profane]
profaned *1798.* 67 thus] close *1798.* 73 sister's . . . own."] mother's."
"Never." "One would think, *1846.* 74 *om. 1846.* 84 sound] sounds *text*
sound *errata 1798.* 90 burden] burthen *1831, 1846.*

"Alas," said Dalica, "tho' all commend
This choice, and many meet with no controul,
Yet, none pursue it! Age, by Care opprest,
Feels for the couch, and drops into the grave.
The tranquil scene lies further still from Youth.
Phrenzied Ambition and desponding Love
Consume Youth's fairest flow'rs; compar'd with Youth
Age has a something something like repose.   100
Myrthyr, I seek not here a boundary
Like the horizon, which, as you advance,
Keeping its form and color, still recedes: *
But mind my errand, and my suit perform.
    Twelve years ago Charoba first could speak.
If her indulgent father asked her name,
She would indulge him too, and would reply
"*What? why, Charoba*"—rais'd with sweet surprize,
And proud to shine a teacher in her turn.
Shew her the graven sceptre; what its use?—   110
'Twas to beat dogs with, and to gather flies.
She thought the crown a plaything to amuse
Herself, and not the people, for she thought
Who mimick infant words might infant toys:
But while she watched grave elders look with awe
On such a bauble, she withheld her breath;
She was afraid her parents should suspect
They had caught childhood from her in a kiss;
She blushed for shame, and fear'd—for she believ'd.
Yet was not courage wanting in the child.   120
For I have often seen her with both hands
Shake a dry crocodile, of equal height,
And listen to the shells within the scales,
And fancy there was life, and yet apply
The jagged jaws wide open to her ear.
Past are three summers since she first beheld
The ocean: all around her earnest wait

* I am not, says Dalica, the pursuer of visionary happiness; I seek not a boundary,
        "Like the horizon, which, as you advance
        "Keeping its form and color, still recedes."
[L. *footnote only in 1803.*]

97 still] stil *1831.*   98 Phrenzied] Frenzied *1831, 1846.*   100 a . . . like] a something like *1846. misp.*   103 color, still] colour, yet *1831, 1846.*   114 mimick]
mimicked *1798.*   116 withheld] witheld *1798, 1831.*   121 For] No; *1831,*
1846.   122 height] highth *1831, 1846.*   127 her . . . wait] the child await *1831, 1846.*

Some exclamation of amazement wild.
She coldly said, her long-lashed eyes abased,
"Is this the mighty ocean? is this all!"   130
That wond'rous soul Charoba once possessed,
Capacious then as earth or heaven could hold,—
Soul discontented with capacity—
Is gone; I fear, for ever: need I say
She was enchanted by the wicked spells
Of Gebir, whom with lust of power inflamed,
The western winds have landed on our coast.
I since have watched her in each lone retreat,
Have heard her sigh, and soften out the name;
Then would she change it for Egyptian sounds   140
More sweet, and seem to taste them on her lips,
Then loathe them—Gebir, Gebir still return'd.
Who would repine, of reason not bereft!
For, soon the sunny stream of Youth runs down,*
And not a gadfly streaks the lake beyond.
Lone in the gardens, on her gather'd vest
How gently would her languid arm recline;
How often have I seen her kiss a flower,
And on cool mosses press her glowing cheek.
Nor was the stranger free from pangs himself.   150
Whether, by spell imperfect, or, while brew'd,
The swelling herbs infected him with foam,
Oft have the shepherds met him wandering
Thro' unfrequented paths, oft overheard
Deep groans, oft started from soliloquies,
Which they believe assuredly were meant
For spirits who attended him unseen.
But when from his illuded eyes retired
That figure Fancy fondly chose to raise,
—For never had she formed so fair an one   160
Herself, till Nature shew'd an architype—
He clasped the vacant air, and stood and gazed.
Then, owning it was folly, strange to tell,
Burst into peals of laughter at his woes:
Next, when his passion had subsided, went
Where from a cistern, green and ruin'd, oozed

---

* When "*the stream of youth has run down*," says Dalica, "there is nothing to break the dull uniformity of life." Dalica lived in a court, and was become an old woman: is there any thing unjust in her reflection? [L. *footnote only in 1803.*]

---

128 wild.] here: *1831, 1846.*   142 still] stil *1831.*   *ll.* 160–1 *om. 1831, 1846.*

A little rill, soon lost; there gather'd he
Violets, and harebells of a sister bloom,
Twining complacently their tender stems
With plants of kindest pliability.   170
These for a garland woven, for a crown
He platted pithy rushes, and ere dusk
The grass was whiten'd with their roots knipt off.
These threw he, finisht, in the little rill,
And stood surveying them with steady smile;
But, such a smile as that of Gebir bids
To Comfort a defiance, to Despair
A welcome, at whatever hour she please.
Had I observ'd him I had pitied him.
I have observ'd Charoba. I have asked   180
If she loved Gebir: "*love him!*" she exclaim'd,
With such a start of terror, such a flush
Of anger, "*I love Gebir? I in love?*"
Then, looked so piteous, so impatient looked—
But burst, before I answer'd, into tears.
Then saw I, plainly saw I, 'twas not love.
For, such her natural temper, what she likes
She speaks it out, or rather, she commands.
And could Charoba say with greater ease
"*Bring me a water-melon from the Nile*"   190
Than, if she lov'd him, "*Bring me him I love.*"
Therefor the death of Gebir is resolv'd."
   "Resolv'd indeed," cried Myrthyr, nought surpriz'd,
"Precious mine arts! I could without remorse
Kill, tho' I hold thee dearer than the day,
E'en thee thyself, to exercise mine arts.
Look yonder; mark yon pomp of funeral;
Is this from fortune or from favoring stars?
Dalica, look thou yonder, what a train!
What weeping! O what luxury! come, haste,   200
Gather me quickly up these herbs I dropt,
And then away—hush! I must, unobserved,
From those two maiden sisters pull the spleen;
Dissemblers! how invidious they surround
The virgin's tomb, where all but virgins weep."

---

170 kindest] tenderest *1798*.   172 He . . . and] Round, pithy rushes platted he—
1798.   173 knipt] nipt *1846*.   181 exclaim'd] exclamed *1831*.   184 Then,]
And *1831, 1846*.   185 But] And *1831, 1846*.   192 Therefor] Therefore *1846*.
194, 196 mine] my *1831, 1846*.

"Nay, hear me first," cried Dalica, "'tis hard
To perish to attend a foreign king."*
   "Perish! and may not then mine eye alone
Draw out the venom drop, and yet remain
Enough? the portion cannot be perceived."   210
Away she hasten'd with it to her home:
And sprinkling thrice fresh sulphur o'er the hearth,
Took up a spindle, with malignant smile,
And pointed to a woof, nor spake a word.
'Twas a dark purple; and its dye was dread.
   Plunged in a lonely house, to her unknown,
Now Dalica first trembled; o'er the roof
Wander'd her haggard eyes—'twas some relief—
The massy stones, tho' hewn most roughly, shew'd
The hand of man had once at least been there.   220
But from this object sinking back amazed,
Her bosom lost all consciousness, and shook
As if suspended in unbounded space.
Her thus intranced the sister's voice recall'd,
"Behold it here! dyed once again, 'tis done."
Dalica stept, and felt beneath her feet
The slippery floor, with moulder'd dust bestrown.
But Myrthyr seized with bare bold-sinew'd arm
The grey cerastes, writhing from her grasp,
And twisted off his horn; nor fear'd to squeeze   230
The viscous poison from his glowing gums:
Nor wanted there the root of stunted shrub †
Which he lays ragged, hanging o'er the sands,
And whence the weapons of his wrath are death:
Nor the blue urchin that with clammy fin ‡
Holds down the tossing vessel for the tides.
   Together these her scient hand combined,

---

* It has been a custom in various countries, and was so in Egypt, on the decease of a monarch, to kill persons that they might accompany him on his journey. Dalica seems unwilling that Gebir should have any attendants. She envies him even the society of the two spleenish sisters. Myrthyr sets her at ease by assuring her that her eye alone will draw out the "venom drop", which will not be missed, and consequently that she would not deprive them of their lives. [L. *footnote only in 1803.*]

  † Bruce mentions the kind of shrub, under which [which mostly *1831*] the cerastes burrows. [L. *1803, 1831*]. *See* Bruce's *Travels*, i. 19. [L. *1803 only.*]

  ‡ The Ancients supposed the echinus marinus could sink ships by fastening itself to the keel. [L. *footnote in 1803, 1831.*]

---

207 foreign] forein *1831.*   210 cannot] can not *1846.*   222 consciousness,]
consciousness' *1798 mispr.*   224 intranced] entranced *1831, 1846.*   227 be-
strown] bestrewn *1831, 1846.*   231 viscous] vicious *text* viscous *errata 1798.*

GEBIR: BOOK V

And more she added, dared I mention more.
Which done, with words most potent, thrice she dipt
The reeking garb, thrice waved it thro' the air: 240
She ceased; and suddenly the creeping wool
Shrunk up with crisped dryness in her hands.
"Take this," she cried, "and Gebir is no more."

END OF BOOK THE FIFTH

THE SIXTH BOOK OF *GEBIR*

ARGUMENT

TAMAR's nuptials—he appears upon the waves, together with the *Nymph*, and receives with modesty and fear the congratulations of the marine deities. They and their occupations described. *Gebir* and the Egyptian ambassadors—his conduct towards them observed—they return that night. *Tamar* awakened by the *Nymph*—her fondness and delicacy—her exhortations and reflections—prognosticates danger. Courage of *Tamar*—sorrowful at hearing it will fall on *Gebir*—dissuaded from enquiry. Their voyage. Several countries described. *Ætna*. *Corsica*—prediction that hence shall descend "A mortal man above all mortal praise." *Tamar*'s joy, however, not unmixt on beholding at a distance, and without any hopes of reaching it, his native land—his apostrophe to *Calpe*. The *Nymph*'s reflections—assures him that his countrymen will have justice, and Egypt enjoy liberty and equality. The Tuscan coast. Description of the sun setting—of a waterfall under the Apennines. Triumphs of *Tamar*'s descendents from the Garonne to the Rhine.

GEBIR

BOOK VI

Now to Aurora, borne by dappled steeds,
The sacred gate of orient pearl and gold,
Smitten with Lucifer's light silver wand,
Expanded slow to strains of harmony;
The waves beneath, in purpling rows, like doves
Glancing with wanton coyness tow'rd their queen,
Heav'd softly: thus the damsel's bosom heaves
When, from her sleeping lover's downy cheek,
To which so warily her own she brings
Each moment nearer, she perceives the warmth   10
(Blithe warmth!) of kisses fann'd by playful Dreams
Ocean, and earth, and heaven, was jubilee.
For 'twas the morning, pointed out by Fate,
When an immortal maid and mortal man
Should share each other's nature, knit in bliss.

Argument. *Only in 1803.*   4 to] in *1798.*   11 (Blithe . . . of] Of coming *1831, 1846.*

39

The brave Iberians far the beach o'erspread
Ere dawn, with distant awe: none hear the mew,
None mark the curlew, flapping o'er the field:
Silence held all, and fond expectancy.
Now suddenly the conch above the sea   20
Sounds, and goes sounding thro' the woods profound.
They, where they hear the echo, turn their eyes;
But nothing see they, save a purple mist
Roll from the distant mountain down the shore.
It rolls, it sails, it settles, it dissolves.
Now shines the Nymph to human eye reveal'd,
And leads her Tamar timorous o'er the waves.
Immortals, crowding round, congratulate
The shepherd; he shrinks back, of breath bereft.
His vesture clinging closely round his limbs   30
Unfelt, while they the whole fair form admire,
He fears that he has lost it; then he fears
The wave has mov'd it; most to look he fears.
Scarce the sweet-flowing music he imbibes,
Or sees the peopled ocean: scarce he sees
Spio, with sparkling eyes, and Beröe
Demure, and young Ione, less renown'd,
Not less divine, mild-natured, Beauty form'd
Her face, her heart Fidelity; for Gods
Design'd, a mortal, too, Ione loved.   40
These were the Nymphs elected for the hour
Of Hesperus and Hymen; these had strewn
The bridal bed: these tuned afresh the shells,
Wiping the green that hoarsen'd them within:
These wove the chaplets; and at night resolved
To drive the dolphins from the wreathed door.
Gebir surveyed the concourse from the tents,
The Egyptian men around him; 'twas observ'd
By those below how wistfully he looked;
From what attention, with what earnestness   50
Now to his city, now to theirs, he waved
His hand, and held it, while they spake, outspread.
They tarried with him, and they shared the feast.
They stoop'd with trembling hand from heavy jars

16 Iberians] Ibericans *text* Iberians *errata 1798.*   36 Beröe] Beréó *text*, Beroe *errata
1798.*   37, 40 Ione] Iöne *1798.*   38 mild-natured] mildnatured *1798.*
2 strewn] strown *1846.*   46 wreathed] wretched *text* wreathed *errata 1798.*
52 outspread] outspred *1831.*

The wines of Gades gurgling in the bowl,
Nor bent they homeward till the moon appear'd
To hang midway betwixt the earth and skies.
'Twas then that leaning o'er the boy beloved,
In Ocean's grot where Ocean was unheard,
"Tamar!" the Nymph said gently, "come, awake!   60
Enough to love, enough to sleep, is given,
Haste we away." This Tamar deem'd deceit,
Spoken so fondly, and he kist her lips;
Nor blushed he then, for he was then unseen.
But she arising bade the youth arise.
"What cause to fly," said Tamar; she replied
"Ask none for flight, and feign none for delay."
  "O am I then deceiv'd! or am I cast
From dreams of pleasure to eternal sleep,
And, when I cease to shudder, cease to be!"   70
She held the downcast bridegroom to her breast,
Look'd in his face and charm'd away his fears.
She said not "wherefor have I then embraced
You, a poor shepherd, or at least, a man,
Myself a Nymph, that now I should deceive?"
She said not—Tamar did, and was ashamed.
Him overcome her serious voice bespake.
"Grief favours all who bear the gift of tears!
Mild at first sight, he meets his votaries,
And casts no shadow as he comes along:*   80
But, after his embrace, the marble chills
The pausing foot, the closing door sounds loud,
The fiend in triumph strikes the vaulted roof,
The uplifted eye sinks from his lurid shade.
Tamar, depress thyself, and miseries
Darken and widen: yes, proud-hearted man!
The sea-bird rises as the billows rise;
Nor otherwise, when mountain floods descend,
Smiles the unsullied lotus glossy-hair'd;
Thou, claiming all things, leanest on thy claim,   90

---

* "And casts no shadow as he comes along." Those who give themselves up to
Grief, which is at first a kind of indulgence, are blind and insensible to the consequence.
That which was a humour grows a torment. [L. *footnote only in 1803.*]

---

56 till] til *1831.*   73 wherefor] wherefore *1846.*   74 least] most *1831, 1846.*
ll. 78–84 *not in 1798.*   78 bear] bring *1846.*   83 vaulted roof,] roof, then
falls *1831, 1846.*   84 uplifted ... sinks] eye uplifted *1831, 1846.*

Till overwhelm'd thro' incompliancy.
Tamar, some silent tempest gathers round!"
  "Round whom," retorted Tamar; "thou describe
The danger, I will dare it."
                    "Who will dare
What is unseen?"
                        "The man that is unblest,"
  "But wherefor thou? It threatens not thyself,
Nor me, but Gebir and the Gadite host."
  "The more I know, the more a wretch am I,"
Groan'd deep the troubled youth, "still thou proceed."
  "Oh seek not destin'd evils to divine,   100
Found out at last too soon! Oh cease the search,
'Tis vain, 'tis impious, 'tis no gift of mine:
I will impart far better, will impart
What makes, when Winter comes, the Sun to rest
So soon on Ocean's bed his paler brow,
And Night to tarry so at Spring's return.
And I will tell, sometimes, the fate of men
Who loos'd from drooping neck the restless arm,
Adventurous, ere long nights had satisfied
The sweet and honest avarice of love: 110
How whirlpools have absorb'd them, storms o'erwhelm'd,
And how amidst their struggles and their prayers
The big wave blacken'd o'er the mouth supine:
Then, when my Tamar trembles at the tale,
Kissing his lips, half-open with surprize,
Glance from the gloomy story, and with glee
Light on the fairer fables of the Gods.
  Thus we may sport at leisure when we go
Where, loved by Neptune and the Naid, loved
By pensive Dryad pale, and Oread,   120
The spritely Nymph whom constant Zephyr woos,
Rhine rolls his beryl-color'd wave: than Rhine
What River from the mountains ever came
More stately! most the simple crown adorns
Of rushes, and of willows, intertwined
With here and there a flower—his lofty brow,

91 Till] Til *1831.* 96 wherefor] wherefore *1798, 1846.* 99 still ... proceed] stil ... procede *1831.* 101 out ... soon!] soon enough when here; *1798.* Oh cease] cease here *1831, 1846.* 108 loos'd] loose *1798;* loost *1846.* 112 amidst] amid *1831, 1846.* 119 Naid] Naiad *1846.* 121 spritely] sprightly *1846.* woos] woes *1798.* 122 beryl-] berry-*text,* beryl- *errata 1798.* color'd] colour'd *1831, 1846.* than] that *text,* than *errata 1798.* 125 intertwined] interwined *mispr. 1831.*

Shaded with vines, and mistleto, and oak,
He rears; and mystic bards his fame resound.
Or gliding opposite, th' Illyrian gulph
Will harbour us from ill." While thus she spake, 130
She toucht his eye-lashes with libant lip
And breath'd ambrosial odours; o'er his cheek
Celestial warmth suffusing: grief dispersed,
And strength and pleasure beam'd upon his brow:
Then pointed she before him: first arose
To his astonisht and delighted view
The sacred isle that shrines the queen of love.
It stood so near him, so acute each sense,
That not the symphony of lutes alone,
Or coo serene or billing strife of doves, 140
But murmurs, whispers, nay, the very sighs
Which he himself had utter'd once, he heard.
Next, but long after, and far off, appear
The cloudlike cliffs and thousand towers of Crete:
Still further to the right, the Cyclades.
Phœbus had rais'd, and fixt them, to surround
His native Delos and aërial fane.
He saw the land of Pelops, host of Gods;
Saw the steep ridge where Corinth after stood,
Beck'ning the serious with the smiling Arts 150
Into the sunbright bay: unborn the maid*
That, to assure the bent-up hand unskill'd,
Look'd oft; but oft'ner fearing who might wake.
He heard the voice of rivers: he descried
Pindan Peneüs, and the slender Nymphs
That tread his banks, but fear the thundering tide:
These, and Amphrysos, and Apidanus,
And poplar-crowned Spercheios, and, reclined
On restless rocks, Enipeus, where the winds
Scatter'd above the weeds his hoary hair. 160
Then, with Pirenè, and with Panopè,
Evenus, troubled from paternal tears;
And last was Acheloüs, king of isles.

127 vines, and] and *not in 1798.*   129 gulph] gulf *1831, 1846.*   137 isle] ile *1831.*
145 Still] And *1831, 1846.*   149 steep] deep *text,* steep *errata 1798.*   150 Beck'ning]
Beckoning *1831, 1846.*   151 maid*] *For footnote see notes at end of vol.*   153 oft'ner]
oftener *1831, 1846.*   157 Apidanus] Apidanos *1846.*   158 Spercheios] Spercheos
1798; Spercheus *1831;* Sperchios *1846 see* Homer, *Iliad,* xvi. 174. W.]   162 Evenus]
Evenos *1846.*   Father of Marpessa. See Scholiast on *Iliad,* ix. 557 and Apollodorus, i.
VII. [W.]   163 Acheloüs] Acheloös *1846.*   isles] iles *1831.*

Zacynthus here, above rose Ithaca,
Like a blue bubble, floating in the bay.
Far onward, to the left, a glimm'ring light
Glanced out oblique; nor vanish'd; he inquired
Whence that arose: his consort thus replied.
   "Behold the vast Eridanus! ere night
We shall again behold him, and rejoice.   170
Of noble rivers none with mightier force
Rolls his unwearied torrent to the main.
And now Sicanian Etna rose to view. *
Darkness with light more horrid she confounds,
Baffles the breath, and dims the sight, of day.
Tamar grew giddy with astonishment,
And, looking up, held fast the bridal vest.
He heard the roar above him, heard the roar
Beneath, and felt it too, as he beheld,
Hurl, from Earth's base, rocks, mountains, to the skies.   180
   Meanwhile the Nymph had fixt her eyes beyond,
As seeing somewhat; not intent on aught.
He, more amazed than ever, then exclaim'd
   "Is there another flaming isle? or this
Illusion, thus past over unobserved?"
   "Look yonder," cried the Nymph, without reply,
"Look yonder!" Tamar look'd, and saw two isles
Where the waves whiten'd on the desart shore.
Then she continued. "That which intervenes†
Scarcely the Nymphs themselves have known from Fame: 190
But mark the furthest: *there* shall once arise,
From Tamar shall arise, 'tis Fate's decree,
A mortal man above all mortal praise.‡
Methinks already, tho' she threatens Heav'n,
Towering Trinacria to my Corsis yields."
   Tamar, who listen'd still amidst amaze,
Had never thought of progeny: he clasped
His arms with extasy around his bride,

† "That which intervenes". Sardinia. [L. *footnote only in 1803.*]

---

164 Zacynthus] Lacynthus *text*, Zacynthus *errata 1798*; Zacynthos *1846*.   167
Glanced , . . oblique] Obliquely glanced *1798*.   169 night] long *1831, 1846*.
170 shall] may *1831, 1846*.   172 main.] main." *1831, 1846*.   173 Sicanian] Sicalian
text, Sicanian *errata 1798*.   Etna] Ætna *1846*.   view *] *For footnote only in 1803 see notes
at end of vol.*   178 *So also in errata 1798 which in text has* it roll above him, heard it
roll   183 exclaim'd] exclamed *1831*.   184 isle] ile *1831*.   187 two isles] afar *1831,
1846*.   188 desart] desert *1831, 1846*.   *ll.* 189–200 *om. 1831, 1846*.   193 praise.‡
For footnote only in 1803 see notes at end of vol.   194 threatens] equals *1798*.
195 my Corsis] Therapnè *1798*.

And pleasure freshen'd her prophetic lips.
He thought too of his ancestors and home.   200
When from amidst grey ocean first he caught
The heights of Calpè, sadden'd he exclaim'd
"Rock of Iberia! fixt by Jove, and hung
With all his thunder-bearing clouds, I hail
Thy ridges, rough and cheerless! what tho' Spring
Nor kiss thy brow, nor deck it with a flower,
Yet will I hail thee, hail thy flinty couch,
Where Valor and where Virtue have reposed."
    The Nymph said, sweetly smiling, "Fickle Man
Would not be happy could he not regret!   210
And I confess how, looking back, a thought
Has touched and tuned, or rather, thrill'd my heart,
Too soft for sorrow, and too strong for joy.
Fond foolish maid, 'twas with mine own accord,
It sooth'd me, shook me, melted, drown'd, in tears.
But weep not thou; what cause hast thou to weep.
Weep not thy country: weep not caves abhorr'd,
Dungeons and portals that exclude the day.
Gebir—tho' generous, just, humane—inhaled
Rank venom from these mansions. Rest O King   220
In Egypt thou! nor, Tamar! pant for sway.
With horrid chorus, Pain, Diseases, Death,
Stamp on the slippery pavement of the great,
And ring their sounding emptiness thro' earth.
The Hour, in vain held back by War, arrives
When Justice shall unite the Iberian hinds,
And equal Egypt bid her shepherds reign.
The fairest land dry-lasht could I forego
Rather than crawl a subject; corals, pearls,
Confine me round, if Nymph can be confined,   230
'Twill not console me! Kindness prest by Power
Gives pride fresh tortures, and fresh bars constraint.
And guard me, Heaven! from that paternal care
Which beats and bruises me with iron rods,
Till I embrace them, and with tears protest

201 amidst] amid *1831, 1846.*   202 heights . . . exclaim'd] hights . . . exclamed *1831*; highths . . . exclaimed *1846.*   206 deck] cool *1831, 1846.*   208 Valor] Valour *1831, 1846.*   217 Weep not] Wouldst thou *1831, 1846;* weep not] wouldst those *1831, 1846.* abhorr'd] abborr'd *mispr. 1831.*   219 inhaled] *So also in errata 1798 which has* exhaled *in text.*   223 great] proud *1831, 1846.*   *After l.* 224 *edd. 1831, 1846 have:*
         Possess the ocean, me, thyself, and peace."
ll. 225–44 *om. 1831, 1846.*

That I am happy! rather, when I sin,
Shut me from love and hide me in the deep."
   Now disappear the Liparean isles
Behind, and forward hang th' Etrurian coasts,
Verdant with privet and with juniper.   240
Now faith is plighted: piled on every hearth,
Crackle the consecrated branches, heard
Propitious, and from vases rough-embost
Thro' the light ember falls the bubbling wine.
And now the chariot of the sun descends!
The waves rush hurried from the foaming steeds:
Smoke issues from their nostrils at the gate;
Which, when they enter, with huge golden bar
Atlas and Calpè close across the main.
They reach th' unfurrow'd Appennines—all hail   250
Clime of unbounded liberty and love!—
And deep beneath their feet, a river flow'd,
Of varied view; yet each variety
So charming, that their eyes could scarce admire
The many beauties that around them throng'd,
Successive as the wave: aspiring elms
O'er the wide water cast a mingled shade
Of tendrils green and grapes of rosy hue.
Among the branches thousand birds appear'd
To raise their little throats, with trilling song   260
Unwearied, but alas their trilling song,
Fast as it flow'd, the roaring torrent drown'd.
Some, unacquainted with the scene, unmoved
By love of tuneful mate, on timid wing
Fly from the eternal thunder of the waves;
But these, content with humid woods, that yield
The choicest moss to warm their callow young,
Brood over them, nor shudder at the damp
That falls for ever round each circled nest.
Here craggy rocks arise; the stream recoils   270
Struggling; but, hurried to the vast abyss
Abrŭptly, reascends in gloomy rain;
Bespangling in its way the scatter'd herbs
That cling around each lofty precipice,

---

238 disappear] disapear *1798.*   245 chariot] charriot *1798.*   246 the] his *1831,*
1846.   249 Calpè [Alube, the Phoenician name for Gibraltar, in Greek καλυβη. καλπη.
W.]   main] sea *1831, 1846.*   *ll.* 250–308 *om. 1831, 1846.*   252 And deep] Deep
down *1798.*   265 from the] from the th' *misp. 1798.*   scatter'd] scatterd *1798.*

Of wintry blasts regardless, and the reeds
Which never shall amuse with shrill essay
The valley or the grove, and tender flowers
On virgin bosom never to repose.
But all around them dart the wandering rays
In myriads, and amid the fresh festoons   280
Of pensile vines a hundred arches bend;
Rais'd by the hand of Phœbus and of Jove,
The seats of Iris.—Rise, Iberian Man!
Rise, maid of Ocean! I myself will rise.
Vigorous with youth, with soaring soul endued,
I feel not earth beneath me—lo I snatch
The sunbeam, scorn the thunder, climb the skies!
What force have you inform'd me with! what sight,
Piercing thro' darkness and futurity.

Yonder, where, sailing slow, the clouds retire,   290
How grand a prospect opens! Alps o'er Alps
Tower, to survey the triumphs that proceed.*
There, while Garumna† dances in the gloom
Of larches, mid her Naids, or reclined
Leans on a broom-clad bank to watch the sports
Of some far-distant chamois silken-hair'd,
The chaste Pyrené, drying up her tears,
Finds, with your children, refuge: yonder, Rhine
Lays his imperial sceptre at their feet.

What hoary form so vigorous vast bends there?   300
Time,—Time himself throws off his motly garb
Figur'd with monstrous men and monstrous gods,
And in pure vesture enters their pure fanes,
A proud partaker of their festivals.
Captivity led captive, War o'erthrown,
They shall o'er Europe, shall o'er Earth extend
Empire that seas alone and skies confine,‡
And glory that shall strike the crystal stars.

END OF BOOK THE SIXTH

† "Garumna", the river Garonne, which rises in the Pyrenean mountains. [L. footnote only in 1803.]
‡ "Empire that seas alone and skies confine." The empire of justice and equality. Great hopes were raised from the French revolution, but every good man is disappointed. God forbid that we should ever be impelled to use their means of amelioration, or that our arms should be attended by success, like theirs,—internal and external subjugation. [L. only in 1803.]

276 essay] assay *text*, essay *errata 1798.*   292 proceed.* *For footnote only in 1803 see notes at end of vol.*   293 Garumna] the Garonne *1798.*

HEROIC POEMS

THE SEVENTH BOOK OF *GEBIR*

ARGUMENT

AGAINST colonization in peopled countries. All nature dissuades from whatever is hostile to equality. The day, according to expectation, of *Charoba's* marriage with *Gebir*. The games of the Tartessians, Gadites, Nebrissans, &c. Sensations of *Gebir*— of *Charoba*. Description of her bath. Preparations. Ardor of the people. She sets out. *Gebir* meets her. Observation by one of her handmaids. The procession. They mount their thrones. *Dalica* appears—throws perfumes over the head and feet of *Gebir*— draws over his shoulders the deadly garment. *Charoba*, who observes, but misinterprets the change in his countenance, with an emotion of tenderness and fear, expects the declaration of his love. He descends from his throne. Astonishment of the Iberians. Horror of *Charoba*—her grief—her love—repeats his name—embraces him in the agonies of despair—calls earth and heaven to attest her innocence—laments most passionately that wretchedness like her's must seem infinitely too great for any thing but guilt—implores instant death—appeals to *Dalica*—acquits *her* of any evil intentions—but accuses the *demons* of tainting the deadly robe—apostrophe to her parents, particularly to her mother—to *Gebir*. He recovers to perceive her sorrows, is consoled, and dies.

GEBIR

BOOK VII

WHAT mortal first, by adverse fate assail'd,
Trampled by tyranny, or scoft by scorn,
Stung by remorse, or wrung by poverty,
Bade, with fond sigh, his native land farewel?
Wretched! but tenfold wretched, who resolv'd
Against the waves to plunge th' expatriate keel,
Deep with the richest harvest of his land!
    Driven with that weak blast which Winter leaves,*
Closing his palace-gates on Caucasus,
Oft hath a berry risen forth a shade: 10
From the same parent plant, another lies
Deaf to the daily call of weary hind—
Zephyrs pass by, and laugh at his distress.
By every lake's and every river's side†
The Nymphs and Naids teach Equality:
In voices gently querulous they ask

---

* Those who have left their country from a sense of injustice or from indifference, have often flourished; while those whom the mother country has sent out with great care and expence, have utterly deceived her expectations. [L. *footnote only in 1803.*]
    † Here are twenty verses which were not in the first edition. They describe the equality which nature teaches, the absurdity of colonizing a country which is peopled, and the superior advantage of cultivating those which remain unoccupied. [L. *footnote only in 1803.*]

Argument. *Only in 1803.*   1 adverse fate] various ills *1798.*   2 scoft] scofft *1846.*
2 tyranny] Tyranny *1798.*   3 poverty] Poverty *1798.*   4 Bade . . . sigh,] Prime
evil! bade *1798.*   farewel] farewell *1831, 1846.*   8 weak] bleak *1798.*   12 hind]
wind *text*, hind *errata 1798.*   *ll.* 14–33 *not in 1798.*   15 Naids] Naiads *1846.*

"Who would with aching head and toiling arms
Bear the full pitcher to the stream far off?
Who would, of power intent on high emprize,
Deem less the praise to fill the vacant gulph　　　　　　20
Than raise Charybdis upon Etna's brow?"
Amidst her darkest caverns most retired,
Nature calls forth her filial Elements
To close around and crush that monster *Void*.—
Fire, springing fierce from his resplendent throne,
And Water, dashing the devoted wretch
Woundless and whole, with iron-colour'd mace,
Or whirling headlong in his war-belt's fold.
Mark well the lesson, man! and spare thy kind.
Go, from their midnight darkness wake the woods,　　　30
Woo the lone forest in her last retreat—
Many still bend their beauteous heads unblest
And sigh aloud for elemental man.
Thro' palaces and porches, evil eyes
Light upon ev'n the wretched, who have fled
The house of bondage, or the house of birth:
Suspicions, murmurs, treacheries, taunts, retorts,
Attend the brighter banners that invade;
And the first horn of hunter, pale with want,
Sounds to the chase; the second to the war.　　　　　40
　　The long awaited day at last arrived,
When, linkt together by the seven-arm'd Nile,
Egypt with proud Iberia should unite.
Here the Tartessian, there the Gadite tents
Rang with impatient pleasure: here engaged
Woody Nebrissa's quiver-bearing crew,
Contending warm with amicable skill:
While they of Durius raced along the beach,
And scatter'd mud and jeers on those behind.
The strength of Bœtis, too, removed the helm,　　　　50
And stript the corslet off, and staunched the foot
Against the mossy maple, while they tore

---

20 gulph] gulf *1831, 1846*. 　　21 Than] Then *misp. 1831.* 　　Etna's] Ætna's *1846.*
22 Amidst] Amid *1831, 1846*. 　　32 still] stil *1831.* 　　　34 Thro' . . . eyes] *After*
l. 33 *ed. 1798 has:*

> So falls it here: and, [*so in text,* one *in errata*] driven forth by Fate,
> On any rock may rest; but evil eyes

35 upon . . . wretched] on the weak, or restless *1798*; upon e'en the wretched *1831, 1846.*
40 second to the] second sounds to *1846.* 　　44 Tartessian] Tartesian *1831.* 　　48 they]
those *1798.* 　　49 those] all *1831, 1846.* 　　50 Bœtis] Bætis *1831, 1846.*

Their quivering lances from the hissing wound.
Others pushed forth the prows of their compeers;
And the wave, parted by the pouncing beak,
Swells up the sides, and closes far astern:
The silent oars now dip their level wings,
And weary with strong stroke the whitening wave.
Others, afraid of tardiness, return.
Now, entering the still harbour, every surge   60
Runs with a louder murmur up their keel,
And the slack cordage rattles round the mast.
Sleepless, with pleasure and expiring fears,
Had Gebir risen ere the break of dawn,
And o'er the plains appointed for the feast
Hurried with ardent step: the swains admired
What could so transversely sweep off the dew,
For never long one path had Gebir trod,
Nor long, unheeding man, one pace preserved.
Not thus Charoba. She despair'd the day.   70
The day was present: true: yet she despair'd.
In the too tender and once tortured heart
Doubts gather strength from habit, like disease;
Fears, like the needle verging to the pole,
Tremble and tremble into certainty.
How often, when her maids with merry voice
Call'd her, and told the sleepless queen 'twas morn,
How often would she feign some fresh delay,
And tell them (tho' they saw) that she arose.*
Next to her chamber, closed by cedar doors,   80
A bath, of purest marble, purest wave,
On its fair surface bore its pavement high.
Arabian gold inclosed the crystal roof,
With fluttering boys adorn'd and girls unrobed,
These, when you touch the quiet water, start
From their aërial sunny arch, and pant
Entangled midst each other's flowery wreaths,
And each pursuing is in turn pursued.
    Here came at last, as ever wont at morn,

* "Tho' they saw." If this were not taken parenthetically, and read so, it would convey a double sense. Charoba told the attendants that she was rising, "tho' they saw"—tho' they were in the apartment, and could perceive that there were no preparations for that purpose. [L. *footnote only in 1803.*]

54 pushed] pused *text 1798,* push'd *in errata,* push *1831, 1846.*   67 could . . . off] so transversely could have swept *1831, 1846.*   79 them] 'em *1831, 1846.*   83 inclosed] enchased *1831, 1846.*   87 midst] mid *1831, 1846.*   flowery] flowry *1798.*

Charoba: long she linger'd at the brink,   90
Often she sighed, and, naked as she was,
Sat down, and leaning on the couch's edge,
On the soft inward pillow of her arm
Rested her burning cheek: she moved her eyes;
She blush'd; and blushing plung'd into the wave.
  Now brazen chariots thunder thro' each street,
And neighing steeds paw proudly from delay.
While o'er the palace breathes the dulcimer,
Lute, and aspiring harp, and lisping reed;
Loud rush the trumpets, bursting thro' the throng,   100
And urge the high-shoulder'd vulgar; now are heard
Curses and quarrels and constricted blows,
Threats and defiance and suburban war.
Hark! the reiterated clangor sounds!
Now murmurs, like the sea, or like the storm,
Or like the flames on forests, move and mount
From rank to rank, and loud and louder roll,
Till all the people is one vast applause.
Yes, 'tis herself—Charoba—now the strife!
To see again a form so often seen.   110
Feel they some partial pang, some secret void,
Some doubt of feasting those fond eyes again?
Panting imbibe they that refreshing sight*
To reproduce in hour of bitterness?
She goes; the king awaits her from the camp.
Him she descried; and trembled ere he reached
Her car; but shudder'd paler at his voice.
So the pale silver at the festive board
Grows paler fill'd afresh and dew'd with wine;
So seems the tenderest herbage of the spring   120
To whiten, bending from a balmy gale.
The beauteous queen alighting he received,
And sighed to loose her from his arms; she hung
A little longer on them thro' her fears,
Her maidens followed her: and one that watch'd,

    * "Panting imbibe they that refreshing sight
      To reproduce in hour of bitterness?"
This metaphor is taken from the country. It alludes to the camel, which is said to be
able to refresh itself with the water which it has imbibed and secreted many days.
[L. *footnote only in 1803.*]

91 Often . . . sighed] she *om. in text 1798, added in errata.*   92 couch's] couchis
1831.   96 chariots] charriots *1798.*   104 clangor] clangour *1831, 1846.*
108 Till] Til *1831.*   116 he] she *text,* he *errata 1798.*

One that had call'd her in the morn, observ'd
How virgin passion with unfuel'd flame
Burns into whiteness; while the blushing cheek
Imagination heats and Shame imbues.
    Between both nations, drawn in ranks, they pass.   130
The priests, with linen ephods, linen robes,
Attend their steps, some follow, some precede,
Where, cloath'd with purple intertwined with gold,
Two lofty thrones commanded land and main.
Behind and near them, numerous were the tents
As freckled clouds o'erfloat our vernal skies,
Numerous as wander in warm moonlight nights,
Along Meander's or Cäyster's marsh,
Swans, pliant-neckt, and village storks, revered.
Throughout each nation moved the hum confused,   140
Like that from myriad wings, o'er Scythian cups
Of frothy milk, concreted soon with blood.
Throughout the fields the savory smoke ascends,
And boughs and branches shade the hides unbroached.
Some roll the flowery turf to form a seat,
And others press the helmet—now resounds
The signal!—queen and monarch mount the thrones.
The brazen clarion hoarsens: many leagues
Above them, many to the south, the hern
Rising with hurried croak and throat outstretched,   150
Plows up the silvering surface of her plain.
    Tottering, with age's zeal, and mischief's haste,
Now was discover'd Dalica: she reached
The throne: she lean'd against the pedestal;
And now ascending stood before the king.
Prayers for his health and safety she prefer'd,
And o'er his head and o'er his feet she threw
Myrrh, nard, and cassia, from three golden urns.
His robe of native woof she next removed,
And round his shoulders drew the garb accurst,   160
And bow'd her head, and parted: soon the queen
Saw the blood mantle in his manly cheeks,
And fear'd, and fault'ring sought her lost replies,
And blest the silence that she wished were broke.

128 whiteness] paleness *1798*.   132 precede] preceed *1798*.   133 cloath'd]
clothed *1846*.   138 Cäyster's] Caÿster's *1798, 1846* Cayster's *1831*.   143 savory]
savoury *1831, 1846*.   145 to form] into *1831, 1846*.   146 press] take *1798*.   149 hern]
heron *1798, 1831, 1846*.   154 lean'd] leant *1831, 1846*.   157 And o'er] And on *1798*.
161 and parted] departing *1846*.   163 fault'ring] faultring *1798*.   faltering *1831, 1846*.

Alas, unconscious maiden! night shall close,
And love, and sovereignty, and life dissolve,
And Egypt be one desert drench'd in blood.
　　When thunder overhangs the fountain's head,
Losing their wonted freshness, every stream
Grows turbid, grows with sickly warmth suffused:　　　170
Thus were the brave Iberians, when they saw
The king of nations from his throne descend.
Scarcely, with pace uneven, knees unnerved,
Reach'd he the waters: in his troubled ear
They sounded murmuring drearily; they rose
Wild, in strange colours, to his parching eyes:
They seem'd to rush around him, seem'd to lift
From the receding earth his helpless feet.
He fell—Charoba shriek'd aloud—she ran—
Frantic with fears and fondness, wild with woe,　　　180
Nothing but Gebir dying she beheld.
The turban that betray'd its golden charge
Within, the veil that down her shoulders hung,
All fallen at her feet! the furthest wave
Creeping with silent progress up the sand,
Glided thro' all, and rais'd their hollow folds.
In vain they bore him to the sea, in vain
Rubb'd they his temples with the briny warmth.
He struggled from them, strong with agony,
He rose half up; he fell again; he cried　　　190
"*Charoba! O Charoba!*" She embraced
His neck, and raising on her knee one arm,
Sighed when it moved not, when it fell she shrieked,
And clasping loud both hands above her head,
She call'd on Gebir, call'd on earth, on heaven.
　　"Who will believe me; what shall I protest;
How innocent, thus wretched?* God of Gods,
Strike me—who most offend thee most defy—
Charoba most offends thee—strike me, hurl
From this accursed land, this faithless throne.　　　200

---

* "How innocent, thus wretched?" How shall I appear innocent in the eyes of mankind, when the Gods have afflicted me with so grievous a calamity? She has no suspicion that Dalica was conscious of the effect which the robe had produced. [L. *footnote only in 1803.*]

---

166 sovereignty] sovranty *1831, 1846.*　　　167 desart drench'd] desert drencht *1831, 1846.*　　　168 fountain's head] fountain heads *1798,* fountain-head *1846.*
169 their] its *1831, 1846.*　　　176 colours] colors *1798.*　　　180 wild] mazed *1831, 1846.*
183 shoulders] shoulder *1846.*　　　188 Rubb'd] Rub'd *1831.*　　　briny] briney *1798.*

O Dalica! see here the royal feast!
See here the gorgeous robe! you little thought
How have the demons dyed that robe with death.
Where are ye, dear fond parents! when ye heard
My feet in childhood pat the palace floor,
Ye started forth, and kist away surprize—
Will ye now meet me! how, and where, and when?
And must I fill your bosom with my tears,
And, what I never have done, with your own!
Why have the Gods thus punish'd me? what harm   210
Have ever I done them? have I profaned
Their temples, ask'd too little, or too much?
Proud if they granted, griev'd if they withheld?
O mother! stand between your child and them!
Appease them, soothe them, soften their revenge,
Melt them to pity with maternal tears.
Alas, but if you cannot!—they themselves
Will then want pity rather than your child.
O Gebir! best of monarchs, best of men,
What realm hath ever thy firm even hand   220
Or lost by feebleness, or held by force!
Behold, thy cares and perils how repaid!
Behold the festive day, the nuptial hour!
Me miserable, desolate, undone!''
   Thus raved Charoba: horror, grief, amaze,
Pervaded all the host: all eyes were fixt:
All stricken motionless and mute—the feast
Was like the feast of Cepheus,* when the sword
Of Phineus, white with wonder, shook restrain'd,
And the hilt rattled in his marble hand.   230
She heard not, saw not; every sense was gone;
One passion banish'd all; dominion, praise,
The world itself was nothing—Senseless man—
What would thy fancy figure now from worlds?
There is no world to those that grieve and love.
She hung upon his bosom, prest his lips,
Breath'd, and would feign it his that she resorbed.
She chafed the feathery softness of his veins,

* "The feast of Cepheus." This story is told at large in the Metamorphoses of Ovid. Phineus was turned into marble by the Gorgon shield. [L. *footnote only in 1803. See* Ovid, *Met.* v.]

213 withheld] witheld *1831.*   217 cannot] can not *1846.*   *l. 224 om. 1831,*
1846.   225 horror] horrour *1831.*   228 sword] Sword *1798.*

54

That swell'd out black, like tendrils round their vase
After libation: lo! he moves! he groans! 240
He seems to struggle from the grasp of death.
Charoba shriek'd, and fell away; her hand
Still clasping his, a sudden blush o'erspread
Her pallid humid cheek, and disappear'd.
'Twas not the blush of shame—what shame has woe?—
'Twas not the genuine ray of hope; it flashed
With shuddering glimmer thro' unscatter'd clouds;
It flash'd from passions rapidly opposed.
    Never so eager, when the world was waves,
Stood the less daughter of the ark, and tried 250
(Innocent this temptation!) to recall
With folded vest, and casting arm, the dove:
Never so fearful, when amidst the vines
Rattled the hail, and when the light of heaven
Closed, since the wreck of Nature, first eclipsed—
As she was eager for his life's return,
As she was fearful how his groans might end.
They ended:—cold and languid calm succeeds.
His eyes have lost their lustre; but his voice
Is not unheard, tho' short: he spake these words. 260
    "And weepest thou, Charoba! shedding tears
More precious than the jewels that surround
The neck of kings entomb'd!—then weep, fair queen,
At once thy pity and my pangs assuage.
Ah! what is grandeur—glory—they are past!
When nothing else, nor life itself, remains,
Still the fond mourner may be call'd our own.
Should I complain of Fortune? how she errs,
Scattering her bounty upon barren ground,
Slow to allay the lingering thirst of Toil? 270
Fortune, 'tis true, may err, may hesitate;
Death follows close, nor hesitates nor errs.
I feel the stroke! I die!" He would extend
His dying arm; it fell upon his breast.
Cold sweat and shivering ran o'er every limb,
His eyes grew stiff; he struggled and expired.

THE END

239 swell'd] swel'd *1798*.   241 death] Death *1798*.   243 Still... o'erspread] Stil...
o'erspred *1831*.   246 hope] Hope *1798*.   *l.* 250 *See note at end of vol*.   253 amidst] amid
1831, 1846.   255 eclipsed] eclipst *1831, 1846*.   258 succeeds] succedes *1831*.   259 lustre]
luster *1831*.   but] bnt *misp. 1798*.   265 grandeur] grandour *1831*.   266 nor] not *1798*,
1831, 1846.   267 Still] Stil *1831*.

HEROIC POEMS

CRYSAOR

[Printed 1800, published in 1802; reprinted 1846, 1847, 1859, 1876. In 1876 "Crysaor" and "Regeneration" beginning "We are what suns and winds and waters make us" were wrongly printed as forming one poem. Text, 1802.]

ADVERTISEMENT TO THE STORY OF CRYSAOR

Hardly any thing remains that made ancient Iberia classic land. We have little more than the titles of fables—than portals, as it were, covered over with gold and gorgeous figures, that shew us what once must have been the magnificence of the whole interior edifice. Lucan has wandered over Numidia, and Virgil too at the conclusion of his Georgics, has left the indelible mark of his footstep near the celebrated Pharos of Egypt. But, in general, the poets of Greece and Italy were afraid of moving far from the latest habitations of their tutelar gods and heroes. I am fond of walking by myself; but others, who have gone before me, may have planted trees, or opened vistas, and rendered my walks more amusing. I had begun to write a poem* connected in some degree with the early history of Spain; but doubtful whether I should ever continue it, and grown every hour more indifferent, I often sat down and diverted my attention with the remotest views I could find. The present is a sketch.

STORY OF CRYSAOR

Come, I beseech ye, Muses! who, retired
Deep in the shady glens by Helicon,
Yet know the realms of ocean, know the laws
Of his wide empire, and throughout his court
Know every Nymph, and call them each by name;
Who from your sacred mountain see afar
O'er earth and heaven, and hear and memorize
The crimes of men and counsels of the Gods;
Sing of those crimes and of those counsels, sing
Of Gades sever'd from the fruitful main;   10
And what befel, and from what mighty hand,
Crysäör, sovereign of the golden sword.

'Twas when the high Olympus shook with fear,
Lest all his temples, all his groves, be crushed
By Pelion piled on Ossa: but the sire
Of mortals and immortals waved his arm
Around, and all below was wild dismay:

* "The Phocæans." [L.]

Advertisement. *Not reprinted.*   *l.* 2 portals] door-posts *1800.*   *l.* 4. The allusion to Lucan and Virgil seems to need correction. See Virgil's reference to Numidia, *Georgics* iii. 339 ff. and Lucan, viii. 445: *petimus Pharon arvaque Lagi.* [W.] 8 opened] entered on *1800.*   10 continue] get thro *1800.*
Title. Story of *om. 1846–1859.* Chrysaor *1846–1859: name so spelt throughout poem.* 7 memorize] *so in errata 1802,* memorate *in text.*   11 befel] befell *1846–1859.* 12 Crysäör, sovereign] Chrysaor, wielder *1846–1859.*   13 *paragraphing mine.* [W.]   14 crushed] crusht *1846–1859.*

56

CRYSAOR

Again—'twas agony: again—'twas peace.
Crysäör still in Gades tarrying,
Hurl'd into ether, tinging, as it flew,   20
With sudden fire the clouds round Saturn's throne,
No pine surrender'd by retreating Pan,
Nor ash, nor poplar pale; but swoln with pride
Stood towering from the citadel; his spear
One hand was rested on, and one with rage
Shut hard, and firmly fixt against his side;
His frowning visage, flusht with insolence,
Rais'd up oblique to heaven. "O thou," he cried,
"Whom nations kneel to, not whom nations know,
Hear me, and answer, if indeed thou can'st,   30
The last appeal I deign thee or allow.
Tell me, and quickly, why should I adore,
Adored myself by millions? why invoke,
Invoked with all thy attributes? men wrong
By their prostrations, prayers, and sacrifice,
Either the gods, their rulers, or themselves:
But flame and thunder fright them from the *Gods*,
Themselves they cannot, dare not—they are ours,
Us—dare they, can they, *us*? but triumph, Jove!
Man for one moment hath engaged his lord,   40
Henceforth let merchants value him, not kings.*
No! lower thy sceptre, and hear Atrobal,
And judge aright to whom men sacrifice.
My children, said the sage and pious priest,
Mark there the altar! tho' the fumes aspire
Twelve cubits ere a nostril they regale,
'Tis myrrh for Titans, 'tis but air for Gods.
Time changes, Nature changes, I am changed!
Fronting the furious lustre of the sun,
I yielded to his piercing swift-shot beams   50
Only when quite meridian, then abased
These orbits to the ground, and there surveyed
My shadow—strange and horrid to relate!
My very shadow almost disappeared!
Restore it, or by earth and hell I swear
With blood enough will I refascinate

---

19 still] stil *1847, 1859.*   38 cannot] can not *1846–1859.*   41 kings*] *for
footnote, only in 1802, see notes at end of vol.*   42 sceptre] scepter *1847, 1859.*
Atrobal] ? *misprint for* Ithobal.   Ethbaal (in the Bible) was high priest of Ashtoreth
and king of the Sidonians. [W.]   49 lustre] luster *1847*

The cursed incantation: thou restore,
And largely; or my brethren, all combined,
Shall rouse thee from thy lethargies, and drive
Far from thy cloud-soft pillow, minion-prest,   60
Those leering lassitudes that follow Love."

   The smile of disappointment and disdain
Sat sallow on his pausing lip half-closed;
But, neither headlong importunity,
Nor gibing threat of reed-propt insolence,
Let loose the blast of vengeance: heaven shone bright,
Still, and Crysäör spurn'd the prostrate land.
But the triumphant Thunderer, now mankind
(Criminal mostly for enduring crimes—)
Provoked his indignation, thus besought   70
His trident-sceptred brother, triton-borne.
"O Neptune! cease henceforward to repine.
They are not cruel, no—the destinies
Intent upon their loom, unoccupied
With aught beyond it's moody murmuring sound,
Will neither see thee weep nor hear thee sigh:
And wherefor weep, O Neptune, wherefor sigh!
Ambition? 'tis unworthy of a God,
Unworthy of a brother! I am Jove,
Thou, Neptune,—happier in uncitied realms,   80
In coral hall or grotto samphire-ciel'd,
Amid the song of Nymphs and ring of shells,
Thou smoothest at thy will the pliant wave
Or liftest it to heaven.—I also can
Whatever best beseems me, nor for aid
Unless I loved thee, Neptune, would I call.
Tho' absent, thou hast heard, and hast beheld,
The profanation of that monsterous race,
That race of earth-born giants—one survives—
The rapid-footed Rhodan, mountain-rear'd,   90
Beheld the rest defeated; still remain
Scatter'd throughout interminable fields,
Sandy and sultry, and each hopeless path
Choaked up with crawling briars and bristling thorns,
The flinty trophies of their foul disgrace.

60 pillow] pillar *text*, pillow *errata 1802*.   67 Still . . . Crysäör] And proud
Chrysaor *1846–1859*.   71 -sceptred] -sceptered *1846–1859*.   77 wherefor *bis*]
wherefore *1846–1859*.   81 -ciel'd] ceil'd *1846*.   91 still] stil *1847, 1859*.

CRYSAOR

Crysäör, Sovereign of the golden sword,
Still hails as brethren men of stouter heart,
But, wise confederate, shuns Phlegrœan fields.
No warrior he, yet who so fond of war,
Unfeeling, scarce ferocious; flattery's dupe   100
He fancies that the gods themselves are his;
Impious, but most in prayer:—now re-assert
Thy friendship, raise thy trident, strike the rocks,
Sever him from mankind." Then thus replied
The Nymph-surrounded monarch of the main.

"Empire bemoan I not, however shared,
Nor Fortune frail, nor stubborn Fate, accuse:
No!—mortals I bemoan! when Avarice,
Plowing these fruitless furrows, shall awake
The basking Demons, and the dormant Crimes,   110
Horrible, strong, resistless, and transform
Meekness to Madness, Patience to Despair.
What is Ambition? What but Avarice?
But Avarice in richer guize arrayed,
Stalking erect, loud-spoken, lion-mien'd,
Her brow uncrost by care, but deeply markt,
And darting downwards 'twixt her eyes hard-lasht
The wrinkle of command.—could ever I
So foul a fiend, so fondly too, caress?
Judge me not harshly, judge me by my deeds."   120

Tho' seated then on Africs further coast,
Yet sudden, at his voice, so long unheard—
For he had grieved, and treasured up his grief—
With short kind greeting, meet from every side
The Triton herds, and warm with melody
The azure concave of their curling shells.
Swift as an arrow, as the wind, as light,
He glided thro' the deep, and now, arrived,
Lept from his pearly beryl-studded car.
Earth trembled—the retreating tide, black-brow'd,   130
Gather'd new strength, and rushing on, assail'd
The promontory's base: but when the God
Himself, resistless Neptune, struck one blow,

---

96 Crysäör, Sovereign] Chrysaor, wielder *1846–1859*.   97 Still] Stil *1847, 1859*.
98 Phlegrœan] Phlegræan *rectius 1846–1859*.   103 rocks] rock *1846–1859*.   114 guize
arrayed] guise array'd *1846–1859*.   117 downwards] downward *1846–1859*.

Rent were the rocks asunder, and the sky
Was darkened with their fragments ere they fell.
Lygea vocal, Zantho yellow-hair'd,
Spio with sparkling eyes, and Beroë
Demure, and sweet Iöné, youngest-born,
Of mortal race, but grown divine by song—
Had you seen playing round her placid neck   140
The sunny circles, braidless and unbound,—
O! who had call'd them boders of a storm!
These, and the many sister Nereïds,
Forgetful of their lays and of their loves,
All, unsuspicious of the dread intent,
Stop suddenly their gambols, and with shrieks
Of terror plunge amid the closing wave:
Still, just above, one moment more, appear
Their darken'd tresses floating in the foam.

Thrown prostrate on the earth, the Sacrilege   150
Rais'd up his head astounded, and accurs'd
The stars, the destinies, the gods—his breast
Panted from consternation, and dismay,
And pride untoward, on himself o'erthrown.
From his distended nostrils issued gore,
At intervals, with which his wiry locks,
Huge arms, and bulky bosom, shone beslimed:
And thrice he call'd his brethren, with a voice
More dismal than the blasts from Phlegethon
Below, that urge along ten thousand ghosts   160
Wafted loud-wailing o'er the firey tide.
But answer heard he none—the men of might
Who gather'd round him formerly, the men
Whom frozen at a frown, a smile revived,
Were far—enormous mountains interposed,
Nor ever had the veil-hung pine out-spread
O'er Tethys then her wandering leafless shade:
Nor could he longer under wintry stars
Suspend the watery journey, nor repose
Whole nights on Ocean's billowy restless bed;   170
No longer, bulging thro' the tempest, rose

136 Lygea] Lygeia *1846–1859.*   137 Beroë] Bervë *text*, Beroë *errata* 1802.   Cf. *Gebir* vi. 36.   138 Iöné] Ione *1846–1859.* Cf. *Gebir*, vi. 37, 40.   140 you] he *1847, 1859.*   150 *paragraphing mine.* [W.]   156 with which] wherewith *errata 1859.* 161 firey] fiery *1846–1859.*   166 out-spread] out-spred, *1847, 1859.*   168 wintry] winter *1847, 1859.*

CRYSAOR

That bulky bosom; nor those oarlike hands,
Trusted ere mortal's keenest ken conceived
The bluest shore—threw back opposing tides.
Shrunken mid brutal hair his violent veins
Subsided, yet were hideous to behold
As dragons panting in the noontide brake.
At last, absorbing deep the breath of heaven,
And stifling all within his deadly grasp,
Struggling, and tearing up the glebe, to turn;   180
And from a throat that, as it throb'd and rose,
Seem'd shaking ponderous links of dusky iron,
Uttering one anguish-forced indignant groan,
Fired with infernal rage, the spirit flew.

    Nations of fair Hesperia! lo o'erthrown
Your peace-embracing war-inciting king!
Ah! thrice twelve years, and longer, ye endured
Without one effort to rise higher, one hope
That heaven would wing the secret shaft aright,
The abomination!—hence 'twas Jove's command   190
That, many hundred, many thousand, more,
Freed from one despot, still from one unfreed,
Ye crouch unblest at Superstition's feet.
Her hath he sent among ye; her, the pest
Of men below, and curse of Gods above:
Hers are the last worst tortures they inflict
On all who bend to any kings but them.
Born of Sicanus, in the vast abyss
Where never light descended, she survived
Her parent; he omnipotence defied,   200
But thunderstruck fell headlong from the clouds;
She tho' the radiant ether overpower'd
Her eyes, accustom'd to the gloom of night,
And quenched their lurid orbs, Religion's helm
Assuming, vibrated her Stygian torch,
Till thou, Astræa! tho' behind the Sire's
Broad egis, trembledst on thy golden throne.

172 oarlike] oerlike *text*, oarlike *errata* 1802.   197 kings] king *1846–1859*.
198 Sicanus] *Sicily was called Sicania after him.* Cf. *Gebir*, vi. 173. [W.]   206 Till
thou] Till then *text*, Till thou *errata* 1802; Til thou *1846, 1859*.   207 golden] heavenly
1846–1859.

HEROIC POEMS

THE PHOCÆANS

[Two fragments (1 and 3) printed in 1800 and published in 1802; a connecting link (2) between them published in 1897; and a sequel (4) published in 1897. Text, fragments 1 and 3, 1802; fragments 2 and 4, 1897. See notes at end of volume.]

[FRAGMENT I]
FROM THE PHOCÆANS

ARGUMENT

[Dedication to Liberty, the Muses invoked. Persian invasion of Ionia. Fall of Priene. Defying Cyrus and his host the Phocæans sail to Iberia and seek aid from the king of Tartessus. Speech of Protis their leader and the king's reply. A minstrel from Miletus at the king's bidding recounts the woes of the Tartessians and how these were happily at an end. Their country was invaded by men of Tyre and Sidon, their elders were slain, many of the younger fled to Calpe. Adventures of Hercules in that region. What befel the invaders is next related by the minstrel. Their wives and daughters, performing religious rites on a river bank, were carried off by Nebrissan hill-men. Meanwhile Tartessian fugitives with restored courage had gone back to Tartessus town and overpowered the garrison. Some of the invaders escaped to their ships, a few sought safety inland, the rest were slain. The minstrel then tells how another party of the invaders which left the town, before its recapture, to join wives and daughters beside Lacippo's fount, learnt their fate. Meeting two Nebrissan boys mentioned earlier in the narrative they sacrificed them in revenge for the abduction of their own kindred. Retracing their steps they found Tartessus again in possession of its rightful masters. Here the minstrel's story and the first fragment of the poem end.—W.]

HEROES of old would I commemorate.
Those heroes, who obeyed the high decree
To leave Phocæa, and erect in Gaul
Empire, the fairest heaven had e'er design'd;
And, borne amidst them, I would dedicate
To thee O Liberty the golden spoils.
For, Liberty, 'tis thou whose voice awakes
Their sons, from slumber in the setting beams
Of sceptered Power, and banishest from Earth
Tho' tardier than hell's heaviest cloud she move,   10
And leave behind the wizard cup and sword—
Circæan soul-dissolving Monarchy.

   Say, daughters of Mnemosyne and Jove,
Speak, hearts of harmony! what sacred cause
United, so long sever'd, in debate,
Pallas and Neptune? 'twas when every god
Flew shuddering from the royal feast accurst,

Title. THE PHOCÆANS, followed in 1802 by a preface, for which see notes at end of volume. A second title, FROM THE PHOCÆANS, and the first fragment of the projected poem, followed the preface.
Argument of Fragment I, written for present edition.

THE PHOCÆANS

With Ceres, most offended, these ordain
Th' eternal terror of proud thrones to rise:
Such among eastern states Phocæa stood,　　　　20
Such, amid Europe's oaken groves retired.

　　Now had Priené mourn'd her murder'd swains,
Who late ascending Mycalé, released
The pipe, and sitting on the way-side crag
Temper'd the tabor to their roundelays:
Of brittle ivy, from the living stone
Stript off with haste, before their partners came,
Chaplets to ward off envy they combined,
To ward off envy, not to ward off death,
Nor to survive themselves: now with amaze　　　30
Meander, rising slow from sedgey bed,
Sees soaring high the white-wing'd multitude
Of cranes and cycnets, like a sunny cloud,
Nor till they circle lower, distinguishes
The aerial blue between, and feeble cries
From thin protended throat: Pactolus tore
His yellow hair with human blood defiled,
And spurn'd his treacherous waves and tempting sand.

　　Of cities, built by heroes, built by Gods,
Throughout the Ægæan, Asia now surveyed　　　40
None but Phocæa free: her bolder youth
The galling yoke of gifted peace disdain.
On far Iberia's friendly coast arrived,
Rich streamers, snatched from conquest, they display;
And Persic spoils, in sportive mockery worn,
Flutter and rustle round the steeds, that rear'd
Amid the caverns of the genial winds,
On Tagrus' top, start side-long from the tide.
All are advanced to manhood for the hour.
With sweet solicitude and fearful joy,　　　　50
Each mother from the shaded ship descries
Her son amid the contest, and her son
Or now excels each rival in the race,
Or if behind them will ere long excel.
Naarchus, whose attemper'd hand heaven-taught,
Directed thro' wide seas and wearying straits

39 *The division into paragraphs here, and at lines* 79, 85, 100, 112, 120, 160, 200, 222, 281, 294, 356, 422 *is now made, for the assistance of the reader.* [W.]

To rich Tartessus the Phocæan sails,
Now, leaning back against a stranded skiff,
Drawn till half upright on the shelving beach,
Turns idly round the rudder in it's rest,   60
And hardly thinks of land; warm youth attracts,
As amber sweet, the wither'd reed of age.
Such, on the banks of Hermus, on the banks
Of that most pleasant of all sacred streams,
For 'twas the nearest to his native home,
And first that exercised his crooked oar,
Now distant, swelling forth with sweet regrets!—
Such was Naarchus! steadfastly he gazed,
And harmless envy heav'd one mindful sigh.

Meanwhile, with Euxenus, and Hyelus,   70
In council sage, but stricken sore by years,
And Cimos, firm in friendship, firm in fight,
And more, whose wisdom, and whose bravery,
The hallowed bosom of but few records,
Men, high in nature, high in sphere, of souls
That burn in battle, or that shine in peace—
Protis, the son of Cyrnus, in the halls
Of Arganthonius, suppliant, thus implores
His peace, and his protection.
                              "Mighty king,
If ever thou injuriously hast borne   80
The rage of ruthless war, and surely war
Hath envied, and hath visited, a realm
So flourishing, so prosperous, behold
The scattered ruins of no humble race."
    Amid these words, a little from the ground
He rais'd his aching eyes, and waved his hand
Where over citron bowers and light arcades
Hung the fresh garlands fluttering from the mast:
Then paused; the hoary monarch, stung with grief,
Sate silent, and observ'd the frequent tear   90
Flow bitterly from off each manly cheek,
Uninterrupted! for the hero's soul
Flew back upon his country's wrongs, and grown
Impatient of the pity it required,
Sunk into sorrow: thus, his foes had said,
Had foes e'er seen him thus, the helpless child

91 Flow] Run *MS. emendation.*   95 Sunk] Sank *MS.*

THE PHOCÆANS

Putting one arm against it's mother's breast,
Holds out the other to a stranger's hand,
But, ere receiv'd, it weeps: th' Iberian king
Then answer'd,

       "Just and holy are the tears   100
Of warriors; sweet as cassia to the Gods,
To man and misery they're the dew of heaven.
But wherefor thus disconsolate! this arm
Might heretofore have rescued and avenged,
And now perhaps may succour." He embraced
The stranger, and, embracing him, perceived
His heart beat heavy thro' his panting vest;
Then thus continued, "we too have endured
Insulting power, insatiate avarice,
But ere the wrongs we suffer'd half were told   110
The sun, more rapid now his rays decline
Would leave the Atlantic wave."

               The patriot chiefs,
Around, burn each to hear his own exploits
And see the history open on his name.
Fain would they seize congenial glances, fain
Force attestation from the question'd eye:
So pants for Glory, Virtue nurst by war,
That, some amongst them to their neighbours turn
Not for their neighbours notice but their king's.

  Hymneus was present, of Milesian race,   120
But he disdain'd his country, and preferr'd
One struggling hard with tyranny, to one
Where power o'er slaves was freedom and was rights,
Nor man degraded could but man degrade.
The harp, his sorrow's solace, he resumed,
Whose gently agitating liquid airs
Melted the wayward shadow of disgrace,
And, bearing highly up his well-stored heart
Above the vulgar, bade him cherish Pride.—
Mother of virtues to the virtuous man,   130
Her brilliant heavenly-temper'd ornaments
Tarnish to blackness at the touch of vice.
Sometimes the sadly quivering soul-struck wires
Threw a pale lustre on his native shore;
When suddenly the sound "*Conspirator,*"
How harsh from those we serve and those we love!—

Burst with insulting blow the enchanting strain,
And the fair vision vanish'd into air.
The pleasant solitude of sunny beach,
The yellow bank scoopt out with idle hands,   140
And near, white birds, and further, naked boys,
That, o'er the level of the lustrous sand,
Like kindred broods, seem ready to unite,
The tempest whirls away,—and where they stood
Up starts a monster, that, with hiss and howl,
Seizes the wretch who runs to loose it's chains.

   When Arganthonius saw him, he exclaim'd
"Hymneus! and thou too here! thy glowing words
Could once, arousing in the warrior's breast
Enthusiastic rage, sublime the soul   150
So far above the rocks where Danger broods,
That she and all her monstrous progeny
Groveling, and breathing fire, and shadow-winged,
Become invisible.—O thou of power
With magic tones Affliction to disarm!
Thou canst conjure up fury, call down hope,
Or whisper comfort, or inspire revenge.
Rise! trace the wanderings of thy comrades, shew
What men, relying on the Gods, can bear."

   He ended here, and Hymneus thus began.   160
"Long has Tartessus left her fertile fields,
And, but by forest beast or mountain bird,
Seen from afar her flocks lie unconsumed;
The maids of Sidon, and the maids of Tyre
To whom proud streams thro' marble arches bend,
Still bid the spindle urge it's whirring flight
And waft to wealth the luxury of our woes.
Thus without lassitude barbaric kings
Shall midst their revels read our history;
And thou too, warm to fancy, warm to grief,   170
In hall and arbour, shade and solitude,
Whose bosom rises at the faintest breath
From dizzy tower, dark dungeon, stormy rock,
But rises not, nor moves, to public pangs—
Woman! our well-wrought anguish shalt admire!
And toy-taught children overtake our flight.
But we have conquer'd:—hear me valiant youth!

66

THE PHOCÆANS

Untired, and pressing for the course; O hear
Ye sires, whom stormy life's vicissitudes
At length, have driven on no hostile shore,   180
O hear me, nor repine; but cherish hope,
And fortune will return and cherish you.
We utter'd soothing words from sickening hearts,
And with firm voice in flight and rout proclaim'd
That we would never yield, would never fly:
While thus, revived by confidence, they rose,
Fortune gave weight to fancy's golden dreams,
And, more than hope dared promise, time perform'd.
Thus from some desert rock, which every tide
Drenches and deluges, the mariner   190
Marks the uneven surges rolling, marks
The black pods rattling as the wave retires,—
And now another!—high he folds his arms,
He groans, looks earnest on, and is resign'd.
Danger and safety this dread interval
Brings close; the billow self-suspended hangs;
The tide had reach'd it's highest, and has ebb'd:
While distant, now appearing, now unseen,
His comrades struggle up the fluted surge,
Their strength, their voices, wreckt!
                                    the spring approach'd;   200
The fields and woods were vocal with the joy
Of birds, that twittering from the thin-leav'd broom
Or close laurustin, or the sumach-tufts
Gay, nest-like, meditated nought but love.
Ah! happy far beyond man's happiness,
Who ever saw them wander o'er the waves
For guilty gold, or shiver on the shore
For life-wrung purple to array their breasts?
Theirs cherish, ours repudiate, chaste desire!
In vain was nature gay; in vain the flocks   210
With fond parental bleatings filled the fold;
In vain the brindled heifer lowed content
To crop the shining herbage, or to brouze
The tender maple in the twilight dell.
Cold, O ye flocks and herds, the hand will be
That fed ye, cold the hand that sweetly tuned
It's pipe to call ye to your nightly home,

208 breasts] *so in errata 1802*; breast *in text.*   214 maple] hazel *MS. emendation.*
216 sweetly] lately *MS. emendation.*

Or gave the feebler dog encouragement
To drive the wolf away! vain care—the wretch
Who slew your shepherd, at the altar's horn 220
Slays you, to celebrate his victory.
  The Tyrians now approach; a thousand oars
Heave with impatient sweep the whitening surge
To seize Tartessus in the noon of peace.
The very zephyr now, that cool'd our coast,
Plays in the bosom of their sail, and smooths
Each rising billow; never more appall'd
The hind that cultivates Vesuvio's slope,
When with dull dash the firey tide o'erflows
The pumice that surrounds his humble cot, 230
Than was Tartessus. Olpis first espied
The naval host advancing; now delay
Were death;—he loosen'd the relapsing rope
From his left elbow, and the toils above
Dropt sounding on the surface of the waves.
He ran; nor enter'd he the city gate
Ere, interrupted oft, by haste, and fear,
In accents loud and shrill he thus began.
"Fly, fly, what madness holds you in your streets?
The Tyrians are behind; they climb the rocks 240
Light and unnumber'd as the brooding gulls.—
O fly, Tartessians! not a hope remains."

  Incontinent, the noisy streets are fill'd
With young alike and old; the mother runs
To save her children, playing in the court,
Improvident of ill, and grasps their wrist,
Hurrying them onward, till they weep, and ask
"*For what?*" and whining plead the promised hour,
Now threaten loud, and now again in tears.
No more the murmuring labor of the loom 250
Detains the virgin, who, with patient hand,
But fluttering heart, the whitest vesture wove
For him she loved so tenderly, for him
Who soon arising from the nuptial couch,
Would scatter mid the warbling wanton choir
The lavish nuts, would hear their bland adieu,
And seize the pleasures they were taught to sing.
Here were the fathers sitting; they were seen

233 relapsing] relaping *mispr. in 1802.*   234 toils *i.e.* toiles: canvas sails. [W.]

To wave their tremulous hand, and bid them go
Whose life is green and vigorous, "for you   260
The sun will ripen many vintages,
But we are prone to tarry, cruel Tyre
Scarcely can drag the dying in her chains."

 The throbs of urgent terror now subside
In all, and every one his earnest arms
With pious anguish throws around them, prays
To lead them into refuge, prays to strow
The bed of age, and close the beamless eye.
Alas! too confident in hoary hairs,
God's gift, but not God's blessing—they refuse   270
The proffer'd kindness; and their parted limbs
Hung upon hooks, with patriot gore distain'd
The walls they once defended! ah! thy day
Rolls on; a victim to the very sword
Thyself unsheathest, I behold thee fall;
Nor help is any near—that help; O Tyre!
Blind to the future, why hast thou destroyed?
Were it not better to extend the hand
T'ward rising states, than proudly crush them? realms
Which stand on ruins insecurely stand.   280
 But wherefor turn our eyes to other climes
Which fate has frown'd on!—tho' her frowns I dread,
I deem it first of human miseries
To *be* a tyrant, *then* to suffer one.
'Tis true, we left our city, left our fields,
O'er naked flints we travel'd, and review'd
What once we held so dear: the eye of youth
Saw, tho' the tear would often intervene,
And shake their branches, and suspend their bowers,
The groves that echoed to his horn, or waved   290
With gales that whilom whisper'd notes of love:
He saw; and linger'd long; for seldom fear
Invades a bosom harbouring regret.
 But others hasten'd to the far-off heights
Of Calpé: there a hundred grottoes gleam
High-archt with massy spar; and hence descend
Columns of crystal, ranged from side to side
In equal order; there the freshest Nymphs

276 is] *so in errata 1802, text has* in. 296 spar *MS. emendation*] spear *1802.*
and hence] *so in errata 1802,* from hence *in text.*

Bring water sweet, and glide away unseen.
But hither few arrive, now darkness reigns   300
Around; but weary of the slow-paced hours
One lifts his eyes above, and, trembling, views
The moss and ivy shake with every wind
Against the yawning cavern; every wind
He deems a spectre's yell; and every beam
Shed from the clouded orbit stops his flight.
One, when molested from their lone abode
The birds of omen rise aloft in air,
Shrill-shrieking, and on whirring pinion borne
Sidelong, and circling o'er the pinnacles,   310
In turbid agitation thinks he hears
His infant, faintly wailing, or his wife
From far, imploring help he cannot give;
And wishes he were dead, yet fears to die.
'Twere piteous now, had pity past ourselves,
To hear sometimes the long-drawn moan of dogs,
Sometimes their quick impatience, while they sought
Fond master, left behind, or headlong dash'd
Where faithless moonshine fill'd the abrupt abyss.
From waken'd nest, and pinion silence-poiz'd,   320
Th' huge vulture drops rebounding;—first he fears;
Looks round; draws back; half lifts his cow'ring wing;
Stretches his ruffled neck and rolling eye,
Tasts the warm blood, and flickers for the foe.

  Some, seated on the soft declivity,
Sink into weary slumber; others climb
The crumbling cliff, and craggy precipice,
To none accessible but him who fears.
Thus, to the mountain-brake, that overhangs
A valley dark and narrow, flies the kid   330
Before a lion: he from far espies
The pensile fugitive, nor dares pursue;
But gazing often, with tremendous roar
Shakes from his thirsty throat the fretful foam.
Here, love, ambition, labor, victory,
Injustice, vengeance, Hercules forgot,
Forgot how proud Laomedon, from Troy's
High summits, knew the hero, knew the steeds
That paw'd the plain beneath, and all the king

315 ourselves] our doors *MS. emendation*.

Shrunk, and the perjurer alone remain'd.   340
Here mournful Thessaly no more occur'd,
Deserted by her shepherds, while the neck
Of roving oxen soften'd from the yoke.
Here hospitable Scyros he forgot;
Here Tempé, fresh with springs, with woods embower'd;
Larissa too, whose glowing children vied
In pæans, vied in tracing where the throng
Around the quiver, markt the hand, of strength
To lift on high the shafts of Hercules.
While thro' the bulrushes the hero stept,   350
Slow, and intently looking round him, waved
His torch, and blue-eyed Lerna, lily-crownd,
Shook at the shadow of a future God.
'Twas there he started, matchless in the race;
The race was run; and Calpé was the goal.
    'Twas here Tartessus, in distraction fled
Before the steel of Sidon; she with Tyre
Unfurl'd the sail of conquest, Oceans rose
To waft her, suns to strow the yielding way.
Here were the realms of Night—each star was hers.   360
But Venus far above the rest, whose orb's
Meek lustre, melting thro' the cedar-sprays
That spire around the lofty Lebanon,
Led forth their matrons all at evening's close
To celebrate the sad solemnity.
There they abided: here, ill-omen'd hour!
Aside Lacippo's stream, with boughs o'erhung,
Dark alder, pearly-blossom'd arbutus,
And myrtle, highest held of earthly flowers,
And mixt with amaranth at the feasts above—   370
Maids snowy-stoled, and purple-mitred boys,
Foregoing each young pleasure—mazy dance,
Where Love most often but most slightly wounds,
Games, where Contention strives to look like Love
Scatter anemonies, and roses, torne
Ere daylight wakes them, from their mossy cell.

    Not thus, Nebrissa, went thy mountaneers.
Mad with religious lust and solemn wine,

354 there] *so in errata 1802*, here *text.*   367 Lacippo] *see* Pliny, iii. 1. *The ruin*
of Aliceppo are near Casares, a few miles north of Gibraltar. [W.]   377 Nebrissa]
the modern Lebrija. Dionysus was worshipped there, see Silius Ital. iii. 393. [W.]

They panted for their orgies, at the fount
Accustom'd: part the mangled heifer tear;   380
Part, stamping on the neck, wrench off it's brow
The horns, and blow them bubbling hoarse with blood:
Some gird themselves with adders: others yell
From pipe far-screeching—trill above their head
The tymbrel—clash the cymbal—others drum
The hollow deeptoned Corybantine brass.
Before them, Sycus and Amphyllion,
Glad to have mixt themselves with men, at hours
When fearful childhood is constrain'd to rest,
Ran tripping for Lacippo; but to see   390
Flowers, that profusely floated down the stream,
Breaking the yellow moonshine as they passed,
Surprized and held them; fixt on this, they heard
No plaintive strain beyond: for childhood's mind
Sits on the eyeball; 'tis her boundary.
But, higher up, those who the orgies led
Hearken'd, at every pause, and each was fill'd
With clear responses winding thro' the vale.

    Old Cheratægon chided this delay.
"Why stood they gaping? had the wrathful Moon   400
Struck them? had any Satyr from the heights,
Had he whom every Season stops to crown,
Whom Hellespontic Lampsacus adores,
Answer'd their carols, kind? if so—reply."
Then, placing to his lips the clarion,
He started, waved it round, and listening
Again, cried out "*a female voice I hear,
Proceed, proceed.*" They hurry on; they view
The choir: the shrieking damsels cannot fly;
Their vesture baffles each attempt of fear.   410
In vain implore they Venus, and adjure
By all she suffer'd when Adonis died,
The rustics knew Adonis not by name
Nor Venus by a tear. They wring their hands
In agony, they clasp them in despair,
Or, those restricted in the strong embrace,
Raise praying eyes to heaven, and bend the neck
Back till, it's tapering column quite convulsed,
The breasts that from their marble sanctuary

400 the] *mispr.* they *here corrected.*

72

THE PHOCÆANS

Stood out, inviting Chastity and Love,   420
By violence and passion are profaned.

   While tumult rages there and wild affright,
Led by avenging deities, and warm'd
With patriot fire, the purest that ascends
Before the presence of those deities,
The caverns we had left, and many a plain
As desolate, where now the wolf, enraged,
Bit the deserted fences of the fold;
And now with plighted faith and pledging vows
Throughout invoke our murder'd countrymen: 430
For now at last the radiant host of heaven
Seem'd, going one by one, to delegate
Peace and repose behind; these oft enchant
The wicked; but whene'er the weary lids
Drop, either dreadful visions they inclose,
Tenacious, or the senseless breast imbibes
The poison'd balm of sweet security.
Seen thro' that porch's pillars, yonder wood
Tho' not far distant, yet from hence appears
More like a grassy slope—by Lybian blasts   440
Distorted—there in ambush, we surveyed
Our battlements, whose friendly shadow stretch'd
O'er half the ruins of old Geryon's tomb:
When silently and quick athwart the dale
Glide ranks of helmets; these alone are seen,
Darkness and distance occupy the rest.
They fade away, and eagerly we catch
The rumour of their march: the hunter, worn
With service, dragging some ignoble weight,
Stops in the passing wind the well-known cry   450
Of hound that, after hard-run chase, hath lept
Up to his nostrils, or against his side
Rested one foot—the other gall'd with thorns—
Like him we, conscious of our former strength,
Quake with the impotence of wild desire.

---

ll. 448–55 *Landor's MS. emendation makes the simile of an aged horse clearer.* For
Stops (*l.* 450) *it reads* Hears; *for* that (*l.* 451) who; *and after* thorns (*l.* 453) *has*:

        And struggles to press forward til returns
        The force that courage even to age imparts.

After desire (*l.* 455) *it has*:

        At first, but soon become what once we were.

Less dangerous now is our determined course
Toward Tartessus: we approach the walls;
We reach them; nor had halted, ere the gates
Fly open: starting at the prodigy,
Encouraged at the fact, the Iberian bands 460
Rush in, and with a dreadful shout proclaim
The vengeance of the Gods; afraid to strike
At first, lest any one of these, conceal'd
In human likeness, at the portal placed,
The force, himself inspired them with, bewail.
Astounded and aghast, the Tyrians rise
From slumber: these imagine it a dream,
Discrediting their senses' evidence;
Those in the portico cry out to arms,
Forgetful of their own, while many, driven 470
By desperation, reckless of their shield
Or buckler, rush amidst us, sword in hand,
Impetuous, covering with their prostrate corse
The spot they fought on: others, overthrown
By numbers pressing forward, under throngs
Of enemies, groan loud; a double pang
Such feel, in dying with no hostile wound.
Hundreds, and fortunate are they, prolong
Sleep into death, nor ever know the change.
The remnant in their hollow ships confide 480
For refuge, close pursued; thrice happy few
Who now, the pitchy, hard, and slippery side
Surmounted, mindless yet of sail or oar,
Embrace their own* Patæcus on the prow.
O'er their companions, in the crouded strand
Death, leading up night's rear, her banner waves,
Invisible, but rustling like the blast
That strips the fallen year: with arms outstretched,
Dismay, before her, pushes on; and Fear

* *Note.* The Patæci were little images, like those which the Spaniards, and others of the same religion, carry about with them at present, to avert calamity. I imagine that those charms and amulets which are also in use among the nations of Africa, and which are called *fetiches*, are of the same origin: they perhaps are the prototypes of the Patæci, and were introduced into Spain by the Carthaginians. When the Tyrians are mentioned here, they must be supposed in great part, Carthaginians; as the people of the United States of America were, during their alliance, indiscriminately [*so in errata 1802*, indiscrimatily *in text*], called Englishmen, by our enemies. [L. *See* Herodotus, iii. 37.]

466 the] *so in errata 1802*, thy *in text*.   486 her] his *MS. emendation.*

Crouching unconscious close beside her, casts   490
A murky paleness o'er her wing black-plumed.
Just liberated from their noisom cells,
Slavery's devoted, thirsting for revenge,
Drink deep; the fetter is at last become
An instrument of slaughter, and the feet
Swoln with it, bathe themselves in hostile blood,
Till from the vallies deep the fogs arise
Perceptible; while, on the summits, Morn
Her saffron robe and golden sceptre lays.
Then of their lofty vessels we descry   500
Nought save the topmost sails, each nether part
By Gades, tho' behind them, was obscured;
These, distant yet, seem'd o'er the town displayed.

'Tis painful, O Phocæans, to unfold
The brazen gates of war, and find Revenge
Bursting her brittle manacles, while Rage
Strikes with impatient spear the sounding floor.
Here Scycus and Amphyllion I behold,
Shivering, and with the back of feeble wrist
Drawn frequently across their swolen eyes,   510
Wiping large tears away—poor harmless pair!
You, playing near life's threshold, strown with flowers,
Common indeed, but sweet, and all your own,
Death snatcht away, and flapt her raven wing.

The Tyrians sally forth, to meet the hour
When woe and darkness yield to light and glee,
And reach Lacippo's fount ere earliest dawn.
No mortal meet they, nor the faintest noise
Hear, but of rustling leaves and tinkling rill.
They wonder; look around them; shudder, seize   520
Each zephyr, and each shadow, which he makes
By nimbly lighting on the pliant boughs
Creep further on the grass: for every man
Imagines, tho' all other may have strayed,
Surely his own must near him still remain.
But all upon the distant hills were drag'd
Thro' wild and winding sheepwalks, into huts
Where, with unsated eye, Nebrissan wives,
Not yet suspicious of supplanting charms,

490 her]him *MS. emendation.* 491 her]his *MS. emendation.* 508 Scycus *here in 1802;*
cf. Sycus *in ll.* 387, 584, 595. 514 her] his *MS. emendation* 517 earliest] early *MS.*
emendation.

Survey their strange attire: one draws the veil 530
Aside, and fancies somewhat in the face
Tho' foreign, like her countrywomen; lips
Rosy, but rather blighted; eyes full-orbed
Ringlets that o'er pellucid temples wave,
As cedars o'er steep snow-drifts; blooming cheeks;
But, courted not by sun or sea-born gale,
Pallid and puny when compared with hers:
Another, hath some broken flower escaped
Mid the dishevel'd hair, with curious hand
Twists round, on tiptoe, it's exotic stem, 540
Exulting high with ingenuity.

   The Tyrians, now, disconsolate, unite
In counsel: each one differs in the way
To follow, each his neighbour's choice amends.
When on the pathway haply one espied
A torch; he whirl'd, he kindled it; he swore
By earth and heaven 'twas happy; he exclaim'd
"We too will sacrifice! Revenge be ours!
Revenge is worthy to succeed to Love.
Each irresistable, immortal each, 550
Not blind—the wretch feigns that—their pupils roll
In fire unquenchable: Pursuasion form'd
Their lips, and raptured at their lively hue
She kist her new creation; hence delight
Breathes thro' the thirsting fibres of the breast,
Like honey from Dodona's prophet-grove,
Sweet and inspiring too—Revenge, revenge."
Silence dwelt shortly with them, ere he touched
This jarring nerve; when suddenly their hearts
Vibrated into dreadful unison. 560
They gape upon him, gathering from his breath
(As manna from the desert men would seize,)
The substance of their wishes; they demand
In sentences imperfect, how to grasp
The phantom set before them, whispering
With eager but with hesitating haste
Together, and awaiting no reply:
Nay, often an enquiry, that commenced

546 whirl'd] *so in errata 1802*, wirl'd *in text.*   552 Pursuasion *so in 1802.*
558 he touched] was toucht *MS. emendation.*   561 upon . . . his] and gathering
each from each ones *MS. emendation.*

76

With one, concluded in another's ear.
They moved; the croud seem'd growing: swift they strode   570
Toward the streamlet, thither where it sprad,
Wider, and (as upon it's bosom fell
The frigid, iron-color'd, unripe light)
Just trembled: here the boy Amphyllion
Stood waiting for the broken garlands, borne
No farther by the current; forward lean'd
The busy idler, under where he stood
Sweeping them gently on with willow wand.
He thought, full sure he thought—such eagerness
His one protended and one poising hand,   580
Half-open lips, and steady lustrous eyes,
Show'd plainly—safe arrived ere others woke,
To deck his mother's door, and be forgiven.
Sycus more weary, on his arm inclined,
Sat peevish by, and, often of the way
Complaining, yet unwilling to arise,
Bit acid sorrels from their juicy stalk.
"Lo yonder!" he exclaim'd, "the morning dawns
Among the junipers, and ill forebodes
Beside such dampness when no dew has fallen—   590
This bursting glare, while all around is shade.
Can it be morning? no; *there* mornings rise:
It is not morning; and the moon is gone;
It cannot be the moon." too rightly judged
Poor Sycus; nearer now flashed redder light
Than rising moons give reapers going home;
Now nearer, and now nearer yet, approach'd
Voices, and armour glimmer'd thro' the glade;
Next, helmets were distinguisht; lastly, vests
Black afar off, their proper crimson shew'd.   600
They tremble at the sight, and deadly drops
Trickle down ankles white like ivory.
Pity and mercy they implore—the soul
Presages ere it reasons—they implore
Pity and mercy, ere the enemy's hand
Seizes them, ere, in painful bondage bent,
Behind them hang so helplessly their own.

    Uprooted smells the hazel underwood,
The verdant pile ascends; upon the top

589 Among] Above *MS. emendation.*   602 like] as *MS. emendation.*

Branches of pitch-tree are arranged, across,   610
And cover'd with their leaves: the cymbals ring;
The tymbrels rough, and doubling drums, reply.

Music, when thunders arm her heavenly voice,
May rouse most other passions—she may rouse
The Furies from their deep Tartarean dens,
Or Wonder from her unseen orbit, fixt
The middlemost of endless myriads—
Terror she stops amid his wild career,
Engages, and subdues. Amphyllion's heart
Flutter'd indeed but flutter'd less confined,   620
He trembled more, yet dreaded less: the boy
Would now with rapturous violence have rubbed
His palms to sparkling, were they but unbound,
His head he would have nestled in the lap
Of Fortune, when he found the budded spoils
Lie innocent, squared well, and garland-hung.
He laugh'd at their device; he look'd around,
And saw the knife, but sought the sacrifice.

Can you, etherial Powers! if any rule
Above us or below, or if concern   630
For human sins and sorrows touches you—
Can you see, quivering, shrinking, shrivelling,
Lips without guile, and bosoms without gall,
Nor pity, succour, save! alas, your will
Was pleaded, and your presence was invoked.
First, 'twas revenge—but, when 'twas done, 'twas heaven!
When others rise in anger, men exclaim
"*Fierce Furies urge them:*" but when they themselves,
"*Righteous inflexible Eumenides.*"
Even thou, Venus! Goddess! even thou,   640
That leadest the Gætulian lioness
From caves and carnage, and on sunny sands
Makest to slumber with satiety—
Thou wreathest serpents as thou wreathest flowers,
Thou silencest the winds without a word,
Thou curbest the black Tempest; and the face
Of Ocean brightens at thy filial smile,
Yet, either thou art cruel or profaned.

617 endless *mispr.* enless *in 1802: here corrected.*   641 That] Who *MS. emenda-*
tion.   644–6 Thou] Who *MS. emendation.*

THE PHOCÆANS

When Cruelty and Youth together dwell
Nature may weep indeed! they also wept.   650
The sons of Tyre and Sidon also wept.
Returning to the gates, they only heard
A few last groans, only a few fond names
Given them long ago: by madness driven,
Like Atys, when he left his father's home,
Never to see it more, nor to admire
His face dim-shining from his olived thigh—
They run into the woods, and are devour'd
By grief and famine, without friend or grave.

655 Atys] *son of Crœsus, see* Herodotus, i. 34.   659 *after* grave *Landor in a copy*
of the volume inserted a slip on which he had written nine additional lines as ending the
recital of Hymneus:

> The cormorants have flown across the strait,   [660]
> Some wealth they carried off, the best remains,
> Confidence in ourselves, in them distrust.
> By the wise serpent, wisdom we are taught,
> We see the hugest of the reptile race
> Uncoil to crush, beslaver to devour,
> No longer we relie on Punic faith,
> But walls and watchtowers raise along the coast
> And fortify stout ships with hearts as stout.

[CONNECTING LINK]

[In the 1802 volume "From the Phocæans" was followed by a second fragment headed "Part of Protis's Narrative". Among the manuscript insertions made by Landor in a copy of the book is one of sixteen lines meant to serve as a connecting link between the two fragments. This insertion, which was first printed in 1897, is given below. Except for a minor variant *l.* 16= *l.* 1 of the "Narrative".]

Here ended Hymneus: and the hall awhile
Was silent, Arganthonius then arose.
"My honored guests! who bravely have endured
The toils of exil and the storms of war,
It will add little to your weariness,"
Said he, "if ye will trace to us the ways
By land and sea ye have gone thro, before
Ye reacht the port wherein ye now shall rest."

Then Protis, he who led them, thus replied:
"O King! the stranger finds in thee a friend   10
Who found none in his kindred. But reproach
Better becomes the weak than firmer breast.
We will not turn to those who past us by
In the dark hour: from such and from the land
Where Pelops, in the days of heroes, reigned,
We speed [turn *1802*] to Delphi: we consult the God . . .   16

HEROIC POEMS

[FRAGMENT II]

PART OF PROTIS'S NARRATIVE

[Printed in 1800, published in 1802.]

[ARGUMENT

Asked by the King of Tartessus to relate the adventures of the Phocæans, their
leader, Protis, begins by telling what happened when their country was threatened by
a Persian invasion. They consulted the Delphic oracle which foretold toil and trouble.
Vainly they sought help from Athens and Sparta. Going back to their sea-port they
were victors in a fight with the invaders but, deserted by their allies, they could not
hold out on the mainland. Terrified by the threats of Cyrus, the Chians denied them
refuge on an island near by. Some of the Phocæans forgot the oath never to return
till molten iron cast into the sea should float on the waves, but the braver set sail for
distant lands. This fragment of Protis's speech ends abruptly with their departure, the
story of their voyage being left untold.—W.]

WE turn to Delphi; we consult the God;
The God, omniscient Phœbus, thus replies.
"Long have your wanderings been o'er wearying seas,
And long o'er earth, Phocæans, must they be—
Where war shall rage around you, treachery lurk,
And kings and princes struggle hard from peace."

   I never shall forget that awful hour,
When Consolation fled Calamity,
And Hope was slow to leave the Delphic shrine.
Scarce half the steps surmounted, sprang the roof;   10
The gorgeous walls grew loftier every step;
In gracile ranks of regular advance
The melting pillars rose like polisht air:
The floor too, seem'd ascending, seemed to wave
It's liquid surface like the heaven-hued sea;
Throughout reflecting, variously displayed,
Deviceful piety and massive prayers.
Above the rest, beside the altar, stood
The Sardian vases, gift of Crœsus, one
Of beaten silver, one of burnished gold,   20
Dazzling without, but dark from depth within.
Alas! for these *Ecbatana should have bowed

* The walls of Ecbatana were built by Deioces. They were seven in number, and
each of a circular form. Each was also raised gradually above the other, just as much
as the battlements were high, and all were of different colors. The first, which equalled
in circumference the city of Athens, was white, from the base of the battlements:
the second, black: third, purple: fourth, blue: fifth, orange: sixth, silver: seventh,
gold. [L. cf. Herodotus, i. 98, and Bradley, *Early Poems of Landor*, p. 51.]

Argument. Written for present ed.   2 Phœbus] *mispr.* Phæbus *here corrected.*
19, 25 Crœsus] *mispr.* Cræsus *here corrected.*

THE PHOCÆANS

Her seven-fold shield, and Lydian flames dissolved
The yielding iris of the embattled crown.
Too soon hath Crœsus found, that once impell'd
By headlong folly or obdurate fate,
All Delphi's tripods, censers, gems, high-piled,
Cannot stop Fortune's swift-descending wheel.
Who but the maniac, then, would strain his throat
And rack his heart beneath capricious birds,   30
And tear disaster from it's bowel'd bed!
I hung o'er these proud gifts, and, rising, felt
A cold hoarse murmur chide the inconscious sigh.
The people heard with horror the decree,
They were undone—and, who himself undo?
This comes from wisdom; woe betide the wise!
Why should they thus consult the oracle
When it could give them only toil and grief?
These were inclined to penance, those to rage.
O how near Nature Folly sometimes leads!   40
Penance seem'd bending with sororial care
To raise the brow of pale Despondency;
And Rage arous'd them, gave them energy,
Made them unjust, perhaps, but made them great.
Not in one city, could we long remain
Ere there occur'd some signal which approved
The Delphic revelation: was the crow
Heard on the left, was thunder on the right,
The starts of terror met the scoffs of scorn.
Taunt, accusation, contumely, curse,   50
Questioning stamp and pale-lipt pious sneer,
Confusion, consternation, mystery,
Procession, retrogression, vortexes
Of hurry, wildernesses of delay:
Each element, each animal, each glance,
Each motion, now, admonish'd them, each bird
Now bore the thunder of almighty Jove,
Each fibre trembled with Phocæa's fate.
Our parting sails far other prospects cheer'd.
Self-courteous Pride, awaiting courtesy,   60
Charm'd with bland whispers half our pangs away.
What Grecian port that would not hail our ships?
'Twas oft debated which high-favor'd land
Should share the honors it might well confer.
Some from Cecropian Athens traced our line,

And said "Minerva's city shall rejoice."
Some Sparta lures—perfection fancy-form'd!
So pure her virtue, and her power so poised,
With Asia's despot how could Sparta join?
Now, from Eurotas driven, whose willows wove   70
His knotty cradle, where should Freedom fly!
Could Freedom exiled cherish exiled Hope?
We leave the plains, then, where the sports and flowers
Are faint, untinged with blood; where naked feet
The mountain snow and woodland hoar condense,
And virgin vestures crack the margent grass.
Resolv'd no longer faithless friends to seek,
And not renouncing, yet, the oracle;
Not yet forgetting, that, from Greece expell'd,
War was to rage around us—could there aught   80
Be markt so plainly as the Enusian isle:
So near our native land too! all exclaim
There take we refuge: here we take revenge.
Again we trust the winds and tempt the waves;
Again behold our country—first ascends
Melæna's promontory, frowning dark,
And threatening woe to foreign mariners.
Now lengthen out thy light unwarlike walls,
And, as the clouds fly over thee or lower,
Leucas! so glance they forward or retire.   90
Myrina next, and Cumæ, and, beyond,
Larissa—nearer still, yet stands unseen,*
(If ought be standing of her blest abodes)
Phocæa: yes!—air, sea, and sky, resound
"Phocæa!"—honor'd o'er the Gods was he
Who the first temple's faintest white descried.
What tears of transport, shouts of extasy,
O what embraces now! foul Enmity
At that sweet sound flew murmuring far away,
And the proud heart the precious moment seized   100
To burst the brutal chains itself imposed.
Dear native land! last parent, last—but lost!
What rivers flow, what mountains rise, like thine?
Bold rise thy mountains, rich thy rivers flow,

---

* Phocæa stands at the furthest end, and at a *curviture*, of the bay, on the borders
and *front* of which are Cumæ, Myrina, and Larissa—the first objects that appear. [L.]

---

101 imposed.] *so in errata 1802, comma in text.*

82

THE PHOCÆANS

Fresh breathes thy air, and breathes not o'er the free!
Love, vengeance, sweet desires, and dear regrets,
Crowded each bosom from that pleasant shore:
We touch the extremest shadow of it's hills,
And taste the fragrance of their flowering thyme.
We see the enemy; we hear his voice;   110
His arrows now fly round us; now his darts:
We rush into the port with pouncing prow.
Faint ring the shields against our hooked poles;
We dash from every pinnace, and present
A ridge of arms above a ridge of waves.
Now push we forward; now, the fight, like fire,
Closes and gapes and gathers and extends.
Swords clash, shields clang; spears whirr athwart the sky,
And distant helmets drop like falling stars.
Along the sands, and midst the rocks, arise   120
Cries of dismay and cries of plangent pain;
Shouts of discovery, shouts of victory—
While, seen amid the ranks, and faintly heard,
Thunders the bursting billow's high-archt bound.
They flee; we follow: where the fray retreats
Torrents of blood run down, and mark it's course,
And seize the white foam from the scatter'd sand,
And bear it floating to the sea unmixt:
While many a breathless corse of warrior bold
Dashes, with hollow sullen plunge, beneath   130
The hostile gods dark-frowning from our prows.

   O how delightful to retrace the steps
Of childhood! every street, and every porch
And every court, still open, every flower
Grown wild within! O worse than sacrilege
To tear away the least and lowliest weed
That rears it's wakeful head between the stones!
He who receiv'd undaunted, and surveyed
With calmly curious eye the burning wound,
And open'd and inspected it, shed tears   140
Upon the deep-worn step, before the gate,
That often whetted, once, his trusty sword.

   The trumpet calling, the Phocæan barks
Reach, with reluctant haste, the Enusian shore.
Here the good Prodicus, whose prudent eye

Foresaw that we were giving to the winds
Our inconsiderate sail, and who advised
To seek our safety from the Delphic shrine,
Died!—those who living fill'd the smallest space
In death have often left the greatest void.   150
The honest crew was gloomy; thro' such gloom
We best discern, and weigh, and value, tears.
When from his dazzling sphere the mighty falls,
Men, proud of shewing interest in his fate,
Run to each other and with oaths protest
How wretched and how desolate they are.
The good departs, and silent are the good.
Here none with labor'd anguish howl'd the dirge,
None from irriguous Ida, cypress-crown'd,
Blew mournfully the Mariandyne pipe;   160
Yet were there myrtles, polisht from the fleece
Of many flocks, successive, and the boughs
Of simple myrtle twined his artless bier.
Some scoopt the rock, some gather'd wonderous shells;
Warm was their study, warm were their disputes;
This was unpolisht; this unsound; 'twas askt
With finger bent, and drawing tacit shame,
Were shells like that for men like Prodicus?
Respect drew back, dishearten'd; Reverence paused:
To features harsh and dark clung first-born tears,   170
And fond contention soften'd where they fell.
Amid these funerals, four aged men
Came out of Chios; olive in their hands,
Around their shoulders flow'd the Persic robe.
They said, report had reacht the Chian state
Of our arrival at it's subject isles;
That, before Cyrus, at his footstool, sworn
In war his soldiers as his slaves in peace,
Charged with the king's high mandate they appear'd.
He said—"Obey me, and ye still retain   180
Freedom; ye loose it when ye disobey.
Therefor ye Grecian states of Asia's realm,
Should ye presume to countenance my curse,
Or dare to sucour him whom I disclaim,
Mark me aright, ye perish! go, demand,
Ye men of Chios, if the isle be yours,
That those who late escaped our scymetar,
Fly thence, or bend submissive to our sway.

THE PHOCÆANS

Should they resist, or hesitate, the fleet
Of every city, from the Sestian stream   190
To Gaza, shall attack them, or pursue,
Nor furl the sail till conquest crown the mast."

  To whom Pythermus, bursting from the throng.
"Go, tell thy master, go, thou self-bound slave,
*Thou subject! soon his dreaded foe departs.
Give him this opiate that thy hoary hairs
Have gather'd from the way—but neither fear
Of Persian swords nor Chian ships will urge
Fresh flight, but famine dire from friends dismayed.
We want not protestations: spare to lift   200
Those eyes to heaven that roll in vows disolved,
Those ready hands that trembling creak with wreaths;
Were not those hands against right counsel rais'd
Were they not joined before the conqueror's throne?
Phocæans venerate not empty age;
Age for the ark of virtue was designed,
And virtuous how they value, best declare
These rites, these robes, and, look around, these tears.
Hast thou forgotten how when Thales spake,
Best of the good and wisest of the wise,   210
And bade aloud the colonies unite
In Teios, middlemost of Asia's marts,
Against his equable and sound demand
Ye stood, and bargain'd freedom for a bale.
Else federal faction and rich rivalry
Had murmur'd, but flow'd down; equality
Had lessen'd danger and diffused success;
And inland Temperance and mountain Strength
Cherisht those arts which Avarice confined—
Confined for riot, ravishment, and spoil.   220
The fruit of commerce, in whatever clime,

* It will probably be thought that, after calling any one a *self-bound* [*so in errata*] *slave,* the word *subject* could hardly be used as a term of severe reproach. But it must also be recollected what people these Phocæans were: that in their hostility to *regular governments*, particularly to that of Cyrus, who generously offered to take them under his *protection*, they were so fierce and refractory [*so in errata*] as in the paroxism of their rage and folly to have reasoned thus—Subjects are by convention what slaves are by compulsion: slaves are unwilling subjects, subjects are willing slaves—they must indeed have reasoned thus, before they could have used any such expression. [L.]

---

194 self-bound] *so in errata 1802*, self-born *in text.*
  207 they value,] *so in errata 1802*, the value *in text.*   209 Thales] (*see* Herodotus, i. 170, and Bradley, *Early Poems of Landor*, p. 54)—W.

Ripening so sweet, so bitter in decay,
Enervates, pampers, poisons, who partake:
Thine, Freedom! rais'd by Toil and Temperance,
Bright as the produce of the Hesperian isles,
Fills the fond soul with sweet serenity,
And mortals grow immortal from it's shade.

O from what height descend I to ourselves!
Alas, for Chios swore our fates to share.
Heaven grant oblivion to the ungenerous race   230
Who spurn'd that Liberty their fathers clasp'd
With extacy, with madness, with despair—
For sure they thought such blessing was not man's:
They felt 'twas theirs—and love was jealousy.
O people, lost to glory, lost to shame,
Neglect the living, but respect the dead,
Your fathers' ghosts the breaking bond will hear.
But, heavenly Powers! whose silent orbs controul
The balanced billows of the boundless sea,
Who framing all things, o'er each state preside,   240
And, ruling all things, rule man's restless heart.—
O! if your servant, still, for follies past,
Unconscious faults, or vices unatoned,
Must suffer,—wander still, still groan repulse,
Ne'er, Powers of Mercy! may from kindred hand
But from the fiercest foe that arrow fly
The men of Chios heard him, and retired.
Again come groundless fears and dark debates.
Part is undaunted; swearing to abide
The threats of Cyrus, anchor'd in the bay: 250
Others walk near, and o'er the crowd descry
The hoary heights of storied Sipylus;
And every tufted lair and tripping stream
Comes from afar before the fondling eye,
Well they remember how the moulten mass
Of ardent iron from Hephestus' fane
Was plung'd into the port, and how they swore
They and their children, while the struggling fire
Seiz'd the white column of the crumbling wave,
That sooner should it rise again, and glow   260
Upon the surface, than would they return,

253 tripping] *so in errata 1802*, trippling *in text.*   254 eye,] eye: *MS. emendation.*
261 than] *so in errata 1802*, then *in text.*

Or e'er, tiara'd Median, bend to thee.
Now it repents them, now it grieves them! years
Are more, and hopes are fewer! they withdraw
One after one, slow creeping to the coast,
Firm against oaths, and fixt to be forsworn.
This when the braver, better part beheld,
First with entreaties, then with threats, they try
To turn the coward counsel back in time:
Those, so intent on ruin, so resolved   270
Against compulsion and against consent,
Would fight their brethren while they court their foe.
Stung by disdain and anguish, I exclaim'd
"What would ye more encounter? ye have borne
War, exile, persecution; would ye bear
(O last calamity of minisht man!)
The hand of pardon on your abject head?
Disease, affliction, poverty, defeat,
Leaving behind them unadopted shame,
Stamp not thus basely low the breathing clay.   280
Man bend to man!—forbid it righteous heaven!
T' endure each other hard calamity
Is great, is glorious; others are from high.
Let us contend in these who best can bear,
Contend in that who bravest can withstand."
Again, appearing shadowingly, return
Spirit, and mild remorse, and decent pride:
The young that waver'd, turn their eyes, and find
Most still unmoved—enough that most remain.
Slow, and abasht, and silent, they rejoin   290
Their bold companions; timorous age believes
They just return to bid their friends farewel:
They join; and unsuspicious youth believes
They only went to bid the old adieu.
None are so stedfast in the servile strife,
As those who, coldly pious, closely draw
The cowl o'er failings from themselves conceal'd;
Who deeming oaths most sacred, deem that oaths
Are made and broken by the same decree:
Wroth at each light-paced laughing folly's name,   300
They lay a nation's counsel'd crimes on heaven:
They think they worship, while they wrong, the Gods,

277 abject] *so in errata 1802,* object *in text.*   293 They] *so in errata 1802,* Their
in text.

And think they pity, while they hate, mankind.
With these go all who, reckoning in themselves
Unfavor'd wealth or wisdom undiscern'd,
Are grown disdainful to have met disdain;
Who, spurning most from others what they most
Hug in themselves, and feed to plethory,
Join stubborn patience with intolerant zeal.
These were the men, who, when the tyrant came   310
Against their country and their freedom, call'd
Debate sedition, acquiescence peace.
Twelve barks, for twelve sufficed them, were decreed
To bear away infirmity and fear,
And falsehood from the crew—twelve feeble barks—
Twice thirty more of stoutest bulk remain.
With these we, buoyant on unbounded hopes,
Ocean's vast wilds by friendly stars retrace.
First, vows and offerings to the powers above,
And to Poseidon, last, were duly paid: 320
Nor seldom, when we saw the cynosure,*
Thales! the grateful heart thy name recall'd.
Blest above men, who gainedst from the Gods
Power, more than heroes, tho' their progeny,
Power over earth, power over sea and sky.
They gave thee wisdom—this thou gavest men,
They gave thee Virtue—this too thou wouldst give:
They called thee aside, and led thy steps
Where never mortal steps were led before,
And shew'd the ever-peaceful realm of light.   330
Amidst the Gods thou lookedst down on Earth—
(Their glory could absorb but half thy soul)
Thou lookedst down, and viewing from afar
Earth struggling with Ambition, didst implore

---

* According to Diogenes Laertius, (1) the poet Callimachus had somewhere attributed to Thales the first discovery, or rather, I should suppose, the first application to any nautical purpose, of the ursa Minor. Whether the mariners observed the Cynosure or Helicé—

"Ex his altera apud Graios *Cynosura* vocatur,
   Altera dicitur esse Helice"—(2)

their remembrance of Thales would be natural. I have preferred the cynosure as the most obvious. The quarter from which they sailed must also be considered. *Major Pelagis apta,* Sidoniis *minor.* (Seneca) (3)—

Regit altera Graias,
Altera Sidonias, utraque sicca, rates. (4) [L.]

[(1) Diog. Laert. i. 23. (2) Translated from Aratus in Cicero, *De Nat. Deor.* ii. 41. (3) Seneca, *Hercules O.* 1539. (4) Ovid, *Trist.* iv. 3. 1.]

THE PHOCÆANS

Now that another country must be sought,
And other counsel taken, (thine disdain'd)
That they would chain up danger from the night,
And strengthen with new stars the watery way.

With surer sail, the daring mariners,
Leaving the green Ægæan, isle-begem'd,   340
Explore the middle main: remembering Greece,
They swell with fiercer pride and fresh disdain;
They scorn the shelter of her mountain-tops,
They curse with closer teeth the bitter blast,
Nor hail the fairest gales that blow from Greece.

345 Greece.] In a copy of the 1802 ed. Landor marked this word with an asterisk,
and appended the following footnote:
"* There would have been a second part of this poem, narrating a sea-fight with
the Carthaginians, recorded in history; then conflicts with the natives. The main
difficulty was to devise names for them. An approximation was attempted from
the welsh and irish, many of which are harmonious in the termination, an essential
in poetry. Druids, Druidesses, Bards, old oaks and capacious wicker baskets were
at hand."
In the same volume Landor wrote and then deleted a passage which he had wished
at first to see inserted in the "Advertisement to the Story of Crysäör". This insertion
is as follows:
"There would have been a second part of the poem entitled *The Phocæans*,
relating the arrival on the coast of Gaul, the first attempt at raising the city of
Massilia, and the conflicts with the High Priest of the Druids and the priests and
people under his influence. The main difficulty lay in the fabrication of proper
names for these impostors and barbarians. Anagrams would look like satire."

[SEQUEL]

[Published in *Letters &c. of W. S. Landor*, 1897. The MS. was found in his
writing-desk. A note was appended saying that the lines would have closed "The
Phocæans".]

O'erpast was warfare: youths and maidens came
From the Ligurian shore, and the Tyrrhene,
And the far Latian, to console the brave
After their toils, and celebrate the rites
Of the same Gods. Hymen stood up aloft;
His torch was brighter than the deadly glare
Lately so reverenced by a crouching throng
In Druid worship, over blacken'd oak
Leafless and branchless: hymns were sung before
That smiling youth whose marble brow was crown'd   10
With summer flowers, and Love's with earlier spring's.
Apollo stood above them both, august,
Nor bent his bow in anger more than Love.
Here was no Python; worse than Python one

Had vext the land before his light came down.
Here stood three maidens, who seem'd ministers
To nine more stately, standing somewhat higher
Than these demure ones of the downcast smile:
Silent they seem'd; not silent all the nine.
One sang aloud, one was absorb'd in grief   20
Apparently for youths who lately bled;
Others there were who, standing more elate,
Their eyes upturn'd, their nostrils wide expanded,
Their lips archt largely; and to raise the hymn
Were lifted lyres; so seemed it; but the skill
Of art Hellenic forged the grand deceit.
Night closed around them, and the stars went down
Advising their departure: when they went
I too had gone, for without them I felt
I should be sad, when from above there came   30
A voice . . it must have been a voice of theirs
It was so musical . . and said, "Arise
Loiterer, and sing what thou alone hast heard."
"Inspire me then, said I, O thou who standest
With the twelve maidens round!"
                                        Was it a dream?
I thought the Delian left his pedestal.
A living God, I thought he toucht my brow;
Then issued forth this hymn, the very hymn
I caught from the full choir, the last they sang,
"Incline a willing ear, O thou supreme   40
Above all Gods! Jove Liberator! Jove
Avenger! to Phocæa's sons impart
The gift of freedom all our days, and peace
To hold it sacred and with blood unstain'd.
And do thou, consort of the Omnipotent!
Bestow thy blessing on our rescued few,
And grant the race, adoring thee, increase."

GUNLAUG AND HELGA

[Scene: Iceland and Sweden, c.1008–11]

[Published with other poems, &c., in *Simonidea*, 1806; reprinted 1831, 1846.]

SOPHIA, pity Gunlaug's fate.
Perfidious friendship, worse than
 hate,
And love, whose smiles are often
 vain,
Whose frowns are never, proved
 his bane.
For war his rising spirit sigh'd,
In foreign realms o'er ocean wide.
 "Illugi, father, let me go,
"I burn to meet my country's
 foe;
"Ere fierce invaders come to spoil
"Our verdant Iceland's native
 soil."   10
 "A blessing, Gunlaug, on thy
 head,"
The fond, afflicted father said.
"If fierce invaders come to spoil
"Our verdant Iceland's native
 soil—
"O son, O warrior, wait till then,
"O man, remember they are men."
 To Thorstein's house, whose
 daring prow
Through ocean pounced upon his
 foe,
Stung with denial, Gunlaug went,
But breathed no word of discon-
 tent.   20
 "Thorstein," he cried, "I leave
 my home,
"Yet not for shelter am I come.

"Thorstein, I come to learn of
 thee
"The dangers of the land and sea.
"Speed thee! together let us go,
"And Thorstein's shall be Gun-
 laug's foe."
 "Rash youth," said Thorstein,
 "wait awhile—
"I love too well my native isle;
"Whether the sandy dog-rose
 blows,
"Or sparkle fierce the starry
 snows;   30
"And never shall this hand again
"Direct the rudder o'er the main."
 Thus as he spake, he would have
 prest
The hand of his aspiring guest.
But Gunlaug cried, "I will not
 here
"Partake thy hospitable cheer;
"For war's, for danger's, gifts I
 came,
"Keep thou thy fears, leave me
 thy fame."
 Aloud the manly veteran
 laugh'd;
"Come! come!" said he, "one
 social draught!   40
"My fears I'll keep that none
 shall see,
"And I will leave my fame to
 thee."

Title and Helga *om. 1831, 1846.* 1 Sophia [*see note at end of vol.*] 4 proved] were
1831. 6 foreign] unknown *1831, 1846.* 7 Illugi, father,] O father, father! *1846.*
8 foe;] foe." *1831, 1846.* 10 "*our verdant Iceland.*"—Iceland was once remarkably
fertile, and celebrated for the verdure of its vallies. [L. *footnote in 1806 only.*] *ll.* 9–10
om. 1831, 1846. 12 The . . . afflicted] Illugi, his fond *1846.* 13 If . . . come] Go.
when invader comes *1831, 1846.* *For ll.* 15–16 *1831, 1846 substitute:*
  But wait with patient zeal til [till *1846*] then
  And learn the deeds of mightier men."
23 of] from *1846.* 27 Rash . . . wait] Brave . . . stay *1831, 1846.*

Out sprang the tears from Gun-
    laug's eyes:
"O noble Thorstein, brave and
    wise!
"To enter how shall Gunlaug
    dare?
"These eyes may meet thy Helga
    fair."
    At Helga's and her father's
    name,
The beauteous blue-eyed virgin
    came.
No word had then the youth to
    say,
But turn'd his downcast face
    away.   50
He heard her sandal sip the floor,
And, ere she reach'd the palace
    door,
His heaving bosom could not
    brook
Reproach or wonder from her look.
    And couldst thou, Gunlaug,
    thus refrain?
And seek'st thou conquests o'er
    the main?
    She saw, but knew not his
    distress,
And eyed him much, nor loved
    him less.
Long stood, and longer would
    have staid
The tender-hearted blue-eyed
    maid;   60
But fear her stifling throat op-
    prest,
And something smote her bound-
    ing breast.

Far off, alone, she would remain,
But thought it time to turn again.
"Yet better not, perhaps," she
    thought,
"For fear the stranger hold me
    nought,
"I dare not wish; they call it sin;
"But—would my father bring him
    in!"
    He came; their friendship grew;
    he woo'd;
Nor Helga's gentle heart with-
    stood.   70
Her milk-white rabbit oft he fed,
And crumbled fine his breakfast-
    bread;
And oft explored, with anxious
    view,
Spots where the crispest parsley
    grew.
Her restive horse he daily rid,
And quite subdued her stubborn
    kid,
Who lately dared to quit her side,
And once, with painful rashness,
    tried
His ruddy horn against her knee,
Bold as his desp'rate sire could
    be.   80
    The cautious father long delay'd
The wishes of the youth and maid.
His patient hand, like her's, unrols
The net to catch the summer
    shoals;
And both their daily task compare,
And daily win each other's hair.
One morn, arising from her side,
He, as he paid the forfeit, cried—

44 brave] bold *1831, 1846.*   *For ll.* 45–6 *1831, 1846 substitute:*
    Shall Gunlaug dare to tarry here?
    Shall Helga see this blush, this tear?"
79 His] Its *1831, 1846.*   80 his desp'rate] its desperate *1831, 1846.*   *Between*
ll. 80–1 *1831, 1846 insert thirty-two lines for which see notes at end of vol.*   83 unrols]
unrolls *1831, 1846.*

"Behold my hair too trimly shine,
"Behold my hands are white as
 thine.   90
"O! could I loose our blissis bar!
"I burn for wedlock and for war."
 "For war," said she, "when
  lovers burn,
"To wedlock, Gunlaug, few return.
"In Samsa, brave Hialmar lies,
"Nor Inga's daughter closed his
 eyes.
"By sixteen wounds of raging fire
"The enchanted sword of An-
 gantyre,
"Withering, laid waste his fruit-
 less bloom,
"And housed the hero in the
 tomb.   100
"'*Oh Oddur*,' said the dying chief,
"'*Take off my ring, my time is
 brief;*
"'*My ring, if smaller, might adorn*
"'*The plighted hand of Ingebiorn!*'
"Swift to Sigtuna flew the friend,
"And sorely wept Hialmar's end.
"By Mæleren's blue lake he found
"The virgin sitting on the ground.
"A garment for her spouse she
 wove,
"And sang '*Ah speed thee, gift of
 love!*'   110
"In anguish Oddur heard her sing,
"And turn'd his face and held the
 ring.
"Back fell the maiden: well she
 knew
"What fatal tidings must ensue.

"When Oddur raised her, back
 she fell,
"And died, the maiden loved so
 well.
"'*Now gladly*,' swore the generous
 chief,
"'*I witness death beguiling grief;*
"'*I never thought to smile agen*
"'*By thy blue waters, Mæleren!*'
"But grant that on the foreign
 strand   121
"Thy bosom meet no biting
 brand:
"Grant that no swift unguarded
 dart
"Lay thee beneath the flooded
 thwart:
"Ah! how unlike a nuptial day,
"To shudder at the hissing spray;
"To wipe and wipe its tingling
 brine,
"And vainly blink thy pelted
 eyen;
"To feel their stiff'ning lids
 weigh'd down
"By toil no pleasure comes to
 crown: 130
"Say, Gunlaug, wouldst thou give
 for this
"The fire-side feast and bridal
 kiss?"
He told the father what he
 said,
And what replied the willing maid.
 "My son," said Thorstein, "now
 I find
"Unfixt, inconstant, is thy mind.

---

91 blissis] bliss's *1846*. [*For footnote only in 1806 see notes at end of vol.*] 119 *agen*] *again 1831, 1846*. 121 foreign] hostile *1831, 1846*. 124 "Thwart."—Bench for the rowers. [L. *footnote in 1806. A thwart* is a bench for rowers *1831*. Footnote *om. 1846*.] 125 Ah!] Yet *1831, 1846*. 126 shudder at] stand amid *1831, 1846*. 127 To] And *1831, 1846*. 128 eyen] eyn *1831, 1846*. 129 To . . . stiff'ning] And . . . stiffening *1831, 1846*. 136 Unfixt . . . thy] Wavering with love the sea-bound *1831, 1846*.

"Away to war, if war delight,
"Be gone three years from Helga's
    sight.
"Then, if perchance at thy re-
    turn
"Thy breast with equal transport
    burn,   140
"Your wishes I no more confine—
"No—darling Helga shall be
    thine."
    Away the tow'ring warrior flew,
Nor bade his Helga once adieu.
He felt the manly sorrows rise,
And open'd wide his gushing eyes:
He stopt a moment in the hall;
Still the too pow'rful tears would
    fall.
He would have thought his fate
    accurst   149
To meet her as he met her first;
So, madly swang the sounding
    door,
And reacht, and reaching left, the
    shore.
Three years in various toils had
    past,
And Gunlaug hasten'd home at
    last.
Rafen at Upsal he had seen,
Of splendid wit and noble mien:
Rafen with pleasure he beheld,
For each in arms, in verse, ex-
    cell'd:
Rafen he heard from sun to sun,

And why? their native land was
    one.   160
    O friends! mark here how
    friendships end!
O lovers! never trust a friend!
    In converse sweet he often told
What treasures would his arms
    infold;
How in the summer he should
    share
The blissful bed of Helga fair.
For, foul suspicion ne'er supprest
One transport of his tuneful breast.
The low and envious past he by,
With scornful or unseeing eye. 170
No words like Gunlaug's words
    could move,
And all his guilt was guilty love.
No, Rafen! crafty traitor, no!
The guilt was thine that made
    him so.
    In Sweden dwelt the manliest
    race
That brighten earth's maternal
    face:
Yet never would proud Gunlaug
    yield
To any man in any field.
The day was fixt for his return,
And crowding friends around him
    burn,   180
Their pomp and prowess to dis-
    play,
And celebrate the parting day.

138 Be gone] Begone *1831, 1846.*   139 Then] And *1831, 1846.*   140 Thy] That
1831, 1846.   141 Your] Its *1831, 1846.*   142 "No . . . be] Thine is my house, My
Helga *1831, 1846.*   143 tow'ring] towering *1846.*   148 pow'rful] powerful *1846.*
158 arms, in verse] arms and verse *1831, 1846.*   163 converse . . . often] fulness of
his heart he *1831, 1846.*   164 infold] enfold *1831, 1846.*   166 Helga] maid so *1831, 1846.*
167 foul] as *1831, 1846.*   169 past he] he past *1831, 1846.*   For *ll.* 171–4 *1831,
1846 substitute:*

    From tales alone their guile he knew,
    Believing all around him true,
    And fancying falsehood flourisht then
    When earth produced two-headed men.

175 dwelt] dwell *1831, 1846.*

94

Amidst them, up a wrestler stood,
And call'd to wrestle him who wou'd.
So still were all, you might have heard
The motion of the smallest bird:
Some look'd, some turn'd away the eye,
Not one amongst them dared reply.
  "Come hither, friend," said Gunlaug bold,
"O ! ne'er in Iceland be it told 190
"I stood, amid the feast, defied,
"Nor skill, nor strength, nor courage tried."
  The wrestler then beheld and smiled,
And answer'd thus in accent mild:—
"O stranger ! though thy heart be stout,
"And none like thee sit round about,
"Thou bringest to unequall'd might
"A form too beauteous and too slight."
  "Well, friend, however that may be,
"Let Gunlaug try his strength with thee." 200
  They closed; they struggled; nought avail'd
The wrestler's skill, his prowess fail'd.

One leg he moved a little back,
And sprang again to the attack.
Gunlaug, in trying to elude
A shock so sudden and so rude,
Avoided half the whelming weight,
But slipt aside, alas! too late.
Though less in force as less in skill,
'Twere better had he quite stood still. 210
His combatant flew headlong past,
Yet round his neck one arm he cast;
And, though beneath he struck the ground,
He mist, and Gunlaug met, the wound.
  The grass and springing flow'rs amid,
A rotten pointed stake was hid.
Swung by the rapid jerk in air,
His nervous leg descended there.
When Rafen saw the spouting blood,
Bewilder'd in new joy he stood:
And scarce his features could controul 221
The rapture of an alter'd soul:
Yet tended ev'ry day his couch,
And emptied there the hawking-pouch:
He brought him game from lake and land,
And fed the falcon on his hand.
At last with doleful look he said—
"We past our time, I fear, have staid;

183 Amidst] Amid *1831, 1846.*   184 wou'd] would *1846.*   188 amongst] among *1831, 1846.*   *ll.* 209–10 *om. 1831, 1846.*   211 headlong] with him *1831.*   *For ll.* 213–14 *1831, 1846 substitute:*
    And threw him headlong [*also 1846*] on the ground,
    Wounded, but with no warrior's wound.

218 nervous] sinewy *1846.*   221 controul] control *1846.*   222 an alter'd] a selfish *1831, 1846.*   223 ev'ry] every *1846.*   225 He] And *1831, 1846.*   *ll.* 227–30 *om. 1831, 1846.*

"And those who waited our return,
"Now, while I speak, our shipwreck mourn." 230
" Go, haste," said Gunlaug, "haste, my friend,
"May peace and love thy steps attend.
"Ah, wretched! thus to stay, alone;
"Ere the day fixt, I too am gone.
"How far more wretched should I be
"If my fair Helga mourn'd for me.
"Each lot were hard; but I prefer,
"If one must be, to mourn for her."
　Away went Rafen: thus he told
The fabled fate of Gunlaug bold.
　"Gunlaug unwillingly I left, 241
"Of reason, as of love, bereft.
"At Upsal, famed for damsels bright,
"And flatter'd wit's bewildering light,
"Him courts and pleasures yet detain,
"And Helga's charms have charm'd in vain."
　"Accursed man!" the father cried,
"My Helga ne'er shall be his bride."

　" O father!"—"Peace!" cried he, "I swear, 249
"Deluded Helga, thou shalt ne'er."
A swoon her swelling bosom smote,
Huge serpents seem'd to clasp her throat;
And underneath the father's chair
Stream'd on his dog her auburn hair.
Quick, Rafen raised her in his arms,
And gazed and gloated on her charms.
　"Gaze; she is thine," said Thorstein fierce,
"If she be Gunlaug's—'tis in verse."
She wept all night; but woes increast
When in the morn she saw the priest. 260
　"O father! pause to break my vow,
"I know his heart; ah, could'st but thou!
"By all divine, all human laws,
"My best beloved father, pause.
"If Rafen loves, he loves the dead,
"I live not for his hated bed."
　At early dawn, the youth she lost
Arrived upon his native coast.

236 fair] sweet *1831, 1846.*　　　*For ll.* 237–40 *1831, 1846* substitute:
　　When twice the sabbath-day had past,
　　Rafen, as one compell'd at last
　　By his impatient listeners, said . .
　　And lower'd his voice and shook his head . .
252 Huge serpents] And serpents *1831*; A serpent *1846.*　　　255 Quick,] Then *1831, 1846.*
259 but woes] her woe *1831, 1846.*　　　261 O] Pause, *1846.*　　　264 My . . . father]
Kindest and best of fathers *1831, 1846.*　　　268 Arrived] Had lept *1846.*　　　*Between*
ll. 268–9 *1831, 1846 insert two lines:*
　　Blessing his fortune to survive,
　　And on the appointed day arrive.

He hung around his father's neck,
And groan'd the thoughts he could
    not speak;   270
And, as his neck he hung around,
The father's tears dropt o'er the
    wound.
The servants watcht with anxious
    heed,
And brought their lord the luscious
    mead.
Then strew'd he bear-skins on the
    stone,
And bade the tardy men begone.
He blest his fortune to survive,
And, on the appointed day,
    arrive.
The servants watcht his eyelids
    close,
They watcht the flush of bland
    repose;   280
Then raised his shaggy pillow
    high'r,
With tender caution trimm'd the
    fire,
And, lest his breath should be
    opprest,
Pickt out the pine-tree from the
    rest:
Then fann'd the flame, nor fear'd
    the smoke
From ash well-dried, and ship-
    wreck oak.

A frolic maid was passing by,
And, as she saw the hero lie,
Removed the clinking hawberk
    mail,
And took a wolf-skin, from a
    nail: 290
Across his throat she placed the
    teeth,
And tuckt the clasping claws be-
    neath;
And would have kist him, but she
    fear'd
To tickle with her breast his
    beard.
    Eight hours he slept: at length
    he woke,
And thus, in hurried accent,
    spoke.
"What means, my men, the
    noise I hear?
"Lead, to the window lead me
    near.
"Aye, Rafen and his friends are
    come,
"I know, to bid me welcome
    home.   300
"Oft has he trod the sunless dew,
"And hail'd at last my bark in
    view.
"O Rafen, my best friend, for this
"Shall Helga give thy brow a
    kiss."

273 watcht] came *1831, 1846.*
for which see notes at end of vol.
279, 280 watcht] watch *1831, 1846.*
282 trimm'd] trim *1831, 1846.*
opprest) *1831, 1846.*   284 Pickt] Pick *1831, 1846.*
1831, 1846.   fear'd] fear *1831, 1846.*
Between ll. 274–5 *1831, 1846 insert twelve lines*
ll. 277–8 *om. 1831, 1846: vide supra ll.* 268–9.
    281 Then raised] They raise *1831, 1846.*
283 lest . . . opprest,] (for his breath might be
    285 Then fann'd] And fan
Between ll. 288–9 *1831, 1846 insert two lines:*
    His arms and armour thrown around,
    Upon the bench, the couch, the ground,
295 Eight . . . slept] Sound was his sleep *1831, 1846.*   *For l.* 298 *1831, 1846*
substitute three lines:
    Nearer the window . . still more near.
    Despach [Despatch *1846*] . . I feel no pain . . despach [despatch *1846*] . .
    Why look upon that idle scratch?
299 Aye] Ay *1831, 1846.*

Then in rusht Thorkell.—"Stay thee, lord!
"Nor blast thee at the sight abhorr'd.
"I thought that heaven could send no curse
"Like slighted love; it sends a worse!
"Now is my joy what was my pain,
"To find so soon I loved in vain.   310
"Rafen leads homeward from the shrine
"Thy Helga—for her heart is thine."
  Gunlaug with pleasure heard him speak,
And smiles relumed his faded cheek.
Thorkell, who watcht him all the while,
With more than wonder saw him smile.
"Thorkell, I thank thee," he replied,
"What, have we both, then, lost the bride?
"No—generous rival, neither quite
"Hath understood the nuptial rite.   320
"Rafen leads homeward from the shrine
"My Helga, for her heart is mine."
  Then Thorkell shook his head, and sigh'd,
"Ill the suspicious soul betide!
"But he whom no suspicions move,
"Loves not, or with ill-omen'd love.

"These eyes, that yet in wonder swim,
"Saw the fair Helga sworn to him."
  His horror Gunlaug could not check,
But threw his arm round Thorkell's neck.   330
"O loose me, let me fall, my friend,
Cried he, "let life and sorrow end."
Now rage, now anguish, seized his soul,
Now love again resumed the whole:
Now would he, fierce, on Helga's name
Pour vengeance: tears for vengeance came.
"Thorkell, two days alone I wait,
"The third shall lour with Rafen's fate.
"I scorn to stay for strength restored—
"Go—at the corner whet my sword."   340
  On the third morn, their friends decreed
That one or both of them should bleed.
On the third morn, what pangs opprest
The tender lover's valiant breast!
His only hope on earth below
To die, and dying slay the foe.
He slept not, nor had ever slept
Since the first day; but said, and wept—
  "Arouse thee, Gunlaug, why complain?
"She never can be thine again!

335 fierce, on] upon *1831, 1846.*   338 lour] close *1831, 1846.*

"The bark shall lean against the
shore,   351
"Nor wave wash off the rested
oar.
"The flowers shall ope their spark-
ling eyes,
"And dance in robes of richest
dyes;
"And, flying back, again shall meet
"The south-wind's kisses, soft and
sweet.
"Young eagles build their first
fond nest,
"And sink from rapine into rest:
"Ah, see them soar above my
head!
"Their hopes are come, but mine
are fled!   360
"Arouse thee, Gunlaug, haste
away,
"And rush into the mortal fray."
From far the list'ning Rafen
heard
His rival's armour ring; nor fear'd.
Fear may be stifled in the breast,
But shame burns fiercer when
supprest.
Onward he rusht.—and dared defy
His arm, but dared not meet his
eye.
Madly he struck, and blind with
guilt,
And his blade shiver'd from the
hilt.   370
O'er Gunlaug's shield, with action
weak,
It fell, and falling rased his cheek.

Away disdainful Gunlaug turn'd,
And cried, while rage within him
burn'd—
"Rafen, take up thy broken
sword;
"Live—see thou Helga be re-
stored.
"Ah, why?" then to himself he
said;
"O Helga, beauteous blue-eyed
maid!
"Such were the tender words of
yore,
"Ah, never can I speak them
more!   380
"By Rafen's side hath Helga
slept,
"Upon my fruit the snail hath
crept,
"The blindworm hath his poison
shed—
"O Rafen! curses on thy head.'
Afar was he, as Gunlaug spoke,
And every tie of honour broke.
Before the court of chieftains old
He stood, and well his story told.
Much for religion and for laws
He pled, and bade them guard his
cause: 390
"Though baffled and disarm'd,"
he cried,
"I gave the wound, and claim the
bride."
Some with disdain his reasons
heard,
While others wisht the cause
deferr'd.

351 against] upon *1831, 1846.*   352 wash] dash *1831, 1846.*   363 list'ning]
listening *1831, 1846.*   372 rased] razed *1831, 1846.*   374 burn'd—] burnt,
1831 rhyme impaired by misp.   379 Such] Sure *1831 misp.*   380 Ah, never]
But never *1846.*   392 bride."] bride."* *1831, 1846 with footnote:*
    * According to the laws of duel in Iceland, he who gave the first wound was
    gainer of the suit. [L.]
393 reasons] reason *1846.*

Then Ormur spake, in speech of scorn,
Ormur, the friend of Asbiorn,
Who, daring singly to engage
A jotun, proved his fatal rage.
  "Go, finish this unmanly strife,
"And keep the vow, but quit the wife. 400
"So neither party shall repine,
"But love be his, and laws be thine.
"Go home, and with the world's applause
"There quaintly kiss the cold-lip laws."
  But Rafen, when he saw the sneer
Run dimpling on from peer to peer,
"Has not the priest then join'd our hands
"In holy everlasting bands?
"One would have thought 'twas thee I wrong'd,
"Right second to the viper-tongued." 410
  The assembly, wishing to compose
The strife of single combat, rose:
But order'd first that none decide
His right by arms o'er Iceland wide.
  "In Auxar then once more we meet,
"And thou shalt never thence retreat."
Swore valiant Gunlaug, when he heard

The suit that Rafen had preferr'd.
"Thy courage shall not screen thy guile,
"When once we meet in Auxar isle." 420
  Urged by his friends, as by his foe,
Again to fight must Rafen go.
But furious winds each pinnace drove
Past little Auxar's lonely cove.
Beyond the strait, their anchors bit
The yellow sand of Agnafit;
Where Inga reign'd, whose daughter's fate
Gunlaug heard Helga once relate.
  Here too the wise and old impede
The brave in lawless fray to bleed.
By Sota's shore their course they take, 431
And anchor near Dyngiunes lake.
There sprad the heath its evener ground,
And purer water there was found.
They meet; and all their friends unite
In the full fury of the fight:
'Till, save the champions, none remain
But the sore wounded, on the plain.
The chiefs had closed; nor space was now
That either urge the deadly blow:
Still, oft they struggle, breast to breast, 441
Oft give, unwilling, mutual rest:

---

398 "*A jotun.*" The jotuns were giants. Their existence is not fabulous. [L. *om.* 1846. *For addition in 1831 see notes at end of vol.*]   406 peer . . . peer] each compeer *1846.*   410 "*Right second to the viper-tongued.*"—Ormstunga. Gunlaug was called so, from the sharpness of his satire [wit *1846*]. [L. Gunlaug was *om. 1846.*] 420 Auxar] Auxar's *1831, 1846.*   433 sprad] spred *1831,* spread *1846.*   437 save] with *1831, 1846.*   441 Still,] But *1831, 1846.*

Then, with fresh force and hate, renew
A combat blood must soon imbrue.
Gunlaug, with desperate strain, recoil'd,
Yet his free force and aim were foil'd:
Else had his sword, athwart the side
Of Rafen, oped life's sluices wide.
The foot he struck; so far he sprung—
The foot upon its tendon hung.
He stagger'd: just within his reach   451
Stood, chosen for the shade, a beech.
He shrunk against it, and his foot
Was resting on the twisted root;
"Now yield thee," loud the hero cried,
"Yield; and resign the blooming bride."
  "True! on these terms we fought before,
Said he, "but now we fight for more.
"This day life only shall suffice,
"And, Gunlaug, he who kills not, dies.   460
"Life still is left me; and the worst
"I suffer now, is fainting thirst."
  Eager the combat to renew,
Fast to the lake brave Gunlaug flew:

There from his neck the helm unbraced,
Nor, though he thirsted, stopt to taste.
Prone, and on tottering knee, he stoopt,
With vigorous arm the surface scoopt,
And swiftly to his rival bore
The clear cold water, running o'er.
By treachery yet untaught to doubt,   471
In his right arm he held it out.
Virtue, and praise, and pride forsook
The soul of Rafen: fierce he strook
His generous rival's naked head,
And gan to triumph o'er the dead.
He fell to earth: the unsated foe
Strove hard to follow up the blow.
His foot denies his deadly hate,
And doubt and horror round him wait.   480
  Gunlaug pusht faintly from his breast
The shield, that struggling life opprest.
The gales that o'er Dyngiunes play
Recal his roving soul to day.
Up would he start; his wound denies
Fresh shadows float before his eyes:

ll. 443–4 *om. 1831, 1846.*   461 still] yet *1831, 1846.*   464 brave] then *1831, 1846.*   466 stopt] staid *1831*; stayed *1846.*   472 In] With *1831, 1846.*   473 Virtue,] Valour *1831, 1846.*   476–7 And . . . earth:] *1831 has:*
  And (for the dying are not dead)
  Gunlaug was fell'd:
1846 has:
  And laught in triumph while it bled.
  Gunlaug was fell'd;
484 Recal] Recall *1831, 1846.*   to day] *misp.* today *1831.*   485 denies denies; *1831, 1846.*

On his right elbow now he leans;
Now brighten the surrounding
    scenes:
Trees, mountains, skies, no more
    are mixt;
The lake, and earth, and foe,
    stand fixt.   490
His silence then he sternly broke,
And thus, his eye on Rafen, spoke.
"Rafen, with powers renew'd I
    rise:
"Yes, traitor!—he who kills not,
    dies.
"Yet would I leave a little space,
"To hear thee own this deed was
    base."
    Now, first, in speech was Rafen
    slow—
Weak from his wound, and wrung
    with woe,
He fixt his eyes upon the ground,
And thus confest, in faultering
    sound.   500
"'Twas base: but how could Rafen
    bear
"That Gunlaug have his Helga
    dear?"

Yet, paused the warrior: fixt
    he stood,
And slowly wiped the welling
    blood.
True love he pitied while he
    heard,
And had but Rafen spared that
    word,
His youthful head had not lain
    low!
Gunlaug scarce felt the fatal
    blow;
But, once repeating "*Rafen bear*
"*That Gunlaug have his Helga
    dear!*"   510
Rage swell'd his heart and fired
    his eye,
And through the forest rang the
    cry,
"*Thou, though thy treachery caught
    her vow,*
"*God's vengeance! Rafen! e'er shalt
    thou?*"
    Then hate rose high with rising
    pain,
And brast the rival's helm in
    twain.

497 in . . . slow—] was Rafen slow in speech, *1846*.   498 Weak . . . woe] Wrung with remorse and weak with woe *1831*. Lowering his brow against the beech *1846*. 500 faultering] faltering *1831, 1846*.   502 have his] be to *1831, 1846*.   503 Yet . . . he] Paus'd had the conqueror: he had *1831, 1846*.   505 True . . . while he] With patience, pity, grief, had *1831, 1846*.   509 , once repeating] hearing *how could 1831, 1846*.   510 *have his*] be to *1831, 1846*.   513 *Thou, though*] *What! tho'* 1831, 1846.   514 *shalt*] *wert 1831, 1846*.   515 hate . . . rising] hatred rising high with *1831*; hatred rising higher than *1846*.   516 And . . . rival's] He smote the traitor's *1831, 1846*.

CORYTHOS

[Published in 1847; not reprinted in same form. For later version, published 1859, reprinted 1876, see notes at end of volume. Text, 1847.]

ARGUMENT

Corythus, Paridis Œnonesque filius, ab Helenâ benigne hospitio exceptus est, quæ, dum patri eum necopinanti vellet intromittere, zelotypiâ correptus est Paris, filiumque vi subitâ adortus interficit. A Philoctete vulneratus, Œnonen veniam orat, datâ moritur.

OENONE had been weeping, but her tears
The bitter blast had dried; for on the top
Of Ida stood she, on that pale short grass
Where the wind whirl'd the pine-cones, rolling them
Along their narrow and hard-pointed leaves.
Hence she beheld the temples and the town
Of Dardanos, now fated, and discern'd
The house of him she loved: then from the woods
She call'd out Corythos; and thus she spake.
   "Go, my child, go. Within the walls of Troy   10
One is there who will love and cherish thee,
Thee, but without thy mother! Yes, there lives
Thy father . . but how short a time to live
Alas! he knows not: for from Lemnos comes
In safety Philoctetes, and he brings
Those arrows with him, those of Hercules,
By which the Fates have sung that he must fall.
Unwelcome thou wilt not be (for no son
Hath she) to Helen, if that head so dear
Thou rescuest from perdition: he himself   20
May not perhaps forget those days serene
That shone on him and me; may not forget
How once the poplar bore upon its bark
Two names united. If unmindful now,
Unmindful he will cease to be at sight
Of thee: if bad the husband, he will be
The better father for that very cause,
And own he owes his life to Corythos,
To thee, deserted Corythos! his son."
   Embracing him, she mingled with embrace   30
Kisses and tears; and then consign'd him, loth,
To an old guide . . but often called him back,
Repeating the same orders; to avoid
The sail-white waters and the secret bays,
And every place where Grecian might abide.

Argument. From the Latin version in *Poemata, &c.*, 1847.

They winde their way down the steep braky road.
Then, when their voices she could hear no more,
Nor see the birds their shouts and stones had scared,
Turn'd she her face, and this lone plaint began!
  "Aërial mountains! woods, where Gods reside,   40
And Corythos was cradled! you I see,
But him I see no longer, to these eyes
Dearer than light! Before him Paris went
And never more return'd: no love remains
For me, no pledge of love! Not only lost
Are former joys, but lost is also he
Who brought them back to me, by step, by mien,
By play, by prattle, and could half-persuade
That nothing was amiss or ought to grieve me.
Him too I now am parted from, and yield   50
Almost without reluctance, tho' the sole
Calmer and comforter of every pang,
That happier days be his than have been mine.
Yet all things (how can I believe my eyes?)
Appear the same as ever: Xanthos flows,
And Simöis, in the morning light as clear,
And Tenedos seems only one vast rock
Upon the whitening reflux of the waves.
In form too and in features I myself
Remain the same; for age can not consume   60
Nor change them. Ah, sad thought! how fugitive
The gifts I catch at! Like the snow beneath
A southern wind, thy form, Œnone, wanes
And wastes, unhappy! in the sight of him
Thou holdest ever lovely, ever dear.
  "How easy it is to mow down the bloom
Of life, and sow the open breast with cares!
How soon, when faith is shaken, youth is shed!
Irrevocable days bear heavily
Upon the sinking heart, but heavier far   70
The future anguish of the fondly loved.
  "Asterope! my sister! happy thou
In thy espousals! Can then Æsacos
Be kin to Paris? brother? But the one
The mild Arisbe bore, the other sprang
From Hecuba, a violent River's child.
I envy not the happy ones alone,
But even the wretched who have left the light

Of upper air; the maiden whose stern sire
Hath turn'd the torch of Hymen from her path,   80
And widow on whose bridal bed there hung
The withering garlands. Grief that death has brought
Time in the course of nature bears away.
   "Where Nile throws open his wide chamber, strewn
With lotus; where, to sight insuperable,
The holy Ganges rolls his stream from high,
If Memnon's mother rise before the sun
To weep for him; if ye too, O ye Nymphs
Of ocean! have beheld how great the grief
Of Thetis; how, when Glaucos would advise,   90
She fled from comfort, fled from Triton's song
And Doris and her daughters who sate round;
If by the walls of Neptune all the maids
And matrons wail'd at Hector's late-rais'd bier,
Stil Hector's was Andromache, as when
Their child was frightened at his nodding crest
And heroes fled before him: his was she
In death, nor severed from him by the tomb.
Deserves Œnone then a harder fate?
   "What is my fault? unless a fault it be   100
To sit secluded at the dens of beasts,
Where bear and wolf break slumbers just begun,
And where the mighty mother of the Gods
Drags the reluctant lions to her wheels;
Unless it be a fault to have remain'd
So faithful to the faithless, nor have breath'd
Complaint to other than the passing wind.
There are kind Gods who may deem otherwise.
Howe'er that happen, brighter be the days
Of Corythos, and nobler his pursuits   110
Than creeping to draw meshes round the nides
Of birds now mute, and gathcr'd close in fields
White with the steril stubble or hard snow.
Happier be thou, my child! if Gods look down
On pious prayers, and children are exempt
From retribution for parental guilt."
   Meanwhile the youth was looking up the walls
And wondering at their highth, and how they stood

82 Grief that . . . .–94 *not in the Latin, 1820.*   111 nides *cf.* avium intendere retia.
nidis. *Poemata, 1847.*

Defiant of so long and fierce a war.
"But where is that old fig-tree? where the spot   120
Whence Hector, my brave uncle, met in fight
Achilles? where did Venus cast the cloud
Around my father?"
                And he siez'd the hand
Of his old guide each time he askt and heard.
Ascending up to Pergama, before
The gate an elder of the town he sees,
And asks him whereabout stands Priam's house.
His guide represses him, and says,
                       "We go
To Helen."
         "Go then," cried the aged man,
"Readily may that fatal pest be found,   130
And none is wanted here to show the way."
  Around his neck sprang the Idæan boy
And "Blessed!" cried he, "blessed be whoe'er
Thus deeply hates my mother's injurer.
With me most virtuous is it to abhor
That Spartan. To none other house go I,
Than the king's own, where with *his* father dwells
My father; where the chaste Andromache
Bemoans her husband on the ground he trod;
Where now a wanton one, who fears not Pan   140
Nor Jove himself, with nimble needle paints
For altars, none of theirs, fine tapestry,
Or plucks the harpstrings with a Sphynxis nail."
  Many had seen and past them as they spake;
One, 'twas a female, hesitated, stopt,
And askt them if from Ida they had seen
The Grecian ships departing? were the winds
So fair? and, while the elder she addrest,
She gazed upon the younger. He was toucht
To see her cheek grow pale and red by turns;   150
Nor quite unmoved the elder: to himself
Said he "When beauty such as this shines forth
From Ilion, who would ever lend his ear
Even when a Goddess may have promist more?"
  Now saw the youth, who saw them not til now,

143 Sphynxis] *cf.* Parisis *l.* 198. In a footnote to *Gunlaug and Helga, l.* 91, Landor gave his reasons for adopting in some cases "the oldest and best manner of spelling" See notes at end of vol.

CORYTHOS

Maidens behind her, beauteous, with succinct
Vesture and braided hair; graceful their form,
And modest their demeanour: not so quick
Bounded his bosom when the boar rusht out
Against the meshes, when the cornel spear   160
Hist on the bristles of his vaulted back,
The curv'd tusk gnasht, and the black blood boil'd o'er.
Whither they bent their way she now inquired.
The elder answered her.
              "We bend our way
Where dwelt Assaracos, and Paris dwells."
Then she.
           "The road is safer if I guide,
And you will easier see whom you require,
Soon coming homeward from the citadel:
For clamour there was heard at early dawn
Along the coast, and then a boat appear'd,   170
And an old man stept out. Ulysses met
This stranger. Now, throughout the orchards, crofts,
And little gardens next the sandy beach,
The sailors gathered vervain, gathered bay,
And with fresh garlands every prow was trim'd.
Our leaders think this surely must denote
Good Fortune, favorable oracles;
And grant, ye Gods! the anchors heave at last."
    The old Idæan shook his head, and spake.
"He who arrives is one they left behind,   180
Is Philoctetes; and the arms he bears
Were once the arms of Hercules: the bow
Of Nessos, and the arrows dipt in blood
Of Hydra, come to light the pyre of Troy."
    Struck by his speech, the more she wisht to ask
The quicker stept she, and the more she urged
The maidens to step on: she flew, but lookt
On Corythos in flying.
             Just below
The citadel a gorgeous palace stood;
She enter'd, followed by the trembling maids;   190
The Idæans followed slower.
              As they pass
The house of Hector, they observe young girls,
Too young for foresight, thence less wretched yet,
And matrons calm, and widows unconsoled,

Bring honey to his Manes: and with these
They mourn, and shudder at the silent hall;
Chilly and lying waste with Hector's death.
　At last to Parisis abode they come.
Bidden to enter here, the spacious courts,
The lofty columns, the resplendent gods　　　　　　　200
Of brass and marble, the smooth steps and wide,
And the vast portals and resounding valves,
Strike them with admiration and with awe.
How many ivory statues breathe around!
How many golden! nor do fewer move
In the warm colours emulous of life.
To the Dictæan king had Dædalos
Given a part of these; his daughter gave
The same to Theseus; Theseus gave the same
To Helen, when he hoped to bear her off　　　　　　　210
To pleasant Athens from her mother's side.
And she afforded no few scenes for art,
No few her mother. Here first recognized
The Idæans Helen. She in every game
Stood forth the fairest with her locks of gold,
While all the potent of the sea and sky
Gazed with proud smile benevolent; but Jove
Above them all: complacently he watcht
His progeny by water and by land
Whatever she was doing. Venus came　　　　　　　220
Close after her, while upon high the swans
Archt their proud necks. Another time (so great
The skill which Venus only could inspire)
You would have thought them circling round and round.
　There is a record in the courts of heaven,
Sometimes brought out and whispered on, that once
Among the reeds and cane-beds Jove assumed
The figure of a swan, and thus beguiled
Her mother Leda; while the river swans,
To kindred strangers evermore averse,　　　　　　　230
Sate silent, and lookt all another way,
So fear'd they that surpassing one, and drave
The swimmer boys afar with threatening beaks
And swinging circuit of expanded vans.
Therefor 'twas his decree that none beside
Should draw her chariot on high days, when moved
By gift of hero or by prayer of God.
　108

CORYTHOS

Tyndaris now told Paris all she knew
From the old shepherd, save what mother bore
The youth, and whose his beauteous face was like.　　240
Such once was Alexander, then the guest
Of Sparta: but not yet ten years of war
Had he encountered, not yet fled the sword
Of Diomed, inglorious and disgraced.
He now sate smiling at the tremulous tones
Of Helen; and then smooth'd her troubled brow,
Touching and kissing it: at last more grave
These words he uttered, and assumed his seat.
"That Philoctetes in a far-off ile
Rests at this moment on a fallen beech　　250
His heavy wound: a bird's wing drives away
The bite of beast and insect. When he feels
Eagle's or vulture's shadow over him,
He tries in vain to lift his weary lids
And cry so weak it drops into his breast.
He who thus suffers from a faithless friend,
Left on the shore to hunger and to thirst,
And hear the oars sound less and less distinct
At every stroke, and songs as they depart
Float on the summer air, so joyously　　260
To them, to him so sadly, first and last,
Deploring that immedicable wound . .
Arrow hath he dipt in Lernæan blood?
But grant he land upon that very coast,
What ills, what dangers, menace us? he sees
That chariot broken which drag'd Hector, sees
The tomb of Ajax, and may know again
The arms that Thetis vainly brought her son.
And this, Neptunian Troy! the man is this
Who comes against thee now and works thy fall;　　270
'Tis time to turn our backs, to leave our homes,
Unshaken wall, unviolated fane,
Rais'd by Minerva, citadel which she
And Venus with her equally protects,
And over which (to Agamemnon's house
For ever hostile) in the light of day
Apollo hath been seen and hath been heard
Exhorting us, and scaring back the foe.
Ulysses, that great queller of our hosts,

250 Rests . . . beech [*In the Latin version*: fagineo solus trunco sedet.]

Brings Philoctetes now! now let us fly   280
Even to Mycenai: let us carry now
Within our quailing bosoms all those Gods
(Among the rest Palladium) who have stood
Stabile and strong against all former wars,
And to Diana let us sacrifice
Upon the summit of Taïgetos.
The rampire of the Achaians, true enough,
Is mingled with the yellow sea-shore sand,
Scattered the Myrmidons, the Dorian camp
Wide open: that is little: but behold   290
How fulminates against our feebleness
The stout successor of Achilles slain!
When their own walls were standing round the Greeks,
When Juno exercised her vengeful sway
And arm'd the fist of Diomed, when safe
Behind his seven-fold shield their Ajax stood,
And the proud man of Nereid mother sprung
Loosen'd with blood the Ætionæan towers,
Such idle terrors with indignant soul
I would spurn from me. Are no gifts of heaven   300
Vouchsafed to me? no Venus marks me out?
And no Apollo breathes into my breast?"
  His boasts encouraged her, his scornful smile
Arous'd her and refresht.
               Some days had past,
And Corythos grew willing to believe
His step-dame was kind-hearted. Not alone
Her countenance, so bland and beautiful,
Rais'd her beyond all mortals: he admired
One who could place herself amid the low,
Could smile with them and weep with them, and view   310
On the same level all, herself above
All things the world's eternal walls contain.
Nor wonderful nor great could aught appear
To one so far supreme, nor would she turn
Her face from Irus at the feasts of Jove.
Corythos now she knew: he did not wish
Concealment of his origin, nor might
Such wish avail him when she saw him more.
The causes of his coming she inquired,
And gave him courage as she gave her hand.   320
At first he was ashamed he could not hate

His step-dame; now, that he had ever tried.
He hangs upon her words; what words! how sweet
In utterance! from what high serenity
Of brow descending on his softened heart!
  "Ever too bold the brave and beautiful!"
Sighed she, "but even the stoutest well may start
At the close graves along the uneven sands,
The scattered bones whitening beneath their pyres
Where sharp winds flake them, and doom'd cypresses   330
That darken Ida's brow, to burn on more.
Surely 'tis sad enough were only joys
And pleasures torne away, without the tomb
With its cold shadows filling up their place."
  Kind words she spake, and kinder deeds prepared,
But doubted when, how, where, she might surprise
Her Paris with his semblance in his child.
Rarely hath any beauteous mother borne
Progeny like herself: the gods who once
Have listened to the prayer, look seldom down   340
A second time upon their supplicant.
She thought of this; she thought of one so young
As not to know her mother's flight; and thick
Came forth her groans; unconsciously the name
Of her first husband followed them.
                              "Ah why
Hath never messager rejoiced my ear
Telling me what thou art, Hermione!
And how thy little playmate hath grown up,
Orestes."
              Seeking how she might retain
The unsteddy love of Paris, oft she wisht   350
A son were hers like Corythos, resolved
To make him hers by gentle offices
And (if there be atonement) to atone
For what his mother suffered by her fault.
  "O Ageläos!" she exclaimed, "thy cares
Have rear'd both sire and son: the fatal torch
Extinguisht thou hast seen, and now wouldst see
Him who was fancied to have brought it home,
Yet who, in Ilion saved, himself is safe.
But haste not, let his son repeat to him   360
His mother's words and have the first embrace."
  "No counsel else" replied the aged man

"Did Cebren's daughter give me: but altho
I may retrace the features so beloved
In childhood, ill may Paris recognise
Old Ageläos, in his wrinkled cheeks,
Grey temples, and that slow and spiritless
Movement where years are crowded upon years.
Perhaps he may not wish to see again
The once familiar who hath followed up   370
A better course than he: the royal heir
May need me not, yet Corythos stil needs
My help . . to fail him but in death alone."
  Various the thoughts of Helen: she resolved
At last that Corythos should meet his sire
When Bacchus has thrown open the warm breast,
And when the harp is ringing, and the room
Round the high lamp is bright and jubilant.
Often she schem'd this interview: at length
The day is come.
              The Trojans sing again   380
Gay songs, long intermitted, half-afraid
Lest skilful Paris gently reprehend
Words ill-remember'd, notes irregular;
The times had deaden'd so the unworthy strings.
Now censers burning all around reflect
The images that hold them, images
Of youths whose left-hand holds long garments back;
Scarlet and purple tapestry glows above
As if the sun had lighted it, and higher
Redden more dim the cedar's vaulted beams,   390
Thro' whose compartments had mimetic art
Displaid the deep clear azure, with its stars,
Where dwell in still serenity the Blest.
Along the hearth shoots forth a lambent flame;
The house-hold Gods smile with it, Paris smiles,
And she, the heaven-descended, whom he loves.
The hearts of both with placid course and full
Joy overflows and every hour expands:
Hour more propitious than the present none
Could meet her wishes. Slight inquietude   400
There is in his delay. Sometimes she breaks
The thread of her discourse to list awhile,
Then takes it up uneven, then replies
Wide of the question she hath seem'd to hear.

CORYTHOS

Silence! here enters Corythos! He starts
At the broad splendour; at the regal form
Of Paris now before him: to approach
His mighty sire he burns, but then draws back
His foot, and looks at Helen. This the prince
Observing . . this . . the bashfulness of youth . .   410
The step so suddenly withdrawn . . the breast
Heaving . . the brow disturb'd . . the voice extinct . .
No colour in the cheek . . no name announced . .
No office . . but from graceful shoulders flowing
The very vest which Helen once had spun
For young Atrides, waiting his return,
In earlier days, when him alone she loved . .
These things together strike him with the force
Of thunderbolt: up springs he: on that vest
He siezes; casts it from him; with his sword   420
Smites the boy's neck, his face, his side; spurns off
His hands to heaven appealing, and hears nought
But, struggling hard with blood, his dying groan.
    Such the last day of Corythos! the last
Of peace to Paris and that gentlest dame
Of stepdames. When she saw the youth sink down
And all the furies urging Paris on,
Her senses left her: on the ivory couch
Cold lay her limbs as though she lay in death.
Her husband's wrath heard not the groan profound   430
When his child roll'd before him and his eyes
Lookt up to him once more, swam, sank, and closed.
    He bursts away and calls upon the Gods
Who punish perjuries; as if no God
Had noticed his; as if 'twere very hard
Deceiver should be in his turn deceived.
    When Ageläos heard the sad report,
Vengeance he called on Helen, vengeance call'd
On Paris: ashes o'er his head he heapt,
And, praying death may intercept him, bent   440
His homeward way. What should he there relate?
Whose thanks bring back? a parent's? overjoyed
To find a son beyond all hope, a son
Long absent, latest, dearest, gift of her
He had deserted! who, of him deprived,
Would miss his voice and face, all day, all night,
Sole solace of those long and weary hours,

But who, to turn aside the death she fear'd
For that most cruel father, bade the boy
Go seek him . . seek him in the stranger's house,   450
The base adulteress who had wrought her woe.
Grief, anger, virtue, shake his breast at once;
Fain would he fly from Ida.
                    When the sire
Knew the sad truth, upon his son's cold cheek
A thousand kisses did his lips impress;
He expiated (if grief could expiate)
His crime with bitter grief, and built up high
A pile of cypress to receive the corse;
And thus the lately found, by name (before
Unknown) in broken accents he bewail'd.   460
  "Wept on no humble or unhonored bier,
Rest, O my Corythos, that placid rest
Which life denied thee!"
                 Scarce hath he invoked
The shade by name before he separates
The ashes of the boughs and of the boy,
And these he places in a golden urn
Nigh his own chamber. Dark is all the house,
And silent all within it. He hath lost,
Utterly lost, his grace in Helen's eyes,
And thro' his tears and anguish none sees he   470
In Leda's daughter: both retort complaints,
And each-one's sorrow is the other's fault.
Again, he rushes forth on the remains
Of the Achaians; his high crest again
Is seen above the combat, and that shield
He shakes which Thetis by her prayers obtain'd
Of the fire-potent God, wherewith she arm'd
To conquer Asia her disdainful son,
And from that conqueror Paris tore away.
Weary of glory, worne with grief, he sought   480
The place where recently he fill'd the urn
With bones, of grace and beauty now disrobed
And brittle to embraces, losing form
And substance (what small remnant they retain'd)
When the first tear fell and sank into them.
In the still sacredness of night, alone
Went he, the stars were shining on the tomb,
And timidly and slowly he explored

With outspred hand if aught might yet remain
Of his lost child, and credulously seiz'd   490
Little black sticks, and bore them in his breast.
Greeks, as they roam'd along the shore, observ'd
His wanderings: these Ulysses had espied,
Epëus too, and, heavy with his wound
And catching the cool air with frequent gasp,
Pæantius. Round a high-piled tomb a trench
Was hollowed: hitherward they steal along
From the Sigæan sands, while yet the stars
Cast a scant light, and thro' the uneven ground
And the dim copses winde their secret way.   500
And here await they Paris, true at last,
And smiting in the anguish of his soul
A breast too long from pious love estranged.
   What bowstring, from what archer's bow unstrung,
Rattles on belt or quiver? Who cries out?
None other voice responding. Hark! he groans;
He calls for enemy; no aid he claims
Of friend; but leaning on one elbow sits
Raging; and often strikes his heel the ground.
   Swift steps run back along the soft sea-shore: 510
For they who smote him in the shade of night,
By the command and with the auspices
Of Gods, had stolen on a man unarm'd
Without their helmets, cuirases, or shields.
He could not follow, for behind his knee
The arrow had gone thro': with desperate twist
He tore it out, and from two apertures
The hissing blood sprang forth: he sinks; he rolls
His limbs, he rolls his heavy eyes, all night,
In the red dew: he sees the city lamps   520
Kindled; he sees them all go out again
From the same spot. But when an iron light
Begins to peer o'er the cold plain, and wakes
From their brief sleep the tamer animals,
They of the household rise, and all around
In grove, in champain, seek their absent lord,
And, as if there the search should be the last,
At his son's tomb. The race that cheers the ear
Of Morning with its voice, and penetrates
With its bold breast the woodland stiff with frost,   530
And, watchful at the gate in life's extreme,

Is faithful to the wretched and the poor,
With eyes as languid on his languid eyes
Looks sorrowing down, and licks them unreproved.
　　When the last hour gleams feebly upon man
Not feebly rise the former: swift and thick
Do they crowd back with all the images
Of his misdeeds in clearest light reveal'd.
Now manifest is every oracle,
Now Lacedæmon's awful Nemesis,　　　　　　　　　540
Now the red torch, now the right-hand that shakes
Its widening vapour over myriad graves,
To settle on the towers of Ilion.
But these all vanish. Thee alone he sees,
Daughter of Cebren! thee, beneath that rock
Where strowed the winds thy nuptial couch with leaves,
Espous'd, deserted, childless! What avail,
Ah what! the promises, the gifts, of Gods?
A better, now he feels, was left in thee.
"Go, ye who once could serve me, go" said he　　　550
"And tell Œnone ye have seen me pierced:
Tell her it is not help I now beseech,
But pardon."
　　　　　　　　When the youths descried her home
Amid the innermost and highest wood,
And found it closed, and heard the wail within,
And saw tame stags raise up their antler'd heads
Suddenly from the threshold, they prepared
To enter.
　　　　　　　They repeat the last command
Of him who sent them. Young, and confident
In ready eloquence, they would adorn　　　　　　560
The wings of Mercury with brighter plumes,
And utter as their lord's what time and place
Forbade his uttering, and (more strongly) grief.
His former love do they commemorate,
And how Œnone was endowed with herbs
Potent to save. She lookt aside, and said
"I could not save my son! nor did he ask
Who asks me now." And, as she turn'd away,
They heard the halls with sob and plaint resound.
　　Meanwhile four stout attendants bear the prince　570
Upon a plank of pliant ash, where rose
The sacred mansion of the Idæan Nymph.

CORYTHOS

And as they bear him thither, toiling up
The narrow path, often the loose round stones
Slip under them and shake him, often spring
The branches back and strike against his wound.
Not long was the delay, but long it seem'd
To him whose day was closing, and before
He could collect the features in his mind
Of her he sought so eagerly. They pass 580
Along the crevices of rocks where hang
The ivy-stems their rigid moss . . of rocks
Which the spear's point, in time gone-by, engraved
With tender verses round about linkt names;
Labour of idle hunter, disinclined
To let that idleness pass soon away.
And into opener places they procede,
For feats remember'd of prevailing strength,
And songs and dances and successful loves.
There Paris paus'd and wept, with both his hands 590
Closed o'er the face: the four who carried him
Placed on the evenest ground the future bier,
And they too, turning back their faces, wept.
The Nymph of Ida came not forth to them,
But on the threshold of the open door
She staid her footstep, that the tears might flow
Within the house unseen one moment more.
   And now the son of Priam views again
His early realm, a realm so peaceable,
And sweet Œnone, then his only care; 600
And now again, again, he hears the sighs
Which heave that faithful bosom: how diverse
From those he sigh'd to in the grot below!
And slowly lifting to that face divine
His eyes, "How many and what years" he cried,
"Since Paris saw Œnone his beloved!"
   Nothing of anger or complaint said she;
For she had prayed of the Eumenides,
Few hours before, that the untimely end
Of Corythos their wrath should vindicate, 610
And that she might not, even if she will'd,
Be help to Paris in his hour of need.
Another prayer she added to these prayers,
With quivering lips, more anxiously, but fear'd
No God would grant it.

              "Jupiter!" she cried,
"And if there be another* who should hear
My last appeal . . grant me the gift of death."
   Thunder was heard upon the left, and signs
Shone forth above her from the sky serene.
But when she saw that son and sire had fared   620
Alike, and that she might have saved the one,
She who alone could save him, she appeared
Cruel and merciless . . to him . . to both.
"No; I deserve not, seek not, to prolong
My life," said Paris. "Only let one urn
Unite us . . me, my Corythos!" He spake
And held the urn toward her: this she caught,
Together with the faint and chilly hand
It had nigh dropt from.
                 Paris had but strength
To add these words,
                "Œnone! it was ours   630
To live united: they . . the Gods alone . .
Sundered us."
           "But they sunder us no more"
Said she. "Behold! the bridal hour is come,
Wherein no wretchedness, no falsehood is,
No separation. Ah! restrain, restrain
Those groans! Let me, my husband, die the first!
Hear me . . the Gods have heard me . . unwithheld,
Give one embrace.
            "Paris is now my own,
Mine, by sure auspices, eternally.
And do not thou in Pluto's house, my child,   640
Disdain the mother whom thy death brings down.
   "Often the cruel gift that Venus gave
Gave me one comfort with it . . that my grief
Could not encrease; and now I lose this one.
From Juno less had been the penalty,
Wroth as she was, than Venus now exacts
In the same Ida . . Venus, crown'd by thee!"
   Her fainting form the sister Nymphs receive,
And from its fountain bring the tepid stream;

* She suppresses the name of Apollo her violator. [L.]

---

637 unwithheld] unwithhel'd *1847 misp. here corrected.*

In vain; then hasten to the mountain-top; 650
And there her father Cebren takes the urn,
To hold fresh ashes gathered by his hand.

THE LAST OF ULYSSES

[Published in "Hellenics" 1847; not reprinted either by Landor or by Forster. A
Latin version was published in "Idyllia Heroica", 1820, and reprinted in "Poemata
etc." 1847. The "Arguments" now prefixed to the Parts are translated from the Latin
version for the present edition. See notes at end of volume.]

FIRST PART

ARGUMENT

[Being made aware that Ulysses was coming home and moved by jealousy of
Minerva, Venus would see Penelope married to some one of the suitors. She ordains
that he who first meets Penelope shall be overcome by love and be loved in his turn.
Ulysses is that man. He departs for Argiripa where Diomed is King.]

SING we the last of that man's days who tore
From Troy its safeguard, not against the will
Of Pallas; Pallas brought him safely home.
   Be with us, daughter of Mnemosyne!
Thou who, altho' thou visitest the abyss
Of Etna, where Enceladus is bound,
Tempestuous giant, mad with impotence,
And darest walk by Styx and Phlegethon,
Nor dreadest, bolt in hand, the Thunderer,
Yet from Sorrento gazest with delight   10
On waves so softly voluble. To these
I also turn: I seek that shore alone
Where stiffens on high rocks the hoary moss,
Too close and hard for idle child to strip
Or singing-bird to twine round slender nest.
When mute the trumpet of Misenus, mute
The Sybil's cave, when o'er Parthenope
Crumbles the bust and scarce her name remains,
Thou holdest up the deeds of glorious men
And followest their funerals with song.   20
Tell us then in what region sank to rest
Ulysses; say, what did he, suffered he,
When he departed homeward from these shores?
   Ogygia's secret, Circe's festive, bower,
Faithless to hospitality, we leave,
And harp that Phœbus scorns, and woof unseen

Argument. Argiripa, *rectius* Argyripa *here and elsewhere.*   16 Misenus] Hector's
trumpeter. See *Æneid*, vi. 162. [W.]

Of Pallas, tho' its shuttle be of gold:
Better by far to mark how pure and firm
Connubial bonds in life and death are blest.
　　Jove pitied him who, after toils which man　　　　30
Had never undergone, was guided now
By Pallas: he decreed in recompense
Penelope not only should retain
Her love and duty, but her youth and charms.
Many the marvels his eventful life
Had witnest; this more marvelous than all
Was unobserv'd; not through ingratitude;
But such he ever thought her; such she seem'd
In grace and beauty at all after-times
As when he left her to depart for Troy,　　　　　　40
Or when he led her, with the fife before,
Under the garlands of her father's gate.
That which the God now gave her seem'd her due,
Her property; he never fear'd that age
Or fate could alter beauty such as hers.
He who sees all things saw the hero's mind.
The crowd of suitors own'd the miracle;
And now the wretched men began to fear
Who rioted so loosely in the house.
How late their piety! how scant their shame!　　　50
How rapidly death's wide and downward road
Opens before them! opens, yet unseen.
　　Indignant that Penelope had borne
So long their importunities and threats,
And that Ulysses had in vain escaped
Calypso's wiles and Circe's bristling caves,
In vain had brought the archer back to Troy
With arrows poison'd in the hydra's blood,
The Sire to Venus "Highth of wickedness!
Those suitors, once so patient, now abstain　　　60
Not even from the choicest of the herd,
Fatten'd, at his return, for us above:
Nor these alone the wretches would consume,
But their fierce lust burns fiercer from delay.
I doubt not . . beauty often counsels ill . .
If hope, if pleasure, give a brighter glow,
Or any deity her charms increase . .
I doubt not . . I fear greatly . . that, subdued
　　　　　　57 archer] *sc.* Philoctetes.　W.]

THE LAST OF ULYSSES: PART I

By ardent prayers she lend a patient ear.
The more I dread it lest Minerva's ire 70
Again be kindled: therefor I abstain,
As thou dost wisely, daughter, from offence.
Within twelve days 'tis destin'd he returns
For whom thou, Venus, hast thro' wars and waves
Preserv'd the flame so vivid. Fate decrees
(What I could wish Fate never had decreed)
That the last comer carry off the prize,
Meeting her earliest on the twelfth day's morn.
A crowd of lovers shakes the faith of few,
He shakes it who stands back and waits his hour. 80
I hope she may not meet the better man
Than her Ulysses: if she should so meet
That better man, I would not he prevail."
    Venus had listened to this wily speech
Fearing lest strong commands might follow it,
But when her father added nothing more
She fancied she could over-reach the wise
And potent, and make Pallas feel her might.
    No hesitation: thro' the air she flies, 90
She stands before Penelope asleep,
And thus, without awakening her.
                              "The first
In the twelfth morn who meets thee, shall be held
By thee in love unbroken, and subdue
Whatever enemy advances near."
    Close to the bed she goes, and there she stops,
Admiring her own gifts: then to herself,
"If Paris had beheld thee . . but just then
Thy husband took thee from the Spartan land . .
I was wrong then . . I am much wiser now . .
But, had he seen thee, he, his house, his realm, 100
Had stil been safe; no guest betraid, no wrath,
By armure ript from heroes drag'd thro' dust,
By temples sunk in ashes, by the wounds
Of Gods, and even their bloodshed, unappeas'd."
Gazing once more ere vanishing, she said
"How beautiful! how modest!"
                              When that morn
Advances, she repents the doom it brings,
And fears him angry whom she little fear'd
So gracious: now she wishes she may fail

In what she most desired: she blames her power 110
Of eloquence, to which Minerva's self
Must yield a victory greater than the last.
What should she do? alas! what had she done?
Unduteous wishes she would now unwish.
Upon no land is rest for her; no land
Can hide, not all Idalia shade her guilt,
Nor clouds of incense from a hundred shrines.
To heaven, where only there is peace, she flies,
Pity of Jove and pardon to implore.
With placid brow he heard his daughter plead. 120
Turning her eyes decorous from his face,
Distantly first she stood, then cast herself
Before his knees: he rais'd her and spake thus:
"Did not thy hand, my daughter, which of late
Covered with cloud Anchises' son, and led
To Africa, lead him whom thou hast blest,
Ulysses? for already hath he past
His city-gate, unknown, and hath approacht
The queen, a welcome unexpected guest.
See what your efforts, in a single day, 130
Applied with such discretion, can achieve!
Yea, I have granted . . if indeed thy power
Hath any need of mine . . that lasting love
Unite the brave and constant: but within
Thy rule this lies, when Juno hath approved.
Seldom with Juno art thou so agreed,
And seldom hast thou sanction'd so her bonds.
Behold what feats conjointly ye perform!
I too, by somewhat, slightly may assist.
Ulysses in the vigour of his youth 140
(Rejoice with me) shall flourish, and shall crush
All enemies he finds beneath his roof:
Moreover (and in this with me rejoice)
Beneath a calmer sky his day shall close.'
Astonisht at these words the Goddess wept
Thro' very shame, and hated Pallas more.
    Ah! we must now away from gentle Gods,
The Muse forbidding us to look behind
Or tarry longer. I would not decline
To sing of shipwrecks, wanderings, battles fought 150
By one against so many, thro' the love
He bore his wife, fought under her defence

THE LAST OF ULYSSES: PART I

Who shatters with her ægis arms unchaste:
For neither song hath fail'd me nor the blast
Of trumpet. Harder is the task, and skill
Greater, to take from age its weariness,
To give slow years fresh movement, and bear up
Sorrows when friends and household Gods are far.
He must himself relate the larger part
Of what befell him: audience will he find   160
In Arpi; there he hopes to close his life
With Diomed, short as that life may be.
    Thither he came, unknown; and there he saw
In a close valley near his narrow walls,
Enjoying young men's games, the generous king.
Pleas'd he lookt on awhile, then took his seat
Among the elders, in the grass by holm
Oershadow'd; and there sate he til the stars
Threw tremulous light among the dusky leaves
And over was the contest: then the prince   170
Distributed the prizes: when the last
Had been awarded, the Dulichian chief
Bespake him thus, from full and throbbing heart.
    "Glorious in war we knew thee; now in peace
Well hast thou garner'd up what best befits
The armury of Mars against foul days,
And Themis best in her old house protects.
Few things are pleasant to my wearied eyes,
But this is pleasant.
             "I have given help
Erewhile, and now I ask it: thou alone,   180
O son of Tydeus! hast deserv'd that Heaven
To all thy wants and wishes should incline."
    He groan'd: more closely Diomed embraced
That brave and faithful breast: he yearn'd to hear
What had befallen him the Greek most Greek.
    From a huge bowl he casts its crown away
And pours out wine to Jupiter, then drinks
And gives it to the guest, and kindly jeers
His temperate draught, and bids the boys around
Fill it again while it is yet half-full.   190
The handmaids gather nigh: one brings the vase
Smoking with water pure; another (white

161 Arpi] Argiripa or Argyripa, founded by Diomed. See *Æneid*, xi. 246. [W.]
172 Dulichian chief] *sc.* Ulysses. [W.]

From dewy meadow what herself had spun)
The soft long napkin; many more are charged
With baskets, such as Ceres smiles to see,
Full of her gifts .. all anxious to behold
That equal chieftain whom their master loved.
From ash and pine high leaps the flame, to glad
A guest beneath chill mountain shade received.
Warm grew the heroes mid redundant bowls,   200
And life-like boar, and black and ridgy hoof
Announcing good old stag, and joke, the growth
Of generous cheer: but moments there were yet
When he of Ithaca could ill suppress
A sigh, a groan .. thus with blithe voice reproved.
   "Do not too much lament that thou hast left
The chaste Penelope: it griev'd thee less
For Circe and Calypso, whom the gods
Endowed with deathless beauty like their own.
If cares which touch all mortals move thee so,   210
And children, and that ill-persuading heed
Of what is future or may never be,
If thou hast lost Telemachus in fight
Or wreckt at sea in seeking thee, my hills
Will soon repair that loss, will soon rebuild
Thy house again: here virgin manners dwell
In virgin bodies active fresh and firm.
Tender are women in a tender age,
The heart grows harder as the years advance.
One thing is constant with them: never laid   220
Is the dread specter of departed youth;
By day, by night, it rises in its pride;
And often wilt thou wonder, often grieve,
To see the necklace of a smooth round neck
From throat ferruginous hang thinly down.
Even the scorpion in its early day
Shows milky whiteness; its pellucid breast
Quivers with gentle fiber; take it up,
And its worst anger is quite innocent;
But thou wouldst shake it off thee when its arms   230
Livid with venom varicate amain."
   Ulysses smiled in silence; to his mind
Ægiale* with Cyllabaros return'd.

---

* Ægiale, the adulterous wife of Diomed. [L.] Cyllabaros, "*Evadnes nepotis*" in the
Latin version, was one of her gallants. [W.]

But Diomed continued, "What forbids
That we should now be comrades, we whom Mars
So soon united when we first bore arms?
If this my house and this my realm were closed,
Or not in common, to the man with whom
Dangers were ever common, day and night,
When most successful prest the Phrygian foe,   240
And the Gods lowered most angrily, because
Of Venus wounded and their pride abased,
I should be such a hoste as Polypheme
Or Polymnestor, nor deserve thy stay.
The aged Daunus bade the Hesperian hinds
Obey my scepter: I engaged to guard
Their cots and pastures with Œtolian arms:
On these conditions I became their king.
Hence the Salentine hills another race
Now holds, and all those regions where once reign'd   250
Iapyx, sprung of Dædalus.
                   "In vain
From the Rutulian king came Venulus,
Swelling with recent war, and bearing high
His crest above its changes, to attract
My arms across the mountains, on a foe
Of other days, whose mother from my spear
Protected him. I envy not the dower
Latinus gives him. That he merited
Wide lands and royal bride even those confess
Who seldom do confess another's worth.   260
Yet fear I not the Dardan: far away
From countries over which his scepter sways,
We rear our castles upon rocks abrupt,
That, none offending us, offending none,
We may enjoy our own . . and unendower'd.
Remote from us be war and cause for war;
And may that pious man his hands abstain,
Nor fancy fate hath given him whate'er
The plenteous fields of Italy produce,
But, above all, stop short in his career   270
Before it reach Messapiusis domain,

247 Œtolian] *rectius* Ætolian *here and elsewhere.* [W.]   252 Venulus] envoy
sent by Turnus, see Ovid, *Met.* xiv. 457. [W.]   255 foe] *sc.* Æneas protected by
Venus. [W.]   271 Messapiusis]=Messapius's; Landor's reasons for spelling the
word as in the text were given elsewhere, see p. 93, *cf.* Messapiaque arva. Ovid, *Met.*
xiv. 513. [W.]

Bounding the lands of Daunus, our allie;
Else he may see the gift of Vulcan hang
Against our temple-walls, and, vanquisht thrice,
May only have the comfort to believe
That, were even Hector living, he had fail'd.
Much has he; let him have it. Trojan spoil
Procures for me the comforts of old-age:
Let those who list remember what I was,
The proud invader what I am shall see.   280
All I desire is to secure my throne
And give my people few and equal laws.
Nor does that people with ungrateful mind
Repay my cares; nor sterile is our glebe,
Nor under influence of malignant star.
If from Œtolia far indeed remote,
If far away Evenus paces slow
Among rich pastures where the quoit sinks deep,
At least Atrides sways no scepter here."
    Then spake Ulysses.
                        "Whence, illustrious son   290
Of Tydeus! whence this hatred? Of all Greeks
Never was one more duteous to his chief;
A great man's no small praise; may this be thine,
And leave to weaker an indocile rage."
    Then smiled the founder of the Arpine walls.
"All things are bearable to him who rose
In valour equal to the first in rank.
Son of Laertes! in those times I held
My peace, thou knowest; valour was enough
For me; worse men commanded. Do those men   300
Restore our kingdoms? Are we not exiled
From our own fields, from our own household Gods?
Did I petition? askest thou? Compel'd
So far not even the exile is, whose shade
Must wander under these Italian skies.
To ask, is buying at too high a price.
Let the spear bring me what is mine, or rest
For ever! Can men's prayers avail when men
Themselves are nothing! Should I try to move
The lofty whom my name could never reach?   310
But, O thou sprung from Mercury! when praise

273 gift of Vulcan] Diomed's cuirass; *see Iliad*, viii. 195. [W.]   287 Evenus]
see Ovid, *Met.* ix. 104 and *Gebir*, vi. 162. [W.]

Descends from thee or any thy compeer,
The lost I seek not, nor do things to come
The present quiet of my soul disturb.
  "From Neritos a pinnace had arrived
And told us thou hadst to thy home return'd,
And found there those who had bemoan'd thee lost,
Sometimes in forein lands, sometimes (as dreams
Or vague reports were prevalent) by death;
Told us not only that thy aged sire   320
Thy boy and thy sweet partner thou hadst found,
But overcome her suitors, slaying all.
Was it not pleasant to thee, looking on,
To see the mistress and her maidens trip
Away to hide the sable vests they wore,
While there was time; and the next morn to hear
How warm and pressing the domestic siege,
To hear the words and voices mockt so well?
It did amuse; and now it should console.
But tell me what good fortune (such is mine)   330
Restores thee to me? Has the wrath of Heaven,
Or prepotence of Circe, been the cause
Of this last absence from thy native land?"
  With downcast eyes Ulysses thus replied.
"She, if she could, would not have done me ill.
She sprinkled my companions with her bane
And changed their figures: me, than bane or spell
More potent, love preserv'd. I am ashamed
To own it . . one whole year . . by love, by hope,
By all vain images her charms could raise . .   340
The fair Persëis my frail heart enthral'd.
Lost all the rest, one only ship, one wreck,
Escaping from the Læstrigons, had reacht
The fatal shore.
           "I yield to sleep my eyes
Weary with watching, rigid with the salt
That hung upon them. In a dream I see
Penelope: I know that golden hair
Braided and bound as usual close behind,
And that green tunic which the Dryads wear
Following Diana thro' the sunny dew.   350
I stretch my arms to clasp her; she escapes
The embrace; not vanishing to empty air;
Her form, her voice, her gentle speech, remain.

' Cease, O Ulysses! cease at length to mourn
My absence, my departure: none among
The Achaian chiefs to happy homes return;
Another torch hath lit beloved wives,
Children so cherisht roam in other lands;
But me, besought until my latest hour
By many suitors, no new love hath toucht   360
(Gods! bear me witness!) nor untimely fate
By Dian's dart oertaken me; but grief
Perpetual for thy loss, thy toils, thy woes,
Thy wanderings over every land and sea,
And rising over all, thy manly breast,
Thy beauteous image . . these, Ulysses! these
Wasted my youth, now mingled with the shades.
Farewell, farewell! enjoy this tranquil land
Blest with eternal spring; remember me;
But not too fondly, lest enjoyment cease.'   370
    "Again I rush to her embrace; I wake.
My eyes see nothing round me, now disturb'd
By weeping, nothing but dark cypresses
And lofty cedars over me, and spred
Along the shore the thin-leav'd olive-tree,
And, wet with tears, the turf whereon I slept.
But somewhat like the presence of that dear
Devoted head remain'd: the chamber-sound
Of her sweet accents warbled in my ear,
Her flower-like hair exhaled its odour stil.   380
'Restore me, O Persephone!' I cried,
'That fond, that faithful one! Why intercept
The coming years of the most beautiful,
O house of Pluto! gladden'd by no grace?'
    "To these complainings evermore renew'd
I added all that grief could add, and all
That madness and impiety could urge.
    "Under this form the daughter of the Sun
Deluded me, rejoicing in the groans
Of spell-bound sleep, and wishing me to share   390
Her bed for life. Time and assiduous love
Softened my sorrow: but my hands and eyes

354 ff. See *Imaginary Conversations*, 1826, i. 373 n., where Landor said that the corresponding passage in the Latin version was imitated from *Odyssey*, xi. 197 ff.; "the only verses I can remember to have imitated from any one". [W.]   388 daughter of the Sun] Circe, *cf.* Ovid, *Met.* xiv. 33.

THE LAST OF ULYSSES: PART I

Often I rais'd to Pallas, and implored
She would not utterly abandon me,
Unworthy, yet desirous to return
Beneath her holy guidance. When the Nymph
Found me devoted to appease that Power
Which in the perils of uncertain war
And on the Ionian and Sicilian sea
Was alway present, she assumed her form   400
And with her voice detain'd me, loth to part.
No longer could Tritonia then endure.
While I was praying that, since Heaven had will'd
Penelope should leave me for the Shades
And nought on earth so cherisht should be mine,
I might in duty prop my father's age,
Suddenly at this prayer from open skies
In gorgon terrors came the Virgin down
And stood before the guilty.
       "'Thou hast dared,
And with impunity' the Goddess cried,   410
'To simulate another: but to lift
Minerva's helmet on a shameless brow,
Minerva's ægis o'er a breast impure,
Themis and he who rules the Gods forbid.
Now then, since thou hast broken every bond
Whereby thou passest human life in years,
Tho' I could justly mulct thee of them all,
Not one I take away from thee; I leave
The number, stripping them of graceful youth
And giving helpless solitary age.'   420
She spake, and rose, and vanisht in the clouds.
The Nymph grew hideous; her indignant voice
Lost its own likeness; and, that nought remain
Of tender to compassionate, her tears
Were taken from her; she could wail, not weep.
Cold, to the inmost chamber, is the air
Of the whole house; still are the grots; the birds
Are silent in the grove; the shrivel'd vine
Drops from the tree, the ivy from the wall.
Stupefied at the sight, with faltering voice   430
I call upon the Goddess, now averse.
Regardless, or forgetting me, not once
Had that stern eye been bent on me, not once
While she was nearer dared I lift up mine.

"I leave the sadden'd shore, lone, helpless, wild
From crowding thoughts. Accurst with guiltiness
I knew not whither I should bend my way,
But was resolved on going. Swift my step
By the blood's tide, and thirsty was my tongue;
I sought the fountain; its perennial source   440
Shrank up before me, and where water flow'd
Nothing was left but one dry black lagoon.
What evils, thought I, had I not deserv'd!
What punishment, that Rhadamanthus dooms
Or Æacus, my ancestors to bear,
Was not alike my due? Such thoughts revolved
In my sad breast; but milder now succede,
And tears, profusely running down, assuage
The storm of grief, and nourish hopes again;
They buoy up distant Ithaca, they bring   450
Before my eyes their fairest first delights,
They bring Eurotas back to me, that stream
Which ran so lucidly along the field
Of good Icarius; I behold afresh
The plighted hand, the overtaken bride,
The cheek upon my shoulder, and the veil
Which stil to Modesty the Spartan maids
At the turf altar dedicate in song.
Above all other thoughts that bride arose,
Chaste, beauteous; and Telemachus her son."   460
    Diomed heard in silence all he said . .
In silence . . not unmoved. As the clear steam
Of wood, however season'd, hurts the eyes,
He backt his seat and turn'd them just aside
And drew his hand across them once or twice,
Then, after short delay, nor late at night,
Wisht placid slumber to his weary guest.

438–9 Swift . . . tide [The Latin version has: *celer ipso sanguinis œstu*. W.]
457 Modesty] *see* "Altar of Modesty", vol. ii, p. 335.

THE LAST OF ULYSSES

SECOND PART

ARGUMENT

[Diomed first relates to Ulysses his own adventures. Then he asks what had befallen
Ulysses after he left Troy for his home. Ulysses begins with the dream which by
Circe's sorcery, a short while before, he had dreamt: notwithstanding he resolved to
go back to Ithaca. His converse with Penelope and Telemachus. Why he left his son
at home, never himself to return. It grieves him to have deceived Penelope, whom he
had persuaded that he was going only to Dodona in order to appease Jupiter after
the visitors had been slain inside the house.]

AT morn the Arpine youth with zeal prepare
Nets, dogs, and whatsoever else the brave
Delight to pass their time in: but at eve
Again did Diomed entreat to hear
(Be there no woman in them) more events.
   "Let Atlas' daughter in sea-sounding woods
Weep on; and farewell Circe. Thy device
With Polypheme hath shaken every side;
But tell us how, a shepherd as he was,
Nor spent, like others of that race, his life   10
In caves, nor struck from anvil all day long
The sparkling splinters of resounding iron,
How could his cruelty all theirs surpass?"
   Ulysses answered.
               "Often I revolv'd
That prodigy; nor would Sicilia's sons
Explane it while he lived: when fear had ceast
They told this story.
             "While his brothers, some
Piped, and some danced, all revel'd, all drank deep,
Polypheme wandered in wild solitudes,
In easy meadow-land or green spring-corn   20
Or Ætna's flowery dells, where fancy chose.
Aglauros led his sportive kids, his goats,
Intractable, his kine, his mother ewes
And lambs aside them, and their wether chief,
Among the groves and fields: as seasons changed
These heard their placid shepherd, whom they lov'd
For change of pasture, and could recognise
His voice, however far; and down they ran
Trooping and stirring up a world of dust.
The Cyclops laught at seeing it, and wisht   30
To bring them in like manner to his call

22 Aglauros] *See note at end of vol.*

And make them sport about him; so he gave
A loud shrill whistle: herds and flocks ran off,
And Polypheme was left with Polypheme.
  "Aglauros laught aloud. The Cyclops cried,
   'What! with thy poisons, with thy eye, thy tongue,
Withdrawest thou my lambs, and drivest thus
My herds, as with a gadfly at the nose?'
  "Fear struck the youth: swift as the wind he ran
To the sea-shore and hid him in its caves.   40
But when the Cyclops found that neither flock
Nor shepherd would return, he went to trace
The footmarks; unsuccessfully: he cast
On his sire Neptune words of scorn, and jeer'd
The trident, which had let the tide prevail
And every print from under disappear.
  "Gentler of aspect soon, throughout the shore
He cries 'Return, Aglauros! By the earth,
The seas, the stars, I swear, and every God
Above me and below! fear not; from harm   50
Safe shalt thou be as thou hast ever been.'
  "Whether he now began to trust in words
All Gods were sworn by, whether hunger prest,
On the fourth day crept out the wretched man.
Now did the giant's bowels yearn with joy
At once and trepidate with bursts of ire.
'Behold the faithless shepherd who withdrew
His master's flocks! Thee never shall my loss
Enrich. Go, seek the shore again; go, find
A deeper cavern, a more sure retreat.'   60
  "Then was the giant seen to seize the youth
In vain imploring; seen to crush his cheeks
With knotty pine; tho' all who saw it ran,
And only know, beside, that round his head
Something was whirl'd, and then a far-off wave
Opened, and closed, and whitened those around.
  "The sheep came back the first, and last the kids,
Long speculating from the highest crags
And closest coverts: to those kids and sheep
Never came back Aglauros, never more   70
Against the empty milk-pail struck his pipe
At eventide, nor oped the wicker gate
Under his hand to free the flock at morn.
Lone, inaccessible, the Cyclops drove

THE LAST OF ULYSSES: PART II

His brethren from him, drove the gentle Nymphs
Napæan, who scarce ventured to approach
In pity of his anguish: with loud shouts
He frighten'd them away, and pelted sore
With cedar cones the slim white backs they turn'd.
Thro' teeth shut close he curses the whole sex,   80
Calls them all malice, calls them all deceit,
Then takes his reed, begins, breaks off, resumes
A hoarse, a strident, an unripen'd song.
When, whether heat or idleness impels,
He plunges with loud plangor from a rock
Or ancient turret on the sea below,
And makes it quail and yield to him, up springs
A griesly specter, and rolls underneath
His heaving bosom, which surmounts the waves
By half its bulk. The shapeless form casts back   90
On the dense foam its dark dishevel'd hair;
Nor can he seize it with his grasp, nor drag
With hooked iron, nor with stones submerge,
Nor crush it with his cypress staff, nor turn
His eyes away from eyes as wildly fixt.
He speaks; he listens; waits; bends down an ear
Now to the right, now to the left; and hears
Remurmur low deep sounds. The shapeless form
Swells on the foam with dark dishevel'd hair;
Sometimes, as waving from it human aid   100
Or imprecation of inhuman foe,
Tosses its arm, circling the surge, reclined;
Sometimes, in power above life's power, erect.
Not only in the daylight, but in sleep
Rises that lurid image; near, more near,
It comes before the gasper's face, and all
The giant's prowess one weak swing throws down.
His whole vast breast flows o'er with bitterness,
From what makes bad men worse, from solitude,
Strength uncontrolable and passion spurn'd.   110
This was (where Scylla and Charybdis rave)
The direst vision of Sicilian seas.
Be sure I quit not Sicily so griev'd
As quitting Circe. This I learnt of her;
Not to be caught with honied words by Nymphs
Or toy with perils.
    "I retrieve a heart

Mindful that pious love once dwelt within,
And only tenderer for its last offence.
Goddess, or woman goddess-like in form
And blandly answering every care and thought, 120
May touch us, and may draw us from ourselves,
Yet always is there something we once had
And have not now; a void we pant to fill.
  "Minerva had admonisht me by night
That a wide water yet remain'd to cross,
And various toils beside; Ogygia's groves,
The evil pleasures of a vacant mind,
The Sirens' rocks, the Sirens too themselves,
Insults and wrongs at home, and other ills,
Again departing, I must undergo. 130
Who with Calypso knows not my sojourn?
For swiftly fly bad actions into fame;
The better follow slowly, and receive
Unwelcome entrance to half-open ears.
  "With little pleasure the Trinacrian coast
And Sirens I remember, and the song
As my prow sounded passing thro' their rocks,
When they came forward and this voice was heard:
  "'Ah! whither art thou hastening? Too severe
Have been thy sufferings, O Laertes' son, 140
By sea and land; too false have been thy joys,
If joys they were. Behold our glebe! behold
Green here is winter, summer here is green,
Nor Sirius burns nor Pleiad deluges
Nor with sharp hailstones Eurus strips our vines,
Nor waste the cattle with disease, nor crops
With mildew. See! how brightly shines our sun,
And far from cities what calm lives we lead.'
  "But when they mark the sail flap past their song,
'O! land at least that thou mayst learn thy fate' 150
Cry all at once and spread their arms to heaven.
I shudder: my companions are intent
On catching more, and loath to turn the prow.
We furl to hearken, and along the thwarts
Sit silent: then upon the breeze is borne
This one clear voice.
              "'O thou, who dost contemn
The Sirens and their pleasures! hasten home,

139 ff. The Sirens' Song, *cf. Odyssey*, xii. 184.

Revisit wife and son: thy son .. mark this ..
Shall be thy death.'
        "My knees sink under me.
Calypso had this very fate foretold   160
In verse unvarying. Tears Calypso shed,
The Siren sang it and her cheek was dry.
And now Atlantia's prophecy came home,
Neglected while deliver'd. For we know
The loving fear sad things when lovers part,
And fancy one weak word may hold them back.
She blusht not, even tho' Mercury stood by,
To waste her bloom with overflow of tears,
Albeit he brought his mighty Sire's command
To hasten my return nor brook delay.   170
Fainting, she thought of me; she sob'd, and said
My fate was harder than my faults deserv'd.
    "Compel'd then am I, wretched! to foreknow·
Inevitable fate, fate so austere
That no impiety could merit it,
While from all other mortals their last hour
Soft shades and kindly darkness have conceal'd.
What should I do? and whither fly? Again
Implore the Goddess whose neglected will
Was manifest?
        "Again did she command: 180
And now am I obedient. Go I will;
I will go home.
        "O powerfulest of Gods!
Avert but this one evil from my house,
From my Telemachus! Long after me
Grant he may live, and ever bear in mind
What was his father .. at whose breast he hung ..
And may his love and virtue equal hers!

    "I reach the rocks of Ithaca, the house
Of old Laertes. Is he yet alive?
Lives yet that good old man? Lives yet that wife   190
So cherisht? Lives that son whom neither threat
Nor omen shall detain from my embrace,
Telemachus?
        "A street I enter, fill'd
With joyous boys whose mothers were unborn

163 Atlantia's] *sc.* Calypso's. [W.]

When last I left it. While my eyes grow dim
By looking out for one of riper age,
Lo, suddenly the Goddess! She arrests
My hurried step, beheld by me alone;
I turn; she teaches what I must perform.
　"Deceived is he who thinks to find at home　　　　　200
The close of his misfortunes. I was griev'd
Now to dissemble; but too great the need.
I did dissemble when that faithful wife
Wept in my presence my sure death, and askt
About the man whom all men must have known,
And whom I had confest to her I met
When Troy was fallen, when the Achaian ships
(Scatter'd by crime in Ajax) all were wreckt,
And many perisht in the Euböic sea.
　"'Ah! 'tis no little' said she 'to have seen,　　　　　210
And only seen, one ever dear, one torne
From my sad youth, one so long hoped in vain.
Until he come, if come he may, my house
Shall cherish thee, and tend thy coming age.
Thy strength is yet unshaken, but will want
A thousand cares one weaker can supply.
For our last days roll like the wintry flood
In rapid course away: at morn, at eve,
We stand and wonder it has not gone down.
No guest more welcome enters thro' our gate　　　　　220
Than one who dares admonish evil minds
How great, how brave, my husband is, how sure
All their transgressions shortly to chastize.'
　"Fixt by her sorrowing constancy I stood.
Open and dry an iron hardness held
My eyes while she was speaking: to relax,
To clasp her, Pallas and the Fates forbade:
In the wide hall the bow must first be bent,
The crowd of daring suitors swept away.
I did indeed at that same hour expect　　　　　230
The fatal weapon me too would transfix,
And yet abstain'd I from admonishing
My son about the prophecy, for fear
That his first feat in arms might be less firm,
Exhorting him however to avoid
The too close columns, lest they intercept
Or turn aside his arrow, when the wrongs

136

Of sire and mother rouse his vengeful wrath.
The Gods have been more gracious: stil I breathe,
Stil we breathe all: the foe alone breathes not.　　　240
　"Then what embraces, then what joys, were ours!
To Pallas, and to Juno, who preserves
The marriage-torch, and to the sire of Gods,
And to thee, Mavors! brother and support
Of Justice! prayers we offer, incense burn.
Nor was the altar cold, before my wife,
Mindful how often to and fro her room
She went to weave and to unweave the web,
Suspended it to Herè. She return'd
And, as Laertes sat enjoying all　　　250
The bliss of sunshine, said to him
　　　　　　　　　　"'Forgive,
Dear father! if thee also I deceiv'd,
Looking each evening at the unravel'd work;
Forgive me if I keep it not to wrap
Thy bones! With better omens time enough
Is there to weave another. May the Gods
Grant me to work as hard and watch as long
Before thou want it, blessed dear old man!'
　"Alas! from what a wife (how brief the space!)
Destiny calls me! Pious, brave, benign,　　　260
I found Telemachus, and loath to bear
The scepter of his sire. I loved to see
One so distrustful of his years, and one
Who counted not his father's.
　　　　　　　　　"Can then youth
Indeed be slow to seize the loosen'd reins?
Willingly less than whom the Gods forsake?
He was .. I led him where green pastures breath'd
With oxen, horses, sheep; where fruit mature
Swel'd on the branches, and where yellow corn
Droopt in luxuriant heaviness of car,　　　270
And said
　　　　"'Look round, Telemachus! the fruit
(Thinkest thou not?) from storm and rain secure,
Is fit to gather and the grain to reap.'
　"'Let it be done' said he. 'I will return
To-morrow for thy orders.'
　　　　　　　"I embrace
The duteous youth, and add in graver voice,

No other is my life: it too hath borne
Its storms, and now is ripened. They to whom
All things must yield, the Gods above refuse
My day to close in Ithaca: I go: 280
This little land is not enough for both,
And there are others that require my care.'
He stood in wonder: then he cast himself
Before my knees, and cried. 'Is then my love
So doubtful? Must worse trial be endured?
Say, father! tell me what thou threatenest.
Can such be thy resolve? We are secure
Now those proud men are slain. Thy sire and thou
Lived with one heart: the land was then enough
For him and thee; ah! why not now for us?   290
A thousand animals thou seest around,
Thou seest the city's flower successively
Spring up: age sinks not at the rise of youth.
Of all this people shall thy son alone,
He who thro' barbarous lands and stormy seas
Sought out his father, shall Telemachus,
Soon as the prayer is heard, the blessing given,
Be wanting to all duty, nor revere
In that beloved father his grey hairs?
For this hath Pallas deign'd to guide my steps   300
Or Jove to regulate my natal hour?
Could he who from Olympus keeps his eye
On guest and hoste, suppresses guilt conceal'd,
Extinguishes guilt manifest, preserves
Fathers . . himself the father of the Gods . .
Could he, the Avenger, see such crimes start up
Nor hurl his lightnings on the guilty head?'
    "Farther he urges me; until he hears
All that the Siren and Calypso sang.
Pale was his face; to heaven his hands he rais'd   310
And 'Milder be the omen' he exclamed,
'Than our fears render it! Ye Gods above,
Look on Ulysses! spare him! Too unblest
Already, never let his house be like
The house of Œdipus! . . I go . . not thou.
The little ile of Capri lies at peace
Under the just Teleboans: Telon prunes
The vines Sebetis planted: opposite,

            316–18 Capri . . . Sebetis] cf. Æneid, vii. 734 ff.

138

The Locrians plow: and farther to the north
The seed of Amphiaräus takes its root   320
Aside the falls of Anien. Let me haste
To any of these regions . . now, alas!
The more remote from native land, from thee,
Unhappy father! and from all we love,
To live the less unhappy. Every land
Will show me many who have known thee great
And glorious. Here Idomeneus commands,
Sprung of Deucalion, leaving sons behind
In distant Crete unwillingly: at hand
Reigns he whom Troy most dreaded of the Greeks,   330
Tydides, equal to the Gods in fight.
Thither the bark which brought thee home again
Shall take me speedily. Like one escaped
From shipwreck, I will hold the altar's horn
Imploring Zeus to mitigate thy doom,
Until the doubtful omen be dissolv'd.'
  "'What wouldst thou?' I exclame. 'Thou viewest things
With youthful eyes, and lookest out for light
Where light ariseth not. Alas, my child!
Little thou know'st how heedless are the safe,   340
To kings how unacceptable a king
Reduced to flight or sunk to poverty.
The sun hates darkness, prosperous men hate woe.
Comfort thy mother, guard thy people, son!
I, trusting in Minerva, will depart.'
  "Thrown on the dust, he would have answer'd; words
Fail'd him, and tears dried up: his breast he smote,
Imploring all the Gods that they would change
What is unchangeable, with looks, with groans,
With sobs, with supplications.
                              "I resist   350
More sternly. Then, in calmer voice and lower,
But turning back his neck that what he felt
Might be the better hidden, then said he,
'The Gods have spoken when my father speaks.
While he was absent, his return I hoped . .
To hope was unforbidden . . now he goes
Casting all hope away, condemns, abjures

320–1 Amphiaräus . . . Anien] Tiburtus, founder of Tibur (Tivoli), on the Anio, is called
by Pliny a son, and by other writers a grandson, of Amphiaraus the Argive seer. [W.]
331 Tydides] sc. Diomed. [W.]

That piety which he and Heaven approved,
No time, no fortune, can assuage my loss.'
Silent and slow he follows to the house. 360
But at what hour and in what words advise
My wife of all I meditate? My mind
Long wavers. I determine to conceal
The worst of ills forthcoming, and pretend
I must consult Dodona's oracle,
There to propitiate Zeus the Hospitable
For blood, tho' traitor's, shed beneath my roof.
To see her credulous of words so false
(Altho' I wisht it) gave my heart a pang
Til then unfelt. I took her hand, and wept. 370
This my fresh-springing grief her cheering voice
Represt, and 'Soon return' was all she said.
Alas! in striving to escape a fault,
A graver I committed. I deceiv'd
Her who deceiv'd not me in word or thought;
Her I deserted who would follow me
In life, in death, nor leave me in the Shades."

366 Zeus the Hospitable] cf. 'Catillus and Salia', l. 241 (p. 155).

THIRD PART

ARGUMENT

[Diomed sends for Penelope. Telegonus, begotten of Circe by Ulysses, seeks his father. As he draws near, Phædon smites him with a stake. Telegonus seizes the stake and hurls it at Phædon fleeing away. Ulysses, hurrying to quell the strife, is pierced through: he gives thanks to the gods for having averted the oracle's threat doubtless because—he thinking only of Telemachus—he was not dying by the hand of his son.]

AFTER some days the vintage had been cull'd,
Which now the rustics celebrate with song,
Dance, merriment, jest, and sonorous laugh.
Diomed their ancestral jokes enjoys
From various wide-mouth'd formidable masks,
Commending to his guest the inventive race
That could devise such wonders. More inclined
Was he to wander in a lonely path,
Where ancient pine-woods to the sloping sun
Redden'd at eventide, or where the downs 10
Were scattered over with low brakes, or where
Garganus whiten'd with the Ionian wave.
The pliant airs that well obey the lip

And those that ivory tames with timely stroke
Sooth'd and dissolv'd his sorrows for awhile,
But, when they left him lonely, these return'd.
   The leader of the Ætolians now perceiv'd
That neither feast nor holiday avail'd,
Nor hound nor horn nor battle won again,
And that from converse, cup, and music's bath   20
(Softener of care) he came out unrefresht.
Wherefor a ship he order'd to set sail
For Ithaca: there should Eurypylos
Tell how Ulysses had once more embraced
Tydides; how he had been warn'd by Zeus
To leave his country, give his son his place,
And meet Penelope where house and home
And regal honours Diomed prepared.
   Soon as he reacht the harbour, in the shade
Of Neritos which overhangs the town,   30
Eurypylos saw there a crowd stand round
A youth; nor was there any who ran down
To hail the ship or moor it on the strand.
Few things this youth seem'd saying, many more
He askt, and to the elders bent his ear,
Better their tremulous voices to receive.
He stood: below him seated were the scribes
On right and left, to seize and crush vague words
That buz about Law's image, and to grave
On brazen tablets what calm minds approved.   40
   "Ay! here is something to delight thy heart,
Ulysses!" said he; for he knew by gest
And feature 'twas Telemachus who spoke
And with his father's wisdom ruled the land.
Where dwells Penelope he now inquires.
One from amid the people, with his hand
Points to the place.
                    "Lo! yonder on the left,
Above the little hill: hers is that house
Which yon old pear-tree's shadow cuts across
And where swells out the hillock from its root."   50
   There finds he, in the inner court retired,
Penelope. She knelt at prayer, that soon
And prosperously her husband may return,
And spend old-age, if but old-age, at home.
Hearing that he was safe, she thought the Gods

Had granted all her wishes: not, to leave
The race that honored her, not peril, toil,
Storm on the water, rocks along the coast,
A stranger's house, a land exposed to war,
Troubled her spirit; not, of wing adverse,   60
Iapyx, fraught with wrecks and darkening heaven,
Nor, pallid from eternal lightning-flash,
Acrokeraunian thunder-rifted crags.
And winter too drew nigh: from every tree
The humid foliage o'er the grove was whirl'd
And the waves shuddered under Auster's blast.
The seventh morn had risen. Eurus, glad
To follow Phœbus, breath'd his favoring gale,
And ship and sailors of his native ile
Telemachus with prudent zeal prepared.   70
With his own hand he heapt upon the deck
Cups, goblets, salvers (strange barbaric signs
Engraven there, strange mystic arguments)
And, laid apart by frugal ancestors,
Much unwrought gold. Slowly and loath the maids
Folded the vestures of their parting queen;
Purple, to robe her husband, once their lord,
And white, befitting both before the Gods.
   Then did Penelope embrace her son
Soothing him with her gladness.
                     "Short the way"   80
She said "that separates thy sire and me,
And safely dwells he in Hesperian fields:
There mayest thou revisit, every year,
Both parents, dearest son! there every spring
I shall look out to see its earliest flowers
Fluttering, a little withered, on the mast."
   He groan'd, he prest her hand, he turn'd away,
And went strait home.
                Now swells the sail, the waves
Plash louder and rise rougher up the prow,
And now the sailors in their hymns implore   90
The Gods presiding over winds and seas.
The anxious wife looks forward: wave and wave
In ceaseless chace advance. She looks behind:
On the hoar surface there the hills subside,
And from the victim a thin smoke ascends.

      61 Iapyx] north-west wind. [W.]

Then . . whether were it for the land she left,
Or hope prefiguring the beloved man,
Or her son's tender piety . . she wept.
   Her mind grew calmer: rest, yet rest confused,
Came stilly over her: the inverted sky   100
Shining cerulean on cerulean sea,
The lapsing pinnace, the perpetual shower
Of golden sun-drops on the rippling wave,
Absorb'd her yielded eyes, no longer sad.
Yet every hour she thought the pinnace sail'd
Slower and slower, the bright day advanced
Less bright: and thus in sunny calm went three.
Upon the third, Ulysses from the sands
Descried a cloud grow whiter with a sail;
Nor long before a prow swells and descends;   110
Then level oars the river's course divide.
Doubtful whence comes that vessel, many shores
And many streams and wealthy marts arise
Before his vision, with their chiefs and kings:
Only one land escapes his mind; that one
His own.
          "Perhaps tho' (for the wind is fair)
It may have left Zacynthos: such the form
And such the colour of Zacynthan sails."
   At length he knew the master; he was born
In little Asteris plow'd by shallow keels.   120
He knew and heard him nearer give command
To lower and furl the sail: but first he warn'd
The maidens to beware the cordage loost.
While as Ulysses ponder'd, at his side
There stood Eurypylos: in lighter skiff
He left the iland, and before the dawn
Arrived at home. From him the hero prest
To hear exactly all that had occur'd.
Royal impatience of long narrative
Confused it: and there presently was that   130
Which brake and scatter'd all . . Penelope.
  Each ran to the embrace.
                   "So swift of foot!
So girlish!" cried he. "Verily I think
The Gods have given back thy youth again!
May . . since the past returns . . may Arpi give,
To show thee welcome, all Amyclai gave!"

And often too when later years advanced
He sported thus; nor knew the truth he spoke.
To make her more contented with her change,
He added, "Sweet as were in other days   140
Täygetos, and woods where pealing horn
Challenged the hunter; sweet beneath the cliffs
Midsummer shade and shade-born moss, retreat
Of maidens equal-aged; yet nought beyond
Regrets that all young hours leave after them
Shall she experience who will tread henceforth
Valleys more soft than all she trod before.
Taburnus robed in roseate light serene
Here meets majestical the setting sun;
Above his folds and swallow-nested roofs   150
Oak-crown'd the ridges of Garganus rise,
And clearest streams from their dark cooms descend.
On stream like these swam Helen's golden hair,
For stream like these her father swan left heaven.
This is the land where thou art to behold,
Born of the Gods, belov'd by them, a man
Whom, if Ulysses, if thy son, be dear,
For-ever thou must venerate. By his arms
Fell Ilion: Deities the most averse
Turn'd round to strengthen him: and he alone   160
Brought those he led to conquest safely home."
    That man himself to greet them now advanced;
But, coming nearer, doubt perplext his mind
Whether he might extend a hand to one
Upon whose brow sat majesty above
The majesty of mortal, to whose step
Modesty lent that quiet stateliness
Which Pride, if Pride were wiser, might assume.
He stops, and fixes on the earth his eyes.
A Goddess seems before him: shield and spear   170
He looks for: sees he Pallas? How presume
To question why the expected stays behind?
A rising sigh betrays the human breast.
    "Penelope! while thy Ulysses breathes"
Cried he "this scepter while Tydides wields,
And while the Father of the Gods and men
Sets right and wrong apart, thy womanhood

152 cooms] ? ridges (Oxford English Dictionary, *s.v.* comb); or dingles (Welsh *cwm*).
By a *cwm* near Llantony Landor had begun to build a mansion. [W.]

Never shall want the spear's true guardianship;
No need of ægis o'er a breast like thine."
   A place there is upon that kingdom's verge   180
O'er which the best of brave Œtolians reign'd,
Near the sea-shore, but in a vale retired,
Where smoke ascended from few cottage-roofs
And the low copses round about; there dwelt
An ancient race in ancient piety;
And there Ulysses with the late restored
Design'd to pass what had not past of life.
And granted was the wish, on compact made
That every year, on their departure's day,
They should return and share the genial feast.   190
   Italy now for many years had paus'd
From war and discord: Fame, who follows war
And discord eagerly, came well receiv'd
By those who rested from them, with her tale
Of each adventure to the heroes since;
And who had died, and how; what better luck
To those, the few, who breath'd in upper air;
Under what auspices Petilia grew;
Antenor's rising realm where loudly sounds
Timavus; the contested Latian bride;   200
The Alban range, and Tiber, on whose stream
Fate had decreed eternal walls should stand.
Another name the winged Goddess loved
To celebrate, one shining over earth,
A name at which all women threw aside
The spindle: ever wretched, ever true,
Was he who bore it: Circe hoped in vain,
In vain Calypso, to possess him, free
From combat, free from converse with mankind,
By seas and rocks enclosed and charms and spells.   210
Certain it is that yet in Italy
He lives, exempt from age and from disease,
Whether by Circe's or Calypso's gift
Uncertain, driven from his realm, receiv'd
In Arpi, guest of Diomed his friend.
   The day appointed for the yearly feast

---

196 luck] luc *misp. in text.* fortuna *in Latin version.* [W.]   198 Petilia] near
Cortona, *see Æneid,* iii. 402.   199 Antenor] mythical founder of Patavium.
Æneid, i. 247.   200 Latian bride] Lavinia, daughter of Turnus. Ovid, *Met.*
xiv. 570.

Of his reception, had recurr'd: the pair
Enter, as wont, the gates of Diomed,
And all around is royal pomp displaid.
The whole house laughs with luxury; the cheer   220
Rejoices it, the bearers of the cheer;
It most is gladdened by its master's face.
Thro' the wide courts and thro' the country round
The lyre and pipe sprinkle and strengthen song.
Staid men warn off the noisier of the crowd
Coming too near the wine-cup's froth and hiss
And savory smoke from salvers. One alone
Resisted. He entreated them to tell
Ulysses that Telegonos was there.
He urged; he call'd him father . . nor miscall'd.   230
After six moons had risen since the flight
Of her beloved husband (thus she named
Ulysses) Circe in her grot had borne
This boy, and, ever mindful of the sire,
Call'd him Telegonos, because his birth
Had happened when Ulysses was afar.
The men of Arpi and of Ithaca,
As the youth presses forward, are alert
In criminations, are alert in blows
Against the impostor who would simulate   240
Telemachus, but blundered in the name;
These, adding to repulse whate'er a love
Of their young lord suggested; those, whate'er
Of coarse and bitter rustic life supplied
And malice's contagion, swiftly spred
When the dense vulgar catches the disease.
Who shall record the rabble? who pronounce
The barbarous names? who care to know, if told?
So loud the clangour of hell's clasping lash
About their sides, 'tis hard to catch them all,   250
But what are audible ye now shall hear.
Gabalus, whence in Italy the name
Of that accursed tree whereon he hung,
Who kept the gold entrusted to his care;
Of pole fox-colored where pink baldness ceast,
Gabbus, who bade escape the thief he caught,
To share with him the spoil he bore away.

252, 256 Gabalus . . . Gabbus] *See poem beginning*: 'Two rival lawyers, Gabb and Gabell', *and note thereon.* [W.]

Bœthamus, bold in plunder, bold in wife,
He, and his sea-spawn brothers; and, of gait
Countenance and demeanour brotherlike,   260
A dismal sister, hired at funerals
To howl in verse the praises of the dead;
Following the father's footsteps all alike,
Who, in proportion to the bribe, from Jove
Or from Ixion traced a chief's descent.
There also stretcht Orsilochos, who knew
The names of horses, but Ulysses' name
He knew not. From the bench where he reclined
Uprear'd a little, heavily he croakt,
"What! and shall we be standing here, and thou   270
Be seated at the feast?"
                                    More eagerly
Urges the youth, more ardently implores,
Calling on Gods and men. Rule, country, son,
Duteous, devoted, his Dulichian sire
Again shall find, not exile. Whether shame
Withheld him, or the Fates, no word said he
Of Circe who had borne him. Staves and clubs
Rattle around him: seamen, craftsmen, rush
Upon one man, and that one man unarm'd.
They close the gate against his issuing out: 280
Nor would it have avail'd: but stones are cast,
Sharp stakes protended. Inborn valour boils;
He catches up and hurls the weapons back,
Wounded by many, sorely too assail'd
By stinging scorn.
                                    While arms are ringing round,
Ulysses, hearing from within the noise,
And that, whatever be the cause, a man
Of his was harrast by assaults and jeers,
That stones were flying in the royal court,
Blows were redoubling, death was breath'd, rusht out   290
So insolent commotion to allay.
In Ithacan and Arpine, young and old,
Clamour and violence, louder, fiercer, swel'd;
But with his eye, his hand, his voice, he checkt

258 Bœthamus] *sc.* Betham, Landor's tenant at Llantony. See note on poem beginning "Hail paragon of T . . .s! hail" [W.]   266 Orsilochos] *see Æneid,* xi. 636 for
the huge Trojan slain by Camilla, but Landor may have been thinking of the Duke
of Beaufort. [W.]

The foremost. One step farther (such respect
All bore toward his dignity and age)
An open way was made. Phædon, escaped
From Apina, found room enough to dart
Against Telegonos, a sharpen'd stake.
Telegonos stoopt, seiz'd it, turn'd, pursued,   300
And hurl'd it, as he mounted up the steps.
Untrue the angry aim! that pointed stake
Transfixt the unknowing and unknown . . transfixt
His father! His knees totter: on the earth
He falls: blood hisses from the gasping wound.
All start with horror, never felt before,
From blood now running thro' the garlands strown
Along the ground; a husband's, guest's, and king's.
Lifting up once his eyes, heavy with death,
"The Omnipotent hath heard my prayer" said he,   310
"The appointed hour is come . . nor brings remorse
To my Telemachus." He turn'd his face
Back on the hall, for thence he seem'd to hear
Confusedly shrill voices, questions sharp.
Whose blood runs there? Ulysses whither gone?
He drew with failing hand the festal robe
Above his head, and sank; no word, no groan.

298 Apina] town in Apulia destroyed by Diomed. [W.]

CATILLUS AND SALIA

[Published in *Hellenics*, 1847. For a shorter version published in 1859 see notes at end of volume. First written in Latin and so published in 1820. Text 1847.]

[ARGUMENT *

Anius, Volsinorum rex, filiam habuit Saliam: Catillus eam abduxit. Pater, cui prædictum erat a genero et hospite periturum esse, frustra insecutus, in Pareusium se jecit, et nomen fluvio Anieni dedit. Catillus a Virgilio et Horatio dictus est, a Plutarcho Cathetos.]

CATILLUS left his spear upon the steps
Of that old temple which from Ciminus
Looks o'er the lake and the dark ilexes.
Often his horse, standing alone before
The columns, starts at sights obscurely seen;
Sometimes at roar of raging beast, sometimes

* Argument. From Landor's Latin version. *See Æneid*, vii. 672; Horace, *Odes*, . 18, 2. [W.]   2 temple] Fanum Voltumnæ, near the Etruscan city Volsinii. [W.]

CATILLUS AND SALIA

At bark that bursts and crackles from the cork,
Or at the rapid whirl of withered leaves
Wafted and rattling on his bridle-bit.
  "Voltumna!" pray'd the youth "reject not thou   10
My vows! for Salia is my heart consumed;
Nor does the sire or maiden disapprove;
But there are ancient oracles that hold
The torch of Hymen back. Thou knowest well,
O Goddess! (for from thy own fane procede
These oracles) what menaces impend.
So great an evil be it mine to ward
From both! Yet how? He who could all foresee,
Amphiaräus, he might have advised;
But earth before him opened, and with flames   20
Enveloping his chariot, drank it in.
Where in far regions, famed Ismenos flows
He left his children and the light of day.
  "The Tuscan shore a race of fugitives
Alights on. O that they had come in guise
Of enemies! not (as they say) of friends:
Because old seers have seen, old prophets sung
That under this the royal house should fall
And royal bride be wedded, to her sire's
And people's ruin. Clearly I discern   30
What Fate before had hidden; nor retreat;
Nor arms, wherever they may lead, refuse;
Nor absence . . long, for ever; nor the gulph
Of Styx, which all must pass; nor, what is worse,
In other lands to wander; be but thou
Mine for one day, O Salia! no one's else
And least of any one an exile's bride!"
  A hollow murmur shakes the beech-tree-tops;
A voice is heard;
                    "Of wretched father, child
More wretched! how wouldst thou have fled before, 40
If thou hadst ever known the curse to come!"
It ceases: loudly, as the portal closed,
Resounded in their depths the woods profound.
  The youth is sunk in prayer, and all again

19 Amphiaräus] King of Argos. Bayle called him "one of the greatest prophets of Paganism" and gives the story of his death during the war of the seven against Thebes. By some writers he was said to be the grandfather of Catillus, Tiburtus, and Coras. [W.] 24 fugitives] Æneas and his companions. [W.]   *ll.* 27–30 Adapted from the story of Turnus and his daughter Lavinia (*Æneid*, vii. 68 ff.). [W.]

Is silent, in the sky, the grove, the fane,
Nor could he see above him any bird
Whose flight should comfort him; for right and left
Rose the huge branches, and afar the swans
Shone out serenely on the lake serene,
Soothing the under-wing with neck reverst.   50
He wishes not for fields of waving vine,
He wishes not for olive-boundary,
Planted when first the blindfold boy had drawn
The lot of each Pelasgian from the urn,
But he does wish for Salia, he does wish
To see Volsinii, blessed land, again.
Then of the king he thinks, and then revolves
Commands which both had given (and one with tears)
Unless Voltumna look with placid smile
Toward the couch of Hymen.
                   Evening came: 60
He threw him on the ground; he sought for dreams,
If haply sleep should calm his weariness,
Dreams that from sire and daughter may remove
The unknown peril that o'ershadows both.
   Sharp was the splendour of the stars; all heaven
Seem'd moving as it never yet had moved;
To mortal power insuperable, fate
Bent easily before him; every word
Of oracles had now grown plain enough;
And he resolv'd to save at once the king   70
And the king's daughter, do they what they would
And fear'd they all that ever could be fear'd.
   Amid these thoughts his yielding senses sleep
Impresses: in his dream he hears the arms
Of guest and ravisher: he sees (can sight
Deceive him?) Salia. With her own consent
Is she borne off? and, when her father calls
Pursuing her, disdains she to return?
He starts, he raves, strikes with his brow the ground,
Springs up, and, siezing on the bridle, leaps   80
Into the saddle, and before 'tis dawn
Reaches the city's outskirt.
                 Long the land
In peace had rested; scanty was its watch;
All knew the cordial youth who, strong of limb,

<hr>

52 olive-boundary] *see* Varro. i. 15. [W.]

CATILLUS AND SALIA

Joyous of countenance and prompt of speech
And large of liberality, and first
On foot or horseback, hurl'd the Argive spear;
Strait went he onward where the palace stood,
And stationed under its first turret found
The friendly Periphas.
                "I haste" he cried,   90
"I haste to Salia. Help me. That is nigh,
That which she fears, her father more than she,
And never may perhaps by arms avert:
Voltumna threatens it. Her father's love
May blind his eyes, but *my* love opens mine.
I bring the Goddesses own words, and these
The dreams she breath'd into my breast confirm."
  Ever to Dian at the break of day
Did Salia bear her sacrifice: the gate
Was this thro' which she past into her grove   100
And little chapel.
               Thickly sound the hoofs
Of fretting horse beneath the turret's arch,
And the last light of lamp that hangs therefrom,
Crackling, now hides now shows the whiten'd iron.
When casts the hind, with broken sleep morose,
The wooden collar round his ox'es neck
And rope athwart the horns, when one red line
Borders the dull horizon, and the fields
Under the drowsy skies lie indistinct,
There stands the royal maiden.
                   "Hence! fly hence!   110
O Salia!" cries Catillus, "and believe
The Gods are now propitious."
                At the word
On his high steed he lifts her, with a leap
Mounts, and redoubles with a rapid spur
His courser's speed.
             "Tremble not" cried the youth:
"A time there was indeed for fear, when flight
Was none, and hope uncertain. From her shrine
Dian inclining to thy prayers and vows

96 Goddesses] Here and in *ll.* 148, 178 Landor may have written "Goddessis",
in conformity with his views on spelling. See notes at end of volume. [W.]
98 Dian] According to G. Dennis (*Cities and Cemeteries of Etruria*) Losna or Lala was
the Etruscan Diana. [W.]   106 ox'es] Perhaps written "oxis". See note on
l. 96. [W.]

Would, if she ever uttered oracle,
Have bidden what Voltumna hath ordain'd.   120
The horse is quiet: see! he frets no more:
And none are following. Is my arm too tight?
Bends it unwelcome round thee? Fearest thou?
Wouldst thou prohibit, wouldst thou chide, my fears?
I loosen it. Why weep and sigh? why doubt?
In Tibur who should envy us a life
Of country peace? To what ferocious man
Canst thou be there a prey? what war molest
Thy father? For no realm we fight; we hold
The only realm we want. I leave behind   130
The Sabines and their ruler to enjoy
Untroubled peace. Instead of fields in dower,
Fields which suspicion everywhere surrounds
With the uncertain faith of hireling arms,
Be there for us the deep repose of woods,
Walls that have never heard the name of Mars,
Tibur, and those green pastures on the banks
Thro' which Pareusius winds his silvery stream.
Look back; how widely spreads the space behind!
Volsinii how remote! the citadel   140
How reddening lower and lower with larger light!"
    At this she raises up her eyes, not quite
Up to his eyes who speaks to her; then looks
Back on her father's city; then they fill
With gushing tears.
                              "Live, father! live in peace!
Voltumna claims me; can then piety
Forbid, or any care obstruct my course?
Follow I must the Goddess'es command.
The desart, the dense darkness of the woods,
The lake, with all their gloom and all its own,   150
I would thro' life inhabit, nor repine,
Let but the Fates grant tranquil days to thee!"
    Moved at her tenderness, Catillus said,
"Behold them granted! and shall she whose prayers
Have won them for her parent, not rejoice?
Voltumna well might choose thee for her own,
But she was silent; nay, she gave commands
Right opposite; she bade thee leave thy home,
Thy father's house: thou wisely hast obey'd,

131 Sabines] *see 1859* ed. *l.* 183. [W.]   138 Pareusius] *see* Argument.

And child so duteous she from far will hear.　　　　160
Meanwhile an aged priestess keeps the fane,
One only: such its holiness, no time
Will ever move it.　Thou shalt see the dells
Of Tibur, the Albunean lake, its shades
And floating ilands, and (what oft thy wish
Shuddering at all the terrors of the tale
Urged thee to see) the fissured rock, the rush
Of angry waters, and, where these subside,
Glens where is heard the song of Nymphs below.
There be our country, there our house, and there　　170
Our early days and later! All thy life
Must thou be happy in a father saved
And faith saved too: and no less happy he,
Obedient to the dictate of the Fates,
In that he gave not (tho' he wisht to give)
Salia to him who holds her to his heart."
　Salia now calmer, bids him to repeat
All that Voltumna said. The Goddess'es
Behest she thinks obscure, the danger clear;
She sighs; but piety distrusts not love.　　　　180
Scarce the first hour of flight had past away
Before the father knew it.　Idle time
He lost not in complaint, nor idle threats
Threw at the fugitive: he gave command
Forthwith that chosen youths surround the woods
And moorlands of Capenus, occupy
Every hill-top, keep equal distances
At certain stations, and from each, right, left,
The subject land, wood, river, lake, survey.
He himself hastened onward, and before　　　190
Noontide he saw, not distant, to the east,
Eretus, its wide woodland overgrown
With speckled arbutus, and, farther on
And higher up, an ancient temple, white
In the sun's splendour, on its mound apart:
Beyond it the Nomentan hills retired.
And now, inclosed by mountains, he approacht
The steep red banks and turbid stream profound
Of Tiber.　Never had that stream been crost
By bridge of stone convex, or mountain pine,　　200
Nor level boats in surging series linkt

164 Albunean lake] *See note at end of vol.*

Made plain the way for horseman and for horse.
He bends, and raises in his hollow hand
The sacred water, and thus prays the God.
 "O father Tiber! if thou hast preserv'd
Thy people quiet by religious awe;
If thou beholdest thy Apollo's hill
Soracte bound in duteous equity;
If the Faliscians, righteous race, impress
The burning ember with unflinching heel;   210
If, when the robber Cacus he had slain,
Alcides (which our sires have seen) washt off
That robber's blood in thy most clensing lymph;
If stolen herds brought vengeance down on him
Whom none consorted with, no host receiv'd;
Shall I in vain implore thee for thy help
Against a wretch who robs his host of all,
Who carries off his child, his only child?
Avenge me: give me only ('tis enough)
To swim in safety o'er thy rapid stream."   220
Thus praying, his huge spear he threw across;
Whereat the steed which bore him shrilly neigh'd,
Rear'd, and with hoof inverted scraped the turf,
And, call'd by name and patted and cheer'd on,
Sprang bravely down and clove the surging waves:
They bent beneath his lusty neck, they broke
At every breath his widening nostril breath'd,
And his rich trappings flasht fresh light around.
 In the late hour of eve the king surveys
The highths of Tibur; to the walls he wends   230
Alone; to Coras, and him only, cries
That he come out.
          But Coras, when he knew
Afar Catillus by his burnisht arms,
Ran from the rampart to embrace the king,
And said "Where is my brother?"
                    Fiercelier burns
His rage at this, and
                "Like a slave he fled;
Nor shall it now avail thee to conceal
His flight; thy walls shall show him in their flames.

ll. 205–20] *cf.* the prayer of Arruns and the allusion to a fire-walking feat in *Æneid,*
xi. 785 ff. [W.]   209 Faliscians] *cf.* æquosque Faliscos, *Æneid,* vii. 695. [W.]
233 Catillus] An uncorrected error. Coras saw, not his brother, but King Anius
approaching. The Latin version has: *agnovit procul hospitis arma Sabini.* [W.]

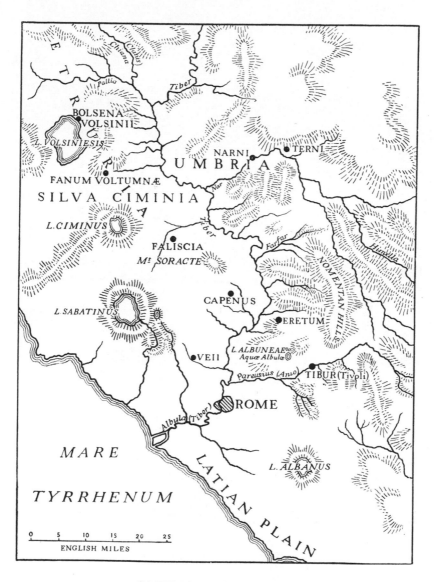

CATILLUS AND SALIA

THE FLIGHT TO TIBUR

CATILLUS AND SALIA

Now let him arm . . a father calls, a guest,
Despoil'd, dishonor'd . . let him arm before   240
The hospitable the avenging Jove
He thinks he may affront, deceive, despise."
    The brother stood astonisht: lifting up
Both hands to heaven,
                   "No brother is with me,
I swear, and therefor lay aside thy wrath,
O king! and under happy auspices
Await in peace and patience his return."
    He answered not, but rudely rusht away.
With angry looks the Argive nobles cried
"What, tyrant! dost thou threaten war? say first,   250
Proud as thy nation is of ancient fame,
Say when on Ciminus hath ever oak
Borne trophy? While the fatten'd heifer shakes
The flowery fillet and salt-sprinkled crown,
Do their round cheeks, well form'd for puffing horns,
Turn into waxen whiteness at the approach
Of level'd spears. If (faith of Gods and men!)
Thou darest threaten us with fire or sword,
We will not wait thee in our walls, but show
Thy city, and all cities leagued with thee,   260
How the proud Tuscans first cried out for peace."
    The last late sunbeam of the summer sky
Had fallen, and with dew far superfused
The fuming meadows of Pareusius paled,
Far as the Albula and Latian plain.
When Tibur's citadel had sunk to view
The king alighted from his horse, and spent
A weary night beneath a peasant's roof.
    Near to Volsinii, with a clear cold stream*
There runs a rivulet and intercepts   270
The little rills that trickle thro' the grove,
And falls into the Tiber where it looks
Into the glades of Umbria; 'twas this course
Catillus followed thro' its whole extent.
Here, where it join'd the Tiber, pusht he forth

---

* Now called Fiume Chiaro. [L.]

241 hospitable . . . avenging] *cf. Jupiter hospitalis* in Cicero, *Jupiter ultor* in
Pliny. [W.]
265 Albula] Ancient name of the Tiber. [W.]

A narrow skiff, tied with a twisted band
Of osier to the tree. The oar's smooth palm
Divided the broad water-leaves and won
An easy way. Now, while the waves it made
With gentle plash and pattering heav'd the bark,   280
Thou, Salia, sattest at thy lover's side
Stiller and calmer than that shady stream.
Catillus then would hoist his little sail,
That he might lay aside the oar, and hold
The rope which turn'd it as the river turn'd
Or the wind caught it, and that he might sit
On the same bench with Salia, and protect
From the hot sun her face beneath its shade.
He fear'd to pass where hinds might see and shout,
He fear'd all voices, most of all he fear'd   290
The irreverent Fescennine's immodest song.
   Volsinii's firm allies, the Sabines held
That country where amid the flowers he rears
Runs Farfar, and that barrener wherefrom
Himella shrinks when Sirius strikes his stream.
So now he took the simple guise of hind
Who had gone early forth, and must return
To hail his household Deities at eve.
Rushes and reeds conceal'd his crest and spear.
Long was the way by land, by water long,   300
Nor would the youth, nor could he had he will'd,
Tell Salia how much farther they must go.
Her dread of any seeing her he calm'd,
Saying,
       "Look up! behold what scanty light
Sheds Hesper, how he swings upon the stream
Alone of all the stars, and what calm gloom
Propitious sits upon the brow of heaven."
They both weave sleepless dreams. In days to come
What will their pleasure be, if touch of hand
Kindles such fires; if at one word, one glance,   310
Disperst is every doubt and every fear.
   Ah! be not wise, ye young! but from bright days
Look into brighter: evermore believe:
Be this your wisdom. At the close of life,
We know too much; we know we are deceiv'd.
   Needless the story were in what converse

294 Farfar] an affluent of the Tiber. *See* Ovid, *Met.* xiv. 30. [W.]

CATILLUS AND SALIA

Hour followed hour; what cultur'd lands, what wilds
Delighted them; how many were the spots
In whose retirement they could spend their lives:
Needless to mention how, amid the pause,   320
A bough impending o'er the stream sometimes
Swept, ere they were aware, the vessel's side,
Startling and reddening her with girlish fright.
The youth too had his fears, but held them in.
He fear'd if any silent matron stole
Down to the river-side, in quest of him
Her children cried for ere they went to bed:
He fear'd if suddenly a lamp-light burst
With long effulgence from some cot unseen
Across the water, or a fisherman   330
Had crown'd his net with flame, and, dipt in pitch,
The feathery cane its finny prey allured.
    Onward they sail all night: when morn appears,
Seeing that friendly Tibur was behind,
He leaves (in view, though distant) on his right
Seven far-famed hills, where stood the residence
Of king Evander, sprung from Arcady;
Janus on one had rear'd a muniment,
And Saturn on another: he admired
How such vast works had ever been destroy'd.   340
Wonder may seize, but can not long detain,
And least the young and ardent. Rowing back,
Catillus rises on the oar and glides
Into his native land.
                  "O mine!" he cries,
"Mine surely now! come, Salia, come, enjoy
In safety and by right our freedom here:
No Gods oppose us: we are here at home."
And as he speaks, swifter he plies the oar.
Soon helmets blaze above the copse; men arm'd
And unarm'd welcome him; stout hinds belay   350
The laboring bark, tugging it where the wind
Baffles the sail; then, smoking from afield,
Laborious oxen and stout-hearted steeds.
But, tho' they aided, slower seem'd the hour
Than yesterday, when lay the oar athwart
And the loose sail flapt idly round the mast.

330 fisherman] For an allusion to fishing nets with cork buoys carrying bells see
poem addressed to W. Linton in Section VI. [W.]

Both wisht to be alone again; nor long
Abstain'd Catillus (when the cliff began
To chafe the water and impede the way)
From ordering to haul the skiff ashore.   360
Alone then were they. He ascends the path,
The well-known path of the old wood; he stops,
Here, lest the stones should hurt her; here, because
The grass is softer than all grass beside;
Here, because sunny hazles most invite;
And here, because no serpent ever coils
Beneath the ashen shade. Such leisure-hour
Fatigue and sense of safety make more sweet.
   "Up! Salia! one more hill we must ascend,
Whence Tibur, now thy own, thou mayst descry."   370
   They reach the summit. What, across yon chasm,
Fixes the maid her eyes upon? A breeze
Whitens the waving willows as they bend,
And ancient elms cast shadows long and dark,
And the lithe tendril of the vine unpruned
Pats and springs up and pats again the stream.
What sees she from the summit there? why gaze?
Why tremble? why turn pale?
                       Behold! there stands
Her father!
           You might have believ'd her knees
Had turn'd to marble.
               "Wretched girl!" he cried,   380
"Whom dost thou fly from?"
                 At that voice she starts.
Swifter and swifter hurried she along
And thought each step was slower than the last.
Ambiguous was it from the fields or town
Whether she tore the youth away (her hand
Holding his spear through terror at the wrath
Of sire and prophet) or his arm made firm
Her step precipitous: but she was first
Where the road narrowed, fit for one alone,
And he where, leaning down for her, his spear   390
Protruded helpt her up the rock abrupt.
   Indignant Anius saw them from below
Receiv'd into the city's double gate
With loud acclaim and trumpet's louder clang;

       381 "Whom] Whom *1847* (*mistake*).

And from the aërial citadel the girls
One to another show'd him, and with taunts
Bade him begone.
                    He rushes to the wood
Resounding o'er the river: but nor clash
Of cataract hears he, nor wild shout, nor dash
Roaring above, redoubled underneath,   400
And far away thro' cavern'd rocks prolong'd:
Nor rage impels him now nor tears dissolve,
He only presses with both hands his brow.
  Ah from what bitter source must flow the grief
Such scenes assuage not! There he stood, nor saw
Pareusius whirl his torrent deep below,
Whence watery dust eternal intercepts
The light of heaven. Dark ilex, bright-hair'd beech,
And, vainly fostering ever-fruitless vine,
The loftier elm, mass above mass, arise.   410
Among the branches thousand birds appear
To raise their little throats, but every song
Fast as it flows the roaring torrent drowns.
Some, by assiduous helpmate undetain'd,
Fly from the eternal thunder of the waves;
These . . leave them only sheltering bough, and moss
To soften for their young the nest they knit . .
Nor rains can chill nor thunders shake their love.
By rocks inclosed, sore fretting, and resolv'd
No force shall quell it, rushes the array   420
Of water, now united, scattered now,
Again to rally: pale is overhead
The mountain, pale and trembling; to its sides
The splasht herbs cling the closer: many a reed
Is there which never shall sigh forth the plaint
Of the lone shepherd, many a flower is there
On virgin bosom never to recline.
But numberless bright intermingled rays
Spring up, whence Jove and Phœbus raise an arch
Lofty and wide, and Iris dwells within.   430
  Wrong, upon earth imperious, may o'erpower
And crush the mortal; Virtue may stand back
Nor help him; even the clemency of Heaven
May fail; the urn, the ashes laid within,
Violence may scatter; but on those who die
Thro' wretchedness, and undeservedly,

Compassionate and faithful verse attends
And drives oblivion from the wasted tomb.
  O why, ye Gods! why, in such lands as these,
Fairest of earth, and where ye chose to dwell,   440
Should burst forth anguish from a father's breast?
Why from the guiltless Anius? Who brought gifts
More gladly to your altars? who more pure?
In part he utter'd this, in part supprest;
Then added,
          "Here is piety! and thus
Doth she requite her father! Duteous, chaste,
Benevolent, all thought her; and to all,
Excepting me, she was so; I alone
Less than a stranger merited her love.
Now know I what (Oh! lesson hard to learn   450
At all times! how much harder for the old!)
A daughter owes a father.
                "O my wife!
If Libitina* had allow'd thy stay,
To see me so far left behind in love
(Our fond contention) thou hadst surely griev'd.
I took the mother's place. When any pain,
However slight, she suffered, could I rest?
Or could I leave her couch?
              "Go, snatch the torch
Of Hymen, run, mingle thy song with theirs,
From tranquil brow draw down the saffron veil,   460
And be thy children, if they can, like thee.
If every other rite thou hast disdain'd,
If scorn'd the dower a royal bride should bring,
If thro' three nations, shameless, thou hast fled,
Blame, blame thy parent for it. He provides
At least a victim for so blest a day."
  He spake; and from the woody mountain-top,
Where by the eternal battery of the waves
A way is cloven, cast himself. From rock
To rock he fell; and all the dew that rose   470
Around was dimly reddened with his blood.
The fact is well recorded: while the name
Of old Pareusius few remember, thine,
O Anius, sounds for ever on that stream.
      * Venus Libitina was an Etruscan Goddess. [L.]

DRAMAS AND DRAMATIC SCENES

COUNT JULIAN: A TRAGEDY

[Published anonymously in 1812; reprinted under author's name 1831, 1846.]

[INTRODUCTION]

The daughter of Count Julian is usually called Florinda—a fictitious appellation, unsuitable to the person and to the period. Never was one devised more incompatible with the appearance of truth, or more fatal to the illusions of sympathy [—a fictitious ... sympathy *om. in 1846*]. The city of Covilla, it is reported, was named after her. Here is no improbability: there would be a gross one in deriving the word, as is also pretended, from La Cava. Cities, in adopting a name, bear it usually as a testimony of victories or as an augury of virtues. Small and obscure places, occasionally, receive what their neighbours throw against them; as Puerto de la mala muger in Murcia. A generous and enthusiastic people [Murcia, but a generous people *1846*], beyond all others in existence or on record [beyond ... record *om. 1846*], would affix no stigma to innocence and misfortune.

It is remarkable that the most important era in Spanish history should be the most obscure. This is propitious to the poet, and above all to the tragedian. Few characters of such an era can be glaringly misrepresented, few facts offensively perverted.

CHARACTERS

Count JULIAN.
RODERIGO, King of Spain.
OPAS, Metropolitan of Seville.
SISABERT, betrothed to COVILLA.
MUZA, Prince of Mauritania.
ABDALAZIS, son of MUZA.

TARIK, Moorish Chieftain.
COVILLA, daughter of JULIAN.
EGILONA, wife of RODERIGO.

Officers.

HERNANDO, OSMA, RAMIRO, &c.

COUNT JULIAN

ACT I. SCENE 1.

Camp of Julian.

OPAS. JULIAN.

Opas. See her, Count Julian: if thou lovest God,
See thy lost child.
Julian.   I have avenged me, Opas,
More than enough: I sought but to have hurled
The brands of war on one detested head,
And died upon his ruin. O my country!

Title : A Tragedy *om. 1846, when* Count Julian *was printed with other matter under a heading :* Acts and Scenes *with note after title :* None of these poems of a dramatic form were offered to the stage, being no better than *Imaginary Conversations* in metre.
Introduction: In 1831 follows after CHARACTERS; *in 1846 as footnote to* COVILLA* *in* CHARACTERS.
3 sought ... hurled] only sought to hurl *1831, 1846.*   5 died] die *1831, 1846.*

O lost to honour, to thyself, to me,
Why on barbarian hands devolves thy cause,
Spoilers, blasphemers!
   Opas.   Is it thus, Don Julian,
When thy own ofspring, that beloved child,
For whom alone these very acts were done   10
By them and thee, when thy Covilla stands
An outcast, and a suppliant at thy gate,
Why that still stubborn agony of soul,
Those struggles with the bars thyself imposed?
Is she not thine? not dear to thee as ever?
   Julian. Father of mercies! show me none, whene'er
The wrongs she suffers cease to wring my heart,
Or I seek solace ever, but in death.
   Opas. What wilt thou do then, too unhappy man!
   Julian. What have I done already? All my peace   20
Has vanished; my fair fame in after-times
Will wear an alien and uncomely form,
Seen o'er the cities I have laid in dust,
Countrymen slaughtered, friends abjured!
   Opas.   And faith?
   Julian. Alone now left me, filling up in part
The narrow and waste intervals of grief:
It promises that I shall see again
My own lost child.
   Opas.   Yes, at this very hour.
   Julian. Till I have met the tyrant face to face,
And gain'd a conquest greater than the last;   30
Till he no longer rules one rood of Spain,
And not one Spaniard, not one enemy,
The least relenting, flags upon his flight;
Till we are equal in the eyes of men,
The humblest and most wretched of our kind,
No peace for me, no comfort, no—no child!
   Opas. No pity for the thousands fatherless,
The thousands childless like thyself, nay more,
The thousands friendless, helpless, comfortless—
Such thou wilt make them, little thinking so,   40
Who now, perhaps, round their first winter fire,
Banish, to talk of thee, the tales of old,
Shedding true honest tears for thee unknown:

    9 ofspring] offspring *1846*.   16 show] shew *1831*.   21 vanished] vanisht
1831, 1846.   after-times] aftertimes *1831;* aftertime *1846*.

162

COUNT JULIAN: A TRAGEDY

Precious be these, and sacred in thy sight,
Mingle them not with blood from hearts thus kind.
If only warlike spirits were evoked
By the war-demon, I would not complain,
Or dissolute and discontented men;
But wherefor hurry down into the square
The neighbourly, saluting, warm-clad race,   50
Who would not injure us, and could not serve;
Who, from their short and measured slumber risen,
In the faint sunshine of their balconies,
With a half-legend of a martyrdom
And some weak wine and withered grapes before them,
Note by their foot the wheel of melody
That catches and rolls on the sabbath dance.
To drag the steddy prop from failing age,
Break the young stem that fondness twines around,
Widen the solitude of lonely sighs,   60
And scatter to the broad bleak wastes of day
The ruins and the phantoms that replied,
Ne'er be it thine.
  Julian.   Arise, and save me, Spain!

49 wherefor] wherefore *1846*.   51 could not] cannot *1831*, can not *1846*.
58 steddy] steady *1846*. Between *ll.* 61–2 Landor had written, he told Southey,
one line:
    Spectres of bliss and avenues of hope
"the meaning being—and destroy all those scenes of privacy and retirement in which
the wretched raise up those illusions which reply and are correspondent with their
distempered imagination." (Forster, *Landor: a Biography*, i. 292 n.)

ACT I. SCENE 2.

Muza *enters.*

Muza. Infidel chief, thou tarriest here too long,
And art, perhaps, repining at the days
Of nine continued victories, o'er men
Dear to thy soul, tho' reprobate and base.
Away!*
 Julian. I follow. Could my bitterest foes
Hear this! ye Spaniards, this! which I foreknew
And yet encounter'd; could they see your Julian
Receiving orders from and answering
These desperate and heaven-abandoned slaves,

   * Muza retires. [1831, 1846 have *He retires* in text.]

They might perceive some few external pangs,   10
Some glimpses of the hell wherein I move,
Who never have been fathers.
    Opas.   These are they
To whom brave Spaniards must refer their wrongs!
    Julian. Muza, that cruel and suspicious chief,
Distrusts his friends more than his enemies,
Me more than either; fraud he loves and fears,
And watches her still footfall day and night.
    Opas. O Julian! such a refuge! such a race!
    Julian. Calamities like mine alone implore.
No virtues have redeemed them from their bonds;   20
Wily ferocity, keen idleness,
And the close cringes of ill-whispering want,
Educate them to plunder and obey:
Active to serve him best whom most they fear,
They show no mercy to the merciful,
And racks alone remind them of the name.
    Opas. O everlasting curse for Spain and thee!
    Julian. Spain should have vindicated then her wrongs
In mine, a Spaniard's and a soldier's wrongs.
    Opas. Julian, are thine the only wrongs on earth?   30
And shall each Spaniard rather vindicate
Thine than his own? is there no Judge of all?
Shall mortal hand seize with impunity
The sword of vengeance, from the armory
Of the Most High? easy to wield, and starred
With glory it appears; but all the host
Of the archangels, should they strive at once,
Would never close again its widening blade.
    Julian. He who provokes it hath so much to rue.
Where'er he turn, whether to earth or heaven,   40
He finds an enemy, or raises one.
    Opas. I never yet have seen where long success
Hath followed him who warred upon his king.
    Julian. Because the virtue that inflicts the stroke
Dies with him, and the rank ignoble heads
Of plundering faction soon unite again,
And, prince-protected, share the spoil, at rest.

    11 wherein] wherin *1831.*   25 show] shew *1831.*   34 armory] armoury *1846.*

COUNT JULIAN: A TRAGEDY

ACT I. SCENE 3.

Guard announces a Herald. Opas *departs.*

Guard. A messager of peace is at the gate,
My lord, safe access, private audience,
And free return, he claims.
    Julian.   Conduct him in.
A messager of peace!* audacious man!
In what attire appearest thou? a herald's?
Under no garb can such a wretch be safe.
    Roderigo. Thy violence and fancied wrongs I know,
And what thy sacrilegious hands would do,
O traitor and apostate!
    Julian.   What they would
They cannot: thee of kingdom and of life   10
'Tis easy to despoil, thyself the traitor,
Thyself the violator of allegiance.
O would all-righteous Heaven they could restore
The joy of innocence, the calm of age,
The probity of manhood, pride of arms,
And confidence of honour! the august
And holy laws, trampled beneath thy feet.
And Spain! O parent, I have lost thee too!
Yes, thou wilt curse me in thy latter days,
Me, thine avenger. I have fought her foe,   20
Roderigo, I have gloried in her sons,
Sublime in hardihood and piety:
Her strength was mine: I, sailing by her cliffs,
By promontory after promontory,
Opening like flags along some castle-towers,
Have sworn before the cross upon our mast
Ne'er shall invader wave his standard there.
    Roderigo. Yet there thou plantest it, false man, thyself.
    Julian. Accursed he who makes me this reproach,
And made it just! Had I been happy still,   30
I had been blameless: I had died with glory
Upon the walls of Ceuta.
    Roderigo.   Which thy treason
Surrendered to the Infidel.

---

* To Roderigo, who enters as Herald. [*1831, 1846* have: Roderigo *enters as a herald.* between *ll.* 3–4.]

10 cannot] can not *1846.*   25 -towers] -tower *1846.*

DRAMAS AND DRAMATIC SCENES

    Julian.   'Tis hard
And base to live beneath a conqueror;
Yet, amidst all this grief and infamy,
'Tis something to have rushed upon the ranks
In their advance; 'twere something to have stood
Defeat, discomfiture; and, when around
No beacon blazes, no far axle groans
Thro' the wide plain, no sound of sustenance   40
Or succour sooths the still-believing ear,
To fight upon the last dismantled tower,
And yield to valour, if we yield at all.
But rather should my neck lie trampled down
By every Saracen and Moor on earth,
Than my own country see her laws o'erturn'd
By those who should protect them: Sir, no prince
Shall ruin Spain; and, least of all, her own.
Is any just or glorious act in view,
Your oaths forbid it: is your avarice,   50
Or, if there be such, any viler passion
To have its giddy range, and to be gorged,
It rises over all your sacraments,
A hooded mystery, holier than they all.
    Roderigo. Hear me, Don Julian; I have heard thy wrath
Who am thy king, nor heard man's wrath before.
    Julian. Thou shalt hear mine, for thou art not my king.
    Roderigo. Knowest thou not the alter'd face of war?
Xeres is ours; from every region round
True loyal Spaniards throng into our camp: 60
Nay, thy own friends and thy own family,
From the remotest provinces, advance
To crush rebellion: Sisabert is come,
Disclaiming thee and thine; the Asturian hills
Opposed to him their icy chains in vain;
But never wilt thou see him, never more,
Unless in adverse war, and deadly hate.
    Julian. So lost to me! So generous, so deceived!
I grieve to hear it.
    Roderigo.   Come, I offer grace,
Honour, dominion: send away these slaves,   70
Or leave them to our sword, and all beyond
The distant Ebro to the towns of France

35 amidst] amid *1831, 1846.*   36 'Tis] 'Twere *1831, 1846.*   rushed] rusht
1831, 1846.   41 sooths] soothes *1831, 1846.*   65 Opposed] Oppose *1846.*

Shall bless thy name, and bend before thy throne.
I will myself accompany thee, I,
The king, will hail thee brother.
   Julian.   Ne'er shalt thou
Henceforth be king: the nation, in thy name,
May issue edicts, champions may command
The vassal multitudes of marshall'd war,
And the fierce charger shrink before the shouts,
Lower'd as if earth had open'd at his feet,   80
While thy mail'd semblance rises tow'rd the ranks,
But God alone sees thee.
   Roderigo.   What hopest thou?
To conquer Spain, and rule a ravaged land?
To compass me around, to murder me?
   Julian. No, Don Roderigo: swear thou, in the fight
That thou wilt meet me, hand to hand, alone,
That, if I ever save thee from a foe—
   Roderigo. I swear what honour asks—First, to Covilla
Do thou present my crown and dignity.
   Julian. Darest thou offer any price for shame?   90
   Roderigo. Love and repentance.
   Julian.   Egilona lives:
And were she buried with her ancestors,
Covilla should not be the gaze of men,
Should not, despoil'd of honour, rule the free.
   Roderigo. Stern man! her virtues well deserve the throne.
   Julian. And Egilona—what hath she deserved,
The good, the lovely?
   Roderigo.   But the realm in vain
Hoped a succession.
   Julian.   Thou hast torn away
The roots of royalty.
   Roderigo.   For her, for thee.
   Julian. Blind insolence! base insincerity!   100
Power and renown no mortal ever shared
Who could retain, or grasp them, to himself:
And, for Covilla? patience! peace! for her?
She call upon her God, and outrage him
At his own altar! she repeat the vows
She violates in repeating! who abhors
Thee and thy crimes, and wants no crown of thine.
Force may compell the abhorrent soul, or want

     78 marshall'd] marshal'd *1846* .   105 she] *she* 1846.

Lash and pursue it to the public ways;
Virtue looks back and weeps, and may return   110
To these, but never near the abandon'd one
Who drags religion to adultery's feet,
And rears the altar higher for her sake.
 Roderigo. Have then the Saracens possest thee quite,
And wilt thou never yield me thy consent?
 Julian. Never.
 Roderigo. So deep in guilt, in treachery!
Forced to acknowledge it! forced to avow
The traitor!
 Julian. Not to thee, who reignest not,
But to a country ever dear to me,
And dearer now than ever: what we love   120
Is loveliest in departure! One I thought,
As every father thinks, the best of all,
Graceful, and mild, and sensible, and chaste:
Now all these qualities of form and soul
Fade from before me, nor on any one
Can I repose, or be consoled by any.
And yet in this torne heart I love her more
Than I could love her when I dwelt on each,
Or clasped them all united, and thanked God,
Without a wish beyond.—Away, thou fiend!   130
O ignominy, last and worst of all!
I weep before thee—like a child—like mine—
And tell my woes, fount of them all! to thee!

  125 any one] anyone *1846*. 127 torne] torn *1831, 1846*. 129 clasped]
claspt *1831, 1846*. thanked] thankt *1831, 1846*.

ACT I. SCENE 4.

ABDALAZIS *enters.*

 Abdalazis. Julian, to thee, the terror of the faithless,
I bring my father's order, to prepare
For the bright day that crowns thy brave exploits:
Our enemy is at the very gate!
And art thou here, with women in thy train,
Crouching to gain admittance to their lord,
And mourning the unkindness of delay!

    1 terror] terrour *1831*.

COUNT JULIAN: A TRAGEDY

*Julian.** I am prepared: Prince, judge not hastily.
Abdalazis. Whether I should not promise all they ask,
I too could hesitate, tho' earlier taught   10
The duty to obey, and should rejoice
To shelter in the universal storm
A frame so delicate, so full of fears,
So little used to outrage and to arms,
As one of these; so humble, so uncheer'd
At the gay pomp that smooths the track of war:
When she beheld me from afar dismount,
And heard my trumpet, she alone drew back,
And, as tho' doubtful of the help she seeks,
Shudder'd to see the jewels on my brow,   20
And turn'd her eyes away, and wept aloud.
The other stood, awhile, and then advanced:
I would have spoken; but she waved her hand
And said, "*Proceed, protect us, and avenge,
And be thou worthier of the crown thou wearest.*"
Hopeful and happy is indeed our cause,
When the most timid of the lovely hail
Stranger and foe—
   Roderigo.†   And shrink, but to advance.
   Abdalazis. Thou tremblest? whence, O Julian! whence this change?
Thou lovest still thy country.
   Julian.   Abdalazis!   30
All men with human feelings love their country.
Not the high-born or wealthy man alone,
Who looks upon his children, each one led
By its gay hand-maid, from the high alcove,
And hears them once aday; not only he
Who hath forgotten, when his guest inquires
The name of some far village all his own;
Whose rivers bound the province, and whose hills
Touch the last cloud upon the level sky:
No; better men still better love their country.   40
'Tis the old mansion of their earliest friends,
The chapel of their first and best devotions;
When violence, or perfidy, invades,
Or when unworthy lords hold wassail there,

* Julian, much [much *om. 1846*] agitated, goes towards [toward *1846*] the door, and returns. [*Transferred in italics to text 1831, 1846.*]
† Unnoticed by Abdalazis. [*Transferred in italics to text 1831, 1846.*]

35 aday] a day *1831;* a-day *1846.*

And wiser heads are drooping round its moats,
At last they fix their steddy and stiff eye
There, there alone—stand while the trumpet blows,
And view the hostile flames above its towers
Spire, with a bitter and severe delight.

   Abdalazis*. Thou feelest what thou speakest, and thy Spain   50
Will ne'er be shelter'd from her fate by thee.
We, whom the Prophet sends o'er many lands,
Love none above another; Heaven assigns
Their fields and harvests to our valiant swords,
And 'tis enough—we love while we enjoy.
Whence is the man in that fantastic guise?
Suppliant? or herald?—he who stalks about,
And once was even seated while we spoke,
For never came he with us o'er the sea.

   Julian. He comes as herald.

   Roderigo.   Thou shalt know full soon,   60
Insulting Moor.†

   Abdalazis.   He cannot bear the grief
His country suffers; I will pardon him.
He lost his courage first, and then his mind;
His courage rushes back, his mind still wanders.
The guest of heaven was piteous to these men,
And princes stoop to feed them in their courts.

---

  * Taking his hand. [*Transferred in italics to text 1831, 1846.*]
  † Julian intercedes. [*Om. 1831, 1846.*]

---

  46 steddy] steady *1846*.   61 cannot bear] ill endures *1846*.   64 still] yet *1846*.
65 guest of heaven] *sc.* Muhammad. See "Koran", *chap.* 17, and Sale's note. [W.]

ACT I. SCENE 5.

Muza‡ *enters with* Egilona.

   Muza.§ Enter, since 'tis the custom in this land.

   Egilona.‖ Is this our future monarch, or art thou?

   Julian. 'Tis Abdalazis, son of Muza, prince
Commanding Africa, from Abyla
To where Tunisian pilots bend the eye

---

  ‡ Roderigo is going out when Muza enters—starts back on seeing Egilona. [*Substituted for headline 1831, 1846.* out when *om. 1846. After* enters *1831, 1846 have* with Egilona: Roderigo starts back. on . . . Egilona *om. 1831, 1846.*]
  § Sternly, to Egilona, who follows. [1831, 1846 om. footnote and have: *sternly to* Egilona in text.]
  ‖ Passing Muza disdainfully, points to Abdalazis, and says to Julian—[*Transferred in italics to text 1831, 1846.* disdainfully *om. 1846.* and . . . Julian *om. 1846.*]

COUNT JULIAN: A TRAGEDY

O'er ruin'd temples in the glassy wave.
'Till quiet times and ancient laws return,
He comes to govern here.
    Roderigo.   To-morrow's dawn
Proves that.
    Muza.   What art thou?
    *Roderigo.**   King.
    Abdalazis.   Amazement!
    Muza.   Treason!
    Egilona. O horror!
    Muza.   Seize him.
    Egilona.   Spare him! fly to me!   10
    Julian. Urge me not to protect a guest, a herald—
The blasts of war roar over him unfelt.
    Egilona. Ah fly, unhappy!
    Roderigo.   Fly! no, Egilona—
Dost thou forgive me? dost thou love me? still?
    Egilona. I hate, abominate, abhor thee—go,
Or my own vengeance—
    Roderigo.†   Julian!—
    Julian.   Hence, or die.

* Drawing his sword. [*Transferred in italics to text 1831, 1846.*]
† Points with his own to the drawn swords of Muza and Abdalazis, who look with malice towards Julian, takes his hand, and seems inviting to attack them. Julian casts his hand away. [1831, 1846 have in text: *takes (taking* 1831) JULIAN's *hand, invites (and inviting* 1831) *him to attack* MUZA *and* ABDALAZIS; rest of footnote om.]

7 'Till] Till *1846.*

ACT II. SCENE 1.

Camp of JULIAN.

JULIAN *and* COVILLA.

    Julian. Obdurate! I am not as I appear.
Weep, my beloved child, Covilla weep
Into my bosom; every drop be mine
Of this most bitter soul-empoisoning cup:
Into no other bosom than thy father's
Canst thou, or wouldst thou, pour it.
    Covilla.   Cease, my lord,
My father, angel of my youth, when all
Was innocence and peace—
    Julian.   Arise, my love,
Look up to heaven—where else are souls like thine!

171

Mingle in sweet communion with its children,   10
Trust in its providence, its retribution,
And I will cease to mourn; for, O my child,
These tears corrode, but thine assuage the heart.
   Covilla. And never shall I see my mother too,
My own, my blessed mother!
   Julian.   Thou shalt see
Her and thy brothers.
   Covilla.   No! I cannot look
On them, I cannot meet their lovely eyes,
I cannot lift mine up from under theirs.
We all were children when they went away,
They now have fought hard battles, and are men,   20
And camps and kings they know, and woes and crimes.
Sir, will they never venture from the walls
Into the plain? Remember, they are young,
Hardy and emulous and hazardous,
And who is left to guard them in the town?
   Julian. Peace is throughout the land: the various tribes
Of that vast region, sink at once to rest,
Like one wide wood when every wind lies hush'd.
   Covilla. And war, in all its fury, roams o'er Spain!
   Julian. Alas! and will for ages: crimes are loose   30
At which ensanguined War stands shuddering;
And calls for vengeance from the powers above,
Impatient of inflicting it himself.
Nature, in these new horrors, is aghast
At her own progeny, and knows them not.
I am the minister of wrath; the hands
That tremble at me, shall applaud me too,
And seal their condemnation.
   Covilla.   O kind father,
Pursue the guilty, but remember Spain.
   Julian. Child, thou wert in thy nursery short time since,   40
And latterly hast past the vacant hour
Where the familiar voice of history
Is hardly known, however nigh, attuned
In softer accents to the sickened ear;
But thou hast heard, for nurses tell these tales,
Whether I drew my sword for Witiza
Abandoned by the people he betrayed,

---

   ll. 16–18 cannot *ter*] can not *1846.*   28 hush'd] husht *1831, 1846.*   34 horrors]
horrours *1831.*   46 Witiza] *See notes at end of vol.*

COUNT JULIAN: A TRAGEDY

Tho' brother to the woman who of all
Was ever dearest to this broken heart,
Till thou, my daughter, wert a prey to grief,   50
And a brave country brooked the wrongs I bore.
For I had seen Rusilla guide the steps
Of her Theodofred, when burning brass
Plunged its fierce fang into the founts of light,
And Witiza's the guilt! when, bent with age,
He knew the voice again, and told the name,
Of those whose proffer'd fortunes had been laid
Before his throne, while happiness was there,
And strain'd the sightless nerve tow'rds where they stood
At the forced memory of the very oaths   60
He heard renewed from each—but heard afar,
For they were loud, and him the throng spurn'd off.
    Covilla. Who were all these?
    Julian.   All who are seen to-day
On prancing steeds richly caparisoned
In loyal acclamation round Roderigo;
Their sons beside them, loving one another
Unfeignedly, thro' joy, while they themselves
In mutual homage mutual scorn suppress.
Their very walls and roofs are welcoming
The King's approach, their storied tapestry   70
Swells its rich arch for him triumphantly
At every clarion blowing from below.
    Covilla. Such wicked men will never leave his side.
    Julian. For they are insects which see nought beyond
Where they now crawl; whose changes are complete,
Unless of habitation.
    Covilla.   Whither go
Creatures, unfit for better, or for worse?
    Julian. Some to the grave—where peace be with them—some
Across the Pyrenean mountains far,
Into the plains of France; suspicion there   80
Will hang on every step from rich and poor,
Grey quickly-glancing eyes will wrinkle round
And courtesy will watch them, day and night.
Shameless they are, yet will they blush, amidst
A nation that ne'er blushes: some will drag
The captive's chain, repair the shattered bark,

51 brooked] brookt *1831, 1846.* 53 Theodofred] *See notes at end af vol.* 59 tow'rds]
tow'rd *1831, 1846.* 84 amidst] amid *1831, 1846.*

Or heave it, from a quicksand, to the shore,
Among the marbles on the Lybian coast;
Teach patience to the lion in his cage,
And, by the order of a higher slave,   90
Hold to the elephant their scanty fare
To please the children while the parent sleeps.
 Covilla. Spaniards? must they, dear father, lead such lives?
 Julian. All are not Spaniards who draw breath in Spain,
Those are, who live for her, who die for her,
Who love her glory and lament her fall.
O may I too——
 Covilla.   ——But peacefully, and late,
Live and die here!
 Julian.   I have, alas! myself
Laid waste the hopes where my fond fancy strayed,
And view their ruins with unaltered eyes.   100
 Covilla. My mother will at last return to thee.
Might I, once more, but—could I now! behold her.
Tell her—ah me! what was my rash desire?
No, never tell her these inhuman things,
For they would waste her tender heart away
As they waste mine; or tell when I have died,
Only to show her that her every care
Could not have saved, could not have comforted;
That she herself, clasping me once again
To her sad breast, had said, Covilla! go,   110
Go, hide them in the bosom of thy God.
Sweet mother! that far-distant voice I hear,
And, passing out of youth and out of life,
I would not turn at last, and disobey.

88 on] of *1831, 1846.* Lybian] Libyan *1831.* 101 thee] you *1846.* 102 now!]
now? *1831, 1846.* 107 show] shew *1831.*

ACT II. SCENE 2.

SISABERT *enters.*

 Sisabert. Uncle, and is it true, say, can it be,
That thou art leader of these faithless Moors?
That thou impeachest thy own daughter's fame
Thro' the whole land, to seize upon the throne
By the permission of these recreant slaves?
What shall I call thee? art thou, speak Count Julian,
A father, or a soldier, or a man?

5 these] those *1831.*

COUNT JULIAN: A TRAGEDY

Julian. All—or this day had never seen me here.
Sisabert. O falsehood! worse than woman's!
Covilla.   Once, my cousin,
Far gentler words were utter'd from your lips;   10
If you loved me, you loved my father first,
More justly and more steddily, ere love
Was passion and illusion and deceit.
  Sisabert. I boast not that I never was deceived,
Covilla, which beyond all boasts were base,
Nor that I never loved; let this be thine.
Illusions! just to stop us, not delay,
Amuse, not occupy!—too true! when love
Scatters its brilliant foam, and passes on
To some fresh object in its natural course,   20
Widely and openly and wanderingly,
'Tis better! narrow it, and it pours its gloom
In one fierce cataract that stuns the soul.
Ye hate the wretch ye make so, while ye choose
Whoever knows you best and shuns you most.
  Covilla. Shun me then: be beloved, more and more.
Honour the hand that showed you honour first,
Love—O my father! speak, proceed, persuade,
Thy voice alone can utter it—another.
  Sisabert. Ah lost Covilla! can a thirst of power   30
Alter thy heart, thus, to abandon mine,
And change my very nature at one blow.
  Covilla. I told you, dearest Sisabert, 'twas vain
To urge me more, to question, or confute.
  Sisabert. I know it—for another wears the crown
Of Witiza my father; who succeeds
To king Roderigo will succeed to me.
Yet thy cold perfidy still calls me dear,
And o'er my aching temples breathes one gale
Of days departed to return no more.   40
  Julian. Young man, avenge our cause.
  Sisabert.   What cause avenge?
  Covilla. If I was ever dear to you, hear me
Not vengeance; Heaven will give that signal soon.
O Sisabert, the pangs I have endured
On your long absence—

12 steddily] steadily *1846*.   26 me] *me* 1846.   27 showed] shewed *1831*;
show'd *1846*.   28 proceed] procede *1831*.   32 blow.] blow? *1831, 1846*.
36 succeeds] succedes *1831*.   37 succeed] succede *1831*.   42 me] me, *1831, 1846*.

175

Sisabert.   Will be now consoled.
Thy father comes to mount my father's throne;
But though I would not an usurper king,
I prize his valour and defend his crown:
No stranger, and no traitor, rules o'er me,
Or unchastized inveigles humbled Spain.   50
Covilla, gavest thou no promises?
Nor thou, Don Julian? Seek not to reply—
Too well I know, too justly I despise,
Thy false excuse, thy coward effrontery;
Yes, when thou gavest them across the sea,
An enemy wert thou to Mahomet,
And no appellant to his faith or leagues.
   Julian. 'Tis well: a soldier hears, throughout, in silence.
I urge no answer: to those words, I fear,
Thy heart with sharp compunction will reply.   60
   *Sisabert.** Then I demand of thee, before thou reign,
Answer me, while I fought against the Frank
Who dared to sue thee? blazon'd in the court,
Trailed not thro' darkness, were our nuptial bands;
No: Egilona join'd our hands herself,
The peers applauded, and the king approved.
   Julian. Hast thou yet seen that king since thy return?
   Covilla. Father! O father!
   Sisabert.   I will not implore
Of him or thee what I have lost for ever,
These were not, when we parted, thy alarms;   70
Far other, and far worthier of thy heart
Were they! which Sisabert could banish then!
Fear me not, now, Covilla! thou hast changed,
I am changed too—I lived but where thou livedst,
My very life was portioned off from thine.
Upon the surface of thy happiness
Day after day, I gazed, I doated—there
Was all I had, was all I coveted,
So pure, serene, and boundless, it appear'd:
Yet, for we told each other every thought,   80
Thou knowest well, if thou rememberest,
At times I fear'd; as tho' some demon sent

---

   * To Covilla. [*Transferred in italics to text 1831, 1846.*]

---

   47 an] a *1831, 1846.*   64 Trailed not] Not trailed *1831, 1846.*   69 ever,]
ever. *1831, 1846.*   77 doated] doted *1831, 1846.*

Suspicion without form into the world,
To whisper unimaginable things;
Then thy fond arguing banished all but hope,
Each wish, and every feeling, was with thine,
Till I partook thy nature, and became
Credulous, and incredulous, like thee.
We, who have met so alter'd, meet no more.*
Mountains and seas! ye are not separation—   90
Death! thou dividest, but unitest too,
In everlasting peace and faith sincere.
Confiding love! where is thy resting-place!
Where is thy truth, Covilla! where?†—go, go,
I should adore thee and believe thee still.‡
   Covilla. O Heaven! support me, or desert me quite,
And leave me lifeless this too trying hour!
He thinks me faithless.
   Julian.   He must think thee so.
   Covilla. O tell him, tell him all, when I am dead—
He will die too, and we shall meet again.   100
He will know all when these sad eyes are closed.
Ah cannot he before! must I appear
The vilest!—O just Heaven! can it be thus?
I am—all earth resounds it—lost, despised,
Anguish and shame unutterable seize me.
'Tis palpable—no phantom, no delusion,
No dream that wakens with o'erwhelming horror;
Spaniard and Moor fight on this ground alone,
And tear the arrow from my bleeding breast
To pierce my father's, for alike they fear.   110
   Julian. Invulnerable now, and unassail'd
Are we, alone perhaps of human kind,
Nor life allures us more, nor death alarms.
   Covilla. Fallen, unpitied, unbelieved, unheard!
I should have died long earlier: gracious God!
Desert me to my sufferings, but sustain
My faith in thee! O hide me from the world,
And from thyself, my father, from thy fondness,

---

  * Takes her hand. [*om. 1831, 1846.*]
  † She attempts, but is unable, to speak. [*om. 1831, 1846.*]
  ‡ Sisabert goes. [Sisabert *om. 1831, 1846 which transfer* Goes. *in italics to text.*]

---

  85 banished] banisht *1831, 1846.*   94 Covilla! where?] Covilla! where! *1831*;
Covilla? where? *1846.*   95 adore ... believe] believe ... adore *1846.*   102 can-
not] can not *1846.*   107 horror] horrour *1831.*   111 now ... unassail'd],un-
assailable *1831, 1846.*   118 thyself ... thy] yourself ... your *1846.*

That opened in this wilderness of woe
A source of tears that else had burst my heart,   120
Setting me free for ever—then perhaps
A cruel war had not divided Spain,
Had not o'erturned her cities and her altars,
Had not endanger'd thee! O haste afar
Ere the last dreadful conflict that decides
Whether we live beneath a foreign sway——
   Julian. Or under him whose tyranny brought down
The curse upon his people. O child! child!
Urge me no further, talk not of the war,
Remember not our country.
   Covilla.   Not remember!   130
What have the wretched else for consolation,
What else have they who pining feed their woe?
Can I, or should I, drive from memory
All that was dear and sacred, all the joys
Of innocence and peace; when no debate
Was in the convent, but what hymn, whose voice,
To whom among the blessed it arose,
Swelling so sweet; when rang the vesper-bell
And every finger ceased from the guitar,
And every tongue was silent through our land;   140
When, from remotest earth, friends met again
Hung on each other's neck, and but embraced,
So sacred, still, and peaceful, was the hour.
Now, in what climate of the wasted world,
Not unmolested long by the profane,
Can I pour forth in secrecy to God
My prayers and my repentance? where beside
Is the last solace of the parting soul?
Friends, brethren, parents—dear indeed, too dear,
Are they, but somewhat still the heart requires   150
That it may leave them lighter, and more blest.
   Julian. Wide are the regions of our far-famed land:
Thou shalt arrive at her remotest bounds,
See her best people, choose some holiest house—
Whether where Castro * from surrounding vines
Hears the hoarse ocean roar among his caves,

   * In Asturia, bordering on Biscay. [*om. 1831, 1876.*]

---

120 that] .. it *1831, 1846.*   124 thee] you *1846.*   126 foreign] forein *1831.*
139 ceased] ceast *1831, 1846.*   147 beside] besides *1831.*   150 still] yet *1846.*

And, thro' the fissure in the green church-yard,
The wind wail loud the calmest summer day;
Or where Santona leans against the hill,
Hidden from sea and land by groves and bowers.   160

    Covilla. O! for one moment, in those pleasant scenes
Thou placest me, and lighter air I breathe;
Why could I not have rested, and heard on!
Thy voice dissolves the vision quite away,
Outcast from virtue, and from nature too!

    Julian. Nature and virtue!—they shall perish first.
God destined them for thee, and thee for them,
Inseparably and eternally!
The wisest and the best will prize thee most,
And solitudes and cities will contend   170
Which shall receive thee kindliest; sigh not so—
Violence and fraud will never penetrate
Where piety and poverty retire,
Intractable to them, and valueless,
And look'd at idly, like the face of heaven.
If strength be wanted for security,
Mountains the guard, forbidding all approach
With iron-pointed and uplifted gates,
Thou wilt be welcome too in Aguilar*—
Impenetrable, marble-turreted,   180
Surveying from aloft the limpid ford,
The massive fane, the sylvan avenue—
Whose hospitality I proved myself,
A willing leader in no impious war
When fame and freedom urged me—or mayst dwell
In Reÿnosas dry and thriftless dale,
Unharvested beneath october moons,
Amongst those frank and cordial villagers.
They never saw us, and, poor simple souls!
So little know they whom they call the great—   190
Would pity one another less than us
In injury, disaster, or distress.

    Covilla. But they would ask each other whence our grief,
That they might pity?

    Julian.   Rest then just beyond,

   * Del Campo, in Castile. [*om. 1831, 1846.*]

---

164 Thy] ? *mispr. 1831, 1846,* have My.   175 look'd] lookt *1831, 1846.*
186 Reÿnosas] Reynosas *1831;* Reÿnosa's *1846.*   187 october] October *1846.*
188 Amongst] Among *1831, 1846.*   194 pity?] pity. *1831, 1846.*

In the secluded scenes where Ebro springs
And drives not from his fount the fallen leaf,
So motionless and tranquil its repose.
   Covilla. Thither let us depart, and speedily.
   Julian. I cannot go: I live not in the land
I have reduced beneath such wretchedness: 200
And who could leave the brave, whose lives and fortunes
Hang on his sword?
   Covilla.   Me canst thou leave, my father?
Ah yes, for it is past; too well thou seest
My life and fortunes rest not upon thee.
Long, happily,—could it be gloriously!—
Still mayst thou live, and save thy country still!
   Julian. Unconquerable land! unrivalled race!
Whose bravery, too enduring, rues alike
The power and weakness of accursed kings—
How cruelly hast thou neglected me!   210
Forcing me from thee, never to return,
Nor in thy pangs and struggles to partake!
I hear a voice—'tis Egilona—come,
Recall thy courage, dear unhappy girl,
Let us away.

    199 cannot] can not *1846.*   202 canst thou] thou canst *1831, 1846.*   207 unrivalled] unrival'd *1831, 1846.*

ACT II. SCENE 3.

Egilona *enters.*

   Egilona.   Remain, I order thee.
Attend, and do thy duty; I am queen,
Unbent to degradation.
   Covilla.   I attend
Ever most humbly and most gratefully
My too kind sovran, cousin now no more;
Could I perform but half the services
I owe her, I were happy, for a time,
Or dared I show her half my love, 'twere bliss.
   Egilona. Oh! I sink under gentleness like thine.
Thy sight is death to me; and yet 'tis dear.   10
The gaudy trappings of assumptive state
Drop, at the voice of nature, to the earth,
Before thy feet—I cannot force myself

    8 show] shew *1831.*   13 cannot] can not *1846.*

To hate thee, to renounce thee; yet—Covilla!
Yet—O distracting thought! 'tis hard to see,
Hard to converse with, to admire, to love,
As from my soul I do, and must do, thee—
One who hath robbed me of all pride and joy,
All dignity, all fondness.—I adored*
Roderigo—he was brave, and in discourse   20
Most voluble; the masses of his mind†
Were vast, but varied; now absorbed in gloom,
Majestic, not austere; now their extent
Opening, and waving in bright levity—
    Julian. Depart, my daughter—'twere as well to bear
His presence as his praise‡—go; she will dream
This phantasm out, nor notice thee depart. §
    Egilona. What pliancy! what tenderness! what life!
O for the smiles of those who smile so seldom,
The love of those who know no other love!   30
Such he was, Egilona, who was thine.
    Julian. While he was worthy of the realm and thee.
    Egilona. Can it be true, then, Julian, that thy aim
Is sovranty? not virtue, nor revenge?
    Julian. I swear to heaven, nor I, nor child of mine,
Ever shall mount to this polluted throne.
    Egilona. Then am I still a queen. The savage Moor
Who could not conquer Ceuta from thy sword,
In his own country, not with every wile
Of his whole race, not with his myriad crests   40
Of cavalry, seen from the Calpian heights
Like locusts on the parched and gleamy coast,
Will never conquer Spain.
    Julian.   Spain then was conquer'd
When fell her laws before the traitor king.

---

  * After a pause. [*This and next two footnotes om. 1831, 1846.*]
  † She walks about, and speaks by fits and abstractedly.
  ‡ Covilla hesitates.
  § She departs. [1831, 1846 have in text: Covilla *goes.*]

---

  18 robbed] rob'd *1831;* robb'd *1846.*   37 still] yet *1846.*   41 heights]
hights *1831;* highths *1846.*   42 parched] parcht *1831, 1846.*

DRAMAS AND DRAMATIC SCENES

ACT II. SCENE 4.

Officer announces OPAS.

O queen, the metropolitan attends
On matters of high import to the state,
And wishes to confer in privacy.
    *Egilona.** Adieu then; and whate'er betide the country,
Sustain at least the honours of our house.†
    Opas. I cannot but commend, O Egilona,
Such resignation and such dignity.
Indeed he is unworthy; yet a queen
Rather to look for peace, and live remote
From cities, and from courts, and from her lord,   10
I hardly could expect, in one so young,
So early, widely, wondrously, admired.
    Egilona. I am resolved: religious men, good Opas,
In this resemble the vain libertine;
They find in woman no consistency,
No virtue but devotion, such as comes
To infancy or age, or fear or love,
Seeking a place of rest, and finding none,
Until it soar to heaven.
    Opas.   A spring of mind
That rises when all pressure is removed,   20
Firmness in pious and in chaste resolves,
But weakness in much fondness; these, O queen,
I did expect, I own.
    Egilona.   The better part
Be mine; the worst hath been; and is no more.
    Opas. But if Roderigo have at length prevail'd
That Egilona willingly resigns
All claim to royalty, and casts away,
—Indifferent or estranged—the marriage bond
His perjury tore asunder, still the church
Hardly can sanction his new nuptial rites.   30
    Egilona. What art thou saying? what new nuptial rites?
    Opas. Thou knowest not?
    Egilona.   Am I a wife; a queen?

* To Julian. [*This and next footnote transferred to text 1831, 1846.*]
† Julian goes before Opas enters.

---

2 matters] matter *1846.*   6 cannot] can not *1846.*   13 resolved] resolv'd
1831, 1846.   24 worst] worse *1846.*

COUNT JULIAN: A TRAGEDY

Abandon it! my claim to royalty!
Whose hand was on my head when I arose
Queen of this land? whose benediction sealed
My marriage-vow? who broke it? was it I?
And wouldst thou, virtuous Opas, wouldst thou dim
The glorious light of thy declining days?
Wouldst thou administer the sacred vows,
And sanction them, and bless them, for another,   40
And bid her live in peace while I am living?
Go then—I execrate and banish him
For ever from my sight: we were not born
For happiness together—none on earth
Were ever so dissimilar as we.
He is not worth a tear, a wish, a thought—
Never was I deceived in him—I found
No tenderness, no fondness, from the first:
A love of power, a love of perfidy,
Such is the love that is returned for mine.   50
Ungrateful man! 'twas not the pageantry
Of regal state, the clarions, nor the guard,
Nor loyal valour, nor submissive beauty,
Silence at my approach, awe at my voice,
Happiness at my smile, that led my youth
Towards Roderigo! I had lived obscure,
In humbleness, in poverty, in want,
Blest, O supremely blest! with him alone;
And he abandons me, rejects me, scorns me,
Insensible! inhuman! for another!   60
Thou shalt repent thy wretched choice, false man!
Crimes such as thine call loudly for perdition;
Heaven will inflict it, and not I—but I
Neither will fall alone nor live despised.
  *Opas.** Peace, Egilona, he arrives; compose
Thy turbid thoughts, meet him with dignity.
  Egilona. He! in the camp of Julian! trust me, sir,
He comes not hither, dares no longer use
The signs of state, and flies from every foe.†

---

  * Sound of trumpet. [1831, 1846 have in text: *A trumpet sounds.*]
  † Egilona retires some distance. [*1831, 1846 om.* Egilona, *and have* Retires . . .
distance *in text.*]

---

56 Towards] Toward *1831, 1846.*

DRAMAS AND DRAMATIC SCENES

ACT II. SCENE 5.

MUZA *and* ABDALAZIS.

*Muza.** I saw him but an instant, and disguised,
Yet this is not the traitor; on his brow
Observe the calm of wisdom and of years.
 Opas. Whom seekest thou?
 Muza.   Him who was king, I seek.
He came arrayed as herald to this tent.
 Abdalazis. Thy daughter! was she nigh? perhaps for her
Was this disguise.
 Muza.   Here, Abdalazis, kings
Disguise from other causes; they obtain
Beauty by violence, and power by fraud.
Treason was his intent: we must admit   10
Whoever come; our numbers are too small
For question or selection, and the blood
Of Spaniards shall win Spain for us, today.
 Abdalazis. The wicked cannot move from underneath
Thy ruling eye.
 Muza.   Right!—Julian and Roderigo
Are leagued against us, on these terms alone,
That Julian's daughter weds the christian king.
 Egilona.† 'Tis true—and I proclaim it—
 Abdalazis.   Heaven and earth!
Was it not thou, most lovely, most high-souled,
Who wishedst us success, and me a crown?   20
 Egilona.‡ I give it—I am Egilona, queen
Of that detested man.
 Abdalazis.   I touch the hand
That chains down fortune to the throne of fate;
And will avenge thee; for 'twas thy command,
'Tis Heaven's—My father! what retards our bliss?
Why art thou silent?
 Muza.   Inexperienced years
Rather would rest on the soft lap, I see,
Of pleasure, after the fierce gusts of war.

---

  * To Abdalazis. [*Transferred to text 1831, 1846.*]
  † Turning round, and rushing forward. [1831, 1846 have in text: *rushing forward.*]
  ‡ Opas, in astonishment, goes abruptly. [1831, 1846 have in text: OPAS *goes abruptly.*]

  Headline. [*Before* MUZA *1831, 1846 have: Enter.*]   13 today] to-day *1846.*
14 cannot] can not *1846.*   18 proclaim] proclame *1831.*

184

O destiny! that callest me alone,
Hapless, to keep the toilsome watch of state;   30
Painful to age, unnatural to youth,
Adverse to all society of friends,
Equality, and liberty, and ease,
The welcome cheer of the unbidden feast,
The gay reply, light, sudden, like the leap
Of the young forester's unbended bow;
But, above all, to tenderness at home,
And sweet security of kind concern
Even from those who seem most truly ours.
Who would resign all this, to be approach'd,   40
Like a sick infant by a canting nurse,
To spread his arms in darkness, and to find
One universal hollowness around.
Forego, a little while, that bane of peace.
Love may be cherished.
 Abdalazis.   'Tis enough; I ask
No other boon.
 Muza. Not victory?
 Abdalazis.   Farewell,
O queen! I will deserve thee; why do tears
Silently drop, and slowly, down thy veil?
I shall return to worship thee, and soon;
Why this affliction? O, that I alone   50
Could raise or could repress it!
 Egilona.   We depart,
Nor interrupt your counsels, nor impede;
O, may they prosper, whatsoe'er they be,
And perfidy soon meet its just reward!
The infirm and peaceful Opas—whither gone?
 Muza. Stay, daughter; not for counsel are we met,
But to secure our arms from treachery,
O'erthrow and stifle base conspiracies,
Involve in his own toils our false allie—
 Egilona. Author of every woe I have endur'd!   60
Ah sacrilegious man! he vowed to heaven
None of his blood should ever mount the throne.
 Muza. Herein his vow indeed is ratified;
Yet faithful ears have heard this offer made,
And weighty was the conference that ensued,

40 approach'd] approacht *1831, 1846.* 44 Forego] Forgo *1831.* 45 cherished]
cherisht *1831, 1846.* 59 allie] ally *1846.* 60 endur'd] endured *1831.*

And long—not dubious—for what mortal e'er
Refus'd alliance with illustrious power?
Tho' some have given its enjoyments up,
Tired and enfeebled by satiety.
His friends and partisans, 'twas his pretence, 70
Should pass uninterrupted; hence his camp
Is open, every day, to enemies.
You look around, O queen, as tho' you fear'd
Their entrance—Julian I pursue no more;
You conquer him—return we; I bequeath
Ruin, extermination, not reproach.
How we may best attain your peace and will
We must consider in some other place,
Not, lady, in the midst of snares and wiles
How to supplant your charms and seize your crown. 80
I * rescue it, fear not: yes, we retire. †
Whatever is your wish becomes my own,
Nor is there in this land but who obeys. ‡

* He takes her hand. [*om. 1831, 1846.*]
† She is reluctant to go with him. [*om. 1831, 1846.*]
‡ Sternly—he leads her away. [1831, 1846 have in text: *He leads her away.*]

67 Refus'd] Refused *1831, 1846.*   70 pretence] pretense *1831.*   74 entrance]
enterance *1831.*

ACT III. SCENE 1.

Palace in XERES.

RODERIGO *and* OPAS.

Roderigo. Impossible! she could not thus resign
Me, for a miscreant of Barbary,
A mere adventurer—but that citron face
Shall bleach and shrivel the whole winter long
There, on yon cork-tree by the sallyport.
She shall return.
  Opas.   To fondness and to faith?
Dost thou retain them, if she could return?
  Roderigo. Retain them? she has forfeited by this
All right to fondness, all to royalty.
  Opas. Consider, and speak calmly: she deserves 10
Some pity, some reproof.
  Roderigo.   To speak then calmly,
Since thine eyes open and can see her guilt—

186

COUNT JULIAN: A TRAGEDY

—Infamous and atrocious! let her go—
Chains—
    Opas. What! in Muza's camp?
    Roderigo.   My scorn supreme!
    Opas. Say, pity.
    Roderigo.   Aye, aye, pity—that suits best.
I loved her, but *had* loved her; three whole years
Of pleasure, and of varied pleasure too,
Had worne the soft impression half away.
What I once felt, I would recall; the faint
Responsive voice grew fainter each reply: 20
Imagination sunk amid the scenes
It labour'd to create; the vivid joy
Of fleeting youth I followed, and posest.
'Tis the first moment of the tenderest hour,
'Tis the first mien on entering new delights,
We give our peace, our power, our souls, for these.
    Opas. Thou hast; and what remains?
    Roderigo.   Myself—Roderigo—
Whom hatred cannot reach, nor love cast down.
    Opas. Nor gratitude nor pity nor remorse
Call back, nor vows nor earth nor heaven controul.   30
But art thou free and happy? art thou safe?
By shrewd contempt the humblest may chastize
Whom scarlet and its ermine cannot scare,
And the sword skulks for everywhere in vain.
Thee the poor victim of thy outrages,
Woman, with all her weakness, may despise.
    Roderigo. But first let quiet age have intervened.
    Opas. N'er will the peace or apathy of age
Be thine, or twilight steal upon thy day.
The violent choose, but cannot change, their end—   40
Violence, by man or nature, must be theirs;
Thine it must be, and who to pity thee?
    Roderigo. Behold my solace! none. I want no pity.
    Opas. Proclaim we those the happiest of mankind
Who never knew a want? O what a curse
To thee this utter ignorance of thine!
Julian, whom all the good commiserate,

---

18 worne] worn *1846.*   21 sunk] sank *1831, 1846.*   23 posest] possest *1831,*
1846.   27 Myself—Roderigo—] Roderigo: one *1846.*   28 cannot] can not *1846.*
32 chastize] chastise *1831, 1846.*   33, 40 cannot] can not *1846.*   44 Proclaim]
Proclame *1831.*

Sees thee below him far in happiness:
A state indeed of no quick restlesness,
No glancing agitation—one vast swell 50
Of melancholy, deep, impassable,
Interminable, where his spirit alone
Broods and o'ershadows all, bears him from earth
And purifies his chasten'd soul for heaven.
Both heaven and earth shall from thy grasp recede.
Whether on death or life thou arguest,
Untutor'd savage or corrupted heathen
Avows no sentiment so vile as thine.
    Roderigo. Nor feels?
    Opas.   O human nature! I have heard
The secrets of the soul, and pitied thee. 60
Bad and accursed things have men confest
Before me, but have left them unarrayed,
Naked, and shivering with deformity.
The troubled dreams and deafening gush of youth
Fling o'er the fancy, struggling to be free,
Discordant and impracticable things:
If the good shudder at their past escapes,
Shall not the wicked shudder at their crimes?
They shall—and I denounce upon thy head
God's vengeance—thou shalt rule this land no more. 70
    Roderigo. What! my own kindred leave me, and renounce me!
    Opas. Kindred? and is there any in our world
So near us, as those sources of all joy,
Those on whose bosom every gale of life
Blows softly, who reflect our images
In loveliness through sorrows and through age,
And bear them onward far beyond the grave.
    Roderigo. Methinks, most reverend Opas, not inapt
Are these fair views; arise they from Seville?
    Opas. He, who can scoff at them, may scoff at me. 80
Such are we, that the giver of all good
Shall, in the heart he purifies, posess
The latest love—the earliest, no, not there!
I've known the firm and faithful; even from these
Life's eddying spring shed the first bloom on earth.
I pity them, but ask their pity too.

---

49 restlesness] restlessness *1846.*   61 confest] confess'd *1846.*   81 giver . . .
good] Giver . . . Good *1846.*   82 posess] possess *1831, 1846.*   84 these]
them *1846.*

I love the happiness of men, and praise
And sanctify the blessings I renounce.
   Roderigo. Yet would thy baleful influence undermine
The heaven-appointed throne.
   Opas.   —the throne of guilt   90
Obdurate, without plea, without remorse.
   Roderigo. What power hast thou? perhaps thou soon wilt want
A place of refuge.
   Opas.   Rather say, perhaps
My place of refuge will receive me soon:
Could I extend it even to thy crimes,
It should be open; but the wrath of heaven
Turns them against thee, and subverts thy sway;
It leaves thee not, what wickedness and woe
Oft in their drear communion taste together,
Hope and repentance.
   Roderigo.   But it leaves me arms,   100
Vigour of soul and body, and a race
Subject by law, and dutiful by choice,
Whose hand is never to be holden fast
Within the closing cleft of knarled creeds;
No easy prey for these vile mitred Moors.
I, who received thy homage, may retort
Thy threats, vain prelate, and abase thy pride.
   Opas. Low must be those whom mortal can sink lower,
Nor high are they whom human power may raise.
   Roderigo. Judge now: for, hear the signal.
   Opas.   And derides   110
Thy buoyant heart the dubious gulphs of war?
Trumpets may sound, and not to victory.
   Roderigo. The traitor and his daughter feel my power.
   Opas. Just God! avert it!
   Roderigo.   Seize this rebel priest.
I will alone subdue my enemies.

   104 knarled] gnarled *1846.*   111 gulphs] gulfs *1831.*   115 *after* enemies.
1831, 1846 have: [*Goes out.*

ACT III. SCENE 2.

RAMIRO *and* OSMA *enter from opposite sides.*

   Ramiro. Where is the king? his car is at the gate,
His ministers attend him, but his foes
Are yet more prompt, nor will await delay.

Osma. Nor need they—for he meets them as I speak—
Ramiro. With all his forces—or our cause is lost.
Julian and Sisabert surround the walls—
    Osma. Surround, sayst thou? enter they not the gates?
    Ramiro. Perhaps ere now they enter.
    Osma.   Sisabert
Brings him our prisoner.
    Ramiro.   They are friends! they held
A parley; and the soldiers, when they saw   10
Count Julian, lower'd their arms and hail'd him king.
    Osma. How? and he leads them in the name of king?
    Ramiro. He leads them; but amidst that acclamation
He turn'd away his head, and called for vengeance.
    Osma. In Sisabert, and in the cavalry
He led, were all our hopes.
    Opas.   Woe, woe is theirs
Who have no other.
    Osma.   What are thine? obey
The just commands of our offended king,
Conduct him to the tower*—off—instantly.
Ramiro, let us haste to reinforce—   20
    Ramiro. Hark! is the king defeated? hark!
    Osma.   I hear
Such acclamation as from victory
Arises not, but rather from revolt,
Reiterated, interrupted, lost.
Favour like this his genius will retrieve
By time, or promises, or chastisement,
Which-e'er he choose—the speediest is the best—
His danger and his glory let us share;
'Tis ours to serve him.
    Ramiro.   While he rules, 'tis ours.
What chariot-wheels are thundering o'er the bridge?   30
    Osma. Roderigo's—I well know them.
    Ramiro.   Now, the burst
Of acclamation! now! again—again.
    Osma. I know the voices; they are for Roderigo.
    Ramiro. Stay, I entreat thee—one hath now prevailed.
So far is certain.
    Osma.   Aye, the right prevails.

    * Guard hesitates. Opas goes. [*Transferred in italics to text 1831, 1846.*]

---

    5 forces—] forces? *1831, 1846.*   13 amidst] amid *1831, 1846.*   27 Which-
e'er] Whiche'er *1846.*   35 Aye] Ay *1831, 1846.*

COUNT JULIAN: A TRAGEDY

Ramiro. Transient and vain their joyance, who rejoice
Precipitately and intemperately,
And bitter thoughts grow up where'er it fell.
    Osma. Nor vain and transient theirs, who idly float
Down popularity's unfertile stream   40
And fancy all their own that rises round?
    Ramiro. If thou still lovest, as I know thou dost,
Thy king——
    *Osma.**   I love him; for he owes me much
Brave soul, and cannot, though he would, repay.
Service and faith, pure faith and service hard,
Throughout his reign, if these things be desert,
These have I borne toward him, and still bear.
    Ramiro. Come, from thy solitary eiry come,
And share the prey so plenteous and profuse
Which a less valourous brood will else consume.   50
Much fruit is shaken down in civil storms,
And shall not orderly and loyal hands
Gather it up? Again!† and still refuse?
How different are those citizens without
From thee! from thy serenity! thy arch,
Thy firmament, of intrepidity!
For their new lord, whom they have never served,
Afraid were they to shout, and only struck
The pavement with their ferrels and their feet;
Now they are certain of the great event   60
Voices and hands they raise, and all contend
Who shall be bravest in applauding most.
Knowest thou these?
    Osma.   Their voices I know well—
And can they shout for him they would have slain?
A prince untried they welcome; soon their doubts
Are blown afar!
    Ramiro.   Yes, brighter scenes arise.
The disunited he alone unites,
The weak with hope he strengthens, and the strong
With justice.
    Osma.   Wait: praise him when time hath given
A soundness and consistency to praise: 70

* Interrupting. [*om. 1831, 1846.*]
† Loud shouts. [*Transferred in italics to text 1831, 1846.*]

42 still] yet *1846.*   44 cannot] can not *1846.*   48 eiry] eyrie *1846.*   50 valourous]
valorous *1831, 1846.*   53 still] stil *1831;* yet *1846.*

He shares it amply who bestows it right.
    Ramiro. Doubtest thou?
    Osma.   Be it so: let us away;
New courtiers come—
    Ramiro.   And why not join the new.
Let us attend him, and congratulate;
Come on, they enter.
    Osma.   This is now my post
No longer: I could face them in the field,
I cannot here.
    Ramiro.   Tomorrow all may change;
Be comforted.
    Osma.   I want nor change nor comfort.
    Ramiro. The prisoner's voice!
    Osma.   The metropolitans?
Triumph he may—not over me forgiven.   80
This way, and thro' the chapel—none are there.

    77 cannot] can not *1846.*   79 metropolitans] metropolitan's *1831, 1846.*
After l. 81 1831, 1846 have [Goes out.

ACT III. SCENE 3.

OPAS *and* SISABERT.

    Opas. The royal threat still sounds along these halls:
Hardly his foot hath past them, and he flees
From his own treachery—all his pride, his hopes,
Are scatter'd at a breath; even courage fails
Now falsehood sinks from under him: behold,
Again art thou where reign'd thy ancestors;
Behold the chapel of thy earliest prayers,
Where I, whose chains are sunder'd at thy sight
Ere they could close around these aged limbs,
Received and blest thee, when thy mother's arm   10
Was doubtful if it loosed thee! with delight
Have I observed the promises we made
Deeply imprest and manfully perform'd.
Now, to thyself beneficent, O prince,
Never henceforth renew those weak complaints
Against Covilla's vows and Julian's faith,
His honour broken, and her heart estranged.
O, if thou holdest peace or glory dear,
Away with jealousy—brave Sisabert,

Smite from thy bosom, smite that scorpion down; 20
It swells and hardens amid mildewed hopes,
O'erspreads and blackens whate'er most delights,
And renders us, haters of loveliness,
The lowest of the fiends: ambition led
The higher on, furious to dispossess,
From admiration sprung and phrenzied love.
This disingenuous soul-debasing passion,
Rising from abject and most sordid fear,
Stings her own breast with bitter self-reproof,
Consumes the vitals, pines, and never dies. 30
Love, Honour, Justice, numberless the forms,
Glorious and high the stature, she assumes;
But watch the wandering changeful mischief well,
And thou shalt see her with low lurid light
Search where the soul's most valued treasure lies,
Or, more embodied to our vision, stand
With evil eye, and sorcery hers alone,
Looking away her helpless progeny,
And drawing poison from its very smiles.
For Julian's truth have I not pledged my own? 40
Have I not sworne Covilla weds no other?
   Sisabert. Her persecutor have not I chastized,
Have not I fought for Julian, won the town,
And liberated thee?
   Opas.   But left for him
The dangers of pursuit, of ambuscade,
Of absence from thy high and splendid name.
   Sisabert. Do probity and truth want such supports?
   Opas. Gryphens and eagles, ivory and gold,
Can add no clearness to the lamp above,
But many look for them in palaces 50
Who have them not, and want them not, at home.
Virtue and valour and experience
Are never trusted by themselves alone
Further than infancy and idiocy;
The men around him, not the man himself,
Are looked at, and by these is he prefer'd:
'Tis the green mantle of the warrener
And his loud whistle, that alone attract

---

23 us,] us *1831.*   25 dispossess] dispossess *1846.*   26 phrenzied] frenzied
1831, 1846.   29 *om. 1846.   ll.* 31–9 *om. 1846.*   41 sworne] sworn *1831, 1846.*
56 looked] lookt *1831, 1846.*   prefer'd:] preferr'd. *1846.*

The lofty gazes of the noble herd:
And thus, without thy countenance and help,   60
Feeble and faint is still our confidence,
Brief perhaps our success.
    Sisabert.   Should I resign
To Abdalazis her I once adored?
He truly, he must wed a Spanish queen!
He rule in Spain! ah! whom could any land
Obey so gladly as the meek, the humble,
The friend of all who have no friend beside,
Covilla! could he choose, or could he find
Another who might so confirm his power?
And now, indeed, from long domestic wars   70
Who else survives of all our ancient house—
    Opas. But Egilona.
    Sisabert.   Vainly she upbraids
Roderigo.
    Opas.   She divorces him, abjures,
And carries vengeance to that hideous highth
Which piety and chastity would shrink
To look from, on the world, or on themselves.
    Sisabert. She may forgive him yet.
    Opas.   Ah Sisabert!
Wretched are those a woman has forgiven;
With her forgiveness ne'er hath love return'd:
Ye know not, till too late, the filmy tie   80
That holds heaven's precious boon, eternally
To those who fondly cherish her; once go
Driven by mad passion, strike but at her peace,
And, tho' she step aside from broad reproach,
Yet every softer virtue dies away.
Beaming with virtue inaccessible
Stood Egilona; for her lord she lived,
And for the heavens that raised her sphere so high:
All thoughts were on her—all, beside her own.
Negligent as the blossoms of the field,   90
Arrayed in candour and simplicity,
Before her path she heard the streams of joy
Murmur her name in all their cadences,
Saw them in every scene, in light, in shade,

61 still] yet *1846.*   67 beside] besides *1831.*   80 till] til *1831.*   82 those who] such as *1831, 1846.*   84 tho'] tho *1831;* though *1846.*   91 Arrayed] Array'd *1846.*

Reflect her image—but acknowledged them
Hers most complete when flowing from her most.
All things in want of her, herself of none,
Pomp and dominion lay beneath her feet
Unfelt and unregarded: now behold
The earthly passions war against the heavenly!   100
Pride against love, ambition and revenge
Against devotion and compliancy—
Her glorious beams adversity hath blunted,
And coming nearer to our quiet view
The original clay of coarse mortality
Hardens and flaws around her.
    Sisabert.   Every germ
Of virtue perishes, when love recedes
From those hot shifting sands, the female heart.
    Opas. His was the fault; be his the punishment.
'Tis not their own crimes only, men commit,   110
They harrow them into another's breast,
And they shall reap the bitter growth with pain.
    *Sisabert.** Yes, blooming royalty will first attract
These creatures of the desert—now I breathe
More freely—she is theirs if I pursue
The fugitive again—he well deserves
The death he flies from—stay! don Julian twice
Called him aloud, and he, methinks, replied.
Could not I have remain'd a moment more,
And seen the end? altho' with hurried voice   120
He bade me intercept the scattered foes,
And hold the city barred to their return.
May Egilona be another's wife
Whether he die or live! but oh!†—Covilla—
She never can be mine! yet she may be
Still happy—no, Covilla, no—not happy,
But more deserving happiness without it.
Mine never! nor another's—'tis enough.
The tears I shed no rival can deride;
In the fond intercourse, a name once cherished   130
Will never be defended by faint smiles,
Nor given up with vows of alter'd love.

* Walking up and down, abstractedly. [*om. 1831, 1846.*]
† Aloud, to Opas. [*om. 1831, 1846.*]

95 acknowledged] acknowledge *1846.*   120 altho'] altho *1831;* although *1846.*
130 cherished] cherisht *1831, 1846.*

And is the passion of my soul at last
Reduced to this? is this my happiness?
This my sole comfort? this the close of all
Those promises, those tears, those last adieus,
And those long vigils for the morrow's dawn.
 Opas. Arouse thee! be thyself. O Sisabert,
Awake to glory from these feverish dreams;
The enemy is in our land—two enemies—   140
We must quell both—shame on us, if we fail.
 Sisabert. Incredible; a nation be subdued
Peopled as ours!
 Opas.   Corruption may subvert
What force could never.
 Sisabert.   Traitors may.
 Opas.   Alas!
If traitors can, the basis is but frail.
I mean such traitors as the vacant world
Echoes most stunningly; not fur-robed knaves
Whose whispers raise the dreaming bloodhound's ear
Against benighted famished wanderers;
While with remorseless guilt they undermine   150
Palace and shed, their very father's house,
O blind! their own and children's heritage,
To leave more ample space for fearful wealth.
Plunder in some most harmless guise they swathe,
Call it some very meek and hallowed name,
Some known and borne by their good forefathers,
And own and vaunt it thus redeem'd from sin.
These are the plagues heaven sends o'er every land
Before it sink—the portents of the street,
Not of the air—lest nations should complain   160
Of distance or of dimness in the signs,
Flaring from far to Wisdom's eye alone:
These are the last! these, when the sun rides high
In the forenoon of doomsday, revelling,
Make men abhor the earth, arraign the skies.
Ye who behold them spoil field after field,
Despising them in individual strength,
Not with one torrent sweeping them away
Into the ocean of eternity,
Arise! despach! no renovating gale,   170

149 famished] famisht *1831, 1846.*   152 own and] own, their *1831, 1846.*
170 despach] despatch *1846.*

No second spring awaits you—up, begone,
—If you have force and courage even for flight—
The blast of dissolution is behind.
    Sisabert. How terrible! how true! what voice like thine
Can rouse and warn the nation! if she rise,
Say, whither go, where stop we?
    Opas.   God will guide.
Let us pursue the oppressor to destruction,
The rest is heaven's: must we move no step
Because we cannot see the boundaries
Of our long way, and every stone between?   180
    Sisabert. Is not thy vengeance for the late affront,
For threats and outrage and imprisonment?
    Opas. For outrage, yes—imprisonment and threats
I pardon him, and whatsoever ill
He could do *me*.
    Sisabert.   To hold Covilla from me,
To urge her into vows against her faith,
Against her beauty, youth, and inclination,
Without her mother's blessing, nay without
Her father's knowledge and authority—
So that she never will behold me more,   190
Flying afar for refuge and for help
Where never friend but God will comfort her—
    Opas. These, and more barbarous deeds were perpetrated.
    Sisabert. Yet her proud father deigned not to inform
Me, whom he loved and taught, in peace and war,
Me, whom he called his son, before I hoped
To merit it by marriage or by arms.
He offer'd no excuse, no plea; exprest
No sorrow; but with firm unfaltering voice
Commanded me—I trembled as he spoke—   200
To follow where he led, redress his wrongs,
And vindicate the honour of his child.
He called on God, the witness of his cause,
On Spain, the partner of his victories,
And yet amidst these animating words
Rolled the huge tear down his unvizor'd face—
A general swell of indignation rose
Thro' the long line, sobs burst from every breast,
Hardly one voice succeeded—you might hear

---

179 cannot] can not *1846.*   205 amidst] amid *1831, 1846.*   206 unvizor'd]
unvisor'd *1831, 1846.*   209 succeeded] succeded *1831.*

The impatient hoof strike the soft sandy plain: 210
But when the gates flew open, and the king
In his high car came forth triumphantly,
Then was Count Julian's stature more elate;
Tremendous was the smile that smote the eyes
Of all he past.—"fathers, and sons, and brothers,"
He cried, "I fight your battles, follow me!
"Soldiers, we know no danger but disgrace!"
    Father, and general, and king, they shout,
And would proclaim him—back he cast his face,
Pallid with grief, and one loud groan burst forth;   220
It kindled vengeance thro' the Asturian ranks,
And they soon scatter'd, as the blasts of heaven
Scatter the leaves and dust, the astonished foe.
    Opas. And doubtest thou his truth?
    Sisabert.   I love—and doubt—
Fight—and believe: Roderigo spoke untruths,
In him I place no trust; but Julian holds
Truths in reserve—how should I quite confide!
    Opas. By sorrows thou beholdest him opprest;
Doubt the more prosperous: march, Sisabert,
Once more against his enemy and ours;   230
Much hath been done, but much there still remains.

   219 proclaim] proclame *1831.*   223 astonished] astonisht *1831, 1846.*   231 still]
yet *1846.*

ACT IV. SCENE 1.

Tent of JULIAN.

RODERIGO *and* JULIAN.

    Julian. To stop perhaps at any wickedness
Appears a merit now, and at the time
Prudence or policy it often is
Which afterward seems magnanimity.
The people had deserted thee, and thronged
My standard, had I rais'd it, at the first;
But once subsiding, and no voice of mine
Calling by name each grievance to each man,
They, silent and submissive by degrees,
Bore thy hard yoke, and, hadst thou but opprest,   10
Would still have borne it: thou hast now deceived;
Thou hast done all a foren foe could do,

    ll. 1–4 *om. 1846.*   12, 14 foren] forein *1831;* foreign *1846.*

COUNT JULIAN: A TRAGEDY

And more, against them; with ingratitude
Not hell itself could arm the foren foe—
'Tis forged at home, and kills not from afar.
Amid whate'er vain glories fell upon
Thy rainbow span of power, which I dissolve,
Boast not how thou conferredst wealth and rank,
How thou preservedst me, my family,
All my distinctions, all my offices,   20
When Witiza was murder'd, that I stand
Count Julian at this hour by special grace.
The sword of Julian saved the walls of Ceuta,
And not the shadow that attends his name:
It was no badge, no title, that o'erthrew
Soldier, and steed, and engine—don Roderigo,
The truly and the falsely great here differ,
These by dull wealth or daring fraud advance,
Him the Almighty calls amidst his people
To sway the wills and passions of mankind.   30
The weak of heart and intellect beheld
Thy splendour, and adored thee lord of Spain—
I rose—Roderigo lords o'er Spain no more.
   Roderigo. Now to a traitor's add a boaster's name.
   Julian. Shameless and arrogant, dost thou believe
I boast for pride or pastime? forced to boast,
Truth costs me more than falsehood e'er cost thee.
Divested of that purple of the soul,
That potency, that palm of wise ambition—
Cast headlong by thy madness from that high   40
That only eminence 'twixt earth and heaven,
Virtue—which some desert, but none despise—
Whether thou art beheld again on earth,
Whether a captive or a fugitive;
Miner or galley-slave, depends on me:
But he alone who made me what I am
Can make me greater, or can make me less.
   Roderigo. Chance, and chance only, threw me in thy power,
Give me my sword again and try my strength.
   Julian. I tried it in the front of thousands.
   Roderigo.   Death   50
At least vouchsafe me from a soldier's hand.
   Julian. I love to hear thee ask it—now my own
Would not be bitter; no, nor immature.

26 —don].. don *1831;* . Don *1846.* 29 amidst] amid *1831, 1846.* 40 high]high, *1846.*

Roderigo. Defy it, say thou rather.
Julian.   Death itself
Shall not be granted thee, unless from God;
A dole from his and from no other hand.
Thou shalt now hear and own thine infamy—
   Roderigo. Chains, dungeons, tortures—but I hear no more.
   Julian. Silence, thou wretch, live on—aye, live—abhor'd.
Thou shalt have tortures, dungeons, chains, enough—   60
They naturally rise and grow around
Monsters like thee, everywhere, and for ever.
   Roderigo. Insulter of the fallen! must I endure
Commands as well as threats? my vassal's too?
Nor breathe from underneath his trampling feet?
   Julian. Could I speak patiently who speak to thee,
I would say more—part of thy punishment
It should be, to be taught.
   Roderigo.   Reserve thy wisdom
Until thy patience come, its best allie:
I learn no lore, of peace or war, from thee.   70
   Julian. No, thou shalt study soon another tongue,
And suns more ardent shall mature thy mind.
Either the cross thou bearest, and thy knees
Among the silent caves of Palestine
Wear the sharp flints away with midnight prayer,
Or thou shalt keep the fasts of Barbary—
Shalt wait amid the crowds that throng the well
From sultry noon till the skies fade again,
To draw up water and to bring it home
In the crackt gourd of some vile testy knave,   80
Who spurns thee back with bastinaded foot
For ignorance or delay of his command.
   Roderigo. Rather the poison or the bow-string.
   Julian.   Slaves
To other's passions die such deaths as those,
Slaves to their own should die—
   Roderigo.   —What worse?
   Julian.   Their own.
   Roderigo. Is this thy counsel, renegade?
   Julian.   Not mine;
I point a better path, nay, force thee on.
I shelter thee from every brave man's sword
While I am near thee: I bestow on thee

     59 abhor'd] abhorr'd *1846.*   69 allie] ally *1846.*

Life: if thou die, 'tis when thou sojournest   90
Protected by this arm and voice no more;
'Tis slavishly, 'tis ignominiously,
'Tis by a villain's knife.
   Roderigo.   By whose?
   Julian.   Roderigo's.
   Roderigo. O powers of vengeance! must I hear? endure?
Live?
   Julian. Call thy vassals. no! then wipe the drops
Of froward childhood from thy shameless eyes.
So! thou canst weep for passion—not for pity.
   Roderigo. One hour ago I ruled all Spain! a camp
Not larger than a sheepfold stood alone
Against me: now, no friend throughout the world   100
Follows my steps or hearkens to my call.
Behold the turns of fortune, and expect
No better; of all faithless men, the Moors
Are the most faithless—from thy own experience
Thou canst not value nor rely on them.
   Julian. I value not the mass that makes my sword,
Yet while I use it I rely on it.
   Roderigo. Julian, thy gloomy soul still meditates—
Plainly I see it—death to me—pursue
The dictates of thy leaders, let revenge   110
Have its full sway, let Barbary prevail,
And the pure creed her elders have embraced:
Those placid sages hold assassination
A most compendious supplement to law.
   Julian. Thou knowest not the one, nor I the other.
Torne hast thou from me all my soul held dear!
Her form, her voice, all, hast thou banish'd from me,
Nor dare I, wretched as I am! recall
Those solaces of every grief, erewhile!
I stand abased before insulting crime.   120
I faulter like a criminal myself.
The hand that hurled thy chariot o'er its wheels,
That held thy steeds erect and motionless
As moulten statues on some palace-gates,
Shakes, as with palsied age, before thee now.
Gone is the treasure of my heart, for ever,

95 vassals.] vassals? *1831;* vassals: *1846.*   116 Torne] Torn *1846.*   121
faulter] falter *1831, 1846.*   124 moulten] molten *1831, 1846.*   -gates] -gate
1846.

Without a father, mother, friend, or name!
Daughter of Julian—Such was her delight—
Such was mine too! what pride more innocent,
What, surely, less deserving pangs like these, 130
Than springs from filial and parental love!
Debarred from every hope that issues forth
To meet the balmy breath of early life,
Her sadden'd days, all, cold and colourless,
Will stretch before her their whole weary length
Amid the sameness of obscurity.
She wanted not seclusion, to unveil
Her thoughts to heaven, cloister, nor midnight bell;
She found it in all places, at all hours:
While, to assuage my labours, she indulged 140
A playfulness that shunn'd a mother's eye,
Still, to avert my perils, there arose
A piety that, even from *me*, retired.
　*Roderigo.** Such was she!—what am I!—those are the arms
That are triumphant when the battle fails.
O Julian, Julian! all thy former words
Struck but the imbecile plumes of vanity;
These, thro' its steely coverings, pierce the heart.
I ask not life nor death; but, if I live,
Send my most bitter enemy to watch 150
My secret paths, send poverty, send pain—
I will add more—wise as thou art, thou knowest
No foe more furious than forgiven kings.
I ask not then what thou woudst never grant:
May heaven, O Julian, from thy hand, receive
A pardon'd man, a chasten'd criminal.
　Julian. This further curse hast thou inflicted; wretch,
I cannot pardon thee.
　Roderigo.　　　　　Thy tone, thy mien,
Refute those words.
　Julian.　　　　　No—I can *not* forgive.
　Roderigo. Upon† my knee, my conqueror, I implore— 160
Upon the earth, before thy feet‡—hard heart!
　Julian. Audacious! hast thou never heard that prayer

---

　* Much agitated—after a pause. [*om. 1831, 1846.*]
　† Julian greatly moved, goes towards him. [*om. 1831, 1846.*]
　‡ Starts back. [*om. 1831, 1846.*]

132 Debarred] Debar'd *1831;* Debarr'd *1846.*　　141 shunn'd] shun'd *1831.*
154 woudst] wouldst *1831, 1846.*

And scorn'd it? 'tis the last thou shouldst repeat.
Upon the earth! upon her knees! O God!
   Roderigo. Resemble not a wretch so lost as I:
Be better; O! be happier; and pronounce it.
   Julian. I swerve not from my purpose: thou art mine,
Conquer'd; and I have sworne to dedicate
—Like a torne banner on my chapel's roof—
Thee to that power from whom thou hast rebelled.   170
Expiate thy crimes by prayer, by penances—
   Roderigo. Hasten the hour of trial, speak of peace.*
Pardon me not, then—but with purer lips
Implore of God, who *would* hear *thee*, to pardon.
   Julian. Hope it I may—pronounce it—O Roderigo!
Ask it of him who can; I too will ask,
And, in my own transgressions, pray for thine.
   Roderigo. One name I dare not——
   Julian.   Go—abstain from that,
I do conjure thee; raise not in my soul
Again the tempest that has wrecked my fame;   180
Thou shalt not breathe in the same clime with her.
Far o'er the unebbing sea thou shalt adore
The eastern star, and—may thy end be peace.

* Julian looks sternly on the ground and does not answer. [*om. 1831, 1846.*]

---

168 sworne] sworn *1831, 1846.*   169 torne] torn *1831, 1846.*   180 wrecked]
wreckt *1831, 1846.*

ACT IV. SCENE 2.

JULIAN *and* HERNANDO.

   Hernando. From the prince Tarik I am sent, my lord.
   Julian. A welcome messager, my brave Hernando.
How fares it with the gallant soul of Tarik.
   Hernando. Most joyfully; he scarcely had pronounced
Your glorious name, and bidden me urge your speed,
Than, with a voice as though it answer'd heaven,
He shall confound them in their dark designs
Cried he—and turn'd away, with that swift stride
Wherewith he meets and quells his enemies.
   Julian. Alas, I cannot bear felicitation,   10
Who shunned it even in felicity.
   Hernando. Often we hardly think ourselves the happy

Heading. 1831, 1846 substitute: RODERIGO *goes:* HERNANDO *enters.* 3 Tarik.] Tarik?
1831, 1846.   5 bidden] bid *1831, 1846.*   10 cannot] can not *1846.*

Unless we hear it said by those around.
O my lord Julian, how your praises cheer'd
Our poor endeavours! sure, all hearts are open
Lofty and low, wise and unwise, to praise.
Even the departed spirit hovers round
Our blessings and our prayers; the corse itself
Hath shined with other light than the still stars
Shedd on its rest, or the dim taper, nigh.   20
My father, old men say, who saw him dead
And heard your lips pronounce him good and happy,
Smiled faintly thro' the quiet gloom, that eve,
And the shroud throbbed upon his grateful breast.
Howe'er it be, many who tell the tale
Are good and happy from that voice of praise.
His guidance and example were denied
My youth and childhood: what I am I owe—
   Julian. Hernando, look not back: a narrow path
And arduous lies before thee, if thou stop   30
Thou fallest; go right onward, nor observe
Closely and rigidly another's way,
But, free and active, follow up thy own.
   Hernando. The voice that urges now my manly step
Onward in life, recalls me to the past,
And from that fount I freshen for the goal.
Early in youth, among us villagers
Converse and ripened counsel you bestowed.
O happy days of (far departed!) peace,
Days when the mighty Julian stooped his brow   40
Entering our cottage door; another air
Breathed thro' the house; tired age and lightsome youth
Beheld him, with intensest gaze—these felt
More chastened joy; those, more profound repose.
Yes, my best lord, when labour sent them home
And midday suns, when from the social meal
The wicker window held the summer heat,
Prais'd have those been who, going unperceived,
Open'd it wide, that all might see you well:
Nor were the children blamed, upon the mat,   50
Hurrying to watch what rush would last arise
From your foot's pressure, ere the door was closed,

20 shedd] shed *1846.*   40 stooped] stoopt *1831, 1846.*   44 those,] they
1846.   50 upon . . . mat,] hurrying to watch *1846.*   51 Hurrying . . . watch]
Upon the mat, *1846.*

And not yet wondering how they dared to love.
Your counsels are more precious now than ever,
But are they—pardon if I err—the same?
Tarik is gallant, kind, the friend of Julian,
Can he be more? or ought he to be less?
Alas! his faith!
    Julian.   In peace or war? Hernando.
    Hernando. O, neither—far above it; faith in God—
    Julian. 'Tis God's, not thine—embrace it not, nor hate it.   60
Precious or vile, how dare we seize that offering,
Scatter it, spurn it, in its way to heaven,
Because we know it not? the sovran lord
Accepts his tribute, myrrh and frankincense
From some, from others penitence and prayer:
Why intercept them from his gracious hand?
Why dash them down? why smite the supplicant?
    Hernando. 'Tis what they do?
    Julian.   Avoid it thou the more.
If time were left me, I could hear well-pleased
How Tarik fought up Calpe's fabled cliff,   70
While I pursued the friends of don Roderigo
Across the plain, and drew fresh force from mine.
O! had some other land, some other cause,
Invited him and me, I then could dwell
On this hard battle with unmixt delight.
    Hernando. Eternal is its glory, if the deed
Be not forgotten till it be surpast:
Much praise by land, by sea much more, he won,
For then a Julian was not at his side,
Nor led the van, nor awed the best before;   80
The whole, a mighty whole, was his alone.
There might be seen how far he shone above
All others of the day: old Muza watched
From his own shore the richly laden fleet,
Ill-arm'd and scatter'd, and pursued the rear
Beyond those rocks that bear St. Vincent's name,
Cutting the treasure, not the strength, away—
Valiant, where any prey lies undevour'd
In hostile creek or too confiding isle:
Tarik, with his small barks, but with such love   90
As never chief from rugged sailor won,
Smote their high masts and swelling rampires down;

        68 do?] do. *1846.*   83 watched] watcht *1831, 1846.*

And Cadiz wept in fear o'er Trafalgar.
Who that beheld our sails from off the hights,
Like the white birds, nor larger, tempt the gale
In sunshine and in shade, now almost touch
The solitary shore, glance, turn, retire,
Would think these lovely playmates could portend
Such mischief to the world; such blood, such woe;
Could draw to them from far the peaceful hinds,   100
Cull the gay flower of cities, and divide
Friends, children, every bond of human life;
Could dissipate whole families, could sink
Whole states in ruin, at one hour, one blow.
    Julian. Go, good Hernando—who *would* think these things?
Say to the valiant Tarik, I depart
Forthwith: he knows not from what heaviness
Of soul I linger here; I could endure
No converse, no compassion, no approach,
Other than thine, whom the same cares improved   110
Beneath my father's roof, my foster-brother,
To brighter days and happier end, I hope;
In whose fidelity my own resides
With Tarik and with his compeers and chief.
I cannot share the gladness I excite,
Yet shall our Tarik's generous heart rejoice.*

  * Egilona enters. Hernando goes. [*om. 1831, 1846.*]

------

      94 hights] highths *1846.*   115 cannot] can not *1846.*

ACT IV. SCENE 3.

JULIAN *and* EGILONA.

    Egilona. O fly me not because I am unhappy,
Because I am deserted fly me not.
It was not so before, it cannot be
Ever from Julian.
    Julian.   What would Egilona
That Julian's power with her new lords can do?
Surely her own must there preponderate.
    Egilona. I hold no suit to them—restore, restore
Roderigo.
    Julian. He no longer is my prisoner.

    Headline. 1831, 1846 substitute: EGILONA *enters:* HERNANDO *goes.*   3 it cannot]
and can it *1846.*   4 Julian.] Julian? *1846.*

Egilona. Escapes he then?

Julian. Escapes he—dost thou say? 10
O Egilona! what unworthy passion—

Egilona. Unworthy, when I loved him, was my passion,
The passion that now swells my heart, is just.

Julian. What fresh reproaches hath he merited?

Egilona. Deeprooted hatred shelters no reproach.
But whither is he gone.

Julian. Far from the walls.

Egilona. And I knew nothing!—

Julian. His offence was known
To thee at least.

Egilona. Will it be expiated?

Julian.* I trust it will.

Egilona. This withering calm consumes me.
He marries then Covilla! 'twas for this
His people were excited to rebell, 20
His sceptre was thrown by, his vows were scorn'd,
And I—and I——

Julian. Cease, Egilona!

Egilona. Cease?
Sooner shalt thou to live, than I to reign.

* After some hesitation. [*om. 1831, 1846.*]

---

14 deeprooted] deep-rooted *1846.*   15 gone.] gone? *1831, 1846.*   16 offence]
offense *1831.*

ACT V. SCENE 1.

Tent of MUZA.

MUZA. TARIK. ABDALAZIS.

Muza. To have first landed on these shores, appears
Transcendent glory to the applauded Tarik.

Tarik. Glory, but not transcendent, it appears,
What might in any other.

Muza. Of thyself
All this vain boast?

Tarik. Not of myself—'twas Julian.
Against his shield the refluent surges rolled,
While the sea-breezes threw the arrows wide
And fainter cheers urged the reluctant steeds.

Muza. That Julian, of whose treason I have proofs,
That Julian, who rejected my commands 10

207

Twice, when our mortal foe besieged the camp,
And forced my princely presence to his tent.
    Tarik. Say rather, who without one exhortation,
One precious drop from true believer's vein,
Marched, and discomfited our enemies.
I found in him no treachery—Hernando,
Who, little versed in moody wiles, is gone
To lead him hither, was by him assigned
My guide, and twice in doubtful fight his arm
Protected me—once on the hights of Calpe,   20
Once on the plain, when courtly jealousies
Tore from the bravest and the best his due,
And gave the dotard and the coward command:
Then came Roderigo forth—the front of war
Grew darker—him, equal in chevalry,
Julian alone could with success oppose.
    Abdalazis. I doubt their worth who praise their enemies.
    Tarik. And theirs doubt I who persecute their friends.
    Muza. Thou art in league with him.
    Tarik.   Thou wert, by oaths,
I am without them; for his heart is brave.   30
    Muza. Am I to bear all this?
    Tarik.   All this, and more:
Soon wilt thou see the man whom thou hast wronged,
And the keen hatred in thy breast concealed
Find its right way, and sting thee to the core.
    Muza. Hath he not foil'd us in the field; not held
Our wisdom to reproach?
    Tarik.   Shall we abandon
All he hath left us in the eyes of men;
Shall we again make him our adversary
Whom we have proved so, long and fatally?
If he subdue for us our enemies,   40
Shall we raise others, or, for want of them,
Convert him into one, against his will?

   15 Marched] Marcht *1831, 1846.*   17 versed] verst *1831.*   20 hights]
highths *1846.*   25 chevalry] chivalry *1831, 1846.*

COUNT JULIAN: A TRAGEDY

ACT V. SCENE 2.

HERNANDO *enters.* TARIK *continues.*

Here comes Hernando from that prince himself——
Muza. Who scorns, himself, to come.
Hernando.   The queen detains him.
Abdalazis. How! Egilona?
Muza.   'Twas my will.
Tarik.   At last
He must be happy; for delicious calm
Follows the fierce enjoyment of revenge.
Hernando. That calm was never his, no other will be!
Thou knowest not, and mayst thou never know,
How bitter is the tear that firy shame
Scourges and tortures from the soldier's eye.
Whichever of these bad reports be true,   10
He hides it from all hearts, to wring his own,
And drags the heavy secret to the grave.
Not victory, that o'ershadows him, sees he!
No airy and light passion stirs abroad
To ruffle or to soothe him; all are quelled
Beneath a mightier, sterner, stress of mind:
Wakeful he sits, and lonely, and unmoved,
Beyond the arrows, views, or shouts of men;
As oftentimes an eagle, when the sun
Throws o'er the varying earth his early ray,   20
Stands solitary, stands immovable
Upon some highest cliff, and rolls his eye,
Clear, constant, unobservant, unabased,
In the cold light, above the dews of morn.
He now assumes that quietness of soul
Which never but in danger have I seen
On his staid breast.
Tarik.   Danger is past, he conquers;
No enemy is left him to subdue.
Hernando. He sank not, while there was, into himself.
Now plainly see I from his alter'd tone,   30
He cannot live much longer—thanks to God!
Tarik. What! wishest thou thy once kind master dead?
Was he not kind to thee, ungrateful slave!
Hernando. The gentlest, as the bravest, of mankind.

8 firy] fiery *1846.*   19 when] ere *1846.*   31 cannot] can not *1846.*

Therefor shall memory dwell more tranquilly
With Julian, once at rest, than friendship could,
Knowing him yearn for death with speechless love.
For his own sake I could endure his loss,
Pray for it, and thank God; yet mourn I must
Him above all! so great, so bountiful,   40
So blessed once! bitterly must I mourn.
'Tis not my solace that 'tis his desire;
Of all that pass us in life's drear descent
We grieve the most for those that wished to die.
A father to us all, he merited
Unhappy man! all a good father's joy
In his own house, where seldom he hath been,
But, ever mindful of its dear delights
He formed one family around him, ever.
    Tarik. Yes, we have seen and known him—let his fame   50
Refresh his friends, but let it stream afar,
Nor in the twilight of home-scenes be lost.
He chose the best, and cherished them; he left
To self-reproof the mutinies of vice—
Avarice, that imps ambition's tone and mien,
Envy, sick nursling of the court; and pride
That cannot bear his semblance nor himself;
And malice, with blear visage half-descried
Amid the shadows of her hiding-place.
    Hernando. What could I not endure, O gallant man,   60
To hear him spoken of, as thou hast spoken!
Oh! I would almost be a slave to him
Who calls me one.
    Muza.   What! art thou not? begone.
    Tarik. Reply not, brave Hernando, but retire.
All can revile, few only can reward.
Behold the meed our mighty chief bestows!
Accept it, for thy services, and mine.
More, my bold Spaniard, hath obedience won
Than anger, even in the ranks of war.
    Hernando. The soldier, not the Spaniard, shall obey.   70
    *Muza.** Into our very council bringest thou

* To Tarik. [*Transferred to text 1831, 1846.*]

---

35 Therefor] Therefore *1846.*   43 that] who *1846.*   44 wished] wisht *1831, 1846.*
53 cherished] cherisht *1831, 1846.*   55 imps] dwarfs *1831, 1846.*   ambition's] Ambition's *1846.*   56 pride] Pride *1846.*   57 cannot] can not *1846.*   58 malice]
Malice *1846.*   70 *After* obey. *1831, 1846 insert in italics* [Goes.

Children of reprobation and perdition?
Darkness thy deeds and emptiness thy speech,
Such images thou raisest as buffoons
Carry in merriment on festivals,
Nor worthiness nor wisdom would display
To public notice their deformities,
Nor cherish them nor fear them; why shouldst thou?
 Tarik. I fear not them nor thee.   *79*

ACT V. SCENE 3.

Egilona *enters.*

 Abdalazis.   Advance, O queen.
Now let the turbulence of faction cease.
 Muza. Whate'er thy purpose, speak, and be composed.
 Egilona. He goes; he is afar; he follows her;
He leads her to the altar, to the throne,
For, calm in vengeance, wise in wickedness,
The traitor hath prevailed, o'er him, o'er me,
O'er you—the slaves, the dupes, the scorn, of Julian.
What have I heard! what have I seen!
 Muza.   Proceed—
 Abdalazis. —And I swear vengeance on his guilty head   *10*
Who intercepts from thee the golden rays
Of sovranty; who dares rescind thy rights;
Who steals upon thy rest, and breathes around
Empoisoned damps o'er that serenity
Which leaves the world, and faintly lingers here.
 Muza. Who shuns thee—
 Abdalazis.   —Whose desertion interdicts
Homage, authority, precedency—
 Muza. Till war shall rescue them—
 Abdalazis.   —And love restore.
 Egilona. O generous Abdalazis! never! never!
My enemies—Julian alone remains—   *20*
The worst, in safety, far beyond my reach,
Breathe freely on the summit of their hopes;
Because they never stopt, because they sprang
From crime to crime, and trampled down remorse.
Oh! if her heart knew tenderness like mine!
Grant vengeance on the guilty; grant but that,
I ask no more; my hand, my crown, is thine.

9 Proceed] Procede 1831.

Fulfill the justice of offended heaven,
Assert the sacred rights of royalty,
Come not in vain, crush the rebellious crew,   30
Crush, I implore, the indifferent and supine.
   Muza. Roderigo thus escaped from Julian's tent?
   Egilona. No, not escaped—escorted—like a king.
The base Covilla first pursued her way
On foot; but after her the royal car,
Which bore me from San Pablos to the throne,
Empty indeed, yet ready at her voice,
Rolled o'er the plain, amid the carcases
Of those who fell in battle or in flight:
She, a deceiver still, to whate'er speed   40
The moment might incite her, often stopt
To mingle prayers with the departing breath,
Improvident! and those with heavy wounds
Groaned bitterly beneath her tottering knee.
   Tarik. Now, by the clement and the merciful!
The girl did well: when I breathe out my soul,
Oh! if compassion give one pang the more,
That pang be mine; here be it, in this land—
Such women are they in this land alone.
   Egilona. Insulting man!
   Muza.   We shall confound him yet.   50
Say, and speak quickly, whither went the king?
Thou knewest where was Julian.
   Abdalazis.   I will tell
Without his answer: yes, my friends! yes, Tarik,
Now will I speak, nor thou, for once, reply.
There is, I hear, a poor half-ruin'd cell
In Xeres, whither few indeed resort;
Green are the walls within, green is the floor
And slippery from disuse; for christian feet
Avoid it, as half-holy, half-accurst.
Still in its dark recess fanatic sin   60
Abases to the ground his tangled hair,
And servile scourges and reluctant groans
Roll o'er the vault uninterruptedly,
Till, such the natural stilness of the place,
The very tear upon the damps below
Drops audible, and the heart's throb replies.

COUNT JULIAN: A TRAGEDY

There is the idol maid of christian creed,
And taller images, whose history
I know not, nor inquired—a scene of blood,
Of resignation amid mortal pangs,
And other things, exceeding all belief.
Hither the aged Opas of Seville
Walked slowly, and behind him was a man
Barefooted, bruized, dejected, comfortless,
In sack-cloth; the white ashes on his head
Dropt as he smote his breast—he gathered up,
Replaced them all, groan'd deeply, looked to heaven,
And held them, like a treasure, with claspt hands.
   Egilona. O! was Roderigo so abased?
   Muza.   'Twas he.
Now, Egilona, judge between your friends
And enemies—behold what wretches brought
The king, thy lord, Roderigo, to disgrace.
   Egilona. He merited—but not from them—from me
This, and much worse: had I inflicted it,
I had rejoiced—at what I ill endure.
   Muza. For thee, for thee alone, we wished him here,
But other hands released him—
   Abdalazis.   —With what aim
Will soon appear to those discerning eyes.
   Egilona. I pray thee, tell what past until that hour.
   Abdalazis. Few words, and indistinct: repentant sobs
Filled the whole space; the taper in his hand,
Lighting two small dim lamps before the altar,
He gave to Opas—at the idol's feet
He laid his crown, and wiped his tears away:
The crown reverts not, but the tears return.
   Egilona. Yes, Abdalazis! soon, abundantly.
If he had only called upon my name,
Seeking my pardon ere he looked to heaven's,
I could have—no! he thought not once on me!
Never shall he find peace or confidence;
I will rely on fortune and on thee
Nor fear my future lot: sure, Abdalazis,
A fall so great can never happen twice,
Nor man again be faithless, like Roderigo.
   Abdalazis. Faithless he may be still, never so faithless.

70

80

90

100

  73 Walked] Walkt *1846.*   **77, 98** looked] lookt *1846.*   **86** wished] wisht *1831,*
1846.   **87** released] releast *1831, 1846.*

Fainter must be the charms, remote the days,
When memory and dread example die,
When love and terror thrill the heart no more,
And Egilona is herself forgotten.   109

ACT V. SCENE 4.

JULIAN *enters.*

Tarik. Turn, and behold him! who is now confounded?
Ye who awaited him, where are ye? speak—
Is some close comet blazing o'er your tents?
Muza! Abdalazis! princes, conquerors,
Summon, interrogate, command, condemn.
   Muza. Justly, don Julian—but respect for rank
Allays resentment, nor interrogates
Without due form—justly may we accuse
This absence from our councils, from our camp;
This loneliness in which we still remain   10
Who came invited to redress your wrongs.
Where is the king?
   Julian.   The people must decide.
   Muza. Imperfectly, I hope, I understand
Those words, unworthy of thy birth and age.
   Julian. O chieftain, such have been our gothic laws.
   Muza. Who then amid such turbulence is safe?
   Julian. He who observes them: 'tis no turbulence,
It violates no peace: 'tis surely worth
A voice, a breath of air, thus to create
By their high will the man, form'd after them   20
In their own image, vested with their power,
To whom they trust their freedom and their lives.
   Muza. They trust! the people! God assigns the charge,
Kings open but the book of destiny
And read their names, all that remains for them
The mystic hand from time to time reveals.
Worst of idolaters! idolater
Of that refractory and craving beast
Whose den is in the city, at thy hand
I claim our common enemy, the king.   30
   Julian. Sacred from justice then! but not from malice!
   Tarik. Surrender him, my friend: be sure his pains
Will not be soften'd.

        10 still] stil *1831.*   15 gothic] Gothic *1846.*

COUNT JULIAN: A TRAGEDY

Julian.   'Tis beyond my power.
Tarik. Tomorrow—if in any distant fort
He lies tonight: send after him.
Julian.   My faith
Is plighted, and he lives—no prisoner.
Egilona. I knew the truth.
Abdalazis.   Now, Tarik, hear and judge.
Was he not in* thy camp? and in disguise?
Tarik. No: I will answer thee.
Muza.   Audacious man!
Had not the Kalif Walid placed thee here,
Chains, and a traitor's death, should be thy doom.   40
Speak, Abdalazis! Egilona, speak.
Were ye not present? was not I, myself,
And aided not this Julian his escape?
Julian. 'Tis true.
Tarik.   Away then friendship; to thy fate
I leave thee: thou hast render'd Muza just,
Me hostile to thee. Who is safe! a man
Arm'd with such power and with such perfidy!
Julian. Stay, Tarik! hear me; for, to thee alone
Would I reply.
Tarik.   Thou hast replied, already.†   50
Muza. We, who were enemies, would not inquire
Too narrowly what reasons urged thy wrath
Against thy sovran lord; beneath his flag
The christians first assailed us from these shores,
And we seized gladly the first aid we found
To quell a wealthy and a warlike king.
We never held to thee the vain pretence
That 'twas thy quarrel our brave youth espoused,
Thine, who hast wrought us much disgrace and woe.
From perils and from losses, here we rest   60
And drink of the fresh fountain at our feet,
Not madly following such illusive streams
As overspread the dizzy wilderness,
And vanish from the thirst they have seduced.
Ours was the enterprise, the land is ours:
What gain we by our toils if he escape
Whom we came hither solely to subdue?

* To Julian. [*om. 1831, inserted in text 1846.*]
† Goes. [*transferred to text 1831, 1846.*]

54 christians ... assailed] Christians ... assail'd *1846.*   57 pretence] pretense *1831.*

Julian. Is there no gain to live in amity?

Muza. The gain of traffickers and idle men;
Courage and zeal expire upon such calms.   70
Further, what amity can Moors expect
When you have joined your forces?

Julian.   From the hour
That he was vanquished, I have laid aside
All power, all arms.

Muza.   How can we trust thee, once
Deceived, and oftener than this once despised?
Thou camest hither with no other aim
Than to deprive Roderigo of his crown
For thy own brow.

Egilona.   Julian, base man, 'tis true.
He comes a prince, no warrior, at this hour.

Muza. His sword, O queen, would not avail him now.   80

Abdalazis. Julian, I feel less anger than regret.
No violence of speech, no obloquy,
No accusation shall escape my lips:
Need there is none, nor reason, to avoid
My questions: if thou value truth, reply.
Hath not Roderigo left the town and camp?
Hath not thy daughter?

Egilona.   —Past the little brook
Toward the Betis—from a tower I saw
The fugitives, far on their way; they went
Over one bridge, each with arm'd men—not half   90
A league of road between them—and had join'd,
But that the olive-groves along the path
Concealed them from each other; not from me:
Beneath me the whole level I surveyed,
And, when my eyes no longer could discern
Which track they took, I knew it from the storks
Rising in clouds above the reedy plain.

Muza. Deny it, if thou canst.

Julian.   I order'd it.

Abdalazis. None could beside: lo! things in such a mass
Falling together on observant minds,   100
Create suspicion and establish proof:
Wanted there fresh—why not employ our arms?
Why go alone?

Muza.   To parley, to conspire,

    73 vanquished] vanquisht *1831, 1846.*   99 beside] besides *1831.*

COUNT JULIAN: A TRAGEDY

To reunite the Spaniards, which we saw,
To give up treaties, close up enmities,
And ratify the deed with Moorish blood.
 Julian. Gladly would Spain procure your safe return,
Gladly would pay large treasures, for the aid
You brought against oppression—
 Muza.   Pay she shall—
The treasures of her soil, her ports, her youth: 110
If she resist, if she tumultuously
Call forth her brigands and we lose a man,
Dreadful shall be our justice; war shall rage
Through every city, hamlet, house, and field,
And, universal o'er the gasping land,
Depopulation.
 Julian.   They shall rue the day
Who dare these things.
 Muza.   Let order then prevail.
In vain thou sendest far away thy child,
Thy counsellor the metropolitan,
And Sisabert—prudence is mine, no less.   120
Divide with us our conquests, but the king
Must be delivered up.
 Julian.   Never by me.
 Muza. False then were thy reproaches, false thy grief.
 Julian. O Egilona! were thine also feigned?
 Abdalazis. Say, lovely queen, neglectful of thy charms
Turned he his eyes toward the young Covilla?
Did he pursue her to the mad excess
Of breaking off her vows to Sisabert,
And marrying her, against the christian law?
 Muza. Did he prefer her so?
 Abdalazis.   Could he prefer   130
To Egilona——
 Egilona.   Her! the child Covilla?
Eternal hider of a foolish face—
Incapable of any thing but shame—
To me? old man! to me? O Abdalazis!
No: he but followed with slow pace my hate.
And cannot pride check these unseemly tears!*

---

* To herself. Goes. [To herself *om.*, Goes *transferred to text 1831, 1846.*]

---

130 her] *wrongly om. 1876.*   133 any thing] anything *1846.*   136 cannot]
can not *1846.*

217

Muza. The most offended, an offended woman,
A wife, a queen, is silent on the deed.

Abdalazis. Thou disingenuous and ignoble man,
Spreading these rumours! sending into exile   140
All those their blighting influence injured most:
And whom? thy daughter and adopted son,
The chieftains of thy laws and of thy faith.
Call any witnesses, proclaim the truth,
And set, at last, thy heart, thy fame, at rest.

Julian. Not, if I purposed or desired to live,
My own dishonour would I e'er proclaim
Amid vindictive and reviling foes.

Muza. Calling us foes, avows he not his guilt?
Condemns he not the action we condemn,   150
Owning it his, and owning it dishonour?
'Tis well my cares prest forward, and struck home.

Julian. Why smilest thou? I never saw that smile
But it portended an atrocious deed.

Muza. After our manifold and stern assaults,
With every tower and battlement destroyed,
The walls of Ceuta still were strong enough*—

Julian.† For what? who boasted now her brave defence,
Or who forbad your entrance, after peace?

Muza. None: for who could? their engines now arose   160
To throw thy sons into the arms of death.
For this erect they their proud crests again.
Mark him at last turn pale before a Moor.

Julian. Imprudent have they been, their youth shall plead.

Abdalazis. O father, could they not have been detained?

Muza. Son, thou art safe and wert not while they lived.

Abdalazis. I feared them not.

Muza.   And therefor wert not safe:
Under their star the blooming Egilona
Would watch for thee the nuptial lamp in vain.

Julian. Never, oh never, hast thou worked a wile   170
So barren of all good! speak out at once,
What hopest thou by striking this alarm?
It shocks my reason, not my fears or fondness.

Muza. Be happy then as ignorance can be;

---

* Stops. [*om. 1831, 1846.*]   † Hastily. [*om. 1831, 1846.*]

144, 147 proclaim] proclame *1831.*   146 purposed] purpost *1831.*   158 defence]
defense *1831.*   167 therefor] therefore *1846.*   170 worked] workt *1831,*
1846.

Soon wilt thou hear it shouted from our ranks.
Those who once hurled defiance o'er our heads,
Scorning our arms, and scoffing at our faith,
The nightly wolf hath visited, unscared,
And loathed 'em as her prey; for famine first,
Atchieving in few days the boast of years,   180
Sunk their young eyes and opened us the gates:
Ceuta, her port, her citadel, is ours.
   Julian. Blest boys! inhuman as thou art, what guilt
Was theirs?
   Muza.   Their father's.
   Julian.   O support me, Heaven!
Against this blow! all others I have borne.
Ermenegild! thou mightest, sure, have lived!
A father's name awoke no dread of thee!
Only thy mother's early bloom was thine!
There dwelt on Julian's brow—thine was serene—
The brightened clouds of elevated souls,   190
Feared by the most below: those who looked up
Saw, at their season, in clear signs, advance
Rapturous valour, calm solicitude,
All that impatient youth would press from age,
Or sparing age sigh and detract from youth:
Hence was his fall! my hope! myself! my Julian!
Alas! I boasted—but I thought on him,
Inheritor of all—all what? my wrongs—
Follower of me—and whither? to the grave—
Ah no: it should have been so! years far hence!   200
Him at this moment I could pity most,
But I most prided in him; now I know
I loved a name, I doated on a shade.
Sons! I approach the mansions of the just,
And my arms clasp you in the same embrace,
Where none shall sever you; and do I weep!
And do they triumph o'er my tenderness!
I had forgotten mine inveterate foes
Everywhere nigh me, I had half forgotten
Your very murderers, while I thought on you: 210
For, O my children, ye fill all the space
My soul would wander o'er—O bounteous heaven!

179 'em] them *1831, 1846.*   180 Atchieving] Achieving *1831, 1846.*   181 sunk]
sank *1831, 1846.*   191 looked] lookt *1831, 1846.*   200 so! years] so years
1831, 1846.   **203 doated**] doted *1831.*   208 mine] my *1831, 1846.*

There is a presence, if the well-beloved
Be torne from us by human violence,
More intimate, pervading, and complete,
Than when they lived and spoke like other men,
And their pale images are our support
When reason sinks, or threatens to desert us.
I weep no more—pity and exultation
Sway and console me: are they—no!—both dead?   220
   Muza. Aye, and unsepulchred.
   Julian.   Nor wept nor seen
By any kindred and far-following eye?
   Muza. Their mother saw them, if not dead, expire.
   Julian. O cruelty!—to them indeed the least!
My children, ye are happy—ye have lived
Of heart unconquered, honour unimpaired,
And died, true Spaniards, loyal to the last.
   Muza. Away with him.
   Julian.   Slaves! not before I lift
My voice to heaven and man: though enemies
Surround me, and none else, yet other men   230
And other times shall hear: the agony
Of an opprest and of a bursting heart
No violence can silence; at its voice
The trumpet is o'erpowered, and glory mute,
And peace and war hide all their charms alike.
Surely the guests and ministers of heaven
Scatter it forth thro' all the elements,
So suddenly, so widely, it extends,
So fearfully men breathe it, shuddering
To ask or fancy how it first arose.   240
   Muza. Yes, they shall shudder—but will that, henceforth,
Molest my privacy, or shake my power?
   Julian. Guilt hath pavilions, but no privacy.
The very engine of his hatred checks
The torturer in his transport of revenge,
Which, while it swells his bosom, shakes his power
And raises friends to his worst enemy.
   Muza. Where now are thine? will they not curse the day
That gave thee birth, and hiss thy funeral?
Thou hast left none who could have pitied thee.   250
   Julian. Many, nor those alone of tenderer mould,
For me will weep—many alas thro' me!
     214 torne] torn *1831, 1846.*   221 unsepulchred] unsepulcred *1831.*

Already I behold my funeral.
The turbid cities wave and swell with it,
And wrongs are lost in that day's pageantry:
Opprest and desolate, the countryman
Receives it like a gift; he hastens home,
Shews where the hoof of Moorish horse laid waste
His narrow croft and winter garden-plot,
Sweetens with fallen pride his children's lore,   260
And points their hatred; but applauds their tears.
Justice, who came not up to us thro' life,
Loves to survey our likeness on our tombs,
When rivalry, malevolence, and wrath,
And every passion that once stormed around,
Is calm alike without them as within.
Our very chains make the whole world our own,
Bind those to us who else had past us by,
Those at whose call brought down to us, the light
Of future ages lives upon our name.   270
   Muza. I may accelerate that meteor's fall,
And quench that idle ineffectual light
Without the knowledge of thy distant world.
   Julian. My world and thine are not that distant one.
Is age less wise, less merciful, than grief,
To keep this secret from thee, poor old man?
Thou canst not lessen, canst not aggravate
My sufferings, canst not shorten nor extend
Half a sword's length between my God and me.
I thank thee for that better thought than fame,   280
Which none however, who deserve, despise,
Nor lose from view till all things else are lost.
   Abdalazis. Julian, respect his age, regard his power.
Many who feared not death, have dragged along
A piteous life in darkness and in chains.
Never was man so full of wretchedness
But something may be suffered after all,
Perhaps in what clings round his breast, and helps
To keep the ruin up, which he amidst
His agony and phrenzy overlooks,   290
But droops upon at last, and clasps, and dies.
   Julian. Altho' a Muza send far underground,

---

258 Shews] Shows *1846.*   268 past] passt *1831.*   278 nor] or *1846.*   284
dragged] drag'd *1831;* dragg'd *1846.*   289 amidst] amid *1831, 1846.*   290 phrenzy]
frenzy *1831, 1846.*

Into the quarry whence the palace rose,
His mangled prey, climes alien and remote
Mark and record the pang; while overhead
Perhaps he passes on his favorite steed,
Less heedful of the misery he inflicts
Than of the expiring sparkle from a stone,
Yet we, alive or dead, have fellow men
If ever we have served them, who collect   300
From prisons and from dungeons our remains,
And bear them in their bosom to their sons.
Man's only reliques are his benefits;
These, be there ages, be there worlds, between,
Retain him in communion with his kind:
Hence is our solace, our security,
Our sustenance, till heavenly truth descends . .
Losing in brightness and beatitude
The frail foundations of these humbler hopes . .
And, like an angel, guiding us, at once   310
Leaves the loose chain and iron gate behind.
  Muza. Take thou my justice first, then hope for theirs.
I, who can bend the living to my will,
Fear not the dead, and court not the unborn:
Their arm will never reach me, nor shall thine.
  Abdalazis. Pity, release him, pardon him, my father.
Forget how much thou hatest perfidy,
Think of him, once so potent, still so brave,
So calm, so self-dependent in distress—
I marvel at him—hardly dare I blame,   320
When I behold him fallen from so high,
And so exalted after such a fall.
Mighty must that man be, who can forgive
A man, so mighty; seize the hour to rise,
Another never comes: O say, my father,
Say, "*Julian, be mine enemy no more.*"
He fills me with a greater awe than e'er
The field of battle, with himself the first,
When every flag that waved along our host
Drooped down the staff, as if the very winds   330
Hung in suspense before him—bid him go

295 pang; while] pang. While *1831, 1846.*   296 favorite] favourite *1846.*
298 stone,] stone; *1831;* stone, *1846.*   303 reliques] relicks *1831;* relics *1846.*
308 Losing in] Covering with *1846.*   318 still] stil *1831.*   326 *mine*] my
1831, 1846.   330 Drooped] Droopt *1831, 1846.*

222

And peace be with him, or let me depart.
Lo! like a god, sole and inscrutable,
He stands above our pity.
    Julian.   For that wish,
Vain as it is, 'tis virtuous—O, for that,
However wrong thy censure and thy praise,
Kind Abdalazis, mayst thou never feel
The rancour that consumes thy father's breast,
Nor want the pity thou hast sought for me.
    Muza. Now hast thou sealed thy doom.
    Julian.   And thou thy crimes. 340
    Abdalazis. O father, heed him not: those evil words
Leave neither blight nor blemish—let him go.
    Muza. A boy, a very boy, art thou indeed!
One who in early day would sally out
To chase the lion, and would call it sport,
But, when more wary steps had closed him round,
Slink from the circle, drop the toils, and blanch
Like a lithe plant from under snow in spring.
    Abdalazis. He who ne'er shrunk from danger, might shrink now,
And ignominy would not follow here.   350
    Muza. Peace, Abdalazis! how is this? he bears
Nothing that warrants him invulnerable,
Shall I then shrink to smite him? shall my fears
Be greatest at the blow that ends them all?
Fears? no! 'tis justice—fair, immutable,
Whose measured step, at times, advancing nigh,
Appalls the majesty of kings themselves.
O* were he dead! tho' then revenge were o'er.

  * Aside. [*om. 1831, 1846.*]

---

339 me.] mine! *1846.*   **349** shrunk] shrank *1831, 1846.*

ACT V. SCENE 5.

    Officer. Thy wife, Count Julian!
    Julian.   Speak!
    Officer.   Is dead!
    Julian.   Adieu
Earth, and the humblest of all earthly hopes,
To hear of comfort, tho' to find it vain.
Thou murderer of the helpless! shame of man!
Shame of thy own base nature! 'tis an act

He who could perpetrate could not avow,
Stained, as he boasts to be, with innocent blood,
Deaf to reproach, and blind to retribution.
    Officer. Julian, be just; 'twill make thee less unhappy.
Grief was her end: she held her younger boy   10
And wept upon his cheek; his naked breast
By recent death now hardening and inert,
Slipt from her knee; again with frantic grasp
She caught it, and it weighed her to the ground:
There lay the dead—
    Julian.   She?
    Officer.   —And the youth her son.
    Julian. Receive them to thy peace, eternal God!
O soother of my hours, while I beheld
The light of day, and thine! adieu, adieu!
And, my Covilla! dost thou yet survive?
Yes, my lost child, thou livest yet—in shame!   20
O agony, past utterance! past thought!
That throwest death, as some light idle thing,
With all its terrors, into dust and air—
I will endure thee; I, whom heaven ordained
Thus to have served beneath my enemies,
Their conqueror, thus to have revisited
My native land with vengeance and with woe.
Henceforward shall she recognise her sons,
Impatient of oppression or disgrace,
And rescue them, or perish; let her hold   30
This compact, written with her blood, and mine.
Now* follow me—but tremble†—years shall roll
And wars rage on, and Spain at last be free.

  * To the guards. [*om. 1831, 1846.*]
  † To Muza, &c. [*om. 1831, 1846.*]

---

23 terrors] terrours *1831.*

THE END.

INES DE CASTRO

[PART I]

[Parts I and III published in 1831; reprinted 1846. Part II published in 1846, when the three parts were put in right order as now but with variants in Parts I and III. See notes at end of volume. Text of Part I, 1831.]

INES DE CASTRO AT CINTRA

INES. PEDRO. CONSTANTIA. BLANCA.

Constantia. Pleasant must be these groves of Cintra, Pedro!
To one who lately left the Moorish sands:
Every thing has its joyance for the eyes
That look from hard-fought and won fields upon it,
As yours do.
Pedro.   Lady! I delight to hear
And see you; so ingenuous, so benign,
So playful!
Constantia. I am then no more *Constantia!*
But *Lady!*
Pedro. You are not the little girl
I left: you have exchanged your childish charms
For others, which require new words, new thoughts,   10
New gazers.
Constantia. Give me one of them awhile;
Cannot you? are you proud? has my mama
Been tutoring you, as she has me?
Pedro.   Constantia!
I ask from you what no man ever had,
Or asked, in my condition . . pity me!
Constantia. O this is then the solemn way to woo!
I have redd something like it, since you went,
But never thought it could be near the same.
Here is my hand . . you take it not!
Pedro.   I kiss it.
My life hangs from it . . and more lives than one.   20
Constantia. O! no, vain man! I love you very well,

Title. 1846 has INES DE CASTRO* with footnote: *The events in these scenes are not
strictly historical.
AT CINTRA transferred to scene heading in 1846, which has:

Act I
Scene I. At Cintra.
Pedro. Constantia.

3 Every thing] Everything *1846.*   12 Cannot you] Can you not *1846.*
15 asked] askt *1846.*   17 redd] read *1846.*

Very sincerely, very tenderly;
For I have seen you often, long together,
Early, and when none knew it; but think not
My life hangs from your ring: you first asked pity,
And fear'd to ask even *that;* you now would grant it,
Perhaps *not* grant it, yet would make me sue . .
And came you then before the hour for this?
   Pedro. I came before the hour, I must confess,
To be with you some moments more, alone.   30
   Constantia. 'Tis very wrong, I hear, at such a time
Of life: when we are children and are wild
'Tis well enough; but when we are grown sage
(As we are) the whole world cries out upon it.
What now have you been doing all these days?
   Pedro. This is the first appointed me for seeing you.
   Constantia. O! I know that: my question was amiss:
I always say the very thing one would not.
Alas! I find, and I am sorry for it,
Too young am I to think of serious things.   40
Surely we might deferr them for a year,
By flattering the king and queen a little
And giving them a kiss or two, each of us.
If you should find me but a child in thought,
Or, what is hatefuller (all say), in manner,
And blush for me, my heart must shrivel under it;
For I would never pain the man I love,
And least of all (for that hurts most) would shame him.
   Pedro. Sure some kind angel breathed into your breast
The words on which I live.
   Constantia.   O! then they pleased you!   50
They were not those that I most hoped to please with.
   Pedro. The queen perhaps has not discourst on all
Of my first passion.
   Constantia.   All? did *you* tell *her?*
There were some silly things: I never told her . .
Why should I? we were very young indeed . .
Do people call *that* passion?
   Pedro.   Have you heard
Perchance of Ines?
   Constantia.   Whom? Ines de Castro?
Not latterly: no one must speak of her.

    25 asked] askt *1846.*   41 deferr] defer *1846.*   57 Ines] Iñes *1846, and so*
throughout.

Pedro. Yes; I must speak of her.
Constantia.   They say you liked her;
And so should I have done (she was so good)   60
If they had let her stay with me: they would not.
    Pedro. O sweetest best Constantia! she is stil
As she was ever . . saving one sad name.
    Constantia. What sad name?
    Pedro.   The betrothed of Don Pedro.
    Constantia. How! faithless man! betrothed?
    Pedro.   So she was:
I have resigned her.
    Constantia.   I resign then you.
What blessing, what prosperity, what peace,
Can rest with perfidy? she is the same,
You tell me . . little matters what you tell me . .
As when you knew her first.
    Pedro.   The very same.   70
    Constantia. Mild, beautiful, affectionate, believing?
    Pedro. All.
    Constantia. Go then! ask forgiveness at her feet,
But never hope it here.
    Pedro.   Stay, princess!
    Constantia.   Go!
The lemon-tyme, geranium, and stiff pinks,
And every tuft in every vase about,
Have lost some leaves while you have been thus speaking;
So, evil spirits must have entered with you:
And tho the curtains swell and fall, and tho
There seems to be a breeze, 'tis not the air!
What air there was, grows hot and tainted round;   80
I scarce can breathe it.
    Pedro.   You will hear the whole . .
    Constantia. I never will.
    Pedro.   The truth . .
    Constantia.   Where?
    Pedro.   From the queen.
    Constantia. The truth, when it left Pedro, left the world.
                                             Goes.
    Pedro alone in the garden. Hated, fled, scorn'd . . I am at least set free
From an affiance which the pure of soul
Abhorr: such marriage-bed appears bestrewn

62 stil] still *1846.*   83 *after* world *1846 omits* Goes—*and inserts* SCENE II.
86 Abhorr] Abhor *1846.*

With the dark flowers and heavy pall that hung
Around the corse, where bloomed their one delight.
She comes .. be strong my heart! thou'rt at thy proof
For the first time .. bear up!
      To Ines.   Sit here by me,   90
Under this cedar.
    Ines.   Where sit under it?
Its branches push the grass away beneath,
Nor leave it room enough to rise amid them;
Easier it were, methinks, to walk along
And rest on them, they are so dense and broad,
And level as the oars are on Mondego
Until the music beckons them below.
    Pedro. Come; I am holding them wide open for thee;
They will close round us.
    Ines.   Have you waited long?
Tell me.
    Pedro. I've other things to tell thee.
    Ines.   What?   100
Oh! I am very chilly in this shade.
    Pedro. Run into the pavilion then.
    Ines.   Now tell me.
Pedro! your hand and brow are sadly parcht,
And you are out of breath, altho' you walked
These twenty paces, more than I who ran ..
And yet you always caught me when we tried.
What would you tell me now, my faithful Pedro!
    Pedro. In one word, Ines! I have ceased to love thee.
Loose me and let me go.
    Ines.   Is this your greeting?
This your first morning salutation? turn ..   110
Can it be? must I (look at me) believe it?
    Pedro. Yes, my sweet .. yes, my Ines .. yes, yes, Ines!
    Ines. And are you stil so generous, O my love,
As to be sorry you have ceased to love me?
To sigh, almost to weep, bending your face
Away from me, lest I should grieve to see
A change in it, and in a change a loss!
Take off that hand from above mine then! take it!

87 dark] ?*mispr.* dank *1846.*   90 *To* Ines] (*To* Ines, *who enters.*) *1846.*
102 *after* then *1846 inserts:*
SCENE III.
PEDRO *and* INES *seated in a Pavilion.*
104 walked] walkt *1846.*   113 stil] still *1846.*   114 ceased] ceast *1846.*

228

I dare not move it from me . . 'tis the prince's,
And not my Pedro's.

    Pedro.   I must go.

    Ines.   I once   120
Might ask you why. Let *me* go.

    Pedro.   Wouldst thou? whither?
Unfortunate! So, thou resignest me,
Light heartless girl!

    Ines.   I would obey: I swore it.

    Pedro. Not yet.

                Aside. Ah! would to God! it were indeed so!

  Ines. Not at the altar yet; but did you not
Force me to say I loved you, ere you went
Against the Moors, telling me you could never
Be half so valiant, half so proud of victory,
Unless I own'd it? Too just punishment!
Why then so long delaid! We oft have met,   130
Oft every day, and no day but in smiles,
(O those three happy ones since your return!)
And I had ceased to fancy it was wrong,
It seemed so little like it and gave *you*
Such pleasure, and such confidence in arms.
Alas! it was unmaidenly! so was it
To leave my arm around your neck: so was it
(And worse) to linger, and not fly at once
For refuge in a cloister, when you prest
My very lips with kisses. You were going,   140
And my poor heart was faint: I thought no ill;
And you, who might have given me more spirit,
Said nothing: no one image was there near,
Or none I saw, of her, the pure, the blessed,
Who might have chastened me with tender look
Compassionate, and dried the tears of both.

  Pedro. I cannot bear these reminiscences,
Rather these presences . . for they who love
As we have done, have but one day, one hour,
In their whole life, in their whole afterlife,   150
In earth, heaven, time, eternity.

    Ines.   What said you?
I know not what you said, and yet your words
Seem'd my own to me.

    Pedro.   Live! live! thou art young,

  130 delaid] delay'd *1846.*   133 ceased] ceast *1846.*   147 cannot] can not *1846.*

Innocent .. none shall hurt thee. Think no more
Of that obedience thou wouldst speak about—
'Twas never promist me.

    Ines.   What else is love?

    Pedro. O Ines! Ines! Ines! must we two
Know nothing more of what love is, than this!

    Ines. Enough for such as I am .. ah! too much ..
It must not be .. and yet it may be, sure!   160
Pedro hath shewn me many of my faults,
And now may shew me all, and bid me mend them.

    Pedro. Forget me, hate me: I am grown ungrateful,
Wild, desperate, the very worst of men.
And (if thou wilt not pity me for saying it)
Most wretched, and most wronged.

                        Hold back thy pity!
I will not have it.

             Is this curse enough
For my consent to leave thee? or what heavier
Would any wish? even thou?

    Ines.   Oh tender Pedro!
If you have ceased to love me (very strange   170
As are your words) I would not argue with you;
I have no power and you no need of it:
But if you ever fancy in yourself
Such blemishes, then be persuaded by me,
O generous Pedro, you have wronged your nature;
They are not to be fear'd or thought of in it.
Enough of breasts are open to them, room
Enough in all, and welcome in too many!
They cannot enter Pedro's.

                  If indeed
You have quite ceast to love me, say it not;   180
Let Watchfulness and Doubt walk slow before
Sad Certainty: let every fibre throb
Daily and nightly in the dim suspense;
Only bid Pity hold the light of Truth
Back, nor break suddenly my dream of bliss;
For fragile is the vase, containing one
Poor simple flower dipt in it by yourself,

161 shewn] shown *1846.*   162 shew] show *1846.*   179 cannot] can not *1846.*
If indeed *and ll.* 180–90 *printed in* Additions *1831 and here inserted in text.* If indeed
om. 1846.   *l.* 180 *om. 1846, which substitutes ll.* 191–4 *of present text and before l.* 181
has:

    Ines. Nought will I ask, nought dare I, nought desire I.

And, if you saw it broken at your feet,
You might weep too, ere you could turn away;
Then never say that you have ceast to love me.   190
    Pedro.   Burst, my heart!
    Ines. One only, in your sorrows, we have stil . .
Speak, and assuage it.
    Pedro.   Dost thou bid me? hear!
Hear me! reproach me! spurn me! but ask nought.
I must not marry thee.
                    What answerest thou?
    Ines. Heaven has decreed it then, O my beloved!
Be calm! unless I have offended you.
    Pedro. I may be calm, no doubt! a curse on those
Who teach me calmness! wouldst *thou* teach me it?
    Ines. Take off the curse! with any pain but that   200
I would; tho others first must teach it *me*.
    Pedro. I thought so! *Others!* What a word is this!
She then has confidents! she asks their counsel!
She talks to them of me! tells of my loves,
My doubts, my fears. . . What fears have I? what doubts? . .
She throws my weaknesses before their feet
To look at, touch, discourse upon, discuss . .
Now I can leave her . . now I can . . and will.
In three strides I am gone beyond a thought
Of such a woman . . dear as she was once!   210
Pooh! I misunderstood her, I perceive.
Monks then and priests invade the sanctuary
Of holiest love, strip down its freshest fruits,
And chew them dry, and call them bad and bitter!
Could it be thus, were dignity in man
Or chastity in woman, as before?
We turn tame foxes into our own vineyards
To yelp the wild ones out; but they the wild
Come only the more numerous at their noise;
And our sleek guardians make the best grapes theirs,   220
Biting the fist that drags them back too late.
    Ines. Revere our holy Church! tho some within
Have erred, and some are slow to lead us right,
Stopping to pry when staff and lamp should be
In hand, and the way whiten underneath.

---

192 stil] still *1846.*   195 *Before* I *1846 has* Pedro *as speaker.*   201 must]
much *mispr. in 1846.*   202 *Pedro*] *Pedro (aside) 1846.*   21 *after* perceive.
1846 has [*To Iñes.*

Pedro. Ines, the Church is now a charnel-house,
Where all that is not rottenness is drowth.
Thou hast but seen its gate hung round with flowers,
And heard the music whose serenest waves
Cover its gulfs and dally with its shoals,   230
And hold the myriad insects in light play
Above it, loth to leave its sunny sides.
Look at this central edifice! come close!
Men's bones and marrow its materials are,
Men's groans inaugurated it, men's tears
Sprinkle its floor, fires lighted up with men
Are censers for it; Agony and Anger
Surround it night and day with sleepless eyes;
Dissimulation, Terrour, Treachery,
Denunciations of the child, the parent,   240
The sister, brother, lover (mark me, Ines!)
Are the peace-offerings God receives from it.
    Ines. I tremble . . but betrayers tremble more.
Now cease, cease, Pedro! Cling I must to somewhat . .
Leave me one guide, one rest! Let me love God!
Alone . . if it must be so!
    Pedro.   Him alone . .
Mind; in him only place thy trust henceforth.
Thy hands are marble, Ines! and thy looks
Unchangeable, as are the wintery stars
In their clear brightness . . and what pangs have I   250
Endured for thee! Gaze, smile at me, sit mute . .
I merit it . . Woman of songs and satires
And sermons, thro the world they point at thee!

                                                     To himself.

I spoke of what I suffered: I spoke ill.
Light as a bubble was the heaviest of it
To what I now endure. Where was there ever
Affliction like love buried thus alive,
And turn'd to hatred by some hellish charm!
So! then thy lips can move! can open too!
When they have leisure, will they deign to speak?   260
    Ines. O Pedro! Pedro! my own agony
Had cast me down; yours will not let me sink.
Uncertain man! once tender, now severe,
Once prodigal of confidence, now prompt

237 Anger] Wrath *1846.*   239 Terrour] Terror *1846.*   249 wintery] wintry
1846.

To snatch it back, rending the heart that held it!
How much true love my grave will hide from you!
Let this dry up my tears!
    Pedro.   Live! and live happy!
    Queen. Perfidious! where are now the promises
You made your father, when at my request
He pardoned that young sorceress? Are your words   270
All spent? am I unworthy of reply?
    Pedro. Madam, no accusation was preferred
Of sorcery; the threat was quite enough.
When you protested by the saints and martyrs,
Angels and confessors, Ines de Castro
Should soon be charged of sorcery before
The competent tribunals of the realm,
Unless she would renounce my plighted vow,
So firm was my reliance on the word
Of royalty, so well I understood   280
What *competent tribunals* are, I swore
Upon my knees, never to marry her
Whom I had sworn to marry. In all this
Is there no merit to a royal mind?
    Queen. Much; if the vow be kept.
    Pedro.   Vows always should be.
    Queen. If made to fathers, made to kings, or saints.
    Ines. Your love, your kindest love then separates us.
Would you not tell me this . . to make me happy!
    Queen. I would prepare this damsel here to loose
(Allowing time . . a day, two days, or more,   290
If need there be . .) her idle unfit ties.
    Pedro. I was more rough, and would have broken them
To save her. Hard as is the alternative,
Rather would I be wanting to my faith
Than see the woman I have loved, and love,
Resign or loosen it. To ask of her
To break my bonds for me, were more than baseness;
'Twere baseness . . which the very weak themselves
Disdain, and love and fear alike brush by.

267 *after* happy! *1846 has:*
ACT II.
AT CINTRA.
BLANCA. PEDRO. INES.
From here to end QUEEN *as speaker is altered in 1846 to* BLANCA.
268 *before* Perfidious *1846 has:*
        Blanca. I who heard all, have brought her back again.
298 baseness . . . weak] what the weakest of the base *1846.*

Queen. Against the course of nature, royal blood   300
Would mingle with plebeian.
    Pedro.   None is here.
    Queen. All blood not royal should to royal eyes
Appear so. Fie! the universe cries out
In condemnation of you.
    Pedro.   I would answer
With calmness your reproof, O queen, if calmness
In such contingencies were not the thing
The most offensive.
    Queen.   Speak: reply you cannot.
    Pedro. Against the course of nature 'tis impossible
To run (a folly you object to me)
Unless we do a violence to others   310
Or to ourselves.
              But then this universe!
This beadle's house, these rotten fangs from fiends,
These imprecation-wallets opening
To blast me with fat air! . .
    Queen.   Scoff at the world!
    Pedro. Saints do it worse.
              The universe of princes,
Lady! is but a narrow one indeed!
Court, church, and camp are its three continents . .
Nothing is there above, below, around,
But air and froth, now quieter, now stormier.
    Queen. Rare manhood! thus to argue with a woman!   320
Rare courtesy! thus to instruct a queen.
    Pedro. Ah! the distracted will for ever reason;
Why will not those sometimes who are not so?
    Queen. What then, unsteddy youth, were your resolves?
    Pedro. If, she who formerly believed so much,
Ines could think me now unworthy of her,
She soon might bear our severance: what care I
How many, great, unmerited, my sufferings,
Be hers but less!
    Queen.   To whom now speaks the boy?
    Ines. Those thoughts, that cannot rest, spring from his heart;   330
And, as they spring, fall into it again,
Like some pure fountain-water, where none heeds
The rift it rises from.
                      To PEDRO, *laying her hand on his.*

307, 330 cannot] can not *1846.*   324 unsteddy] unsteady *1846.*

INES DE CASTRO

Was it to me,

Or to yourself, or to the queen, you spoke?

   Pedro. In Nature's voice I spoke alone with Nature.

To the QUEEN.

Madam! protect this innocent sweet girl!

I, who would have abandoned her, implore it!

   Ines. Too generous soul! O Pedro! O my prince!

Let the unworthiest of your father's vassals

Clasp, on the ground, your knee!

   Queen. How! in my presence   340

Thou leanst thy forehead on thy keeper's knee!

   Pedro (raising Ines). Rise!

To the QUEEN.

           Madam, I have not yet learnt castilian.

My royal father has confer'd on me,

For my poor humble service, no such title.

I am but Pedro, prince of Portugal.

Towns, provinces, have been entrusted to me,

And kept; but never have I undertaken

The weighty charge, to be a woman's keeper.

   Ines. Crave pardon of the queen!

   Queen. Of me? what need?

His father will forgive him at my suit;   350

He loves him, and hath shewn it in the choice

He has approved and sanctioned, of his wife.

   Ines. O happy father! happy Portugal!

And, whatsoe'er befall thee, happy Ines!

   Queen. Has the audacious chatterer ceased at last?

Constantia, sir, is royal, is your equal,

Is your superior.

   Pedro. Who is not? that wears

The graces of her sex, the goodness of it,

The mildness, and sometimes the pitying tears.

Constantia knows my passion.

   Queen. Knows your passion?   360

What! before marriage? Yes, yes, you are right . .

I told her of it when I gave it her . .

How twas devoted to her . . Prove my words,

If loyalty and knighthood are within you.

   Pedro. Strong the appeal: and any other words

The queen might dictate . .

341 Thou leanst] Leaning *1846.*   342 castilian] Castilian *1846.*   343 confer'd] conferr'd *1846.*   351 shewn] shown *1846.*   363 twas] 'twas *1846.*

235

Queen.   These will do quite well;
Confirm them to my daughter: that is all:
Say them in your own way . . with some few more,
As princes do, by precedent . . or not . .
I would drop any form, to make you easy   370
And put this boyish fancy out of mind.

   Ines. I must not throw myself again before you,
I must not hear those royal words again,
They hurt you so, they almost made you angry . .
Ah! how you blush at being wroth so soon! . .
But let me pray, and let me once more move you,
Be duteous! be obedient! O how lovely
Is the young princess who expects your hand!

   Queen. Does it require an effort to espouse
The princess of Castille?

   Pedro.   Nor to espouse,   380
Nor to abandon whom we *should* espouse,
Is thought an effort in the court of kings.

   Queen. Plebeian soul! ill-sorted with its state!

   Ines. Into what errors have I led you, Pedro!
The princess may retrieve you . . she alone.

   Queen (seizing INES). Come then . . resist not, think not, hang not
     back . .
Along with me! There is no other way
To give him freedom. We may find for you
A match more equal and less perilous.
I will adorn your nuptials with my presence,   390
To satisfy your pride, and his, unworthy!
No earthly thing is wanting to the bridegroom.
He has estate, youth, person, rank, court-favour . .
What! thankless, graceless, uncompliant girl,
Will nothing serve you under royalty?

   Ines. O were there none on earth! I then were happy.

   Queen. Abomination! treason! heresy!
My duty now compels me . . call the guard . .

   Pedro. Forbear, forbear, justly offended queen!

   Ines. Well may you blush, who never blusht for me   400

---

*ll. 372–415 taken in part and with variants from metrical passage in an Imaginary
Conversation published 1828. See notes at end of volume.*   373 I] You *1828.*
again] repeated *1828.*   375 Ah! how] Well do *1828.*   wroth] moved *1828.*
385 The princess] Constantia *1828.*   393 estate . . . rank] youth, estate, rank,
person, and *1828.*   394 graceless, uncompliant] uncompliant! Graceless *1828.*
395 you] thee *1828.*   397 Abomination . . . heresy] Impiety! abomination!
treason! *1828.*

Before! I lost my senses when I said it.
I may love God: I may not love *you*, Pedro!
And hence the worst and wildest wish that ever
Distraction wrencht from passion . . for my warmth
To draw the sun ('twas nothing less) from heaven.
O what were Portugal, what were earth, without you!
Inanimate, or trampled, or distraught,
Or self-opprest, like one in wicked slumber.
Reign, bravest Pedro, teaching first obedience . .
Be every thing that kings have ever been . .   410
Unless they should have loved!
                                        O that, before
We part, I must not touch those cheeks with mine,
To catch their modesty and beauteousness!
    Queen. Mad impudence! am I then but a fly
Or bird, or vacant unobservant air,
That every sigh should strip itself before me?
Thy wanton ardour, girl, shall have its range
Elsewhere.
    Ines.   Most gracious lady! let me follow,
I am unworthy of the hand that leads me . .
    Queen. That drags thee to thy doom, if thou resist.   420
Choose; death or marriage!
    Ines.   Marriage! never, never!
Help me, O help me, Pedro! not to fly,
Not to resist, but to obey in all
Save that one thing where life and death are one.
Of that speak not, tho you should speak from heaven.
    Pedro. What can I? Wilt thou claim me? I am thine . .
One fire, before the populace, burns both.
    Queen. Atheist and heretic! shame, shame o'erwhelm thee!
A prince of Portugal, in robes of flame!
Before the populace! and own his fault!   430
                                        To INES.

Come, come along! these horrors must not be.
God, Sant-Iago, and Castille, forbid!
    Ines. Grant me, O queen, a cloister.

401 Before] *not in 1828.*   when I said] to have uttered *1828.*   402 may . . .
may] might . . . might *1828.*   *For ll.* 404–5 *1828 had:*
            Distraction wrung from love . . . to draw the sun
            ('Tis nothing less) from heaven for my own warmth.
406 what were] or *1828.*   407 trampled, or distraught] trampled on, or waste *1828.*
408 like] as *1828.*   409 bravest] gracious *1828.*   412 We . . . must] O that
I may *1828.*   416 sigh should] wish shall *1828.*   421 Marriage!] Marriage? *1846.*

Queen. With the pure?
The consecrated? the resigned?
   Ines. A grave
Then grant me! there the fit and unfit meet.
   Queen. I will grant that which girls like thee wish more,
And pray for less aloud: my word is given:
The bridegroom waits: thou'rt his ere the last mass:
In time for dinner at his father's house.
Haste; do not keep the valets round the board   440
To drive away the flies which mar your feast,
Nor make the elder guests more grave than age
Has made them, that their wine grows warm apace.
   Ines to PEDRO. O then you cannot save me!
   Pedro. Save I will,
If my own life can do it.
   Queen. How should that?
   Ines. No branch so leafless but it gives a shade
To some poor insect at some hour of day.
Many has that sword slain who wisht to live,
And there was glory from it; was it then
Because they wisht to live, that there was glory   450
In stripping them of life? are friendly deeds
Less glorious than unfriendly? is less brave
The blow that liberates than the force that binds?
   Pedro. What sayst thou!
   Ines. I dare neither say nor do,
Yet wish . . and more than wildest love e'er wisht.
   Pedro to himself. I will not ask again, lest one desire,
As ever, come between us and seize both.

                                  To INES.

What thou hast spoken of inanimate things
Levels me with them, nay, casts me beneath.
Lo! here am I, and cannot lend protection   460
To those whom God's right-hand placed at my side
Rather to strengthen and admonish *me*,
And whom their virtue should have raised above it.
   Queen. Virtue! ay, where obedience and religion
Are wanting, there comes virtue! by my faith
Never a word on earth I like so ill:
Who taught you it?
   Pedro. The word I have forgotten
Who taught me: if you ask or heed who taught

            444, 460 cannot] can not *1846*.

238

The thing, behold her here! and here the heart
Wheron, beneath her image, 'tis engraven.   470
  Queen. Blessed are they who walk in innocence,
And fear the Lord, and only know his saints,
And only do his will! The arts of Hell,
The powers of darkness, be they far from me,
From you, my son, and all our royal house?
I would not even mention them, lest woe
Fall upon some one at the searching sound.
Treason, rebellion, wishes undisguised,
Bold boisterous exclamations, not against
One King, and him the very best on earth,   480
Our natural lord and master, but against
The form, the power, the name, of royalty . .
Royalty! God's appointed, God's own work,
God's own resemblance, need no charge of sorcery.
You are the witness, prince! I would hurt none . .
You on your oath must answer to our liege
For the state's weal: and let us drop the rest.
  Pedro. Spare her! or, by the Christ that died for me,
I die for her, and on this sword, before you.
  Queen. Abstain, rash youth!
  Pedro.   Merciless queen, abstain!   490
  Ines. O call none merciless! all *must* have mercy;
All need it.
  Queen.   Hold thy peace! art thou in church,
Profane one! or are words like these for thee!
  Pedro. Forgive her! swear upon the crucifix
That you will never urge against her aught
Endangering life, or liberty, or fame,
Then give me to the axe or to the stake
As best beseems you . .
  Queen.   You will then obey?
  Pedro. Swear; due obedience follows.
  Queen.   To my lips
I lift my blessed Lord, and call his name   500
In witness; not a thought of ill is left
Within my sinful breast against the life,

470 Wheron] Whereon *1846.*   *after* engraven *1845 inserts one line:*
      Drown'd, drown'd are all my senses in deep love.

475 house?] house! *1846.*   484 resemblance . . . sorcery.] resemblance. Need
we charge of sorcery? *1846.*

Or liberty, or fame, of that young maid,
Ines de Castro.

Ines.　　　　　　Gracious queen! kind Pedro!
To think of me!

　　　　　　　　I too have courage . . strength . .

Queen. She falls upon my knees: she faints: 'tis nothing;
Call . .

Pedro. Let my arms, for the last time, sustain her!　　　　507

506 *before* She falls *1846 inserts one line:*
　　　　　What confidence! what impropriety!

[PART II]

[Added and published in 1846 with heading as below.]

ACT III.

AT CINTRA

KING ALFONSO *and* QUEEN BLANCA.

Blanca. She hath been known to favor the suggestion
That he is wiser, handsomer, and younger
(We know what that word points to) than your majesty.

Alfonso. There is irreverence in it. Well; but sons
May be, nay, must be, younger than their fathers.

Blanca. O well-pois'd thought! how kindly! how considerate!
I am no enemy of hers; we both
Agree, the wily Iñes hath her charms;
God grant they all be innocent, they all
Be such as holy church may countenance,　　　　10
Better than it can do her foul alliance.

Alfonso. The church can give us purity of life,
Devotion and obedience, and strong miracles
To make us stedfast in our true belief.

Blanca. The Devil may prevail.

Alfonso.　　　　　　　　No, no; not he;
I will not have it so.

Blanca.　　　　　Against the church
I did not say, but against us frail creatures.

Alfonso. Ay, let him stick but there, and small harm done.

Blanca. Thus, thus it is; all pious men are wise:
None other.

　　240

Alfonso. Not a mother's son of them. 20

Blanca. How shall we bear to think then of those spells,
Those conjurations and those incantations?
Yes, cross yourself until your coat be tatters,
It will not countervail them.

    Alfonso. Who 's at work?

    Blanca. Iñes.

    Alfonso. And did she write her name in blood?

    Blanca. She would; and even in yours.

    Alfonso. Bad! bad! but mine
Would not be half so wicked as her own:
The Devil would find savour in that sop,
And kiss a seal so precious ten times over.

    Blanca. He has already.

    Alfonso. How! you do not say so! 30

    Blanca. I say it; I am sure of it; and they
Imitate that abomination.

    Alfonso. Who?
Iñes and Pedro? Ten times over?

    Blanca. Twenty.

    Alfonso. God help him!

    Blanca. O my liege! what word was that?

    Alfonso. It must be lust.

    Blanca. Worse.

    Alfonso. Even than lust? I've thought
Upon it much, and the more years I think
Upon it, worse and worse it seems to me.

    Blanca. Odious! most odious! Princes thus descend!

    Alfonso. Yet, Blanca, they are young! young too were we!

    Blanca (aside). I have no patience.
    Still the charms of youth 40
Surround your majesty.

    Alfonso. I have been younger.

    Blanca. Chroniclers may assert it.

    Alfonso. I am hale.

    Blanca. Ah! there are powers that sap all human strength!
Even words can do it, words, the froth of wishes
Boiling in venom.

    Alfonso. Saints above! would Iñes
Compass my death? that beauteous one? she, Iñes?

    Blanca. Look to her.

    Alfonso. Do you think so?

    Blanca. God avert it!

Alfonso. Nay, if it come to that, I must protect
With all my strength of courage and of wisdom
My royal house most royally against her,   50
And call upon the church to stand and guard us.

[PART III]

[Published in 1831 where it follows *Ines de Castro at Cintra l.* 507 (Part I, p. 225);
reprinted 1846 where it follows Part II. Text 1831.]

INES DE CASTRO AT COIMBRA

PEDRO. INES. QUEEN.

Pedro. INES! we have not loved in vain: this day
Rewards thy many sufferings for my sake,
And places our sweet children where they ought
To stand, in their own brightness.
                              Once I said
The king will do it: 'twas some heavenly voice
Prompted my words; yet my heart own'd them not,
And I was slow to speak and thou to hear
The comfort this hour brings.
      Ines.   The holy Father
Sanctioned our vows, the bishop joined our hands,
In vain, if the parental blessing on us   10
Be wanting.
            Many are the tears we shedd
For poor Constantia, who, upon the brink
Of death, took our right-hands, and claspt them hard,
And sighed, *Be never sundered, faithful pair!*
Not even this avails us: when the king
Calls us his children, and the queen too hers,
Then, and then only, are the rites complete.
      Pedro. Sweet was the friend thou gavest me; more sweet
The friend she gave: heroic was her gift,
More than heroic thine; she loved me well,   20
I loved her only that she loved me so:
Thou wert my soul's delight from the first day
My eyes had opened on thee, and thy life

Title and sub-title, Ines . . . Queen. *om. 1846, which substitutes:*
Act IV.
At Coimbra
PEDRO. INES.

11 shedd] shed *1846.*   12 who] when *1846.*   13 took . . . -hands,] she took
our hands *1846.*

Kept mine on earth but to watch over it.
Now it is safe.

                 Something yet troubles thee;
What can it be?

   Ines.   I wonder why the children
Are not yet brought to us. The king and queen
Will soon be here; and we without the flowers
To offer them!

   Pedro.   The fault is mine. A child,
Now almost four years old, remarks, remembers.   30

   Ines. Surely he should.

   Pedro.   Humiliation? no.
He shall not scorn *his* father, nor curse *mine.*
What I must do, Ines, I do for thee . .
Hard else the service . . hard! . . ay, unperformed.
The king will see the children in the park,
(He must ride through it) and let that suffice!

   Queen Blanca entering. Don Pedro! I rejoice that our liege lord
Hath well considered what becomes his house,
And, in his tenderness of heart, embraced
This lady, to whom on my part I pray   40
Heaven grant its loving mercies.

   Pedro.   I await
The presence of my father, to pour forth
Whatever gratitude, whatever zeal,
Soldier or son may offer: late last night
His orders came that we await him here;
And the most gracious presence of our queen
Alike detains me from the hoped embrace.

   Queen. The king, my husband, met before the castle
The children which they told him are his son's,
And he was taken with . . I know not which . .   50
The elder, or the younger, and would fain
Have them with him and talk with them and love them,
And may perhaps, in time, provide for them.

   Pedro. Madam, when they are stronger, their own swords
Will do it.

   Ines apart. O! hush! Pedro! is this right,
After such kindness?

        After l. 36 Queen ... *entering. om. 1846 which has:*
                 ACT V.
             At Coimbra
         Blanca. Pedro. Ines.
    ll. 46–7 *om. 1846.*   49 which] who *1846.*

Queen.   But until they *are*
Stronger, and carry swords (which may do harm),
Shall we not look to them, and merit thanks?
    Pedro. God grant it!
    Queen.   All must give up some designs,
Some wishes too long nurst, some ill-grown thoughts.   60
After five years many would not repine
To yield a mistress, but would bless the eyes
That winkt upon the fault, like mine, like his,
The fond indulgent father's, the wise king's.
    Pedro. I have no mistress, save whom holy Church
And love as holy gave me. Gifts like her
Heaven seldom gave, and never man resigned.
    Ines. Surely no longer is there any cause
For separation.
    Pedro.   Cause be there or not,
No power on earth can separate us now.   70
    Queen. He who permitted can release your bonds;
To him belongs all power in earth and heaven.
    Pedro. Hath God none left? have vows and sacraments
No force in them?
    Queen.   God leaves this nether world
To his vicegerent.
    Pedro.   So it seems!
    Queen.   Then bow
Obedient to the rod.
    Pedro.   Is there no time
When rods shall shed their knots, and we arise
From under them, and when the bloody hand
Shall drop them, will consent to clench our gold
In preference, and be kist on the outside   80
For form-sake, letting us stand up, and walk?
    Queen. I understand not this opprobrious speech.
We are vile worms: how can we stand erect?
    Pedro. God made us not vile worms.
    Queen.   We make ourselves
None other, by our passions.
    Pedro.   Not by those
The Church hath sanctified.
    Queen.   For its own ends.
    Pedro. Ay, truly!
    Queen.   For its peace . .

             79 will] shall *1846*.

INES DE CASTRO

Pedro.   And plenteousness.
Queen. God's house should be well stored.
Pedro.   God's law well kept.
His house be it his to keep, his law be it ours.
 Queen. Assertor of illegibilities   90
In law, the sense wherof but one can tell,
No longer do I wonder that my poor
Constantia died so soon: died ere the crown
Circled her fine black hair! . .
 Pedro.   . . And King Alfonso
Was gathered to his fathers!
 Queen.   Miscreant!
Who thought of that?
 Pedro.   Worthy was your Constantia
Of any crown; but none (had life been spared)
Could have been hers before my father left it.
 Queen. And shall that creature there, that half-espous'd,
Wear it instead?
 Pedro.   That creature there descends 100
Of royal lineage; and from her hath sprung
A royal lineage not below the past.
Adversity hath nurst it, and just Heaven
Placed it, you say, beneath my father's smile.
 Ines. Nothing is wanting, now, most glorious queen!
Beside your blessing.
 Queen.   Curses on the brood . .
. . I had well-nigh been prompted to exclame
Under my wrongs . . but wrongs we all must bear.
 Ines. If any of them seem to rise from me,
Punish me, O kind lady! and point out   110
How I may expiate my offense at last.
 Queen. De Castro! Set not thou thy heart upon
The crown! it may fall from thee . . nay, it shall.
 Ines. For crowns I care not.
 Queen to PEDRO.   Carest *thou* for crowns?
 Pedro. I value that of Portugal above
All earthly things, saving my faith and sword.
 Queen. Above this woman?
 Pedro.   On this woman rests
My faith, and o'er her pillow hangs my sword.
The crown is, and God grant it long may be,

105 glorious] gracious *1846.* 107 exclame] exclaim *1846.* 111 offense]
offence *1846.*

Another's; and no thought can dwell theron   120
Of mine, but hopes of love from him who wears it,
A subject's, soldier's, son's obedience.

    Queen.   *An officer brings a letter.*
Prove it: the speech was spoken opportunely.

                        After some time reading.

" She spoils me! what would one much better do?
Give me my own mama! I'll run away . .
I'll never have another . . very good ones
Would only make me cry the more for mine."
And words like these confound and shake the wise!
Patience! . . I have no patience for his folly.
" Beauty."

              Young things are always beautiful.   130
" Such innocence."

               Can they be otherwise?
" Like me a little."

               Ha! there lies the spell.
Doating old man! I'll break it, if I live.
Like thee?

            Constantia's children may become so;
Legitimately born, them sponsor kings
Have held, and heard their titles, at the font.

    Pedro. Madam, the former words you spoke less loud:
They may not have concern'd me; but these last
Strike at my honour.

               Since the nuptial rites
First held together those whom love had joined,   140
None have been ever holier than were ours.
The pontif, to whose power you have appeal'd,
Ordered the best of bishops, him of Guarda,
To join our hands and bless us; which he did;
Shedding the tears that virtuous old men shed
On those whom they think virtuous, both when joy
Showers from above, and when grief strikes them low.

    Queen. The pontif did it lest a scandal lie
Against the Church: he was deceived: some doubts
Have risen in his mind, which you shall hear,   150
Of this young person who was named your wife.

    Pedro. Named! by the name of God! she is my wife,

---

    120 theron] thereon *1846.*   123 *after* opportunely *1846 has:* [*Reading.*   *l.* 128
om. *1846.*   129 *after* folly *1846 has* [*Reads on.*   134 thee] thee *1846.*
142, 148 pontif] pontiff *1846.*   149 deceived] deceiv'd *1846.*

And shall be so for ever! Earth, Hell, Rome,
Shall never separate us.
                         Courage! girl!
Thou hast heard worse from her.
   Queen.   . . And worse shalt hear.
Some time ago, when we first met, at Cintra,
I was too tender-hearted; so the king
Assured me: now he leaves me my own way
To follow.
   Ines.   When he comes . .
   Queen.   He comes not hither.
   Pedro. Can kings deceive?
   Queen.   No, they can not deceive,   160
But they can promise and observe the promise
Or drop it, as they will.
                   Who shall controll
Or question them?
   Pedro.   Their God.
   Queen.   God hath approved
From Rome (if you will read it) our resolves.

                                        Holding a paper.

   Pedro. Madam, I read not any thing from Rome
That violates our sacraments.
   Queen.   Rome made
And can unmake them, and does every day.
   Pedro. Only where kings are rich and nations weak.
   Queen. Some deference must be paid in solid gold,
Some in obedience: the more weighty part   170
We undertake, the lighter is for you.
   Pedro. Rare image, by my troth, is this of Heaven!
Odin and Thor shattered the bones, and drank
Of beer and mead what the crackt skull could hold;
Too generous were their mighty hands to filch
The purse, had any purse been in the way . .
The bridge of Mahomet has no shops upon it.
The very Jew eats up his meal morose
Apart from God, nor robs us in God's name.
   Queen. Who would have thought this cursed sect should count   180
Among its friends a prince of Portugal!
   Pedro. There are no sects in subjects: all are one;
One protects all.

   162 controll] controul *1846.*   165 any thing] anything *1846.*   179 God]
God's *1846.*

The world will never flourish
Under crowned priests or water-sprinkling kings.
 Queen. O horrible! O blasphemy! O lust
Of change in princes! You would fain become
(Tho' prince) what people call, I think, a patriot,
Hard husky thing with little kernel in it,
And bitter as the water of Hell-streams.
 Pedro. No, Madam! I abjure the uncleanliness   190
Of name so prostituted: prince I am,
And claim my birthright, and wish others theirs.
Two cackling mothers hatch two separate broods
Of patriots; neither shall infest my house.
I shun the noisier, but I loathe far more
Patriots with tags about their carcases
Bedolled with bits of ribbon and rag-lace,
And dangling, dainty, jeweled crucifix.
The puffed heart's pride and not its purifier . .
Limbs, lives, and fortunes, all before the king,   200
Until he ask the hazard of the same;
Then the two broods unite . . one step, one voice . .
For their dear country in its sad estate.
These, these are changeful.
         Ines! do not weep!
I want thy word.
 Ines.   I have no word to speak,
Now every one I utter gives offense.
 Pedro. I am then fond of change! Say this against me
And thou wilt not offend.
 Ines.   O! may God love me
As does my Pedro! may at length the queen
Pardon me as God pardon'd me, who made him!   210
 Queen. . . Over the grave of my dear child!
              Ay, sob!
Hide thy white face! pull thy loose curls around,
Exactly like . . I know not what they're like,
They are so frightful . . tossing here and there
By their own rustic untamed springiness,
Even when thou movest neither head nor body!

Eighteen lines from You would (*l.* 186) *to* changeful (*l.* 204) *printed in* ADDITIONS, *1831, and here in position then indicated. ll.* 193–203 *removed from context and printed as separate poem in* 'Works', *1846,* ii. 664: *remainder of* ADDITION *reprinted 1846 in position indicated in 1831 with one variant, i. e.* 204 These . . . are] I am less *1846.*   206 offense] offence *1846.*   *ll.* 213–16 *printed in* ADDITIONS *1831 and here in position then indicated, and so reprinted 1846.*   216 nor *1846, mispr.* not *1831.*

248

INES DE CASTRO

Darkening them (for they want it) with thy tears,
If tears will serve, to make them look becoming.
Vain wretch! thy features are some poor Biscayan's,
Some mountain girl's, half-Spanish; and thy soul   220
Has nothing royal, nothing noble, in it.
Now am I forced to say what shocks my soul
In utterance . . first because it places thee
Too near our royal house, and then because
It covers it with incest . . can I speak
The words I would? Speak them I must! for these,
These only, could strike down thy lofty hopes,
And shew thee what abyss, what hell, of guilt
Lies under to engulf thee. Didst thou not
Stand with don Pedro here, and hold the prince   230
Don Luis with him at the sacrament
Of baptism? By the saints in Paradise!
Thou art his sister in the Churchis eye.
   Pedro. The Church had wiped, I fancied, from her eye
This grain of dust . . I gave the kerchief for it . .
Many, and somewhat worse, she throws in ours.
   Queen. Arguing with him who argues against God,*
As thou dost, were a folly: this at least,
Ines! is not among thy many sins:
Yet little as thou hast deserved of me,   240
I make thee what amends thy broken marriage
(For such in courtesy I will express it)
Admits of.
   Pedro.   I am then, it seems, to die . .
Since nothing but the stroke of death can break it.
   Ines. Sweet husband! shall false dangers overshadow
Whom true and great ones blazed upon and guided?
   Pedro. And shall these false ones make thee weep? did those?
Bear up, my Ines! bear up bravely, girl!
We have been happy: happy we shall be.

* Pedro must have been thought a very profane man by the religious: for, even when
he was king, he insulted the bishop of Oporto, for appearing at court after he had been
tried for adultery and found guilty. Mariana records this terrible outrage of his on
the privileged orders. In other things he was not amiss. It was his saying that a king
who permitted a single day to pass without a beneficent action, deserved not the kingly
name. [L. *See* "General History of Spain" by Juan de Mariana, translated by Captain
John Stevens, 1699, p. 285.]

ll. 217–20 om. 1846.   221 Has] There's *1846.*   *See footnote to l. 256 and
notes at end of volume for thirty-four lines in* ADDITIONS, *1831, to follow* noble, in it.
227 could] can *1846.*   228 shew] show *1846.*   233 Churchis] Church's *1846.*
See note to p. 93 at end of vol.   248 girl! *so in 1846*: *mispr.* girl? *1831.*

Thou seest me not, withering with age, cast down   250
By weight of wrongs, consumed by grief, distraught
By envy and ambition, worse than one
Whom penal horses sever limb from limb,
Nor, what were worse than all, bereft of thee;
For Heaven will give me thoughts and views of Ines,
As Ines gave me, in this world, of Heaven.

Goes to the window.

Ha! there they stand below, agape for me.
One walked but half the length of the house-front
And turn'd again, and askt his fellow slave
(I do believe, for they have hungry scrips)   260
When will the prey be ours? and the prey's price?
Their plumes and brims ill hide them, tho they keep
As near as may be under us: perhaps
Twere well to call three more and better men.
Pacheco is too lank; the shrewd Coello
And spruce Gonzales would not like their doublets
To have another slash in them.
 Queen.   What mean
These foul insinuations?
 Pedro.   What mean they
Under my window?
 Queen.   Your own good; the king's
True service.
 Pedro. Let them enter then.
 Queen.   This room?   270
 Pedro. Yea, and within one pace of their king's son;
Covered; with dirk and rapier .. but in front.
 Ines. Escape, O dearest Pedro!
 Pedro.   He who dies
Escapes .. and some shall beat the path before.
I would not willingly try any flight:
The only one I know, the only one
Where Honour can go with me, will be mine
Whatever hour I choose.
 Queen.   Most heathenish!
To talk of Honour and of Death so lightly!
 Pedro. Madam, we may lose one, but not the other; 280
Therefor we need not mind it.

256 *after* Heaven *1846 inserts thirty-five lines for which see notes at end of volume.*
Before l. 257 *1846 has* [Pedro *goes to the window.* 258 walked] walkt *1846, 1876.*
264 Twere] 'Twere *1846.*

INES DE CASTRO

Queen.   Not when Hell
Opens before us?
    Pedro.   Hell too we may close
And its enormous portals, with less effort
Than infants push aside ungrateful food.
We have but to maintain our sense of right,
Which of all senses is the pleasantest,
And which must bear most violence ere expell'd.
    Queen. I understand not a fantastic speech
Appliant to no person, to no purport.
I will speak plainer; and I speak to both . .   290
Obey!
        It seems not decent that men's hands
Should touch with little gentleness, should lead
Compulsively, young women who have stood
Behind and near the daughter of Castille.
Long-suffering is my merit, if the grace
Of God vouchsafes me one: but oaths of fealty
On all are binding, and on queens the most.
My conscience hath upbraided me severely
For not disclosing to our king the part
Whereto (in tears I own it) I was privy,   300
Against his crown and dignity.
               Come now!
Hear reason, donna Ines! I no more
Urge any choice which may displease you both . .
    Pedro. Displease us! urge a choice!
    Queen.   We must avoid
Scandal at least.
          There are formalities . .
Mere abjuration now of marriage-rites,
And nothing more than living separate,
One in a cloister, t'other in a camp . .
The very choice the brave and chaste all make . .
    Pedro. Ay, by the Saints! and some perhaps too soon   310
Shall find my choice made firmly.
    Queen.   Now delay
Were madness, pardon perjury: such threats
Are traitorous and parricidal too.
             She calls from the window.
Coello! Diego! with your band upstairs . .

302 donna] dona *1846*.   304 us! . . choice!] us? . . choice? *1846*.   314 Coello]
Coelho *1846*. [Pedro Coelho and Alvaro Gonzales, two of the murderers of Ines, were

251

With your whole band . . two timid women wait . .
Your queen commands . . your king . . your friend the bridegroom . .
Force! murder!

To PEDRO. Stop me? hold me? grasp my wrist?

Audacious! and let that foul fiend escape?

 Ines (*just out of the door*). Good soldier! I am not escaping from
  you . .
Push me not back! *that* was not the command . .   320
Strike! you must act no otherwise . . let fall
This halbert, or I run from under it . .
The word is given . . 'twas the queen gave it . . strike,
Irresolute!

 Pedro. What fell?
 Queen.   Where is she?
 Pedro.   Fled.
 Queen. Hold me not; pray me not; I will pursue . .
 Pedro. The guard hath stopt her.
 Queen.   At the door?
 Pedro.   With force
More than is manly, thrusting her against it.
Ho! Ines! art thou hurt? speak! art thou speaking?
What sobbest thou, my love! is then my name
Uncall'd upon in any grief of thine!   330
Where is she?
      Ho! throw open, sentinel,
This door.
 Queen.   Stand further off . . he does his duty . .
Further back yet . . have you no decency!
To tread upon her blood! it runs thro fast,
And will ('tis to be fear'd) leave marks behind.
Who, hearing your insensibility,
Will pity you?
 Pedro.   None! none!
        Ines is dead!
My father! you are childless! fare you well!
Unbar the door!   *Aloud to the sentry.*
 To the QUEEN. Command him, madam!
        Who
Shall keep me here, while steel is in my grasp   340
And vengeance strengthens it and justice guides it.

given up to Pedro after his accession to the throne and put to death in his presence.
Diego Lopez Pacheco escaped. W.]
 339 *To the* QUEEN] *om. 1846 which after* madam! *has:* [*To* BLANCA.

INES DE CASTRO

Queen. Sentry, unbar!

Looking at the corpse.

The scene quite saddens me.
'Twas her own fault, rash child! God's will be done!

IPPOLITO* DI ESTE

[FIRST PART]

[Scene. Ferrara, 1505–6.]

[Published in 1831; reprinted 1846. Text 1831.]

Ippolito. Now all the people follow the procession
Here may I walk alone, and let my spirits
Enjoy the coolness of these quiet ailes.
Surely no air is stirring; every step
Tires me; the columns shake, the cieling fleets,
The floor beneath me slopes, the altar rises.
Stay! . . here she stept . . what grace! what harmony!
It seemed that every accent, every note
Of all the choral music, breathed from her:
From her celestial airiness of form   10
I could have fancied purer light descended.
Between the pillars, close and wearying,
I watcht her as she went: I had rusht on . .
It was too late; yet, when I stopt, I thought
I stopt full soon: I cried, *is she not there?*
She had been: I had seen her shadow burst
The sunbeam as she parted: a strange sound,
A sound that stupefied and not aroused me,
Filled all my senses; such was never felt
Save when the sword-girt Angel struck the gate,   20
And Paradise wail'd loud and closed for ever.
She should return; the hour is past away.
How can I bear to see her (yet I will)
Springing, she fondly thinks, to meet the man
I most abhorr, my father's base-born son,
Ferrante!

* Ferrante and Giulio were brothers, by the father's side, to the Duke Alfonso and
the Cardinal Ippolito di Este. The cardinal deprived Ferrante of his eyes for loving
the same object as his Eminence, and because she had praised the beauty of them.
[L. *See note at end of vol.*]

3 ailes] aisles *1846.*   5 cieling] ceiling *1846.*   16 She had] She *had 1846.*
25 abhorr] abhor *1846.*

253

Rosalba entering. What! I called him! in my haste
To languish at his beauty, to weigh down
His eyelids with my lips for gazing on me:
Surely I spoke the name, and knew it not
Until it bounded back and smote me so! 30
 Ippolito. Curses upon them both!
      Advancing toward her. Welcome, sweet lady!
 Rosalba. Lord Cardinal! you here! and unattended!
 Ippolito. We wait the happy lover! do we not?
 Rosalba. Ferrante then betrayed the secret to you!
And are you come to honour with your presence . .
 Ippolito. Has the Duke signed the contract?
 Rosalba.   For what bride?
Ferrante writes *Ferrante* plain enough;
And I do think, altho I once or twice
Have written it instead of mine, at last
I am grown steddier, and could write *Rosalba.* 40
 Ippolito. Sport not with one your charms have cast too low.
 Rosalba. Sport not with one your hand would raise too high.
 Ippolito. Again that taunt! the time may come, Rosalba,
When I could sanctify the blissful state
I have aspired to.
 Rosalba.   Am not I mere ice?
Shew not I girlish frowardness, the fears
Of infancy, the scruples of old age?
Have not you said so? and said more . . you hate them?
How could you bear me, or what wish from me?
 Ippolito. That which another will not long retain. 50
 Rosalba. You know him little, and me less.
 Ippolito.   I know
Inconstancy in him.
 Rosalba.   And what in me?
 Ippolito. Intolerance for his betters.
 Rosalba.   Ignorance,
But not intolerance of them, is my fault.
 Ippolito. No?
 Rosalba.   Call it thus, and cast it on the rest.
 Ippolito. Some are there whose close vision sees but one
In the whole world, and would not see another
For the whole world, were that one out of it.
 Rosalba. Are there some such? O may they be my friends!
O how, before I know them, I do love them! 60

    40 steddier] steadier *1846.* 46 Shew] Show *1846.*

IPPOLITO DI ESTE

Ippolito. After no strife, no censure, no complaint,
Have not your tears been seen, when you have left him,
Thro tediousness, distaste, dislike, and grief,
(Ingenuous minds must feel it, and may own it)
That love, so rashly promist, would retire,
Hating exaction, circumvention, bonds?
   Rosalba. Such grief is yet unknown to me; I know
All tears are not for sorrow: many swell
In the warm depths of gratitude and bliss;
But precious over all are those that hang   70
And tremble at the tale of generous deeds.
These he relates when he might talk as you do
Of passion: but he sees my heart, he finds
What fragrance most refreshes it.
                         How high,
O Heaven! must that man be, who loves and who
Would stil raise others higher than himself
To interest his beloved!
                  All my soul
Is but one drop from his, and into his
Falls, as Earth's dew falls into Earth again.
   Ippolito. Yet would it not be wise to trust a friend   80
Able to counsel in extremes and straits?
   Rosalba. Is it not wise in darkness and in storm
To trust the wave that lashes us and pray
Its guidance on the rocks whereto it tends?
I have my guide, Lord Cardinal! he alone
Is ship and pilot to me, sea and star:
Counsel from others, knowing him, would be
Like worship of false gods; in me no less
Than profanation and apostasy.
   Ippolito. We may retire; he comes not here to day.   90
   Rosalba. Then will I not retire, but lay my head
Upon the feet of any pitying saint
Until he comes, altho it be tomorrow?
   Ippolito. Tomorrow he may fail: the sovran will
By rescript has detained and must delay him.
   Rosalba. Lead, lead me to Ferrante.
   Ippolito.   Were I worthy.
   Rosalba. Proud cruel man! that bitter sneer bodes ill.
May not I see him?
   Ippolito.   He may not see you.

        76 stil] still *1846.*   98 you] *you 1846.*

Rosalba. O let him! well my memory can supply
His beauteous image. I can live on love   100
Saturate, like bees with honey, long drear days.
He must see me, or cannot rest: I can.

102 me ... cannot] *me,* or can not *1846.*

SECOND PART

Ippolito, Ferrante, *and* Giulio, *in prison.*

Ippolito. Reasons of state, I fear, have dictated
This something like severity; God grant
Here be no heresy: do both avow it,
Staring in silence at discovery?
    Giulio. No order forced me hither; I am come
To share my brother's fate, whate'er it be,
And mitigate his sufferings.
    Ippolito.   May they cease!
    Giulio. Those words would have dissolved them into air,
Spoken but twenty furlongs from these bars.
    Ippolito. I would do much to serve you; but my faith   10
And my allegiance have two other lords,
The duke my brother, and the pope my God.
Ferrante then says nothing?
    Ferrante.   He well knows
Thy hatred and its cause.
    Ippolito.   Why should I hate you,
My father's son, they say?
    Ferrante.   *They say!* His blood
Runs in these veins, pure; for pure blood was hers
Who loved the youthful lover, and who died
When falser vows estranged the matchless prince.
    Ippolito. He saw his error.
    Ferrante.   All men do when age
Bends down their heads, or gold shines in their way.   20
    Ippolito. Altho I would have helpt you in distress,
And just removed you from the court awhile,
You called me tyrant.
    Ferrante.   Called thee tyrant? I?
By heaven! in tyrant there is something great
That never was in thee. I would be killed
Rather by any monster of the wild

Than choked by weeds and quicksands, rather crusht
By maddest rage than clay-cold apathy.
Those who act well the tyrant, neither seek
Nor shun the name; and yet I wonder not   30
That thou repeatest it, and wishest me;
It sounds like power, like policy, like courage,
And none that calls thee tyrant can despise thee.
Go, issue orders for imprisonment,
Warrants for death: the gibbet and the wheel,
Lo! the grand boundaries of thy dominion!
O what a mighty office for a minister!
(And such Alfonso's brother calls himself),
To be the scribe of hawkers! Man of genius!
The lanes and allies echo with thy works.   40
   Giulio. Ah! do not urge him; he may ruin you;
He may pursue you to the grave.
   Ferrante.   He dares not:
Look at his collar! see the saint he wears!
The amber saint may ask too much for that.
   Ippolito. Atheist! thy scoffs encourage every crime,
And strip thee, like a pestilence, of friends:
Theirs is the guilt to march against the law,
They mount the scaffold, and the blow is thine.
   Ferrante. How venom burnishes his adder's crest!
How eloquent on scaffolds and on laws!   50
If such a noisome weed as falsehood is
Give frothy vigour to a worm like thee,
Crawl, eat, drink, sleep upon it, and farewell.
   Ippolito (*to Giulio*). Take you the sentence, and God be with
     both!   *Goes.*

   Giulio. What sentence have we here?
   Ferrante.   Unseal and read it.
   Giulio (*reading*). Of sight! of sight! of sight!
   Ferrante.   Would you escape,
My gentle Giulio? Run not thus around
The wide light chamber, press not thus your brow
Against the walls, with your two palms above.
Seek you the door then? you are uncondemned   60
To lose the sight of one who is the bloom
And breath of life to you: the bolts are drawn
On me alone. You carry in your breast

27 choaked] choakt *1846.*   33 that] who *1846.*

Most carefully our brother's precious gift:
Well, take it anywhere, but do not hope
Too much from any one. Time softens rocks,
And hardens men!
   Giulio.   Pray then our God for help.
   Ferrante. O my true brother, Giulio, why thus hang
Around my neck and pour forth prayers for me!
Where there are priests and kinsmen such as ours,   70
God hears not, nor is heard. I am prepared
For death.
   Giulio.   Ah! worse than death may come upon you,
Unless Heaven interpose.
   Ferrante.   I know the worst,
And bear one comfort in my breast that fire
And steel can ne'er force from it: she I love
Will not be his, but die as she hath lived.
Doubt you? that thus you shake the head, and sigh.
   Giulio. Far other doubt was mine: even this shall cease.
   Ferrante. Speak it.
   Giulio.   I must: God pardon me!
   Ferrante.   Speak on.
   Giulio. Have we not dwelt in friendship from our birth,   80
Told the same courtier the same tale of joy,
And pointed where life's earliest thorn had pierced
Amid the sports of boyhood, ere the heart
Hath aught of bitter or unsound within?
   Ferrante. We have indeed.
   Giulio.   Has my advice been ill?
   Ferrante. Too often ill-observed, but always good.
   Giulio. Brother, my words are not what better men
Would speak to you; and·yet my love, I think,
Must be more warm than theirs can ever be . .
   Ferrante. Brother's, friend's, father's, when was it like yours!   90
   Giulio. Which of them ever said what I shall say!
   Ferrante. Speak; my desires are kindled, my fears quencht.
   Giulio. Do not delay to die, lest crueller
Than common death befall you.
   Ferrante.   Then the wheel
Is ordered in that schedule! Must she too
Have her chaste limbs laid bare? Here lies the rack;
Here she would suffer ere it touch the skin . .
No, I will break it with the thread of life

94 befall] befal 1846.

Ere the sound reach her. Talk no more of Heaven,
Of Providence, of Justice . . Look on her!   100
Why should she suffer? what hath she from Heaven
Of comfort, or protection?
   Giulio.   Talk not so!
Pity comes down when Hope hath flown away.
  Ferrante. Illusion!
  Giulio.   If it were, which it is not,
Why break with vehement words such sweet illusion?
For were there nought above but empty air,
Nought but the clear blue sky where birds delight,
Soaring o'er myriad worlds of living dust
That roll in columns round the noontide ray,
Your heart would faint amid such solitude,   110
Would shrink in such vacuity: that heart
(Ferrante! can you hide its wants from me?)
Rises and looks around and calls aloud
For some kind Being, some consoling bosom,
Whereon to place its sorrows, and to rest.
   Ferrante. Oh! that was here . . I cannot look beyond.
   Giulio. Hark! hear you not the people? to the window!
They shout and clap their hands when they first meet you
After short absence; what shall they now do?
Up! seize the moment; shew yourself.
   Ferrante.   Stay, Giulio!   120
Draw me not thither! speak not of my wrongs . .
I would await but not arouse their vengeance,
And would deserve but court not their applause.
Little of good shall good men hope from them,
Nothing shall wiser.
              Aside. O were he away!
But if I fail, he must die too, being here.
   Giulio. Let me call out: they are below the grate.
They would deliver you: try this one chance.
Obdurate! would you hold me down! They're gone!
   Ferrante. Giulio! for shame! weep not, or here I stay   130
And let vile hands deform me.
   Giulio.   They shall never.
   Ferrante. What smoke arises? Are there torches under?
Surely the crowd has passed . . 'tis from the stairs.
   Giulio. Anticipate the blow.
   Ferrante.   One more must grieve!
133 passed] past 1846.
s 2

And will she grieve like you, too tender Giulio!
Turn not away the head, the hand . . what hold you?
Give, give it me . . 'tis keen . . they call you forth . .
Tell her . . no, say not we shall meet again,
For tears flow always faster at those words . .
May the thought come, but gently, like a dream.   140

FROM THE PENTALOGIA

DRAMATIC SCENES

[Published with a Dedication in 1837; reprinted without Dedication 1846. For two of the Scenes see Vol. ii, pp. 217, 219. The first three are as follows: Text 1837.]

TO ROBERT SOUTHEY, Esǫ. LL.D. &c. &c. &c.

You and two others will read these dramatic scraps with pleasure.

Jam satis terris: [Horace, *Carm.* i. 2.]

You are almost the only public man, of either party, whom I would give a farthing to please by anything I write. But never shall I cease to eulogise those of either, who are friends to liberal economy, fair conciliation, and watchful peace.

I publish no more in my lifetime. I may, however, throw off my fingers'-ends a few drops to lay the dust; a few to make the point-lace lie closer on the lawn, which others must wash and mend. As you will not enter the laundry or tire-room with me, pray accept these lumps of sugar-candy, to remove any bitterness left in the mouth by the astringency of my conservatism.

I never write more than a scene or two of the same drama, giving too short a hold for the rabble to seize and pull at; one calling me quaint, another pushing unlucky Canning against me.

In all this licentiousness of electioneering, the worst that has happened to me from our light-fingered literators, is an ineffectual tug at my seals (with a trifle of scurrility) by an Irishman out of place, and a kick on the skin (between two compliments) by his Scotch associate.

While the smile is on your lips, adieu! God bless you.

W. S. L.

literators,] *cf.* literators of the town, *Works, 1846,* ii. 101. [W.]   An Irishman] ? William Maginn, LL.D., identified as Captain Shannon in Thackeray's *Pendennis.* [W.]   skin] shin *Ablett's MS. emendation.*   Scotch associate] ? John Wilson ("Christopher North") [W.]

FROM THE PENTALOGIA

ESSEX AND BACON

[Published in 1837; reprinted 1846.]

[ROBERT DEVEREUX, EARL OF ESSEX, beheaded February 25, 1601.
FRANCIS BACON.]

Essex. I did believe, sir, I had helpt to raise
Many to wealth and station, some to fame,
And one to friendship.
    Bacon.   You, my noble earl,
Have done it; and much more. We must lament
A power thus past (or rather thrown) away.
    Essex. Thou? thou lament it, Bacon?
    Bacon.   To my soul.
    Essex. Why then, with energy beyond the pitch
Of brawling law, cry vengeance? when my fortune
Was pierced with every bolt from every hand,
Soon as the golden links were snapt asunder   10
Which those who rule the earth held round that bird
Who bore their lightnings and struck down their foes.
    Bacon. My gracious lord! were always their commands
Well waited for?
    Essex.   Nay, by my troth, my zeal
Outflew them.
    Bacon.   Your return was unadvised.
    Essex. Unwelcome: that is worse.
    Bacon.   The worst of all
Was summoning to arms a loyal land,
Basking in peace and plenteousness.
    Essex.   How far
Extended this your basking? court indeed
And inns of law were warm enough; on those   20
The sun beats all the day, through all the year;
Everything there so still and orderly,
That he who sneezes in them is caught up
And cudgell'd for his pains.
    Bacon.   Should he awake
Trumpets by sneezing, should he blow up banners,
'Twere well if only cudgels fell on him:
Our laws have sharper instruments, my lord!
    Essex. I know it; and I knew it ere I rose.

11 those] they *1846.*   24 cudgell'd] cudgel'd *1846.*

Bacon. O! had this never happened!

Essex.   Then wouldst thou
Have lost some smiles, some parlyings, some tags   30
Of ermine, and, what more thou valuest
(As any wise man would) some little gold.

Bacon. Dross!

Essex (*smiling*). Very true! . . as men are dust and ashes.

Bacon. Such thoughts become all mortals; most of all
Those who have fallen under high displeasure,
Who have their God and Prince to reconcile,
And are about to change this brief vile life . . .
Nay, nay, my lord! your life may rest unchanged
For years to come, if you, upon your knees,
Humbly ask pardon . .

Essex (*fiercely*).   Pardon!
          (*After hesitation.*) I will ask it . .   40

Bacon. . . Before the privy council, and the court
Especially assembled.

Essex (*indignantly*).   Not before
The best among them, were he quite alone,
No, by the soul of Essex! were he Raleigh . .
The only great man there.

Bacon.   Are we so scorned?

Essex. Bacon! I did not say the only wise one:
So, do not break thy ring, or loose the stone.

Bacon. My lord! my finger might have been uneasy
Without such notice from that once high peer
Erewhile the Earl of Essex . . until treason   50
Leveled him lower than burgess or than churl.

Essex. I will not say thou liest; for thy tongue
Lags far behind thy heart; thy strongest wit
May stretch and strain, but never make them yoke-mates.

Bacon. This cork appliance, this hard breathing, served
While there was water under for support,
But cut a dismal figure in the mud.

Essex. To servile souls how abject seem the fallen!
Benchers and message-bearers stride o'er Essex!

Bacon. Unmasted pinnace may row safely under   60
No high colossus, without pricking it.
But, sure, the valiant Earl is somewhat chafed . .
Who could have thought it! . . by a worm like me!

30 parlyings] parleyings *1468.*   61 No high] A mean *MS. emendation in Ablett's copy.*

ESSEX AND BACON

Essex. Begone! I have fairly weighed thee.
    Bacon (alone).   He weigh me!
No man is stout enough* to trim the balance,
Much less to throw the weight in . .
                   He weigh me!
Flaunting and brittle as a honeysuckle,
Sweet in the chamber, in the field blown down,
Ramping in vain to reach again its prop,
And crusht by the first footfall.
                 Arrogance   70
Stares, but sees badly . . snatches with quick gripe
What seems within the reach, and, being infirm
Of stand, is overbalanced.
              Shall I bear
Foul words upon me?
            I have thrown them back
Manfully to the beard that wagged with them . .
My courage is now safe beyond suspicion . .
Myself can hardly doubt it after this . .
Yet that audacious criminal dared spit
Reproaches! seldom are they bearable,
But, springing up from reason, sting like asps . .   80
Not that the man has reason . . he has none . .
For, what had I to do with it? I spoke . .
And, when we are commanded, we must speak.
It was her Grace . . and surely she knows best.
I may now wash my hands of him at last,
I have but done my duty . . fall who may.

* Bacon little knew or suspected that there was then existing (the only one that ever did exist) his superior in intellectual power. Position gives magnitude. While the world was rolling above Shakspeare, he was seen imperfectly: when he rose above the world, it was discovered that he was greater than the world. The most honest of his contemporaries would scarcely have admitted this, even had they known it. But vast objects of remote altitude must be looked at a long while before they are ascertained. Ages are the telescope-tubes that must be lengthened out for Shakspeare; and generations of men serve but as single witnesses to his claims. [L.]

70 footfall] footfal *1846.*

DRAMAS AND DRAMATIC SCENES

WALTER TYRREL AND WILLIAM RUFUS

[Published in 1837; reprinted 1846.]

[*Scene: The New Forest, August* 2, 1100.]

Rufus. Tyrrel, spur onward! we must not await
The laggard lords: when they have heard the dogs
I warrant they will follow fast enough,
Each for his haunch. Thy roan is mettlesome;
How the rogue sidles up to me, and claims
Acquaintance with young Yorkshire! not afraid
Of wrinkling lip, nor ear laid down like grass
By summer thunder-shower on Windsor mead.
    Tyrrel. Behold, my liege! hither they troop amain,
Over yon gap.
    Rufus.   Over my pales! the dolts   10
Have broken down my pales!
    Tyrrel.   Please you, my liege,
Unless they had, they must have ridden round
Eleven miles.
    Rufus.   Why not have ridden round
Eleven miles? or twenty, were there need.
By our Lady! they shall be our carpenters
And mend what they have marred. At any time
I can make fifty lords; but who can make
As many head of deer, if mine escape?
And sure they will, unless they too are mad.
Call me that bishop . . him with hunting-cap   20
Surcharged with cross, and scarlet above knee.
    Tyrrel (*galloping forward*). Ho! my lord bishop!
    Bishop.   Who calls me?
    Tyrrel.   Your slave.
    Bishop. Well said, if toned as well and timed as well.
Who art thou? citizen or hind? what wantest?
    Tyrrel. My lord! your presence; but before the king;
Where it may grow more placid at its leisure.
The morn is only streakt with red, my lord!
You beat her out and out: how prettily
You wear your stocking over head and ears!
Keep off the gorse and broom! they soon catch fire!   30
    Bishop. The king shall hear of this: I recognise
Sir Walter Tyrrel.

22 me] me 1846.

264

TYRREL AND RUFUS

Tyrrel.   And Sir Walter Tyrrel
By the same token duly recognises
The Church's well-begotten son, well-fed,
Well-mounted, and all well, except well-spoken,
The spiritual lord of Winchester.
    Bishop. Ay, by God's grace! pert losel!
    Tyrrel.   Prick along
Lord bishop! quicker! catch fresh air! we want it;
We have had foul enough till dinner-time.
    Bishop. Varlet! I may chastise this insolence.   40
    Tyrrel. I like those feathers: but there crows no cock
Without an answer. Though the noisiest throat
Sings from the bellfrey of snug Winchester,
Yet he from Westminster hath stouter spurs.
    Bishop. God's blood! were I no bishop. . .
    Tyrrel.   Then thy own
Were cooler.
    Bishop. Whip that hound aside! O Christ!
The beast has paw'd my housings! What a day
For dirt!
    Tyrrel. The scent lies well; pity no more
The housings; look, my lord! here trots the king!
    Rufus. Which of you broke my palings down?
    Bishop.   God knows,   50
Most gracious sir.
    Rufus.   No doubt he does; but you,
Bishop! could surely teach us what God knows.
Ride back and order some score handicrafts
To fix them in their places.
    Bishop.   The command
Of our most gracious king shall be obeyed.
(*Riding off.*) Malisons on the atheist! Who can tell
Where are my squires and other men! confused
Among the servitors of temporal lords!
I must e'en turn again and hail that brute.
Sir Walter! good Sir Walter! one half-word!   60
                        [*Tyrrel rides toward him.*

Sir Walter! may I task your courtesy
To find me any of my followers!
    Tyrrel. Willingly.

---

43 bellfrey] belfrey *1846*.   Winchester] Since Bishop Walkelin's death in 1098
the see of Winchester had been vacant. [W.]

Rufus.   Stay with me; I want thee, Tyrrel!
What does the bishop boggle at?
Tyrrel.   At nothing.
He seeks his people, to retrieve the damage.
    Rufus. Where are the lords?
Tyrrel.   Gone past your Grace, bare-headed,
And falling in the rear.
    Rufus.   Well, prick then on.
I care but little for the chase to-day,
Although the scent lies sweetly. To knock down
My paling is vexatious. We must see   70
Our great improvements in this forest; what
Of roads blockt up, of hamlets swept away,
Of lurking dens called cottages, and cells,
And hermitages. Tyrrel! thou didst right
And dutifully, to remove the house
Of thy forefathers. 'Twas an odd request,
To leave the dovecote, for the sake of those
Flea-bitten blind old pigeons. There it stands!
But, in God's name! what mean these hives? the bees
May sting my dogs.
    Tyrrel.   They hunt not in the summer.   80
    Rufus. They may torment my fawns.
    Tyrrel.   Sir! not unless
Driven from their hives: they like the flowers much better.
    Rufus. Flowers! and leave flowers too?
    Tyrrel.   Only some half-wild,
In tangled knots; balm, clary, marjoram.
    Rufus. What lies beyond this close briar hedge, that smells
Through the thick dew upon it, pleasantly?
    Tyrrel. A poor low cottage: the dry marl-pit shields it,
And, frail and unsupported like itself,
Peace-breathing honeysuckles comfort it
In its misfortunes.
    Rufus.   I am fain to laugh   90
At thy rank minstrelsy. A poor low cottage!
Only a poor low cottage! where, I ween,
A poor low maiden blesses Walter Tyrrel.
    Tyrrel. It may be so.
    Rufus.   No; it may not be so.
My orders were that all should be removed,
And, out of special favour, special trust
In thee, Sir Walter, I consigned the care

TYRREL AND RUFUS

Into thy hands, of razing thy own house
And those about it; since thou hast another
Fairer and newer, and more lands around.   100
Tyrrel. Hall, chapel, chamber, cellar, turret, grange,
Are level with the grass.
   Rufus.   What negligence
To leave the work then incomplete, when little
Was there remaining! Strip that roof, and start
Thy petty game from cover.
   Tyrrel.   O my liege!
Command not this!
   Rufus.   Make me no confidant
Of thy base loves.
   Tyrrel.   Nor you, my liege! nor any:
None such hath Walter Tyrrel.
   Rufus.   Thou 'rt at bay;
Thou hast forgotten thy avowal, man!
   Tyrrel. My father's house is (like my father) gone: 110
But in that house, and from that father's heart
Mine grew into his likeness, and held thence
Its rich possessions . . God forgive my boast!
He bade me help the needy, raise the low . .
   Rufus. And stand against thy king!
   Tyrrel.   How many yokes
Of oxen, from how many villages
For miles around, brought I, at my own charge,
To bear away the rafters and the beams
That were above my cradle at my birth,
And rang when I was christened, to the carouse   120
Of that glad father and his loyal friends!
   Rufus. He kept good cheer, they tell me.
   Tyrrel.   Yonder thatch
Covers the worn-out woman at whose breast
I hung, an infant.
   Rufus.   Ay! and none beside?
   Tyrrel. Four sons have fallen in the wars.
   Rufus.   Brave dogs!
   Tyrrel. She hath none left.
   Rufus.   No daughter?
   Tyrrel.   One.
   Rufus.   I thought it.
Unkennel her.
   Tyrrel.   Grace! pity! mercy on her!

Rufus. I will not have hot scents about my chase.

Tyrrel. A virtuous daughter of a virtuous mother
Deserves not this, my liege!

Rufus.   Am I to learn   130
What any subject at my hand deserves?

Tyrrel. Happy, who dares to teach it and who can!

Rufus. And thou, forsooth!

Tyrrel.   I have done my duty, sire!

Rufus. Not half: perform the rest, or bide my wrath.

Tyrrel. What, break athwart my knee the staff of age!

Rufus. Question me, villain!

Tyrrel.   Villain I am none.

Rufus. Retort my words! By all the saints! thou diest,
False traitor.

Tyrrel.   Sire, no private wrong, no word
Spoken in angriness, no threat against
My life or honour, urge me . .

Rufus.   Urge to what?   140
Dismountest?

Tyrrel.   On my knees, as best beseems,
I ask . . not pardon, sire! but spare, oh spare
The child devoted, the deserted mother!

Rufus. Take her; take both.

Tyrrel.   She loves her home; her limbs
Fail her; her husband sleeps in that churchyard;
Her youngest child, born many years the last,
Lies (not half-length) along the father's coffin.
Such separate love grows stronger in the stem
(I have heard say) than others close together,
And that, where pass these funerals, all life's spring   150
Vanishes from behind them, all the fruits
Of riper age are shrivelled, every sheaf
Husky; no gleaning left. She would die here,
Where from her bed she looks on his, no more
Able to rise, poor little soul! than he.

Rufus. Who would disturb them, child or father? where
Is the churchyard thou speakest of?

Tyrrel.   Among
Yon nettles: we have levelled all the graves.

Rufus. Right: or our horses might have stumbled on them.

Tyrrel. Your grace oft spares the guilty; spare the innocent!   160

Rufus. Up from the dew! thy voice is hoarse already.

152 shrivelled] shrivel'd *1846.*   158 levelled] level'd *1846.*

TYRREL AND RUFUS

Tyrrel. Yet God hath heard it. It entreats again,
Once more, once only; spare this wretched house.
  Rufus. No, nor thee neither.
  Tyrrel.   Speed me, God! and judge
O thou! between the oppressor and opprest!
                    [He pierces Rufus with an arrow.

THE PARENTS OF LUTHER

[Published in *The Tribute*, 1837, and in *Pentalogia*, 1837; reprinted 1846. Text
Pentalogia.]

[*Scene: Eisleben in Mansfeld, 1483.*]

[CHARACTERS.

JOHN [HANS] LUTHER and his wife MARGARETTA ZEIGLER.]

John Luther. I left thee, Margaretta, fast asleep,
Thou, who wert always earlier than myself,
Yet hast no mine to trudge to, hast no wedge
To sharpen at the forge, no pickaxe loose
In handle.
           Come, blush not again: thy cheeks
May now shake off those blossoms which they bore
So thick this morning, that last night's avowal
Nestles among them stil.
              So, in few months
A noisier bird partakes our whispering bower.
Say it again.
  Margarella. And, in my dream, I blushed!   10
  John. Idler! wert dreaming too? and after dawn?
  Margarella. In truth was I.
  John.   Of me?
  Margaretta.   No, not of you.
  John. No matter; for methinks some Seraph's wing
Fann'd that bright countenance.
  Margaretta.   Methinks it did,
And stir'd my soul within.
             How could you go
And never say good-bye, and give no kiss?
  John. It might have waken'd thee. I can give more

Title. Luther's Parents. By Walter Savage Landor, Esq. *Tribute.*
Scene. Characters. *Not in any ed.*
8 Nestles] Nestled *T.*   stil] still *T., 1846.*   9 bower.] bower? *1846.*

269

Kisses than sleep: so thinking, I heav'd up
Slowly my elbow from above the pillow,
And, when I saw it woke thee not, went forth.   20
 Margaretta. I would have been awaken'd for a kiss,
And a good-bye, or either, if not both.
 John. Thy dreams were not worth much then.
 Margaretta.   Few dreams are;
But . . . . .
 John. By my troth! I will intrench upon
The woman's dowry, and will contradict,
Tho' I should never contradict again.
I have got more from dreams a hundred-fold
Than all the solid earth, than field, than town,
Than (the close niggard purse that cramps my fist)
The mine will ever bring me.
 Margaretta.   So have I,   30
And so shall each indeed, if this be true.
 John. What was it then? for when good dreams befall
The true of heart, 'tis likely they come true . .
A vein of gold? ay? silver? copper? iron?
Lead? sulphur? alum? alabaster? coal?
Shake not those ringlets nor let down those eyes,
Tho' they look prettier for it, but speak out.
True, these are not thy dainties.
 Margaretta.   Guess again.
 John. Crystalline kitchens, amber-basted spits
Whizzing with frothy savory salamanders,   40
And swans that might, so plump and pleasant-looking,
Swim in the water from the mouths of knights;
And ostrich-eggs off coral woods (the nests
Outside of cinnamon, inside of saffron,
And mortar'd well, for safety-sake, with myrrh,)
Serv'd up in fern leaves green before the Flood?
 Margaretta. Stuff! you will never guess it, I am sure.
 John. No? and yet these are well worth dreaming of.
 Margaretta. Try once again.
 John.   Faith! it is kind to let me.
Under-ground beer-cascades from Nuremberg?   50
Rhine vintage stealing from Electoral cellars,
And, broader than sea-baths for mermaid brides,
With fluits upon the surface strides across,
Pink conchs, to catch it, and to light it down;

25 dowry] dowery T.   32 befall] befal 1846.

THE PARENTS OF LUTHER

And music from basaltic organ-pipes
For dancing; and five fairies to one man.
   Margaretta. Oh his wild fancies! . . . Are they innocent?
   John. I think I must be near it by that shrug.
Spicy sack-posset, roaring from hot springs
And running off like mad thro' candied cliffs,   60
But catching now and then some fruit that drops . . . . . .
Shake thy head yet? why then thou hast the palsy.
Zooks! I have thought of all things probable
And come to my wit's end.
                       What canst thou mean?
   Margaretta. Nay, I have half a mind now not to tell.
   John. Then it is out . . . Thy whole one ill could hold it.
A woman's mind hates pitch upon its seams.
   Margaretta. Hush! one word more! and then my lips are closed.
   John. Pish! one more word! and then my lips . . .
   Margaretta.   O rare
Impudent man! . . . and such discourse from you!   70
I dreamt we had a boy . . .
   John.   A wench, a wench . . . .
A boy were not like thee.
   Margaretta.   I said a boy.
   John. Well, let us have him, if we miss the girl.
   Margaretta. My father told me he *must* have a boy,
And call him Martin (his own name) because
Saint Martin both was brave and cloth'd the poor.
   John. Hurrah then for Saint Martin! he shall have
Enough to work on in this house of ours.
   Margaretta. Now do not laugh, dear husband! but this dream
Seem'd somewhat more.
   John.   So do all dreams, ere past.   80
   Margaretta. Well, but it seems so stil.
   John.   Aye, twist my fingers,
Basketing them to hold it.
   Margaretta.   Never grave!
   John. I shall be.
   Margaretta.   That one thought should make you now.
   John. And that one tap upon the cheek to boot.
   Margaretta. I do believe, if you were call'd to Heaven
You would stay toying here.
   John.   I doubt I should.
Methinks I set my back against the gate,

56 fairies] faeries *T.*   64 wit's] wits' *1846.*   81 stil] still *T., 1846.*

Thrown open to me by this rosy hand,
And look both ways, but see more heaven than earth:
Give me thy dream: thou puttest it aside: 90
I must be feasted: fetch it forth at once.
   Margaretta. Husband! I dreamt the child was in my arms,
And held a sword, which from its little grasp
I could not move, nor you: I dreamt that proud
But tottering shapes, in purple filagree,
Pull'd at it, and he laught.
   John.   They frighten'd thee!
   Margaretta. Frighten'd me! no: the infant's strength prevail'd.
Devils, with angel's faces, throng'd about;
Some offer'd flowers, and some held cups behind,
And some held daggers under silken stoles. 100
   John. These frighten'd thee, however.
   Margaretta.   He knew all;
I knew he did.
   John.   A dream! a dream indeed!
He knew and laught!
   Margaretta.   He sought his mother's breast,
And lookt at them no longer.
                    All the room
Was fill'd with light and gladness.
   John.   He shall be
Richer than we are; he shall mount his horse . .
A feat above his father; and be one
Of the duke's spearmen.
   Margaretta.   God forbid! they lead
Unrighteous lives, and often fall untimely.
   John. A lion-hearted lad shall Martin be. 110
   Margaretta. God willing; if *his* servant; but not else.
I have such hopes, full hopes, hopes overflowing.
   John. A grave grand man, half collar and half cross,
With chain enough to hold our mastiff by,
Thou fain would'st have him. Out of dirt so stiff,
Old Satan fashioneth his idol, Pride.
   Margaretta. If proud and cruel to the weak, and bent
To turn all blessings from their even course
To his own kind and company, may he
Never be great, with collar, cross, and chain; 120

---

95 filagree] *so in 1846*, filigree *T*, filagee P. (*mispr.*).   96 thee!] thee?
1846.   98 angel's] angels' 1846.   111 *his*] his *T*.   112 overflowing]
overflowed *T*.

THE PARENTS OF LUTHER

No, nor be ever angel, if, O God!
He be a fallen angel at the last.
                (After a pause.)
Uncle, you know, is sacristan; and uncle
Had once an uncle who was parish priest.
    John. He was the man who sung so merrily
Those verses which few scholars understand,
Yet which they cannot hide away, nor drive
The man from memory after forty years.
    Margaretta. (sings) *Our brightest pleasures are reflected pleasures,*
And they shine sweetest from the cottage-wall.   130
    John. The very same.
    Margaretta.   We understand them, John!
    John. An inkling. But your uncle sacristan
Hath neither sword nor spur.
    Margaretta.   It was a sword,
A flaming sword, but innocent, I saw;
And I have seen in pictures such as that,
And in the hands of angels borne on clouds.
He may defend our faith, drive out the Turk,
And quench the crescent in the Danaw stream.
    John. Thou, who begannest softly, singest now
Shrill as a throstle.
    Margaretta.   Have we then no cause   140
To sing as throstles after sign thus strange?
    John. Because it was so strange, must we believe
The rather?
    Margaretta. Yes; no fire was in the house,
No splinter, not a spark: the virgin's chin
Shone not with rushlight under it; 'twas out,
For night was almost over, if not past,
And the Count's chapel has not half that blaze
On the Count's birth-day, nor the ball at night.
Ah surely, surely fare like our's sends up
No idle fumes; nor wish nor hope of mine   150
Fashion'd so bright a substance to a form
So beautiful . . . . There must be truth in it.
    John. There shall be then. Your uncle's sacristy
Shall hold the armour quite invisible,
Until our little Martin some fine day

121, 122 angel] Angel *T.*   125 sung] sang *T.*   127 cannot] can not *1846.*
131 We] *We 1846.*   136 angels] Angels *T.*   138 crescent] Crescent *T.*
144 virgin's] Virgin's *T., 1846.*   148 ball] hall *1846.*

Bursts the door open, spurr'd, caparison'd,
Dukes lead his bridle, princes tramp behind.
He may be pope . . . . who knows?
   Margaretta.   Are you in earnest?
But if he should be pope, will he love *us?*
Or let us (O yes sure he would!) love *him?*   160
Nor slink away, ashamed? Pope, no; not pope,
But bishop (ay?) he may be? There are few
Powerfuller folks than uncle Grimmermann.
Promise he scarce would give us, but a wink
Of hope he gave, to make a chorister.
   John. If thou wilt find materials, were his words.
   Margaretta. I did not mark the words; they were too light:
And yet he never breaks his troth.
   John.   Not he:
No, he would rather break his fast ten times.
Do not look seriously . . . . when church allows,   170
I mean; no more; six days a week; not seven.
I *have* seen houses where the Friday cheese
Was not (in *my* mind) cut with Thursday knife.
   Margaretta. O now for shame! such houses cannot stand.
Pr'ythee talk reason . . . . As the furnace-mouth
Shows only fire, so your's shows laughter only.
Choristers have been friars . . . . our's may be . . . .
And then a father abbot.
   John.   At one leap,
As salmon up Schaffhausen.
   Margaretta.   Just the same . . . .
Then . . . .
   John. Ring the bells! Martin is pope, by Jove!   180

170 church] Church *T, 1846.*   174 cannot] can not *1846.*   180 pope]
Pope, *1846.*

TWO DRAMATIC SCENES

By Walter Savage Landor, Esq.

[Published in 1838 in *The Book of Beauty* for 1839; reprinted 1846. Text *Book of Beauty*.]

[*Scene, Tower of London*, May 18, 1536.

CHARACTERS.
Anne Boleyn. Sir William Kingston. Constable of the Tower.]

Anne Boleyn. Is your liege ill, sir, that you look so anxious?
Constable of the Tower. Madam!
Anne.   I would not ask what you may wish
To keep a secret from me; but indeed
This right, I think, is left me . . I would know
If my poor husband is quite well to-day.
Constable. Pardon me, gracious lady! what can prompt
To this inquiry?
Anne.   I have now *my* secret.
Constable. I must report all questions, sayings, doings,
Movements, and looks of yours. His Highness may
Be ruffled at this eagerness to ask   10
About his health.
Anne.   I am used to ask about it.
Beside, he may remember . . .
Constable.   For your Highness
Gladly will I remind our sovran Lord
Of any promise.
Anne.   Oh, no! do not that!
It would incense him: he made only one,
And Heaven alone that heard him must remind him!
Last night, I do suspect, but am not sure,
He scarcely was what kings and husbands should be.
A little wine has great effect upon
Warm hearts (and Henry's heart *was* very warm)   20
And upon strong resentments . . . I do fear
He has those too . . But all his friends must love him.
He may have past (poor Henry!) a bad night,
Thinking upon his hasty resolution.
Constable. Lady! I grieve to tell you, worse than that . .
Far worse!
Anne.   Oh, mercy, then! the child! the child!
Why not have told me of all this before?

Title. 1846 substitutes: HENRY THE EIGHTH AND ANNE BOLEYN.
Sub-titles. By . . . Esq. *om. 1846, which has for first scene:* Scene in the Tower. Anne
Boleyn and a Constable of the Tower. [a *deleted by Landor in a copy of 1846 ed.*]

What boots it to have been a guiltless wife,
When I, who should have thought the first about it,
Am an ill mother? Not to think of thee,   30
My darling! my Elizabeth! whose cradle
Rocks in my ear and almost crazes me.
Is she safe? Tell me, tell me, is she living?
  Constable. Safe, lady, and asleep in rosy health,
And radiant (if there yet be light enough
To shew it on her face) with pleasant dreams,
Such as young angels come on earth to play with.
  Anne. Were I but sure that I could dream of her
As I, until last autumn, oft have done,
Joyously, blithely, only waking up   40
Afraid of having hurt her by my arms
Too wildly in my rapture thrown around her,
I would lay down my weary head, and sleep,
Although the pillow be a little strange,
Nor like a bridal or a childbed pillow.
  Constable. Oh, spare those words!
  Anne.   Why spare them? when I feel
Departure from this world would never be
Departure from its joys: the joys of heaven
Would mingle with them scarcely with fresh sweetness.
  Constable (*falling on his knees*). My queen!
  Anne.   Arise, sir constable!
  Constable.   My queen!
Heaven's joys lie close before you.
  Anne.   And you weep?   51
Few days, I know, are left me; they will melt
All into one, all pure, all peaceable . .
No starts from slumber into bitter tears,
No struggles with sick hopes and wild desires,
No cruel father cutting down the tree
To crush the child that sits upon its boughs
And looks abroad . . too tender for suspicion,
Too happy even for hope, maker of happiness.
I could weep too, nor sinfully, at this.   60
    Thou knowest, O my God! thou surely knowest
'Tis no repining at thy call or will.
      (Constable, *on his knees, presents the Writ of Execution.*)
  I can do nothing now . . take back that writing,

36 shew] show *1846*.   46 Oh, spare] O lady! spare *1846*.   I feel] *om.* 1846.
51 weep?] weep! *1846*.   57 boughs] bough *1846*.

And tell them so, poor souls! Say to the widow
I grieve, and can *but* grieve for her; persuade her
That children, although fatherless, are blessings;
And teach those little ones, if e'er you see them,
They are not half so badly off as some.
Fold up the paper .. put it quite aside ..
I am no queen; I have no almoner ..   70
Ah, now I weep indeed! Put, put it by.
Many .. I grieve (yet, *should* I grieve?) to think it,
Many will often say, when I am gone,
They once had a young queen to pity them.
Nay, though I mention'd I had nought to give,
Yet dash not on your head, nor grapple so
With those ungentle hands, while I am here,
A helpless widow's innocent petition.
Smoothe it; return it with all courtesy:
Smoothe it, I say again: frame some kind words   80
And see they find their place, then tender it.
What! in this manner gentlemen of birth
Present us papers? turn they thus away,
Putting their palms between their eyes and us?
Sir! I was queen .. and you were kind unto me
When I was queen no longer .. why so changed?
Give it .. but what is now my signature?
Ignorant are you, or incredulous,
That not a clasp is left me? not a stone
The vilest; not chalcedony; not agate.   90
Promise her all my dresses, when .. no, no ..
I am grown superstitious; they might bring
Misfortune on her, having been Anne Boleyn's.
    Constable. Lady! I wish this scroll could suffocate
My voice. One order I must disobey,
To place it in your hand and mark you read it.
I lay it at your feet, craving your pardon
And God's, my lady!
    Anne.   Rise up; give it me;
I know it ere I read it, but I read it
Because it is the king's, whom I have sworn   100
To love and to obey.
    Constable (*aside*).   Her mind 's distraught!
Alas, she smiles!
    Anne.   The worst hath long been over:
Henry loves courage; he will love my child

277

For this; although I want more than I have;
And yet how merciful at last is Heaven
To give me but thus much for her sweet sake.

SCENE IN EPPING FOREST

[May 19, 1536.]

HENRY, *Courtiers, Hounds, &c.*

Henry. Northumberland! pray tell me, if thou canst,
Who is that young one in the green and gold?
Dost thou not see her? hast thou left both eyes
Upon the bushes?
   Northumberland.   There are many, sir,
In the same livery.
   Henry.   *Her* I mean; her yonder
On the iron-gray with yellow round his ears.
Impudent wench! she turns away her cheek!
   Northumberland.   (*after inquiring.*)
The Lady Katharine Parr, an' please your Highness.
   Henry. Faith! she *doth* please me. What a sap is rising
In that young bud! how supple! yet how solid!   10
What palpable perfection! ay, Lord Arundel!
   Arundel. A bloom well worthy of a monarch's bower,
Where only one more lovely smiles beside him.
   Henry. Though spring is stirring, yet give me the summer . .
I can wait yet . . though, some day, not far off,
I would confer with her at Hampton-Court . .
Merely to ask her how she likes the chase:
We shall not have another all this season:
The stag alone can help us on in May:
To-morrow is the twentieth.
                 Hark! the knell   20
From Paul's! . . the Tower-gun, too!
                   I am right enough!
                    (*Claps his hands.*)
I am a widower!   [*Again claps his hands.*
     By this hour to-morrow

SECOND SCENE.
For Epping Forest *in heading of second scene 1846 substitutes;* Richmond Chase.
[*See notes at end of volume.*]
     5 *Her* I mean;] I mean *1846.*   11 Arundel!] Surrey? *1846.*   12 *Arundel.*]
Surrey [as speaker] *1846.*   15 yet . . . day,] yet. Some day, one *1846.*

ANDREA OF HUNGARY

Sunny Jane Seymour's long and laughing eyes
Shall light me to our chamber.

Lords! prick on!

The merry hounds are chiding! To the chase
To-day! our coronation for to-morrow.   26

After l. 26 1846 adds:

> How sweetly that bell warbled o'er the water.
> *Norfolk.* I like it better than the virginals.
> *Suffolk.* They are poor music.
> *Norfolk.*   Songs but make them worse.
> *Henry.* Come; prick we onward. Shall we have a race?
> *Surrey.* We are well mounted; but the youngest man
> Will win, for majesty sits lightly on him.
> *Henry.* It may well be. I have lost half my weight
> This morning, lithesome as I was before.
> Away!
> *Norfolk.* His saddle swells its bolstered back
> Already full two hundred yards before us.

ANDREA OF HUNGARY

AND

GIOVANNA OF NAPLES

[Published 1839; reprinted 1846. The Prologue was also printed in Madden's *The Countess of Blessington*, 1855. Text, 1839. See notes at end of volume.]

MALE CHARACTERS.

ANDREA.   KLAPWRATH, ⎱
FRA RUPERT.   ZINGA,   ⎰ *Hungarian Officers.*
CARACCIOLI.   PSEIN,
CARAFFA.   PAGE.
BOCCACCIO.   GARISENDO, *a Peasant.*
MAXIMIN, *a Soldier.*

FEMALE CHARACTERS.

GIOVANNA, *Queen.*   MARIA OF SICILY, *Half-sister.*
SANCIA, *Queen Dowager.*   FILIPPA, *Foster-mother.*
MARIA, *Sister of Giovanna.*   PETRONILLA, *a Peasant.*

PROLOGUE.

MY verse was for thine eyes alone,
Alone by them was it repaid;
And stil thine ear records the tone
Of thy grey minstrel, thoughtful maid!

Title. AND *om. 1846, which after* NAPLES *adds:*, AND FRA RUPERT: A TRILOGY.
Headlines: MALE *om. 1846.*   *heading* FEMALE CHARACTERS *om. 1846.*   3 stil] still
1846.   4 thoughtful] gentle *1855.*

279

Amid the pomps of regal state,
　Where thou, O Rose! art call'd to move,
Thee only Virtue can elate,
　She only guide thy steps to Love.

Sometimes, when dark is each saloon,
　Dark every lamp that crown'd the Seine,　　　　　10
Memory hangs low Amalfi's moon
　And lights thee o'er Salerno's plain,

And onward, where Giovanna bore
　Keen anguish from envenom'd tongues:
Her fame my pages shall restore,
　Thy pity shall requite her wrongs.

ANY profits which may arise to the Author from this Edition, he has
requested the Publisher will transmit to Grace Darling. [L.; *om. 1846.*]

6 Rose] *1855 has blank space.* The prologue was addressed to Miss Rose Paynter
afterwards Lady Graves Sawle. [W.]　　*For ll. 7–8 1855 substitutes:*
　　　　Nothing wilt ever thou deem great
　　　　But virtue—nothing bright, but love.
12 Salerno's] Sorrento's *1855.*　　　　13 where] when *1855 (misp.).*　　　　14 Keen
. . from] Corroding chains *1855.*

ANDREA OF HUNGARY

ACT I.

SCENE I. PALACE AT NAPLES [? 1342].

ANDREA *and* GIOVANNA.

Andrea. What say you now, Giovanna! shall we go
And conquer France? Heigho! I am sadly idle;
My mighty mind wants full activity.
　Giovanna. Andrea! be contented; stay at home;
Conquer? you've conquer'd me.
　Andrea.　　　　　　　　　Ah rebel queen!
I doubt it: we have had war first, however,
And parleys, and all that.
　Giovanna.　　　　　　You might have more
Before you conquer the strong cities there.
　Andrea. England, they tell me, hath as much of France
As France hath. Some imagine that Provenza　　　　　10
Is half-and-half French land. How this may be
　　　　　2 Heigho!] Heigho? *1846.*

280

I cannot tell; I am no theologian.
Giovanna . . in your ear . . I have a mind
To ride to Paris, and salute the king,
And pull him by the beard, and make him fight.
    Giovanna. Know that french beards have stiffer hairs than german,*
And crackle into flame at the first touch.
    Andrea. 'Sblood! like black cats! But only in the dark?
    Giovanna. By night or day, in city or in field.
    Andrea. I never knew it: let the Devil lug them   20
For me then! they are fitter for his fist.
Sure, of all idle days the marriage-day
Is idlest: even the common people run
About the streets, not knowing what to do,
As if they came from wedding too, poor souls!
This fancy set me upon conquering France.
    Giovanna. And one hour only after we are united?

  * Hungary and Germany were hostile. [L.]

---

12 cannot] can not *1846.*   16 french] French *1846.*   german] German *1846.*

[ACT I.] SCENE II.

MARIA *enters.*

    Andrea. Maria! where are you for? France or Naples?
She heard, she smiled . . Here's whispering! This won't do . .
                       [Going; but stops, pacified.
She may have secrets . . they all have . . I'll leave 'em.   *[Goes.*
    Giovanna. Unsisterly! unfriendly!
    Maria.   Peace! Giovanna!
    Giovanna. That word has sign'd it. I have sworn to love him.
    Maria. Ah, what a vow!
    Giovanna.   The harder to perform
The greater were the glory: I will earn it.
    Maria. How can we love . . .
    Giovanna, interrupting.   Mainly, by hearing none
Decry the object; then, by cherishing
The good we see in it, and overlooking   10
What is less pleasant in the paths of life.
All have some virtue if we leave it them
In peace and quiet; all may lose some part
By sifting too minutely bad and good.
The tenderer and the timider of creatures
Often desert the brood that has been handled

Or turn'd about, or indiscreetly looked at.
The slightest touches, touching constantly,
Irritate and inflame.

 Maria, touching her shoulder. Giovanna mine!
These rhetoric-roses are supremely sweet,   20
But hold! the jar is full. I promise you
I will not steal up with a mind to snatch,
Or pry too closely where you bid me not,—
But for the nest you talk about . .

 Giovanna.   For shame!
What nest?

 Maria. That nest your blushes gleam upon.
O! I will watch each twig, each feather there,
And, if my turning, tossing, hugging, does it,
Woe to Giovanna's little bird, say I.

 Giovanna. Seriously, my sweet sister!

 Maria, interrupting.   Seriously
Indeed! What briars ere we come to that!   30

 Giovanna. I am accustomed to Andrea's ways,
And see much good in him.

 Maria.   I see it too.

 Giovanna. Fix upon that your eyes; they will grow brighter,
Maria, for each beauty they discover.

  17 Or] And *1846.* looked] lookt *1846.*   19, *touching . . . shoulder*] om. *1846.*

[ACT I.] SCENE III.

ANDREA, FRA RUPERT.

 Andrea. Well met again, Fra Rupert! Why not, though,
At church with us? By this humility
You lost the prettiest sight that ever was.

 Fra Rupert. I know what such sights are.

 Andrea.   What?

 Fra Rupert.   Vanity.

 Andrea. Exact the thing that everybody likes.

 Fra Rupert. You young and heedless!

 Andrea.   We pass lightly over,
And run on merrily quite to the end;
The graver stumble, break their knees, and curse it:
Which are the wiser? Had you seen the church!
The finest lady ever drest for court   10
A week-day peasant to her! By to-morrow

  After heading SCENE III. *1846 has* ANOTHER ROOM IN THE PALACE.

There's not a leg of all the crowd in Naples
But will stand stiff and ache with this day's tiptoe;
There's not a throat will drop its paste-tape down
Without some soreness from such roaring cheers;
There's not a husband but whose ears will tingle
Under his consort's claw this blessed night
For sighing *"What an angel is Giovanna!"*
   Fra Rupert. Go, go! I cannot hear such ribaldry.
   Andrea. Rather should you have heard, as there you might,   20
Quarrelsome blunder-headed drums, o'erpowered
By pelting cymbals; then complaining flutes,
And boy-voiced fifes, lively, and smart, and shrill;
Then timbrels, where tall fingers trip, but trip
In the right place, and run along again;
Then blustering trumpets, wonder-wafting horns,
Evvivas from their folks, *hurrahs* from ours,
And songs that pour into both ears long life
And floods of glory and victory for ever.
   Fra Rupert. What signify these fooleries? In one word,   30
Andrea, art thou king?
   Andrea.   I fancy so.
The people never give such hearty shouts
Saving for kings and blunders.
   Fra Rupert.   Son! beware,
Lest, while they make the one, they make the other.
   Andrea. How must I guard against it?
   Fra Rupert.   Twelve whole years
Constantly here together, all the time
Since we left Hungary, and not one day
But I have labored to instill into thee,
Andrea! how wise kings must feel and act.
   Andrea. But, father, who let *you* into the secret?   40
   Fra Rupert. I learnt it in the cloister.
   Andrea.   Then no doubt
The secret is worth knowing; many are
(Or songs and fables equally are false)
Among those whisper'd there.
   Fra Rupert.   Methinks, my son,
Such words are lighter than beseems crown'd heads,
As thine should be, and shall be, if thou wilt.

19 cannot] can not *1846*   21 o'erpowered] o'erpower'd *1846.*   35 Twelve]
so in errata 1839 and text 1846; first printed Ten.   38 labored] labour'd *1846.*
46 shall] shalt *1839 (corr. in errata).*

Andrea. Ay, father, but it is not so as yet;
Else would it jingle to another crown,
With what a face beneath it! What a girl
Is our Giovanna!
    Fra Rupert.   By the saints above!   50
I thought it was a queen, and not a girl.
    Andrea. There is enough in her for both at once.
A queen it shall be, then, the whole day long.

                    [FRA RUPERT *impatient.*

Nay, not a word, good Frate! the whole day,
Ave-Maria ends it, does it not?
I am so glad, so gamesome, so light-hearted,
So fond, I (sure!) am long steps off the throne.
    Fra Rupert. And ever may'st be, if thou art remiss
In claiming it.
    Andrea.   I can get anything
From my Giovanna. You would hardly guess   60
What she has given me. Look here!
    Fra Rupert.   A book?
    Andrea. King Solomon.
    Fra Rupert.   His *Song?* To seculars?
I warrant she would teach it, and thou learn it.
    Andrea. I'll learn it thro', I'll learn it every verse.
Where does the *Song* begin? I see no rhymes.
    Fra Rupert. The Proverbs! Not so bad!
    Andrea.   Are songs then proverbs?
And what is this hard word?
    Fra Rupert.   *Ecclesiastes.*
    Andrea. But look! you have not seen the best of it.
What pretty pictures! what broad rubies! what
Prodigious pearls! seas seem to roll within,   70
And azure skies, as ever bent above,
Push their pink clouds, half-shy, to mingle with 'em.
    Fra Rupert. I am not sure this book would do thee harm,
But better let me first examine it.   [*He takes it.*
    Andrea. You shall not have it; give it me again.
    Fra Rupert. Loose it, I say, Andrea!
    Andrea.   I say no!
    Frá Rupert. To me?
    Andrea.   Dost think I'd say it to Giovanna?
Beside, she gave it me: she has read in it
With her own eyes, has written latin in it

       64 thro'] through *1846.*   76 no!] *no! 1846.*

With her own fingers, . . for who else could write   80
Distinctly such small letters? . . You yourself,
Who rarely have occasion for much latin,
Might swear them to be latin in ten minutes.
Another thing . . the selfsame perfume clings
About those pages as about her bosom.
   Fra Rupert, starts. Abomination! Know all that!
   Andrea.   Like matins.
Thence, tho' she turn'd quite round, I saw her take it
To give it me. Another thing . . the people
Bragg'd of my mettle half an hour ago,
And I will show I have it, like the best.   90
Another thing . . forgettest thou, Fra Rupert,
I am a husband?
   Fra Rupert.   Seven years old thou wert one.*
   Andrea. Ha, but! ha, but! seven years upon seven years
Could not make me the man I am to-day.
   Fra Rupert. Nor seventy upon seven a tittle wiser.
   Andrea. Why did not you then make me while you could?
You taught me nothing, and would let none teach me,
No, not our king himself, the wisest man
In his dominions, nor more wise than willing.
Forsooth! you made a promise to my father   100
That nobody should filch my faith and morals,
No taint of learning eat skin-deep into me!
And good king Robert said, *If thus my brother*
Must have it . . if such promise was exacted . .
   Fra Rupert. All have more knowledge than they well employ.
Upbraidest thou thy teacher, guardian, father?
   Andrea. Fathers may be, alas! too distant from us,
Guardians may be too close . . but, teacher? teacher?
   Fra Rupert. Silence!
   Andrea, retreating.   He daunts me: yet, some day *cospetto!*
   Fra Rupert. What mutterest thou?
   Andrea, to himself.   I will be brave, please God!   110
   Fra Rupert, suppressing rage. Obstinate sinners are alone unpardoned:
I may forgive thee after meet repentance,
But must confer with thee another time
On that refractory untoward spirit.

* Andrea and Giovanna were contracted when he was seven, she five. [L.] But in September 1333, when they were affianced, Andrea was five and Giovanna seven. [W.]

103–4 *itals.*] rom. quoted *1846.*

Andrea, to himself. He was then in the right (it seems) at last.
Fra Rupert. I hear some footsteps coming hitherward.

[ACT I.] SCENE IV.

GIOVANNA *and* FILIPPA.

Fra Rupert, turns his back to them. O those pestiferous women!
Andrea.   Ay, well spoken.
The most religious of religious men
Lifts up his arms and eyes, my sweet Giovanna,
Before your wonderous charms.
                              [*The Friar looks at him with rage and scorn.*
    Giovanna.   Simple Andrea!
Are they more wonderous than they were before?
Or are they more apparent now the robes
Are laid aside, and all those gems that made
My hair stand back, chiefly that mischievous
Malignant ruby (some fierce dragon's eye
Turn'd into stone) which hurt your finger so   10
With its vile crooked pin, for touching me,
When you should have but lookt, and not quite that.
    Fra Rupert, who had listened. Come hither; didst thou hear her?
    Andrea.   Every word;
And bear no rancour to her, tho' she scolds.
    Fra Rupert. She might have waited twenty years beyond
This day, before she thought of matrimony;
She talks so like a simpleton.
    Andrea.   She does
Indeed: yet, father! it is very true:
The pin did prick me: she is not a simpleton
As far as memory goes.
                    [*The Friar looks up, then walks about impatiently.*
                        Now, won't you mind me?   20
She is but very young, scarce seventeen;
When she is two years older, just my age,
Then shall you see her! more like me perhaps.
She might have waited . . you say well . . and would
Willingly, I do think; but I am wiser,
And warmer. Our Hungarian blood (ay, Frate!)
Is not squeez'd out of March anemones.
    Filippa. Since, friar Rupert! here are met together
The lofty and the lowly, they and we,
If your austerity of life forbade   30
5 wonderous] wond'rous *1846.*   19 not a] no *1846.*

To mingle with the world's festivities,
Indulge, I pray you, in that luxury
Which suits all seasons, sets no day apart,
Excludes from its communion none, howe'er
Unworthy, but partakes of God indeed . .
Indulge in pardon.
    Fra Rupert.   Does a seneschal's
Wife bend before me? Do the proud ones beg?
    Filippa. Too proud I may be: even the very humblest
May be too proud. I am, 'tis true, the widow
Of him you mention. Do I beg? I do.   40
Our queen commands me to remove ill-will.
    Fra Rupert. There are commands above the queen's.
    Filippa.   There are,
O holy man! obey we both at once!
    Giovanna, calls ANDREA. Husband!
    Fra Rupert.   And not our king? most noble lady!
    Giovanna. He, or I much mistake him, is my husband.
    Andrea. Mistake me! not a whit: I am, I am.
    Giovanna. If, O my husband! that dear name has power
On your heart as on mine, now when first spoken,
Let what is love between us shed its sweets
A little wider, tho' a little fainter;   50
Let all our friends this day, all yours, all mine,
Be one another's, and not this day only.
Persuade them.
    Andrea.   Can I?
    Giovanna.   You persuaded *me.*
    Andrea. Ay, but you did not hate me; and your head
Is neither grey nor tonsured; these are odds.
I never could imagine well, how folks
Who disagree in other things, agree
To make each other angry. What a game!
To toss back burs until the skin is full
On either side! Which wins the stake, I wonder?   60
    Fra Rupert, bursting away. I have no patience.
    Andrea.   I have, now he's gone.
How long were you contriving this grand scheme
To drive away the friar? Do you think   [*Whispers to* GIOVANNA.
He won't come after supper? Does he know
Our chamber?
    Giovanna.   Hush! Andrea!
    Andrea.   In good earnest

I fear him, and the fleas about his frock.
Let me go after him: he went in wrath:
He may do mischief, if he thinks it right,
As these religious people often do.   [ANDREA *goes*.
   Filippa. Happy Andrea! Only fleas and friars   70
Molest him. Little he suspects the snares
About his paths; the bitter jealousies
Of Hungary; how pertinaciously
Mail'd hands grasp sceptres, how reluctantly
Loose them; how tempting are our milder clime
And gentler nation! He deserves our pity.
   Giovanna. O! more than pity. If our clime, our nation,
Bland, constant, kind, congenial with each other,
Were granted him, how much more was withheld!
Sterile the soil is not! hard! hard! 'tis waste.   80
What buoyant spirits and what pliant temper!
How patient of reproof! how he wipes off
All injuries before they harden on him,
And wonders at affronts, and doubts they can be!
Then, his wild quickness! O the churl that bent it
Into the earth, colourless, shapeless, thriftless,
Fruitless, for ever! Had he been my brother,
I should have wept all my life over him;
But, being my husband, one hypocrisy
I must put on, one only ever will I.   90
Others must think, by my observance of him,
I hold him prudent, penetrating, firm,
No less than virtuous: I must place myself
In my own house (now indeed his) below him.
   Filippa. I almost think you love him.
   Giovanna.   He has few
Even small faults, which small minds spy the soonest;
He has, what those will never see nor heed,
Wit of bright feather, but of broken wing;
No stain of malice, none of spleen, about it.
For this, and more things nearer . . for the worst   100
Of orphancy, the cruellest of frauds,
Stealth of his education while he played
Nor fancied he could want it; for our ties
Of kindred; for our childhood spent together;
For those dear faces that once smiled upon us
At the same hour, in the same balcony;

         80 not . . . 'tis] not, but sadly *1846.*

288

Even for the plants we rear'd in partnership,
Or spoil'd in quarrel, I do love Andrea.
But, from his counsellors! . . .
 Filippa.   We shall elude
Their clumsy wiles perhaps. The youth, methinks,   110
Is tractable.
 Giovanna. May wise men guide him then!
It lies beyond my duty.
 Filippa.   But the wise
Are not the men who guide the tractable.
The first bold hand that seizes, holds them fast;
And the best natures melt into the bad
'Mid dances and carousals.
 Giovanna.   Let Andrea
Be sparing of them!
 Filippa.   Evil there may be
Where evil men preside, but greatly worse
Is proud austerity than princely glee.
 Giovanna. Heaven guard us! I have entered on a course 120
Beleaguered with dense dangers: but that course
Was first ordained in earth, and now in heaven.
My father's spirit fill'd his father's breast,
And peace and union in our family,
They both foresaw, would be secured by ours.
 Filippa. She who forgets her parent will forego
All later duties: yes, when love has lost
The sound of its spring-head, it grows impure,
Tortuous, and spent at last in barren sand.
I owe these generous kings the bread I broke,   130
The letters I pickt up: no vile sea-weed
Had perisht more neglected, but for them.
They would heap affluence on me; they did heap it;
Next, honours: for these only I am ungrateful.
 Giovanna, smiling. Ungrateful? thou? Filippa!
 Filippa.   Most ungrateful.
With humble birth and humbler intellect
The puff-ball might have bounced along the plain
And blinded the beholder with its dust:
But intellect let down on humble birth
Writhes under titles, shrinks from every glance,   140
At every question turns one fibre fresh
For torture, and, unpullied and adrift,
Burns its dull heart away in smouldering scorn.

Giovanna. Where no etherial spirit fills the breast . .
Filippa. . . Honours are joys great as such breast can hold.
Giovanna. The happy then in courts are numberless;
We hear the contrary.
   Filippa.   Never believe
This, nor another ill report of them.
   Giovanna. What?
   Filippa.   That the great are not great to their valets;
'Tis but their valets who can find their greatness.   150
   Giovanna. I know that you have enemies.
   Filippa.   Thank God!
I might have else forgotten what I am,
And what he gave me ere he placed me here.
   Giovanna. I never shall, Filippa!
   Filippa.   Think of those
Who rais'd our souls above us, not of me.
   Giovanna. Oh! if my soul hath risen, if the throbs
Of gratitude now tell it me, if they
Who rais'd it must be thought of . . to my heart,
Filippa! for the heart alone can think.
   Filippa. I first received thee in these arms; these arms   160
Shall loose thee last of living things, Giovanna.

ACT II.

SCENE I. IN THE PALACE.

Giovanna, Fiammetta, Maria.

Maria. And now, Fiammetta, tell me whence that name
Which tickles thee so.
   Fiammetta.   Tell indeed! not I.
   Maria, to Giovanna. Sister! you may command.
   Giovanna.   Command a sister?
Secrets are to be won, but not commanded.
I never heard the name before . . *Fiammetta* . .
Is that it?
   Maria.   That is it.
   Fiammetta.   For shame, Maria!
Never will I entrust you with a secret.
   Maria. I do believe you like this one too well
Ever to let another mingle with it.
   Fiammetta, to herself. I do indeed, alas!
   Giovanna.   Some gallant knight   10
Has carried off her scarf and bared her heart.

But to this change of name I must withhold
Assent, I like *Maria* so much better.
    Fiammetta, points to MARIA. There is Maria yet.
    Giovanna.   But where twin-roses
Have grown so long together, to snap one
Might make the other droop.
    Fiammetta.   Ha! now, Maria!
Maria! you are springed, my little quail!
    Giovanna. Fiammetta! if our father were here with us,
He would suspect some poet friend of his,
Dealer in flames and darts, their only trade,   20
Enchanted his Sicilian.
    Maria.   Ho! ho! ho!
Proserpine never blusht such damask blushes
When *she* was caught.
    Fiammetta.   I am quite cool.
    Maria.   The clouds
May be quite cool when they are quite as red;
Girls' faces, I suspect, are somewhat less so.   [FIAMMETTA *runs off.*
    Giovanna. Maria! dear Maria! she is flown.
Is the poor girl in love then?
    Maria.   Til this hour
I thought it but a fancy, such as all
We children have: we all choose one; but, sure,
To run out of the room at the mere shadow!   30
    Giovanna. What would *you* do?
    Maria.   Wait till he came himself.
    Giovanna. And then?
    Maria.   Think seriously of running off,
Until I were persuaded it was civil.
27 Til] Till 1846.

[ACT II.] SCENE II.

    Andrea. What have ye done to little Sicily?
She ran so swiftly by me, and pusht back
My hand so smartly when I would have stopt her,
I think you must have vext her plaguily
Amongst you.
    Maria.   She was vext, but not by us.
    Andrea. Yes, many girls are vext to-day. One bride
Sheds fifty thorns from each white rose she wears,
I did not think of that. (*To Maria.*) *You* did, no doubt?
5 Amongst] Among 1846.

Maria. I wear white roses too, as well as she:
Our queen's can have no thorns for us.
    Andrea.   Not one?   10
    Maria. No, nor for any in this happy realm.
    Andrea. Ah now! this happy realm! Some people think
That I could make it happier.
    Giovanna.   I rejoice
To hear it.
    Andrea. Are you glad, my little bride?
    Giovanna. Most glad. O never disappoint their hopes!
The people are so kind! they love us so!
    Andrea. They are a merry race: ay, very crickets,
Chirruping, leaping. . . What they eat, God knows;
Sunshine and cinders, may-be: he has sent
Plenty of these, and they are satisfied.   20
    Giovanna. Should *we* be, if they are?
    Andrea.   O then! a boon!
To make them happy all their lives.
    Giovanna.   The boon
To make them happier Heaven alone can grant.
Hearken! If some oppressions were removed,
Beyond my strength to manage, it were done.
    Andrea. Nothing so easy. Not your strength indeed,
But mine, could push a buffalo away.
I have a little favour to request.
    Giovanna. Speak.
    Andrea.   Give me then this kingdom, only this.
I do not covet mountains to the north,   30
Nor cities over cities farther west,
Casal or Monferrato or Saluzzo,
Asti or Coni, Ceva or Torino,
Where that great river runs which spouts from heaven,
Nor Aix nor Toulon, nor Marseille nor Nice
Nor Avignon, where our good pope sits percht;
I only want this tidy little kingdom,
To make it happy with this sword upon it.
    Giovanna. The people and their laws alone can give it.
    Andrea. Well, we can make the laws.
    Giovanna.   And people too?   40
    Andrea. Giovanna! I do think that smile could make
A thousand peoples from the dullest clay,
And mould them to thy will.
    Giovanna.   Pure poetry!

Andrea. Don't say it! or they knock me on the head!
I ought to be contented; but they would
Insist upon it. I have askt: here ends
My duty: I don't want it for myself . .
And yet those cities lookt like strings of bird-eggs,
And tempted me above my strength. I only
Repent of learning all their names for nothing.   50
Let them hang where they are.
    Giovanna.   Well said.
    Andrea.   Who wants 'em?
I like these pictures better. What a store!
Songs, proverbs, and a word as hard as flint,
Enough for fifty friars to ruminate
Amid their cheese and cobnuts after dinner.
Read it me.
    Giovanna. Which?   [ANDREA *points.*
    Giovanna.   *Ecclesiastes.*
    Andrea.   Right!
As you pronounce it, scarce a word of ours
In Hungary is softer. What a tongue!
Round, juicy, sweet, and soluble, as cherries.
When Frate Rupert utter'd the same word,   60
It sounded just as if his beard and breast,
And all which there inhabit, had turn'd round
Into his throat, to rasp and riddle it.
I never shall forget *Ecclesiastes!*
Only two words I know are pleasanter.
    Giovanna. And which are they?
    Andrea, saluting her.   *Giovanna* and *Carina.*
    Maria. Unmanner'd prince!
    Andrea.   Now the white rose sheds thorns.

55 dinner.] dinner, *1846.*

[ACT II.] SCENE III.

SANCIA *and* FILIPPA.

Sancia, smiling. Step-mothers are not always quite at home
With their queen-daughters.
    Giovanna.   Yet queen-mothers *are.*
Step-mother you have never been to me,
But kindest, fondest, tenderest, truest mother.
    Maria. Are we not all your children?

Sancia.   All: where then
Is fled our lively Sicily?
  Giovanna.   She is gone
To her own chamber.
  Maria.   To read poetry.
  Sancia. Where poetry is only light or flattering,
She might read some things worse, and many better.
I never loved the heroes of Romance,   10
And hope they glide not in among the leaves.
  Maria. And love you then their contraries?
  Sancia.   Those better.
What clever speech, Maria, dost thou ponder?
I see we differ.
  Maria.   Rather.
  Sancia.   Why so grave?
Surely no spur is tangled in *thy* hem!
  Maria. No, my regrets were all for you. What pity
Andrea dropt upon our globe too late!
A puissant antipode to all such heroes!
  Giovanna, smiling. Intolerable girl! sad jealous creature!
  Sancia. Where is he? I was seeking him.
  Maria.   There now.   20
  Sancia. Or else I should not have return'd so soon
After our parting at the Benediction.   [*Goes.*
  Maria. Sister! I fear my little flippancy
Hurried Queen Sancia: why just now want *sposo?*
  Giovanna. She did not smile, as you do, when she went.
Fond as she is, her smiles are faint this morning.
A sorrowing thought, pure of all gloom, o'ersprad
That saintly face.
  Maria.   It did indeed.
  Giovanna.   She loves
Us all, she loves our people too, most kindly.
  Maria. Seeing none other than Hungarian troops   30
At church about us, deeply did she sigh
And say *"Ah! where are ours?"*
  Giovanna.   You pain me sadly.
Queens, O Maria! have two hearts for sorrow;
One sinks upon our Naples. Whensoever
I gaze ('tis often) on her bay, so bright
With sun-wove meshes, idle multitudes

---

5 All: where] All. Where *1846.*   27 o'ersprad] *so in errata 1839;* o'erspread *in text 1839, 1846.*

ANDREA OF HUNGARY

Of little plashing waves; when air breathes o'er it,
Mellow with sound and fragrance, of such purity
That the blue hills seem coming nearer, nearer,
As I look forth at them, and tossing down   40
Joyance for joyance to the plains below . .
To think what mannerless, unshorn, harsh-tongued
Barbarians from the Danube and the Drave
Infest them, I cast up my eyes to Heaven
Impatiently, despondently, and ask
Are such the guests for such festivities?
But shall they dare enthrall my poor Andrea?
Send, send for him: I would not he were harm'd,
Much less degraded. O for ministers
To guide my counsels and protect my people!   50
I would call round me all the good and wise.
   Sancia, returning. Daughter! no palace is too small to hold them.
The good love other places, love the fields,
And ripen the pale harvest with their prayers.
Solitude, solitude, so dread a curse
To princes, such a blight to sycophants,
Is *their* own home, their healthy thoughts grow in it.
The wise avoid all our anxieties:
The cunning, with the tickets of the wise,
Push for the banquet, seize each vacant chair,   60
Gorge, pat their spaniel, and fall fast asleep.
   Giovanna. Ah then what vigils are reserved for me!
   Maria. Hark! spears are grounded.
   Giovanna.   Officer! who comes?
   Officer. Lady! the friar mounts the stairs; behind him
Those potent lords, Caraffa and Caraccioli.
   Giovanna. Your chair, Queen Sancia, stands unoccupied:
We must be seated to receive the lords.
Is it not so?
   Sancia.   The queen must.
   Giovanna.   One queen only?
The younger first? we cannot thus reverse
The laws of nature for the whims of court.   70
                        [SANCIA *is seated.*
There's our kind mother! Just in time! they come.

47 enthrall] enthral *1846.*   52 *Sancia, returning*] *so in errata 1839 and*
text 1846; first printed FILIPPA.   69 cannot] can not *1846.*

DRAMAS AND DRAMATIC SCENES

[ACT II.] SCENE IV.

FRA RUPERT, CARAFFA, and CARACCIOLI.

Fra Rupert. Lady! these nobles bring me with them hither,
Fearing they might not win an audience
On what concerns the welfare of the state,
In such an hour of such a day as this.
   Giovanna. Speak, gentlemen! You have much wronged yourselves,
And me a little, by such hesitation.
No day, methinks, no hour, is half so proper,
As when the crown is placed upon my brow,
To hear what are its duties.
   Caraffa.   Gracious queen!
We come to represent . .
   Fra Rupert, behind. Speak out . . wrongs . . rights . .   10
Religion.
   Caraffa to him. You distract me.
   Fra Rupert, to CARACCIOLI.   Speak then thou.
See how attentively, how timidly,
She waits for you, and blushes up your void!
   Caraccioli. 'Tis therefore I want words.
   Fra Rupert.   Hear mine then, boys!
                       [Walks toward GIOVANNA.

Imprest with awe before such majesty,
The hopes of Naples, whom their fathers deem
On this occasion, this gay hour, from high
Nobility, from splendour of equipments,   20
Beauty of person, gracefulness of mien,
And whatsoever courts are courtly by,
Most fitted, and most likely to prevail
Against those ancient frauds and artifices
Which certain dark offenders weave about them . .
These unsophisticated youths, foredoom'd
Longest and most impatiently to suffer,
Lay humbly at the footstool of your throne
A list of grievances yet unredrest.
   Giovanna. Give it me, gentlemen, we will peruse it
Together.
   Fra Rupert. They are more than scribe could pen.
   Giovanna, to FRA RUPERT. Are they of native or imported growth? 30
Your Reverence hath some practice in the sorting.
Permit me to fill up your pause, Fra Rupert!

ll. 1–4 Fra Rupert speaks but is not named as speaker in either ed.

296

ANDREA OF HUNGARY

On this occasion, this gay hour, methinks
To urge impatience and foredoom of suffering
Is quite untimely. High nobility
And splendour of equipment are the last
Of merits in Caraffas and Caracciolis.   [*To them.*
The delicacy that deferr'd the tender
Of your important service, I appreciate,
Venturing to augur but a brief delay.   40
Gentlemen! if your fathers bade you hither,
I grieve to owe them more than I owe you,
And trust, when next we see you, half the pleasure,
Half, if not all, may be your own free gift.   [*She rises, they go.*

[ACT II.] SCENE V. PALACE GARDEN.

FRA RUPERT, CARAFFA, *and* CARACCIOLO.

Fra Rupert. The losel!
Caraccioli.   Saints! what graciousness!
Caraffa.   Was ever
So sweet a girl? He 's uglier than old Satan,
Andrea . . I abhor him worse than ever. . .
Curse on that Tartar, Turk, Bohemian,
Hungarian! I could now half-strangle him.
     Fra Rupert. We are dismist.
     Caraffa.   My speech might have done wonders.
     Fra Rupert. Now, who (the mischief!) stops a dead man's blood?
Wonders! ay truly, wonders it had done!
Thou wert agape as money-box for mass,
And wanted'st shaking more. What are our gains?   10
     Caraffa. A vision the strain'd eyes can not inclose,
Or bring again before them from the senses,
Which clasp it, hang upon it, nor will ever
Release it, following thro' eternity.
     Caraccioli. I can retain her image, hear her words,
Repeat, and tone them on each fibre here,
Distinctly stil.
     Caraffa.   Then hast thou neither heart
Nor brain, Caraccioli! No strife so hard
As to catch one slight sound, one faintest trace,
Of the high beauty that rules over us.   20
Who ever seized the harmony of heaven,
Or saw the confine that is nearest earth?

10 wanted'st] wantedst *1846.*   17 stil] still *1846.*

Fra Rupert. I can bear youthful follies, but must check
The words that run thus wide and point at heaven.
We must warn laymen fairly off that ground.
Are ye both mad?
    Caraffa.   One is; I swear to one:
I would not be the man that is not so
For empires girt with gold, worlds starr'd with women.
A trance is that man's life, a dream be mine!
Caraccioli's an ice-pit, covered o'er   30
With straw and chaff and double-door'd and thatch'd,
And wall'd, the whole dark space, with earthen wall.
Why! Frate! all those groans of thine for heaven?
Art toucht?
    Fra Rupert. I have been praying fervently . .
Despairingly I fear to say . . 'twere rash,
Ungrateful, and ungodly.
    Caraffa.   He has brought
The whole Maremma on me at one breath.
My cold fit now comes over me. But, Frate!
If we do feel, may we not say we do?
    Fra Rupert. To feel is harm; to say it, may be none,   40
Unless 'tis said with levity like thine.
    Caraffa. Ah faith! I wish 'twere levity! The pagan
That heaves up Etna, calls it very differently:
I think the dog is better off than I am:
He groans upon the bed where lies his torment,
I very far away from where lies mine.
    Fra Rupert. Art thou a Christian?
    Caraffa.   Father! don't be serious.
    Fra Rupert. I must be.
    Caraffa.   Have not I most cause?
    Fra Rupert.   Yea truly.
    Caraffa. I am not over-given to complain,
But nettles will sting all . .
    Fra Rupert.   . . who put their hands in.   50
Caraccioli! be warn'd by this our friend
What sufferings may arise from lawless love.
Thine passeth its due bounds; it doth, Caraccioli!
But thou canst conquer every wild desire;
A high emprize! what high emprize but suits
A true Caraccioli! We meet again . .
I have some warnings, some reproofs, for him.   [CARACCIOLI *goes.*

     31 thatch'd] thatcht *1846.*   42 pagan] *sc.* Typhoeus [W.]

ANDREA OF HUNGARY

FRA RUPERT, CARAFFA.

Fra Rupert. Where walls are living things, have ears, eyes, mouths,
Deemest thou, son Francesco! I alone
Heard those most violent words about Andrea?
   Caraffa. What words? I never thought about the man . .
About his wife some little . . true enough.
Some little? criminal it were to say it:
He who thinks little of such . . such perfection,
Has left his thoughts among the worms that creep
In charnel-houses, among brainless skulls,
Dry bones, without a speck of blood, a thread   10
Of fibre, ribs that never cased a heart.
The volumes of the doctors of the church
Could not contain a tithe of it: their clasps,
Strong enough to make chains for Saracens,
Their timbers to build argosies, would warp
And split, if my soul's fire were pent within.
   Fra Rupert. Remember, son Francesco! prince Andrea,
King rather (such the husband of a queen
Is virtually, and should be) king Andrea
Lives under my protection.
   Caraffa.   Well, what then?   20
   Fra Rupert. What? Into mine own ear didst thou not breathe
Traitorous threats?
   Caraffa.   I? Threats? About his queen?
   Fra Rupert. Filthy! most filthy!
   Caraffa.   No, no: wandering thoughts
Fluttered in that direction; one thought, rather.
Doves have hot livers.
   Fra Rupert.   Be adultery
Bad as it will, yet treason, son Francesco!
Treason is far more difficult to deal with.
   Caraffa. I do suspect it may be.
   Fra Rupert.   Saidst thou not
Thou couldst half-strangle that Hungarian?
   Caraffa. Spake I so rashly?
   Fra Rupert.   I am a Hungarian.   30
   Caraffa. Evident: but that noble mien would daunt
Moor, Usbeck, Abyssinian: and that strength!
A Switzer bear could not half-strangle it.

     2 Francesco *1846*] *mispr.* Francisco *1839.*

Fra Rupert. 'Twere martyrdom, 'twere martyrdom. The life
Of kings hath swords and scaffolds round about it;
A word might fling thee on them.
 Caraffa.   Such a word
Must fall from holy lips, thenceforth unholy.
 Fra Rupert. Guided by me and courage, thou art safe.

ACT III.

SCENE I. IN THE PALACE.

ANDREA *and* FILIPPA.

Andrea. Many the stories you've repeated to me,
Lady Filippa! I have clean forgotten 'em;
But all the bloody giants every girl
Before our bed-time threw into my night-cap,
Lie safe and sound there stil.
 Filippa.   I quite believe
You've not the heart to drive them out, my prince.
 Andrea. Not I indeed. And then your sage advice!
 Filippa. Is all that too forgotten?
 Andrea.   No, not all;
But, dear Filippa, now that I am married,
And sovran (one may say) or next door to it,   10
You must not give me any more advice . .
Not that I mind it; but to save appearances.
        [*She bends: he goes, but returns suddenly.*
Lady Filippa! lady seneschal!
 Filippa. My prince, command me.
 Andrea.   Solve me one more question.
How happens it (while old men are so wise)
That any foolish thing, advice or story,
We call it an old woman's?
 Filippa.   Prince Andrea!
I know not as for stories and advice;
I only know, when *we* are disappointed
In any thing, or teazed with it, we scoff   20
And call it an old man's.
 Andrea.   Ah spiteful sex!
 Filippa. Here comes Maria: ask her no such questions.
 Andrea. I wish Fra Rupert heard your words.
 Filippa.   To prove them?
 Maria. Give him a nosegay at the door.
      5 stil] still *1846.*

ANDREA OF HUNGARY

Andrea.   He spurns
Such luxury.
  Maria.   Since his arrival here,
Perfumes, they tell me, are more general
And tenfold dearer. Everybody wears them
In self-defence: men take them with their daggers;
Laundresses sprinkle them on vilest linen,
Lest they be called uncleanly; round the churches   30
What once were clouds of incense, now are canopies
Of the same benzoin; kites could not fly thro';
The fainting penitents are prone to catch
At the priest's surplice as he passes by,
And cry, above their prayers to Heaven for mercy,
Stop! stop! turn back! waft me a little yet.
  Andrea. The father is indeed more fox than civet,
And stinks out sins like sulphur and stale eggs.
[*To* MARIA.] You will not run away with him?
  Maria.   Tarantola!
Worse than most venomous tarantola,   40
He bites, and will not let us dance for it.

      27 dearer. Everybody] dearer: everybody *1846.*

[ACT III.] SCENE II. IN THE GARDENS OF CAPO DI MONTE.

BOCCACCIO *and* FIAMMETTA.

  Fiammetta. I do not know whether it be quite right
To listen, as I have, day after day
And evening after evening.
  Boccaccio.   Are my sighs
Less welcome in the garden and the bower,
Than where loud organ bellow'd them away,
And chorister and waxlight ran between?
  Fiammetta. You sadly interrupted me at vespers:
Never do that again, sir! When I pray
I like to pray with all my heart. Bold man!
Do you dare smile at me?
  Boccaccio.   The bold man first   10
Was smiled at; was he not?
  Fiammetta.   No, no such thing:
But if he was, it was because he sigh'd
At the hot weather he had brought with him.

      2 day . . . day] morn after morn *1846.*

Boccaccio. At the cold weather he fear'd coming on
He sighed.
 Fiammetta. And did it come?
 Boccaccio.   Too gracious lady!
 Fiammetta. Keep *gracious lady* for dull drawing-rooms;
Fiammetta is my name; I would know yours.
 Boccaccio. Giovanni.
 Fiammetta.   That I know (*aside*). I ought, alas!
Often with Acciaioli and Petrarca
I've seen you walking, but have never dared   20
To ask your name from them; your house's name
I mean, of course; our own names stand for nothing.
You must be somebody of high estate.
 Boccaccio. I am not noble.
 Fiammetta, shrinking back. Oh! . . then! . .
 Boccaccio.   I must go!
That is the sentence, is it not?
 Fiammetta, runs and takes his hand. Don't tell me
Thou art not noble: say thou art most noble:
Norman . . half-Norman . . quarter-Norman . . say it.
 Boccaccio. Say an untruth?
 Fiammetta.   Only this one; my heart
Will faint without it. I will swear to think it
A truth, wilt thou but say it. 'Tis a truth: 30
Thy only falsehood thou hast told already,
Merely to try me. If thou art not noble . .
Noble thou art, and shalt be!
      [*She sobs and pauses: he presses her hand to his bosom.*
         Who gainsays it?
 Boccaccio. A merchant's son, no better, is thy slave,
Fiammetta!
 Fiammetta, smiling. Now art thou disguised indeed.
Come, show me specimens of turquises,
Amethysts, emeralds, diamonds . . out with 'em.
 Boccaccio. A merchant's, and poor merchant's, son am I;
Gems I have none to offer, but pure love
Proof to the touchstone, to the crucible.   40
 Fiammetta. What then or who is noble, and thou not?
I have heard whispers that myself am not so
Who am king Robert's daughter. We may laugh
At those who are, if thou and I are none.

37 'em] them 1846.

Thou art my knight, Giovanni! There now; take [*Giving him her scarf.*
Thy patent of nobility, and wear it.
   Boccaccio, kisses it. What other but were cobweb after this?
   Fiammetta. Ha! kiss it! but take care you don't kiss me. [*Runs away.*

[ACT III.] SCENE III. IN THE PALACE.

SANCIA *and* FILIPPA.

Sancia. Even you, my dear Filippa, are alert
As any of the girls, and giddy too:
You have dropt something now you cannot find.
   Filippa. I have been busy, looking here and there
To find Andrea.
   Sancia.   Leave him with his bride,
Until they tire of saying tender things.
   Filippa. Untender things, I fear, are going on.
He has been truant to the friar Rupert
Of late, who threatens him with penances
For leaving some injunction unperform'd.   10
And more perhaps than penances are near:
For sundry captains, sundry nobles, meet
At friar Anselm's cell; thither had sped
Fra Rupert. In the garden of Saint Clara
Voices were heard, and threats; then whispers ran
Along the walls. They walkt out, one by one,
Soldiers with shuffling pace unsoldierly,
Friars with folded hands, invoking heaven,
And hotly calm as night ere burst Vesuvius.
   Sancia. Beyond the slight affronts all princes bear   20
From those who miss what others have obtain'd,
Andrea shall fear nothing. Heaven protects him.
   Filippa. Heaven, in its equal dispensation, gives
The pious palms, the prudent length of days.
We seek him not then with the same intent
Of warning?
   Sancia.   With the same of warning; you,
Where the good angels guard; I, where the bad
Seduce him. Having reign'd, and having heard
That thither tend his wishes . .
   Filippa.   Momentary.
   Sancia. But lawless wishes have returning wings   30
Of speed more than angelic. I would win

         3 cannot] can not *1846.*

His private ear, lest courtiers take possession;
I would persuade him, with his lovely bride
To share all other troubles than the crown's.

[ACT III.] SCENE IV. IN THE PALACE.
ANDREA *and* MARIA.

Andrea. Are we then going up to Capo-Monte?
How long shall we remain there? all the night?
   Maria. Until the evening.
   Andrea.   And where then?
   Maria.   Aversa.
   Andrea. Ay, because there I askt her if she loved me:
Besides . . the strangest thing on earth . . young brides
Fly from the altar and roost anywhere
Rather than near it. What should frighten them?
But, if we go, why not set off directly?
   Maria. We stay because the people round the gates,
Who left too late their farms and villages   10
To see our queen and you, expect at noon
To follow the procession . .
   Andrea.   What procession?
Is there another marriage? O rare sport!
   Maria, continuing. From Castel-Nuovo far as Capo-Monte.
   Andrea. O glorious! But we really shall be let
Into the gardens and the groves?
   Maria.   Why not?
Who should prevent us?
   Andrea.   Into all? Among
The marble men and women who stand there,
And only stir by moonlight? I don't think
They stir at all: I am half-sure they don't.   20
   Maria. I have been always of the same opinion.
   Andrea, shakes his head. Although he said it who says mass, I
    doubt it.
   Maria. Ah! but to doubt is not to be half-sure:
The worst end may stick fast, like broken tooth.
   Andrea. Now if you laugh, you make an unbeliever.
You girls are . .
   Maria.   Pray what are we?
   Andrea.   Cunninger.
Fra Rupert told me he would break their bones.
   Maria Did he?

Andrea.   As bad. He'd tumble them down headlong,
If ever he once caught me looking up
Again at those who stood alert for swimming.   30
    Maria. When?
    Andrea.   Four years back. To me they seem'd pure marble,
But Frate Rupert never could have spited
Mere marble so, altho' they lookt like women.
I scarcely would believe him when he said
They once were devils, but could do no harm
(Now the salt water had been sprinkled on 'em)
Unless we look at them as worshippers.
    Maria. I am sure you did not.
    Andrea.   No; upon my faith!
    Maria. We never stand about them; we walk on.
    Andrea, in a low voice. What! when you are but one or two to-
        gether?
I like their looks: the women are quite lovely,   41
And the men too (for devils) not amiss.
I wonder where they laid their plaguy scourges;
They must have had them, or were never worshipt.
    Maria. Did not the Frate tell you?
    Andrea.   Ask the Frate!
He would have found them in a trice, and held
The scourges good enough, tho' not the devils.
    Maria. I think you mind him less than formerly.
    Andrea. I am a married man.
    Maria.   But married men
Fear priests and friars more than single ones.   50
    Andrea. He is the holiest monk upon God's earth,
And hates you women most.
    Maria.   Then the least holy.
    Andrea. Dost think it? If I thought him so, I'd fear
The beast no longer, broad as are his shoulders,
His breath .. pho! .. like a water-snake's, his fist
Heavy as those big books in chapter-houses,
And hairy as the comet; for they say
'Twas hairy; tho' I saw no hairs upon it.
    Maria. Whenever love comes upon *thee*, Andrea,
Art thou not kinder?
    Andrea.   Kinder, but not holier.   60
    Maria. Is not thy heart more grateful?
    Andrea.   As may happen;
A little thing would make it so.

Maria.   And, tell me
Art thou not readier to give alms?
Andrea.   Tell *me*
How long, Maria, those bright eyes have seen
Into my thoughts? Fra Rupert knows not half one
Unless he question for an hour or better
And stamp and threaten, nor then more than half one.
I'll never fear him now: I'll tell him so.
  Maria. Be not too hasty: tell him no such thing.
But fear him not; fear rather those about him.   70

                        [FRA RUPERT *is seen prying.*

  Andrea. Whom?
  Maria.   His Hungarians.
  Andrea.   They're my countrymen.
  Maria. Should they make all us dread them?
  Andrea.   Me?
  Maria.   Even you,
Under Fra Rupert, like the best, or worst.
Should they possess our kingdom?
  Andrea.   My wife's kingdom?
No, by the Saints! they shall not touch her kingdom.
  Fra Rupert, crossing the farther part of the stage. They shall not touch
    her kingdom! . . and shalt thou?
  Andrea. I heard a voice.
  Maria, laughing.   No doubt, no doubt, the Frate's.
  Andrea. I hear and feel him farther off than thou dost.
  Maria. Andrea! were thy ears as quick to hear
Thy friends as enemies!
  Andrea.   Stil would that eye   80
Glare over me, like the great open one
Above the throne at church, of gold and azure,
With neither brows nor lashes, but black clouds
Round it, and nought beside.
  Maria.   The three eyes match,
May be; but is there anything in church
So like his voice?
  Andrea.   The organ-bellows are,
Without the keys. That was not much unlike it . .
A little softer . . and not too soft, neither.
  Maria. I heard no voice whatever, not a sound.
Are you stil half-afraid?
  Andrea.   No, if thou art not.   90

            ll. 80, 90 Stil . . . stil] Still . . . still *1846.*

    306

Maria. Are you convinced?

Andrea.   I was not very soon.
Men weigh things longer than you women do.
Maria! take my word, I am quite sated
Of fearing, tho' (thank God!) the worst is past.

   Maria. I praise this manliness, this resolution.

   Andrea. Dost thou? Already am I grown more manly,
More resolute. O! had your praise come earlier,
And heartily as now, another man
In thought and action might have been Andrea!
But will you tell Giovanna what you think?   100

   Maria. I will indeed, and joyfully.

   Andrea.   Her praise
Is better stil: your's screws the spur on heel,
Hers scarfs the neck, and lifts the lance to hand.
What 's all this tinkling?   [*Guitars in the next chamber; the door open.*

   Maria, smiling.   O! again Fra Rupert!
One of these voices surely must be his!
Which of them? cannot you distinguish it?

   Andrea, calls out. Who sings there?

   Maria.   Do not stop them: let us hear.

Petronilla.

Ah! do not go! ah do not go
   Among the silly and the idle!
A lover surely should not so   110
   From her who loves him slip and sidle.

Garisendo.

The *saltarella** waits for me,
   And I must go and I must play . .
Come! do not dance, but hear and see,
   To-morrow we will love all day.

   Andrea. Now she is reasonable, he might spare her
A handful of his ribbons, or that net
Silver and blue there dangling down his nape.
Who is he? I don't know him.

   Maria.   Garisendo.

   Andrea. And t'other?

   Maria.   Petronilla.

   Andrea.   Nor her neither.   120

   Maria. I and Giovanna know here every face.

   Andrea. And every name?

_____
* The favorite [favourite *1846*] Neapolitan dance. [L.]
_____
102 stil] still *1846*.

Maria. Every one.
Andrea. Clever creatures!
Maria. By all those twitchings at the two guitars,
And tappings of fore-finger on the wrist,
They seem to be at fault.
Andrea. No harm, no matter,
Zooks! they are up again; he first . . that 's odd.
Maria. Nay, but he only tells her what to sing.

Petronilla.

There is a lad upon the sea,
There is, O Mary! such a lad!
And all he thinks of, it is me.   130

Garisendo.

Why then, my jewel! he is mad.

Petronilla.

Mad! he is no more mad than you.

Garisendo.

Unless he stamps, and stares, and cries,
As certain pretty creatures do,
And stain their cheeks and spoil their eyes.

Petronilla.

I love, I love him with my whole . .   [*Sobbing.*

Garisendo.

Go on, go on: you mean to say
(I'd lay a wager) heart and soul,
And very well, no doubt, you may.

Petronilla.

No, I may not, you cruel man!   140
He never did what you have done,
Yet, say and do the worst you can,
I love, I love, but you alone.

Maria. He has not much offended.
Andrea. Who can tell?
I am quite sorry they have fallen out.
What almanack can calculate fine weather
In those strange fickle regions where God plants
A man and woman, and sticks love between!
Maria. All the man's fault.
Andrea. All hers. She went and teazed him:
With my own eyes I saw it; so might you.   150
Maria. You do not always look so melancholy
At music; yet what music can be gayer
Than this is?

Andrea. Gayer, say you? Ay, the music.
But if folks quarrel so in joke, what will they
In earnest? If, before they're man and wife . .
Ah! Heaven be praised! there 's time to break it off.
Look, look at them!
    Maria. She seems more reconciled.
    Andrea. Reconciled! I should say . .
    Maria. Pray, don't say anything.
    Andrea. Ready for . . By my troth! 'twas a salute!
    Maria. Now what things run into your head, Andrea!   160
    Andrea. It was as like as pea to pea, if not . .
However, let them know, another time
They must not sing about the house, in that way.
    Maria. Why not?
    Andrea. Giovanna might not like it now.
    Maria. So! you would do then all she likes?
    Andrea. I would:
But if she ever hears that wicked song,
She might not do all *I* like. Sweet Maria!
Persuade them, when you see them, to forget it;
And, when you go to bed, turn on your pillow,
First drop it from one ear, then from the other,   170
And never pick it up again, God love you!
    Maria. I'll run to them directly with your wishes.
    Andrea. Stay: the last verse is clever; pick out that.
    Maria. And nothing more?
    Andrea, anxiously. Don't overload your memory.

[ACT III.] SCENE V.—FRA RUPERT'S CELL.

ANDREA *and* FRA RUPERT.

Fra Rupert. What! am I never to be left alone,
Andrea? Let me have my pleasures too,
Such as they are.
    Andrea. They're very much like mine.
Have we not prayed and scourged and wept together?
    Fra Rupert. Ah! were that now the case!
    Andrea. Well, father, well!
I would not stand between you and your duty:
But I thought, being prince . .
    Fra Rupert, sneering. Thou, being prince,
Thoughtest! Thou verily not only toppest

Thyself, but most among thy fellows, lad!
And so, Andrea! being prince, thou thoughtest?   10
   Andrea. Good-bye! thou art as brave and blithe as ever.

[Goes, but turns back.

I had one little thing upon my conscience.
   Fra Rupert. I am quite ready: let me know the whole:
Since yesterday? Nod! wink! to me!
   Andrea to himself.   He chafes me.
   Fra Rupert. And throw your head back thus?
   Andrea.   My head's my own.
   Fra Rupert. Wonderful! Be not over-sure of that.   [*Aside.*
If thou art contrite, go!
   Andrea.   I will not go;
I am not contrite.
   Fra Rupert.   I am in a maze!
   Andrea. A scrape thou'rt in.
   Fra Rupert.   A scrape! Who could betray me?

[*To himself.*

   Andrea. Thou'st lost thy lamb, old shepherd! no great pet.   20
   Fra Rupert, recovering himself. No, nor great loss: when lambs, tho',
    lose their shepherd
They find the shambles nearer than the fold.
   Andrea. Father! you said you must confer with me
Another time?
   Fra Rupert.   I did so.
   Andrea.   Why not now?
   Fra Rupert. I see not why: but soon Caraccioli,
And first Caraffa, must unbosom here.
Thou hast much power, Andrea! thou canst do
Anything now to glorify thy country.
   Andrea. Suppose I wish to swim to Ischia;
Could I?
   Fra Rupert. Thou hast not wind enough for that.   30
Am I to be evaded, taunted, posed?
Or thinkest thou, Andrea, that because
A silly girl espouses thee . .
   Andrea.   By Peter!
She who espouses me shall ne'er be call'd
A silly girl. I am a husband, Frate!
I am a boy no longer: I can cope
With women: and shall men then, even tho' friars,

14 Nod! . . . me!] Nod? wink? to me? *1846.*   15 your] thy *1846.*   21 *recovering himself*] om. *1846.*   30 Could I?] *ends l.* 29. *in 1846.* Thou] My boy! thou *1846.*

Pretend to more? . . I will go back and call
The maidens: they shall pelt you from the palace,
If ever you set foot within its walls.   40
   Fra Rupert. Should every stone from maiden hit my nose,
A grain of dust would hurt it tenfold more.
   Andrea. Know, they have tongues that yours could never meet.
   Fra Rupert. Andrea! wouldst thou kill me with unkindness?
   Andrea. Gad! he sheds tears! . . Now at him! . . Yes, I would.
   Fra Rupert. And bring down these grey hairs . .
   Andrea.   Which hairs are they?
The skull's are shaven, and the beard's are dirty;
They may be grey though.
   Fra Rupert.   Shame upon thy mirth!
I am a poor old man.
   Andrea.   'Tis your vocation.
Beside, I have heard say that poverty   50
Is the best bargain for the best place yonder
In Paradise. All prick their feet before
They clamber upward into that inclosure.
'Tis well worth while.
   Fra Rupert.   Age too (alas how heavy!)
To serve my loving ward, my prince's son,
I would support stil longer, willingly.
   Andrea. Frate! 'tis more than I can say for it.
                    [Rupert *creeps supplicatingly toward him.*
Out of my sight! crawl back again . . I loathe thee.

[ACT III.] SCENE VI.

   Fra Rupert alone. I have no malice in me: if I know
My secret heart, no heart so pure of malice:
But all my cares and vigils, hopes and dreams,
Blown by a boy, spurn'd by a brute, away!
So ends it? Blessed Stephen! not so ends it.
It ends with him, and with him only: me
No sword can touch. Why are not come those fools?
I thought the other would have kept them off.
I will have power without him, and not thro' him.
They must have clean forgotten. 'Tis the hour . .   10
'Tis past it . . no, not past it . . just the hour;
The bell now strikes for noon.   [*A knocking.*
             One comes at last.
                [*Opens the door:* Caraffa *enters.*
    56 stil] still *1846.*

Fra Rupert. Exactly to the moment.

Caraffa.   I was walking
About the cloister till I heard the bell,
For Father Rupert's hours are golden ones.

Fra Rupert. May my friends spend them profitably for me!
Caraffa! thine are number'd.

Caraffa.   All men's are.

Fra Rupert. But some are not notch't off like schoolboys' days,
Anxious to see his parent. Thou may'st see
Thy parent too.

Caraffa.   I left him but just now.   20

Fra Rupert. We all have one, one whom we all have left
Too often. Hast thou not some sins for me?

Caraffa. As many as a man could wish to have.

Fra Rupert. Are there none dangerous? none involving life?
Hast thou forgotten our last conference?

Caraffa. No, nor shall ever. But what danger there?

Fra Rupert. Need I to say, Francesco, that no breath
Transpired from me? We both were overheard.

Caraffa. I think you hinted it.

Fra Rupert.   I fear'd it only.
Thou knowest my fond love . . I will not say   30
For thee . . thou art but second in my breast . .
Poor, poor Andrea!

Caraffa.   Never fear about him.
Giovanna, even tho' she did not love,
(O that she did not!) yet would never wrong him.

Fra Rupert. Nay, God forbid she should! 'Twas not for me
To mark her looks, her blushes, gestures, . . how
Faltered the word *Caraffa* as she spoke it.
Thy father then said nothing?

Caraffa   Not a word;
What should he?

Fra Rupert.   Not a word. Old men are close:
And yet I doubted . . I am apt to doubt . .   40
Whether he might not . . for ambition stirs
Most fathers . . just let slip . . Why didst thou falter?
For never faltered child as thou didst falter.
Thou knowest then her mind better than we?

Caraffa. I know it? I divine it? Would I did!

Fra Rupert. Nay, rather let the bubble float along
Than break it: the rich colours are outside.

18 schoolboys'] schoolboy's *1846.*

ANDREA OF HUNGARY

Everything in this world is but a bubble,
The world itself one mighty bubble, we
Mortals, small bubbles round it!
   Caraffa.   Frate! Frate!   50
Thou art a soapy one! No catching thee!   [*aside.*
[*Aloud.*] What hopes thou showest me! If these were solid
As thou, most glorious bubble who reflect'st them,
Then, then indeed, to me from this time forth
The world, and all within the world, were bubbles.
   Fra Rupert. A knight art thou, Caraffa! and no title
(Secular title, mind! secular title)
Save only royalty, surpasses knighthood.
There is no condescension in a queen
Placing her foot within the palm of knight,   60
And springing from it on her jewel'd saddle:
No condescension is there if she lend
To theirs the sceptre who lent hers the sword.
Knights there have been, and are, where kings are not,
Kings without knights what are they?
   Caraffa.   Norman blood
Runs in my veins as in her own: no king
(Savage or tame) shall stand above those knights
Who raised his better to the throne he won:
Of such am I. But what am I before
Giovanna! to adore, to worship her,   70
Is glory far above the chiseling
Of uncouth kings, or dashing them to earth:
O be it mine!
   Fra Rupert. Perhaps some other Norman
May bear less tamely the new yoke; perhaps
A Filangieri may, this very night . .
   Caraffa.   No Filangieri ever stoop't to treachery,
No sword of Norman ever struck by night.
Credulous monk! to me name Filangieri!
Quellers of France and England as we are,
And jealous of precedency, no name
(Offence to none) is higher than Filangieri.   80
   Fra Rupert. Boaster!
   Caraffa.   I boast of others; few do that
Who merit such a title.
   Fra Rupert.   Lower thy crest;
Pause! thou art in my hands.

     71 chiseling] chiselling *1846.*   76 stoop't] stoopt *1846.*

Caraffa.   I am in God's.

Fra Rupert, mildly, after hesitation. Who knows but God hath chosen
    thee, amid
His ministers of wrath, to save thy country
And push oppression from her! Dreams and signs
Miraculous have haunted me.

    Caraffa.   Thee, Frate!

    Fra Rupert. Me, even me. My ministry is over:
Marriage ends pupilage, and royalty
Ends friendship. Little is it short of treason   90
To say that kings have friends.

    Caraffa.   How short of treason
I know not, but I know how wide of truth.

    Fra Rupert. Listen! There are designs against the life
Of young Andrea.

    Caraffa.   By the saints above!
I hope there are not.

    Fra Rupert.   If thy name be found
Among conspirators (and those are call'd
Conspirators who vindicate their country)
Where thy sword is, there must thy safety be.
The night for vengeance is the marriage-night.

    Caraffa. I draw the sword without defiance first?   100
I draw the sword uninjured? Whom against?
Against a life so young! so innocent
Of any guile! a bridegroom! in his bed!
O! is this horror only at the crime?
Or is it . . No, by Heaven! 'tis Heaven's own horror
At such unmanly deed. *I*, Frate! *I*,
Caraffa, stain with tears Giovanna's cheek!
I sprinkle poison on the flowers she smells!

    Fra Rupert, resolutely. Hark ye, Caraffa! If the public good . .

    Caraffa. Away with public good! Was never book   110
Put in my hand? was never story told me?
Show me one villain vile beyond the rest,
Did not that villain talk of public good?

    Fra Rupert. Only at friars are Caraffa's stabs.
Valiant and proud and wealthy as thou art,
Thou may'st have nothing left on earth to-morrow.

    Caraffa. I shall have more to-morrow than to-day.
My honour may shoot up all in one night,
As did some tree we read of.

    Fra Rupert.   Thou art rash.

Caraffa. Rashness may mellow into courage; time   120
Is left me.

Fra Rupert. For thy prayers.

Caraffa.   My prayer then is,
Peace, safety, glory, joy, to our Giovanna!

Fra Rupert. Thou may'st depart.

Caraffa, indignantly.   For ever.   *[Goes.*

Fra Rupert.   He says well.

CARACCIOLI *enters.*

Fra Rupert, smiling and embracing him. Caraccioli! without our
    friend Caraffa!

Caraccioli. He should have been here first.

Fra Rupert, aside.   Perfectly safe!
I did not follow him into the cloister.

Caraccioli. Father! you seem as pondering to yourself
How that wild fellow kept his word so ill;
Caraffa-like!

Fra Rupert. I keep mine well with him.

Caraccioli. He should have thought of that.   130

Fra Rupert.   He had no time.

Caraccioli. Always so kind! so ready with your plea
For little imperfections! Our Francesco,
Somewhat hot-headed, is warm-hearted too.

Fra Rupert. His petty jealousy about the queen
(Were there no sin behind it) we might smile at.
Caraffa stands not with Caraccioli.

Caraccioli. On the same level . . there particularly.

Fra Rupert. Ho! ho! you laugh and jeer about each other?

Caraccioli. We might. How she would laugh at two such ninnies!

Fra Rupert. At one, most certainly. But laughing girls   140
Often like grave men best. There's something grand,
As well as grave, even in the sound "Caraccioli."

Caraccioli. I have no hopes.

Fra Rupert.   How I rejoice to hear it!
Hopes are but wishes, wishes are but sin,
And, fed with ranker exhalations, poison.

Caraccioli. The subtilest consumes me.

Fra Rupert.   What?

Caraccioli.   Despair.

Fra Rupert. Violets and primroses lie under thorns
Often as asps and adders; and we find
The unexpected often as the expected,
The pleasant as the hideous.

315

Caraccioli.   That may be,   150
But what avails your lesson? whither tends it?
   Fra Rupert. My son! I hear from those who know the world
And sweep its noisome litter to my cell,
There are mild days when love calls love abroad
As birds call birds, and even leaves call leaves:
Moments there are, my poor Caraccioli!
Moments in which the labyrinth of the ear
At every turn of its proclivity
Grows warmer, and holds out the clue, itself:
Severity should not beget despair.   160
I would not much encourage thee, nor yet
Dash all thy hopes, however inconsiderate,
For hopes there may be, though there should not be,
Flickering even upon despondency.
There may be sounds in certain names to smite
The stagnant heart, and swell its billows high
Over wide spaces, over distant years . .
There may; but who would utter them and know it?
Delicate is the female sense, yet strong
In cherishing and resenting; very prompt   170
At hiding both, and hating the discoverer.
Never, my Paolo! look too deeply in,
Or thou may'st find what thou art looking for.
Not that she ever said one word against thee;
She even lower'd her voice in naming thee.
Seeing her sister and the rest sit giggling,
Anything else! anything else! said she,
And snapt the thread she workt with, out of spite.
A friend, who hopes the best, may tell the worst.
Patience will weary; even Giovanna's patience.   180
I could go farther, and relate . . but why
Why ('tis too light to touch upon) relate
The little hurt she gave Filippa's ancle
With that lark heel of hers, by twitching it
Uneasily? O the impatient sex!
She did shed . . tears I will not say . . a tear . .
Shed it! no; I am wrong: it came, it stayed,
As hangs one star, the first and only one,
Twinkling, upon some vernal evening.
   Caraccioli. I am but clay beneath her feet. Alas!   190
Clay there would quicken into primal man,
Glorified and immortal once again.

ANDREA OF HUNGARY

Fra Rupert. Thou art too hot, my Paolo! One pulse less
In the half-hour might have been rather better.
Lovest thou our Francesco?
    Caraccioli.   Like a brother.
Fra Rupert. He should not then have brought thy life in peril.
Andrea is quite furious: all at court
Are sworn upon thy ruin.
    Caraccioli.   Upon mine?
I will then calmly tell them they are wrong.
    Fra Rupert. Will they as calmly hear? Francesco said,   200
Imprudent youth! you boasted of remembering
Every the lightest mole about Giovanna.
    Caraccioli. I say it?
    Fra Rupert.   Those were not your words.
    Caraccioli.   My words!
    Fra Rupert. Certainly not . . precisely.
    Caraccioli.   Holy Mary!
Is there in Naples, Hungary, or Hell,
The monster who dares utter them?
    Fra Rupert.   'Tis hard
Our friend should be the very man.
    Caraccioli.   'Tis false,
Frate! 'tis false: my friend is not the man.   [*Bursts away.*
    Fra Rupert, sneering. I will not follow *him* into the cloister.

ACT IV.

SCENE I. IN THE GARDEN OF CAPO DI MONTE.

BOCCACCIO *and* FIAMMETTA.

BOCCACCIO, *sings.*
If there be love on earth, 'tis here,
  O maid of royal line!
Should they who spring from heroes, fear?
  Be scornful the divine?

Shine not the stars upon the sea,
  Upon the fountain too?
O! let your eyes then light on me,
  And O! let mine see you.

    [FIAMMETTA *comes forward.*
How kind, to come!
    Fiammetta.   To come into the air?
I like it. They are all at their *merenda**.   10
The smell of melon overpowers me quite;

    * *Merenda* (meridiana) the mid-day repast. [L.]

317

I could not bear it; therefor I just come
Into the air to be revived a little.
And you too here! Sly as the satyr-head   [*Affecting surprise.*
Under yon seat!
 Boccaccio. Did you not tell me?
 Fiammetta.   *I?*
You dreamt it.
 Boccaccio. Let me dream then on! Without
Such dreams, Fiammetta, dull would be the sleep
Call'd life.
 Fiammetta, looking round timidly. I must be broad awake.
 Boccaccio.   You must.
 Fiammetta, nodding. And you. All are indulgent to me; most
Of all, queen Sancia and Giovanna.
 Boccaccio.   One   20
A saint, the other better.
 Fiammetta.   Then the grave
Filippa . .
 Boccaccio. Grave and watchful.
 Fiammetta.   Not a word
Against her! I do hold her in my heart,
Although she gives me good advice sometimes.
 Boccaccio. I'm glad to hear it; for the very worthy
Are very rarely general favorites.
 Fiammetta. Some love our friend most cordially; those know her:
Others there are who hate her; those would know her
And cannot; for she stands aloof and thanks them;
Remoter, idler, neither love nor hate,   30
Nor care about her; and the worst and truest
They say of her, is, that her speech is dark.
 Boccaccio. Doubtless, the vulgar eye will take offence
If cedar chambers are unwasht with lime.
 Fiammetta. But why are you come here?
 Boccaccio.   To gaze, to sigh,
And, O Fiammetta! tell me if . . to live.
 Fiammetta, laughing. I never saw more signs of life in any.
 Boccaccio. Cruel!
 Fiammetta. To find the signs of life in you?
 Boccaccio. To scoff them out.
 Fiammetta.   I am incapable.
  [Boccaccio *rises, and steps back gazing fondly.*

12 therefor] therefore *1846.* 14 here!] here? *1846.* 26 favorites] favourites *1846.* 29 cannot] can not *1846.*

O now, Giovanni! I am terrified!   40
Why! you sprang up . . as if you sprang to kiss me!
Did ever creature think of such a thing!
   Boccaccio. The drooping blades of grass beneath your feet
Think of it; the cold runlet thinks of it;
The pure sky (how it smiles upon us!) thinks of it . .
I will no more then think of it.   [*Kisses her*.
   Fiammetta.   Giovanni!
Ah! I shall call you (wretch!) to task for this.
   Boccaccio. Call; and, by Heaven! I'll come, tho' from the grave.
   Fiammetta. Any-one, now, would say you thought me handsome.
   Boccaccio. Earth has two beauties; her Bellagio   50
And Anacapri; earth's inhabitants
Have only one among them.
   Fiammetta.   Whom?
   Boccaccio.   Fiammetta.   [*Going*.
   Fiammetta. Where are you running now? Stay! tho' quite angry,
I am not yet so angry as I should be:
But, if you ever take such liberties
Again!
   Boccaccio. O never! . . till we reach Aversa.
   Fiammetta. And will you there? and tell me to my face?
                             [*Is departing*.
Wait, wait for pardon. Must we part? So soon?
So long a time?
   Boccaccio.   Til star-light.
   Fiammetta.   Stay a moment.
   Boccaccio. Gladly a life: but my old mule loves walking   60
And meditation. Now the mask and dress,
And boy to carry them, must all be found.
   Fiammetta. Boy, mask, dress, mule! speed, gallop, to Aversa!
   Boccaccio. So many kisses lie upon this hand,
Mine hardly reach it.
   Fiammetta.   Lips there may have been;
Had there been kisses, I must sure have felt them,
As I did yours . . at least I thought I did . .
But go, for I am half afraid of you . .
That is, of your arriving yonder late.
Go, else the crowd may stop you; and, perhaps,   70
I might delay you for some sudden fancy,
Or . . go your ways . . not let you go at all.

---

   42 thing!] thing? *1846*.   49 Any-one, now,] Any-one now *1846*.   59 Til]
Till *1846*.

Fra Rupert alone. I wisht him power; for what was his was mine;
I wisht him jealousy, distrust, aversion
For his pert bride, that she might have no share.
I never fail'd before this wretched day.
Fail'd! I have not: I will possess my rights,
Spring over him, and never more be spurn'd.
They who had rais'd his seat, shall stablish mine,
Without those two vain boys. O! had they done it!
And not been where they are! The fault was theirs.

MAXIMIN *enters.*

Fra Rupert. Maximin! since thy services may soon   10
Be call'd for, satchel on thee my experience,
Then set about thy work. My Maximin!
Mind how thou liest! Know, if lie thou must,
Lies, while they sap their way and hold their tongues,
Are safe enough: when breath gets into them,
They, and the work about them, may explode.
Maximin! there are more lies done than said.
Son! when we hesitate about the right,
We're sure to do the wrong.
    Maximin.   I don't much hesitate.
    Fra Rupert. To chain a dog and to unchain a dog   20
Is hazardous alike, while the deaf beast
Stands barking: he must sleep; then for the cord.
    Maximin. What! are my services in some farm-yard?
I am a soldier.
    Fra Rupert. All great statesmen have been.
How large a portion of the world is each
In his own eyes!
    Maximin.   Am I so proud in saying
I am a soldier?
    Fra Rupert.   *I* am proud of thee;
Be that sufficient. Give thou every man
What he requires of thee.
    Maximin.   A world to each?
    Fra Rupert. Not so: yet hold not up to him a glass   30
That shows him less, or but some digits greater.
    Maximin. Honestly now, Fra Rupert, by my cross!
No gull art thou. I knew that trick myself,
And (short the digits) told it word for word.
    Fra Rupert. I will be sworn for thee. Being minister
(Not that I think it certain just at present,

For when the sage and honest are most wanted,
That is the chink of time they all drop through)
But when thou art so, mind this precept. One
Not wise enough to keep the wiser off   40
Should never be a minister of state.
    Maximin. Fra Rupert! presto! make me one to-day.
Give fifty precepts, there they go! [*blowing*] but this
I'll kiss the cross and the queen's hand, and keep.
    Fra Rupert. I make thee minister!
    Maximin.   You can make kings.
    Fra Rupert. Not even those! I might have made Andrea
What thou and every true Hungarian
Wisht him to be, ere he show'd hoof for claw,
And thought to trample down his countrymen.
    Maximin. Andrea bloody-minded! turtle-doves   50
Are bloody-minded then, and leave their elm,
The first day's mating, for the scent of gore.
    Fra Rupert. Maximin! here is no guitar for thee,
Else mightest thou sip that pure poetry,
Preciously warm and frothy from the udder.
    Maximin. Father! if any in our troop call'd me
A poet, he should sing for it.
    Fra Rupert.   Thou'rt brave,
Maximin! and Andrea is not bloody.
But there are princes, or have been within
Our memory, who, when blood gusht forth like water   60
From their own people, stood upon some bridge
Or iland, waving their plumed caps, and drank
The cries of dying men with drunken ears.
    Maximin. Curses, eternal curses, man's and God's,
Upon such heathens!
    Fra Rupert.   Nay, they were not heathens;
Happily they were christians, Maximin!
Andrea, though myself instructed him,
Is treacherous. Better were this pasty people
Dissolved, washt down, than brave Hungarians perish.
    Maximin. No truer word prophet or saint e'er spoke.   70
    Fra Rupert, sighing. Saint hath not spoken it: O may not pro-
    phet!
    Maximin. I, being neither, cannot understand you.
    Fra Rupert. The innocent, the helpless, are surrounded.

---

54 sip] *so in errata 1839 and text 1846; first printed* sing.   62 iland] island *1846.*
72 cannot] can not *1846.*

Maximin. Andrea?

Fra Rupert.   My Andrea would betray us.

Maximin. To whom? Are we the helpless? we the innocent?

Fra Rupert. While he is yonder at Aversa, we
Are yelling thro' these very streets for mercy.

Maximin. I cry *you* mercy, father! When I yell,
I'll borrow whistles from some thirty good
Neapolitans, who'll never want them more.   80

Fra Rupert. Be ready then! be ready for Aversa!
Glory stands there before thee; seize the traitor,
Win wealth, win jewels, win . . What have not palaces
For brave young men upon such nights as these!

Maximin. Would'st bid me stick Andrea?

Fra Rupert.   Hungary,
Not I; our country, not revenge.

Maximin.   Bids murder!
I will proclaim thy treason thro' the camp.

Fra Rupert. Unhappy son, forbear! By thy sweet mother!
Upon my knees! Upon my knees before
A mortal man! Yea, Rupert! bend thy head;   90
Thy own son's hand should, and shall, spill thy blood.

          [MAXIMIN *starts, then hesitates, then rushes at him.*

Maximin. Impudent hound! I'll have thy throat for that.

Fra Rupert, guards his throat. Parricide! make me not cry Murder . .
          love
Forbids it . . rather die! My son! my son!
Hide but thy mother's shame; my shame, not hers.

                              [MAXIMIN *relaxes his grasp.*

Maximin! stand between the world and it!
Oh! what avails it! sinner as I am!
Other worlds witness it.   [MAXIMIN *looses hold.*
          My Maximin!   [RUPERT *embraces him.*

Maximin. Why, how now, Frate! hath some wine-vault burst
And fuddled thee? we know thou never drinkest.   100

Fra Rupert. That lighter sin won't save me.

Maximin.   If light sins
Could save us, I have many a bushelful,
And little need your sentry-boxes yonder.

Fra Rupert, very mildly. I must reprove (my own dear child!)
          (*Passionately*) . . I must
Reprove, however gently, such irreverence.

84 these!] these? *1846.*   96 it!] it? *1846* (*mispr.*).   ˉ 98 Maximin!] Maximin?
1846.

Confessionals *are* sentry-boxes! true!
And woe betide the sentry that naps there!
Woe, if he spare his voice, his prayer, his curse!
  Maximin. Curses we get dog-cheap; the others, reasonable.
  Fra Rupert. Sweet Maximin! whatever my delight   110
In gazing on those features (for sharp shame,
When love blows over it from lands afar,
Tingles with somewhat too, too like delight!)
We must now part. Thy fortune lies within
My hands. To-night, if thy own officers
Command thee to perform a painful office . .
  Maximin. Good father! what know we of offices?
Let them command a duty, and 'tis done.
  Fra Rupert. Discreet tho'! Maximin! discreet! my marrow!
Let not a word escape thee, not a breath.   120
Blessings, my tender kid! We must walk on
(I love thee so!) together thro' the cloister.
  Maximin. No, father! no; too much!
  Fra Rupert.   Too much for thee?
        [RUPERT *precedes, speaks to three men, who bow and retire; he*
                                                       disappears.
  Maximin, loitering in the cloister. Incredible! yet friars and cock-
    roaches
Creep thro' all rooms, and like the closest best.
Let me consider! can it be? how can it?
He is bare fifty; I am forty-one.
                125 closest] closet *1846.*

[ACT IV.] SCENE III. THE GARDEN OF FRIAR ANSELM'S CONVENT.

FRA RUPERT, KLAPWRATH, ZINGA, *and* PSEIN.

  Fra Rupert. Ye brave supporters of Hungarian power
And dignity! O Zinga! Klapwrath! Psein!
Becomes it me to praise (we may admire
Those whom to praise were a temerity)
Such men as you.
  Psein.   Us? we are only captains.
  Zinga. After hard service we are nothing more.
  Klapwrath. Twenty-three years hath Klapwrath rid and thirsted.
  Fra Rupert. Ingratitude! the worst of human crimes,
Hardly we dare to say; so flat and stale,
So heavy with sick sobs from mouth to mouth,   10
        7 rid] *so in errata 1839 and text 1846; first printed* rode.

The ejaculation. To my mind scarce witchery
Comes up to it.

Psein.   Hold! father! For that sin
Either we deal with devils or old women.

Fra Rupert. Man was created of the dust; to make
The fragile mass cohesive, were employed
The bitter waters of ingratitude.   [*Affects to weep.*

Klapwrath. Weeping will never rinse that beaker, Frate!

Fra Rupert. It is not for myself.

Zinga.   We see it is not.

Fra Rupert. Ye cannot see deep into me.

Psein.   Few can.

Fra Rupert. Ye cannot see the havoc made within   20
By ever-dear Andrea.

Zinga.   Havoc?

Fra Rupert.   Havoc!

Klapwrath. I like the word: purses and rings hang round it,
Necklaces, broches, and indented armlets.

Psein. But, ere we reach 'em, ugly things enough,
Beside the broken swords that lie below
And brave men brandisht in the morning light.

Klapwrath. Brave men then should not cross us; wise men don't.

Fra Rupert. Your spirit all attest; but those the least
Whose safety hangs upon your saddle-skirts.
Men are not valued for their worth in Italy: 30
Of the same price the apple and the peach,
The service and the fig.

Zinga.   Well, there they beat us.

Psein. Whatever they may be, we cannot help it.

Fra Rupert. Help it, I say, ye can; and ye shall help it,
Altho' I perish for ye.

Klapwrath.   Then indeed,
Frate! some good might come of it; but wilt thou?

Fra Rupert. Abandon to his fate my poor Andrea!
Has he not slept upon this bosom?

Klapwrath.   Has he?
He must have had some scratches on his face.

Fra Rupert. Has he not eaten from this hand?

Klapwrath.   Why then,   40
He'll never die for want of appetite.

Fra Rupert. Have we not drunk our water from one bowl?

19, 20, 33 cannot] can not *1846.*   23 broches] brooches *1846.*

ANDREA OF HUNGARY

Klapwrath. Father! you were not very liberal;
He might have drunk the whole of mine, and welcome.
    Fra Rupert. How light ye make of life!
    Zinga.   Faith! not so light;
I think it worth a tug, for my part of it;
Nor would I leave our quarters willingly.
    Psein. O the delight of floating in a bath,
One hand athwart an orange-bough, the other
Flat on the marble pavement, and our eyes   50
Wandering among those figures round the arch
That scatter flowers, and laugh at us, and vie
With one another which shall tempt us most!
Nor is it undelightful, in my mind,
To let the curly wave of the warm sea
Climb over me, and languishingly chide
My stopping it, and push me gently away.
    Klapwrath. Water, cold, tepid, hot, is one to me.
The only enemy to honest wine
Is water; plague upon it!
    Zinga.   So say I.   60
    Fra Rupert. Three braver friends ne'er met. Hei! hei! hei! hei!
The very name of friend! You cannot know
What love I bear Andrea!
    Psein.   All the world
Knows it.
    Fra Rupert. The mischief he designs, who guesses?
    Psein. All boys are mischievous.
    Fra Rupert.   Alas! but mischief
There might be without treachery.
    Psein.   Poor Andrea!
So little fit for it!
    Fra Rupert.   Frank generous souls
Always are first to suffer from it, last
To know it when they meet it.
    Klapwrath.   Who shall harm
Our own king's colt? Who moves, speaks, looks, against him,   70
Why! that man's shroud is woven, and spred out.
    Fra Rupert. Let mine then be! would it had been so ere
I saw this day!
    Psein.   What has he done?
    Fra Rupert.   To me
All kindness ever. Why such mad resolves

        62 cannot] can not *1846.*   71 spred] spread *1846.*

Against the lives of his most sure defenders?
Against his countrymen, his guards, his father's
Most chosen friends?

Zinga.   Against your life?

Fra Rupert.   No, no!
Heaven protects *me*; he sees it; nor indeed
(To do him justice) has he such a heart.
But why ask *me* to aid him? Why ask *me*   80
Whether he was as strong at heart as Zinga,
Dexterous at sword as Klapwrath, such a fool . .
Pardon! your pardon, gentlemen!   [*Looking at* PSEIN.

Psein.   As Psein.

Fra Rupert. The very word! Who else dared utter it?
I give him up! I almost give him up!

Klapwrath. He shall not rule us. The best blood of Hungary
Shall not be poured this night upon the wine.

Fra Rupert. If you must leave the country . . and perhaps
No worse may reach the greater part of you . .

Psein. I have no mind to leave it.

Zinga.   None shall drive us.   90

Klapwrath. The wines of Hungary strive hard with these,
Yet Klapwrath is contented; he hates change.

Zinga. Let us drink these out first, and then try those.

Fra Rupert. Never will come the day when pine-root fire
And heavy cones puff fragrance round the room,
And two bluff healthy children drag along
(One by the ear, the other by the scut)
A bulging hare for supper; where each greyhound
Knows his own master, leaps up, hangs a foot
Inward, and whimpers piteously to see   100
Flagons go round; then off for bread and lard.
Those were your happy times; unless when foray
Stirr'd ye to wrath, and beeves, and swine, and trulls,
(Tempting ye from propriety) heapt up
A mount of sins to strive against; abduction
Of linen-chests, and those who wove the linen;
And shocking oaths obscene, and well-nigh acts;
Fracture of cellar-doors, and spinning-wheels;
And (who can answer for you) worse, worse, worse!

Klapwrath. 'Sblood! Frate! runs no vine-juice in our arteries;   110
Psein's forehead starts wry veins upon each side;
His nostrils blow so hot they'll crack my boots.

Zinga. Must we move hence?

326

ANDREA OF HUNGARY

Fra Rupert.   To die like sheep? like conies?
Ye shall not die alone; I will die with you.
There have been kings who sacrificed their sons . .
Abraham would have done it; Pagans have;
But guardians such as I am!
  Klapwrath.   Frate! Frate!
Don't tear those tindery rags, or they will quit thee
With only horse-hair under, and some stiffer.
  Fra Rupert. You conquer me, you conquer me, I yield.   120
He was not bloody. Would it end with one!
And we knew which . . or two, or three.
  Zinga.   But *us?*
  Fra Rupert. "*If once the captains of the companies,*"
Said he . . and then, I own, he said no more:
He saw me shudder, and he sped away.
  Klapwrath. Are we to hold our throats out to the knife?
  Fra Rupert. Patience! dear doubtful Klapwrath! mere suspicion!
He did not say the knife, or sword, or halter,
He might have meant the scaffold; nothing worse;
Deprive you he might not of all distinction,   130
Nay, might spare one or other of you yet:
Why then prevent what may need no prevention?
Slyer are few; many more sanguinary:
Must we (don't say it) give him up? I hope
He 's mischievous through weakness, not malignity.
  Zinga. What matters that? A feather-bed may stifle us
(If we will let it) with a babe to press it.
Is there no other prince in Hungary
Fit to maintain us here?
  Fra Rupert.   The very thought
That came into my head!
  Psein.   But when ours fall,   140
What matters it who leaps upon his horse
To overlook our maintenance? A fool
I may be, can his wisdom answer that?
  Zinga. He doubts my courage, bringing thus his own
Against it. He 's a boy: were he a man,
No injury, no insult, no affront . .
Every man is as brave as I . . Stop there!
By all my saints! [*He shows several about him.*] by all my services!
This hilt shall smash his teeth who dares say, *braver.*

121 Would] Could *1846.*   148 *so in errata 1839 and text 1846.*   *As first printed the stage direction followed* services!

327

Klapwrath. What I am you know best, at battling it;   150
Nothing is easier: but I've swum two nights
And days together upon Baian wine,
And so have ye: 'twould swamp that leaky nump-skull.
Behead us; good! but underrate us; never!
   Fra Rupert. Having thus clear'd our consciences, and shown
Our purity in face of day, we swear . .   *[Hesitates.*
   Zinga. Frate, if *you* don't grudge an oath or two . .
   Fra Rupert. Death to Andrea! loyalty to Lewis!
   All. Hurrah!
   Fra Rupert.   Sweet friends! profane not thus the cloister!
Leave me to weep for him! the cruel boy!   160

[ACT IV.] SCENE IV.
PALACE OF AVERSA; SALOON OVERLOOKING THE GARDEN.

SANCIA, FILIPPA, MARIA, FIAMMETTA.

Maria. Ha! here they come again. See! Lady Sancia
Leaning upon Filippa. They are grown
Wiser, and will not barter songs for griefs.

BOCCACCIO *sings.*
A mellow light on Latmos fell,
It came not from the lowly cell,
   It glided from the skies;
It lighted upon one who slept,
Some voice then askt him why he wept,
   Some soft thing prest his eyes.

Another might have wonder'd much,   10
Or peer'd, or started at the touch,
   But he was far too wise;
He knew the light was from above,
He play'd the shifting game of love,
   And lost at last three sighs.

Fiammetta. (*to* FILIPPA). I wish he would come nearer, just to see
How my hair shines, powder'd with dust of gold:
I think he then would call me . .
   Maria.   What?
   Fiammetta.   Fiammetta.
   Filippa. He hardly . . poet as he seems to be . .
Such as he is . . could feign a better name.   20
He does not seem to be cut out for singing.
   Fiammetta. I would not have his voice one tittle altered.
The poetry is pretty . . She says nothing.
The poetry is charming . . Now she hears me.
     10 wonder'd] wondered *1846.*

328

ANDREA OF HUNGARY

The most delightful poetry! .. O Lady
Filippa! not one praise for it! not one!
I never dreamt you were yourself a poet.
  Filippa. These summer apples may be palatable,
But will not last for winter; the austere
And wrinkle-rinded have a better chance.   30
Throw a whole honeycomb into a haystack,
It may draw flies, but never will feed horses.
From these same cogs (eternally one tune)
The mill has floured us with such dust all over
As we must shake off, or die apoplectic.
Your gentle silken-vested swains may wish
All poetry one sheepfold.
  Maria.   Sheep are well,
Like men and most things, in their proper places,
But when some prancing knight would entertain us,
Some gallant, brightening every gem about him,   40
I would not have upon the palace steps
A hind cry out, "*Make way there for my sheep.*"
They say (not speaking of this woolsy race)
They say that poets make us live for ever.
  Filippa. Sometimes the life they lend is worse than none,
Shorn of its glory, shrivel'd up for want
Of the fresh air of virtue.
  Fiammetta.   Yet, to live!
O! and to live by those we love so well!
  Filippa. If such irregularities continue
After to-night, when freedoms are allowed,   50
We must lock up the gardens, rigorously
Forbidding all the inmates of the palace
To use the keys they have.
  Fiammetta.   The good king Robert
Sooner had driven out the nightingales
Than the poor timid poets.
  Filippa.   Timid poets!
What breed are they of?
  Fiammetta.   Such as sing of love.
  Filippa. The very worst of all; the boldest men!
  Maria. Nay; not the boldest; very quarrelsome,
Tragic and comic, hot and cold, are so;
And so are nightingales; the gardener   60
Has told me; and the poets do no worse
       33 From] With *1839* (*corr. in errata*).

Than they do. Here and there they pluck a feather
From one another, here and there a crumb;
But, for hard fighting, fair straight-forward fighting,
With this one nosegay I could beat them all.
In good king Robert's day were lute and lyre;
Now hardly dare we hang them on the nail,
But run away and throw them down before
The blustering drum and trumpet hoarse with rage.
Let poetry and music, dear Filippa,   70
Gush forth unfrozen and uncheckt!
 Filippa.   Ah child!
Thy fancy too some poet hath inflamed:
Believe me, they are dangerous men.
 Maria.   No men
Are dangerous.
 Filippa.   O my child!
 Maria.   The very creatures
Whom God has given us for our protection.
 Filippa. But against whom?
 Maria.   I never thought of that.
 Fiammetta. Somebody told me once that good king Robert
Gave keys to three or four, who neither were
Nor would be constant inmates of the court.
 Maria. Who might and would not! This is an enigma.   80
They must have felt, then, very low indeed.
Among our glass-house jewels newly-set
I have seen vile ones, and have laught to think
How nicely would my slipper pat their faces;
They never felt thus low.
 Sancia.   We feel it for them.
Prescriptively, we leave to our assayers
To stamp the currency of gold and brass.
 Fiammetta to FILIPPA. Have you not prais'd the king your very self
For saying to Petrarca, as he did,
"*Letters are dearer to me than my crown,*   90
And, were I forced to throw up one or other,
Away should go the diadem, by Jove!"
 Sancia. Thou art thy very father. Kiss me, child!
His father said it, and thy father would.
When shall such kings adorn the throne again!
 Fiammetta. When the same love of what Heaven made most lovely

69 blustering] boisterous *1846*. [This line with variants also occurs in *The Examination of Shakespeare*, 1834, p. 196. W.]

330

ANDREA OF HUNGARY

Enters their hearts; when genius shines above them,
And not beneath their feet.   *[Goes up to* GIOVANNI.
   Sancia to FILIPPA.   Rapturous girl!
Warmth ripens years and wisdom. She discourses
Idly as other girls on other things.   100
   Filippa. That ripening warmth fear I.
   Sancia.   Portending what?
   Filippa. Ah, gracious lady! sweetest fruits fall soonest . .
   Sancia. (Who sweeter?)
   Filippa.   And are bruised the most by falling.
   Maria joining them. Sicily and myself are disagreed.
Surely the man who sang must have thick fingers,
He play'd so badly: but his voice is sweet,
For all its trembling.
   Fiammetta.   Now I think the trembling
Makes it no worse. I wish he would go on.
   Maria. Evidently the song should finish there.
   Fiammetta. Evidently it should go on . . (*aside*) for ever.   110
   Maria. Ho! ho! you are not cruel to the knight?
   Fiammetta. It is no knight at all.
   Sancia.   How know you that?
   Maria. You would be frightened . .
   Fiammetta.   He could never frighten.
   Maria. If tilting . .
   Fiammetta.   Nobody would hurt Giovanni.

---

98 *stage direction* [*Goes . . .* GIOVANNI. *marked in errata 1839 for deletion but retained in text 1846.*]   101 warmth] *mispr.* warmht *1839.*

[ACT IV.] SCENE V.

ANDREA, MARIA, *and* FIAMMETTA.

   Andrea. So! you too have been listening, every soul,
I warrant ye.
   Maria.   And have you too, Andrea?
   Andrea. From that snug little watch-tower. 'Twas too high;
I only lookt upon the tops of trees.
See! him there! maskt! under the mulberry!
   Fiammetta. I do not see him. Look for him elsewhere.
That is a shadow.
   Andrea.   Think you so? It may be.
And the guitar?
   Fiammetta. What! that great yellow toad-stool?
   Andrea. How like is everything we see by starlight!

Fiammetta, aside. If there were not a star in all the sky,   10
Every one upon earth would know Giovanni!
    Andrea. I wish the mulberries were not past, that dozens
Might drop upon him, and might speckle over
His doublet: we should see it like a trout
To-morrow, white and crimson, and discover
The singer of this nonsense about light.
    Fiammetta. If you don't like it, pray don't listen to it.
    Maria, maliciously. Then let us come away.
    Fiammetta.   Pray do.
    Maria, taking her arm.   Come.
    Fiammetta, peevishly.   No.
    Maria. Listen! another song!
    Fiammetta.   Hush! for Heaven's sake!
O! will you never listen? All this noise!   20
    Maria. Laughter might make some; smiles are much too silent.
    Fiammetta. Well; you have stopt him! Are you now content?
    Maria. Quite, quite; if you are.
    Fiammetta.   He begins again!
Hush! for the hope of Paradise! O hush!

BOCCACCIO *sings.*
List! list ye to another tale!

FIAMMETTA.
No; he who dares tell one
To other ears than one's, shall fail.

BOCCACCIO.
I sing for her alone.

    Andrea. I have a mind to be . .
    Maria.   What? prince!
    Andrea.   What? angry.
    Maria. Not you.
    Andrea.   Not I? Why, who should hinder me?   30
    Maria, coaxing. No, no; you won't be angry, prince!
    Andrea.   I said
Half-angry, and resolve to keep my word.
    Maria. Anger is better, as pomegranates are,
Split into halves, and losing no small part.
    Andrea. I never heard such truth about pomegranates!
What was the other thing we reason'd on?
Ho! now I recollect, as you shall see.   *[Goes: all follow.*

ANDREA OF HUNGARY

ANDREA, MARIA, FIAMMETTA, *and* BOCCACCIO.

Andrea. Keep back: where thieves may be, leave men alone.
Now for drawn swords! Where are they; slipt behind
The mulberry: wisely schemed! 'twon't do! come forth!
Yield! tremble like a poplar-leaf! Who art thou?   [*Seizing* BOCCACCIO.
   Boccaccio. King Robert, sir, respected me.
   Andrea.   Did *he?*
Did *he?* Then far more highly should Andrea.
Sicily! treat him kindly. We may all,
Even you and I, commit an indiscretion.
How the stars twinkle! how the light leaves titter!
And there are secret quiverings in the herbs,   10
As if they all knew something of the matter,
And wisht it undisturb'd. To-night no harm
Shall happen to the worst man in Aversa.

ACT V.

SCENE I. PALACE OF AVERSA.

ANDREA *and* GIOVANNA.

Giovanna. How gracefully thou sattest on thy horse,
Andrea!
   Andrea. Did I?
   Giovanna.   He curveted so,
Sidled and pranced and croucht and plunged again,
I almost was afraid, but dared not say it.
   Andrea. Castagno is a sad curvetting rogue.
   Giovanna. 'Twas not Castagno; 'twas Polluce.
   Andrea.   Was it?
How canst thou tell, Giovanna?
   Giovanna.   I can tell.
   Andrea. All at hap-hazard: I am very sure
'Twas not the horse you look'd at; nor did I
Think about riding, or about the palfrey,   10
Crimson and gold, half palfrey and half ostrich.
But thou too ridest like a queen, my dove!
   Giovanna. So very like one? Would you make me proud?
   Andrea. God forbid that! I love thee more for beauty.
Ne'er put on pride, my heart! thou dost not want it;

9 look'd] lookt *1846.*

333

Many there are who do; cast it to them
Who cannot do without it, empty souls!
Ha! how you look! is it surprise or pleasure?

Giovanna. Pleasure, my love! I will obey with pleasure
This your first order. But, indeed, my husband,   20
You must not look so fondly when the masks come,
For you and I, you know, shall not be maskt.

Andrea. A pretty reason for not looking fond!
Must people then wear masks for that?

Giovanna.   Most do.
I never saw such fondness as some masks
Presented.

Andrea.   Thou hast never seen half mine;
Thou shalt; and then shalt thou sit judge between us.
We have not spoken more to-day, my chuck,
Than many other days, yet thou appearest
Wiser than ever. I have gain'd from thee   30
More than I gave.

Giovanna.   And, without flattery,
I am more pleased with your discourse than ever.

Andrea, fondly. No, not than ever. In this very room
Didst thou not give to me this very hand
Because I talkt so well?

Giovanna.   We foolish girls
Are always caught so.

Andrea.   Always kept so, too?
Well, we must see about it then, in earnest.

Giovanna. Andrea! one thing see to: pray inquire
If, in the crowd that rusht so thro' the gates,
No accident has happen'd. Some cried out,   40
Some quarrel'd; many horses started off
And bore amidst them.

Andreas.   Never fear.

Giovanna.   But ask.   [*He goes.*

17 cannot] can not *1846.*   22 maskt] masked *1846.*   32 pleased] pleas'd
1846.   35 talkt] talked *1846.*   39 rusht] rushed *1846.*   41 quarrel'd]
quarrell'd *1846.*   42 amidst] amid *1846.*

[ACT V.] SCENE II.

FIAMMETTA, MARIA, FILIPPA, *and* SANCIA, *enter.*

Maria. The bridegroom is among the other grooms,
Asking odd questions: what man's horse broke loose,

ANDREA OF HUNGARY

Who was knockt down, what fruit-stall overturn'd,
Who quarrel'd, who cried out, struck, ran away.
   Giovanna. Maria! this is pleasantry.
   Andrea, returning hastily.   They say,
Caraffa and Caraccioli are dead.
   Giovanna. It cannot be: they were both well this morning.
   Filippa. The west-wind blew this morning . . no air now.
   Giovanna. O but, Filippa! they both came together.
Did not queen Sancia tell you?
   Filippa.   I have seen   10
Two barks together enter the port yonder,
And part together.
   Giovanna.   But to die at once!
   Filippa. Happy the friends whom that one fate befalls!
   Giovanna. So soon!
   Filippa.   Perhaps so soon.
   Giovanna.   It may be happy,
It must be strange; awfully strange indeed!   [FIAMMETTA *goes out.*
   Andrea. My darling! how you pity those two youths!
I like you for it.
   Giovanna.   Both have fathers living:
What must they suffer! Each . . I never heard,
But may well fancy . . loved some girl who loves him.
I could shed tears for her.
   Maria.   My dear Giovanna!   20
Do queens shed tears? and on the wedding-day?
   Sancia. I see no reason why they should not.
   Filippa, aside.   I,
Alas! see far too many why they should.
   Andrea. What did Filippa say? that brides should cry?
   Filippa, to GIOVANNA *and* MARIA. Not idly has the genial breath of
     song
Turn'd into pearls the tears that woman sheds:
They are what they are call'd: some may be brighter
Among your gems, none purer, none become
The youthful and the beautiful so well.
   Andrea, as FIAMMETTA *enters.* Here enters one you never will teach
     that,   30
She is too light for grief, too gay for love,
And neither salt nor misletoe can catch her,
Nor springe nor net: she laughs at all of them

   4 quarrel'd] quarrell'd *1846.*   7 cannot] can not *1846.*   26 woman sheds]
women shed *1846.*   32 misletoe] mistleto *1846.*

Like any woodpecker, and wings away.
I know you women; I'm a married man.
    Fiammetta. They will not give the story up: they draw
All different ways, but death they all will have.
    Andrea. Ay, and one only will not satisfy them.
                   [An officer enters, and confers apart with him.
Certain?
    Giovanna. Some other accident less heavy,
Heaven! let us hope!
    Andrea.   Strangled! O what a death!   40
One of them . . one (no matter now which of them)
Disliked me, shunn'd me; if we met, look'd at me
Straiter and taller and athwart the shoulder,
And dug his knuckles deep into his thigh.
I gave him no offence . . yet, he is gone . .
Without a word of hearing, he is gone!
To think of this! to think how he has fallen
Amid his pranks and joyances, amid
His wild heath myrtle-blossoms, one might say,
It quite unmans me.
    Sancia.   Speak not so, my son!   50
Let others, when their nature has been changed
To such unwonted state, when they are call'd
To do what angels do and brutes do not,
Sob at their shame, and say they are unmann'd:
Unmann'd they cannot be; they are not men.
At glorious deeds, at sufferings well endured,
Yea, at life's thread snapt with its gloss upon it,
Be it man's pride and privilege to weep.

    42 look'd] lookt *1846.*   43 Straiter] Straighter *1846.*   55 cannot] can
not *1846.*

[ACT V.] SCENE III. GRAND SALOON.

Masks passing.

ANDREA, GIOVANNA, MARIA, FIAMMETTA, FILIPPA.

    Filippa. It may be right, my lady, that you know
What masks are here.
    Giovanna.   I have found out already
A few of them. Several waived ceremony
(Desirably at masks) and past unnoticed.
The room fills rapidly.
    Filippa.   Not to detain

ANDREA OF HUNGARY

My queen (for hundreds anxiously approach),
Pardon! I recognised the Prince Luigi.
   Giovanna. Taranto? Tell our cousin to keep on
His mask all evening. Hither! uninvited!
   Maria, out of breath. Think you the dais will keep the masks from
     hearing? 10
   Giovanna. Why should it?
   Maria.   Oh! why should it? He is here.
Even Filippa could distinguish him.
Every one upon earth must know Taranto.
   Giovanna. Descend we then: beside the statue there
We may converse some moments privately.
   Maria. Radiant I saw him as the sun . . a name
We always gave him . . rapid as his beams.
I should have known him by his neck alone
Among ten thousand. While I gazed upon it,
He gazed at three mysterious masks: then rose 20
That graceful column, ampler, and more wreathed
With its marmoreal thews and dimmer veins.
The three masks hurried thro' the hall; Taranto
After them (fierce disdain upon his brow)
Darted as Mercury at Jove's command.
No doubt, three traitors who dared never face him
In his own country, are courageous here.
   Giovanna. Taranto, then, Taranto was unmaskt!
Against my orders!
   Maria.   Rather say, *before.*
Luigi never disobeyed Giovanna. 30
   Giovanna. Filippa carried them.
   Maria.   I know his answer.
   Giovanna. Repeat it then, for she may not to-night.
   Maria. "*Tell her I come the cousin, not the prince,*
Nor with pretension, nor design, nor hope;
I come the loyal, not the fond, Taranto."
Why look you round?
   Giovanna.   The voice is surely his.
   Maria. The thoughts are . .
   Giovanna, pressing her hand. May, O Heaven! the speaker be!
                            [*Both walk away.*
   Fra Rupert, maskt and disguised, to one next. I heard our gracious
     queen, espoused to-day,
Give orders that Taranto keep well maskt.

           38 *maskt*] *masked* 1846.

Next Mask, to another. Ho then! Taranto here!
Second Mask.   What treachery!
Fra Rupert, maskt. He could not keep away. Tempestuous love 41
Has tost him hither. Let him but abstain
From violence, nor play the jealous husband,
As some men do when husbands cross their roads.
   Second Mask. Taranto is a swordsman to the proof.
   First Mask. Where is he?
   Fra Rupert, maskt.   He stood yonder, in sky-blue,
With pearls about the sleeves.
   Second Mask.   Well call him Phœbus!
I would give something for a glimpse at what
That mask conceals.
   Fra Rupert, maskt. Oh! could we catch a glimpse
Of what all masks conceal, 'twould break our hearts.   50
Far better hidden from us! Woman! woman!   *[Goes off.*
   First Mask to second. A friar Rupert! only that his voice
Breathes flute-like whisperings, rather than reproofs.
   Second Mask. Beside, he stands three inches higher; his girth
Slenderer by much.
   First Mask.   Who thought 'twas really he?
I only meant he talkt as morally.
   Third Mask coming up to FOURTH. I am quite certain there is Frate
     Rupert.
   Fourth Mask. Where is he not? The Devil's ubiquity!
But, like the Devil, not well known when met.
How found you him so readily? What mark?   60
   Third Mask. Stout is he, nor ill-built, though the left shoulder
Is half a finger's breadth above the right.
   Fourth Mask. But that man's . . let me look . . that man's right
     shoulder
Stands two good inches highest.
   Third Mask.   Doubt is past . .
We catch him! over-sedulous disguise!

41 *maskt*] *masked* 1846.   46, 49 *maskt*] *om. 1846.*

SCENE IV.

Andrea, enters. We have a cousin in the house, my queen!
What dost thou blush at? Why art troubled? Sure
We are quite grand enough for him: our supper
(I trust) will answer all his expectations.

ANDREA OF HUNGARY

Maria. So, you have lookt then at the supper-table?

Andrea. 'Twould mortify me if Giovanna's guests
Were disappointed.

Giovanna.   Mine! and not yours too?

Andrea. Ah sly one! you have sent then for Taranto
And would not tell me! Cousin to us both,
To both he should be welcome as to one.   10
Another little blush! Why, thou art mine,
And never shalt, if love's worth love, repent it.

Giovanna. Never, my own Andrea! for such trust
Is far more precious than the wealthiest realms,
Or all that ever did adorn or win them.

Andrea. I must not wait to hear its value told,
We shall have time to count it out together.
I now must go to greet our cousin yonder,
He waits me in the balcony; the guards
Have sent away the loiterers that stood round,   20
And only two or three of his own friends
Remain with him. To tarry were uncourteous.

Maria, earnestly to him. I do believe Luigi is below.

Andrea. Do not detain me: we have never met
Since your proud sister spoke unkindly to him,
And, vaulting on his horse, he hurried home.   *[Goes.*

Maria. The soldiers there do well to guard the balcony,
And close the folding-doors against intrusion.   *[Cry is heard.*

Fiammetta. Ha! some inquisitive young chamber-lady,
Who watcht Luigi enter, pays for it.   30
Those frolicsome young princes are demanding
A fine for trespass.

Giovanna.   Nay, they are too rude,
Permitting any rudeness. Struggles! sobs!
Andrea never caused them.

Maria.   Shame, Taranto!

Giovanna. Stifling of screams! Those nearer are alarm'd;
Those farther off are running for the staircase;
And many come this way! What can they mean?
See! they look angry as they run, and dash
Their hands against their foreheads! (*Very alarmed.*)
                    Where 's a page?

A page stands maskt in the doorway: crowds of unmaskt behind him.

Maria. A page! a page!

23 *to him*] om. *1846.*   35 alarm'd] alarmed *1846.*   *maskt . . . unmaskt*]
masked . . . unmasked 1846.

Page, to himself.   I am one; and discovered!   [*Advances.*

Giovanna.   Run; see what those young courtiers round the
     princes

Are doing in the balcony. Below;   42

Not there.

Page.   I might mistake the prince Andrea,

Not having ever seen him, quite a stranger,

Being prince Luigi's page, whom I awaited,

To say his groom and horse are near at hand.

Maria. He goes then?

Page.   Ere it dawn.

Giovanna.   Oh! hasten! hasten

Below, and instantly run back again,

Telling me what you can discover there.

Page, returns. Lady! the lamps about the balcony   50

Are all extinguisht.

Giovanna.   Is the wind so high?

What didst thou hear, what didst thou note, beside?

Page, hesitating. Against the gentlest, the most virtuous queen,

Opprobrious speech, threats, imprecations . .

Giovanna, earnestly.   Pass it.

Page, continues. Upon the stairs; none from the gardens.

Giovanna.   There

What sawest thou?

Page.   Over the balcony

Downward some burden swang.

Giovanna.   Some festive wreath

Perhaps.

Page.   Too heavy; almost motionless.

Maria. Several damask draperies thrown across.

Page. May-be. The wind just stirr'd the bottom of them: 60

I had no time to look: I saw my prince

Fighting.

Maria. O heaven! was ever night like this.

Page. For gallant sword! it left two proofs behind:

The third man, seeing me (poor help for arm

So valiant!) fled.

Maria.   O! we are safe then, all!   [*Very joyous.*

---

44 him,] him. *1846.*   quite a stranger,] *om. 1846, which after* him. *inserts :*
           Maria. Who then are you?
           Page. The Prince Luigi's [*&c. as in 1839.*]
49 Telling] Reporting *1846.*   54 *earnestly*] *om. 1846.*   55 *continues*] *om. 1846.*
62 this.] this . . *1846.*

ANDREA OF HUNGARY

Page. No cap lost they, nor did the one who fled:
Whose, in the world of Naples, can be this?
   [*He takes from under his richly embroidered cloak the cap of* ANDREA.
   GIOVANNA *clasps it to her face, and falls with a stifled scream.*
   Another Page, brings in ANDREA'S *ermine cloak.* This cloak fell near
   me from the balusters.
   Maria. His own! Ha! this dark speck is not the ermine.
   Filippa. See! she revives! hide it away! O guests   70
Of our unhappy festival, retire.

69 ermine] ermine's *1846.*

NOTES

SECTION I. HEROIC POEMS

P. 1. GEBIR. The second edition (Oxford, 1803) instead of the first (London, 1798) is given in the present volume. When the Oxford edition was issued, the text had been carefully revised by Landor and his brother Robert, while new notes and the Arguments prefixed to each book removed much of the obscurity of the poem. The 1803 preface with variants from that of 1798 is as follows:

PREFACE.*

IT may possibly save some trouble, and obviate some errors, if I take a cursory review of my own performance. Not that I would prevent any other from [prevent others from *1798*] criticising it, but that I may explain at large, and state distinctly, its origin and design. This Poem, the fruit of Idleness and Ignorance—for had I been a botanist or mineralogist it never had been written—was principally written in Wales. The subject was taken, or rather the shadow of the subject, from a wild and incoherent, but fanciful, Arabian Romance. On the shelf of a circulating library, I met with a Critique on the various Novels of our Country. Though the work itself had nothing remarkable in it, except indeed we reckon remarkable the pertness and petulance of female criticism, yet it presented to me, at the conclusion, the story of Gebirus and Charoba. [A poem, like mine, descriptive of men and manners, should never be founded totally on fiction. But that which is originally fiction may cease in effect to be so: the tears of Andromache are as precious as those of Sapphira. A poem . . . Sapphira, *only in 1798*.]

Not a sentence, not a sentiment, not an image, not an idea, is borrowed from that work. [Not . . . work *not in 1798*] I have availed myself merely of the names, and taken but few bare circumstances. I have followed no man closely; nor have I turned from my road because another stood in it; though perhaps I have momentarily, in passing, caught the object that attracted him. I have chosen [written in *1798*] blank verse, because there never was a poem in rhyme that grew not tedious in a thousand lines. [My choice is undoubtedly the most difficult of the two: for, how many have succeeded in rhyme, in the structure at least; how few comparatively in blank verse. There is Akenside, there is, above all, the poet of our republic. But in most others we meet with stiffness instead of strength, and weakness instead of ease. I am aware how much I myself stand in need of favor. I demand some little from Justice; I entreat much more from Candor. If there are, now in England, ten men of taste and genius who will applaud my Poem, I declare myself fully content:

---

* The former was incomplete, and was sent to the printer by mistake. Having been fairly written out, instead of another more enlarged and corrected and in several places blotted and interlined, it was hastily put into the press—which the author, from the distance of sixteen miles, and without any regular post, could not easily superintend. [L. *Footnote only in 1803*.]

NOTES

I will call for a division; I shall count a majority. My choice . . . majority, *only in 1798 where the preface ends at* majority. *In 1803 it continues:*]

In the moral are exhibited the folly, the injustice, and the punishment of Invasion, with the calamities which must ever attend the superfluous colonization of a peopled country. Gebir, the sovereign of Bœtic Spain, is urged by an oath, administered in childhood, to invade the kingdom of Egypt. He invades it. Passions, the opposite to those which he has cherished, are excited by his conference with the queen Charoba. On the other hand, her apprehensions, of which at the first alarm she had informed her attendant Dalica, from whom, as having been her nurse, she implores advice and assistance, decrease at this interview with Gebir. But women communicate their fears more willingly than their love. Dalica, all this time, intent on one sole object, and never for a moment doubting that the visible perturbation of Charoba's mind proceeded, as at first, from her terrors, is determined to restore her tranquillity. She executes the plan which she had long been forming, nor discovers the love of Charoba but by the death of Gebir. [L.]

[END OF 1803 PREFACE]

A preface to "Gebir, Count Julian, and other poems" 1831, begins with the following statement about "Gebir" not reprinted:

Gebir was written in my twentieth year. Many parts were first composed in Latin; and I doubted in which language to complete it. I had lost the manuscript: finding it four years after in a box of letters, I reduced it nearly to half, inserting a few verses in some places to give it its proportions.

The work in which Landor met with the story of Gebirus was Clara Reeve's "Progress of Romance", Dublin, 1785. This contains "the History of Charoba Queen of Egypt" taken by Miss Reeve from Pierre Vattier's translation of an Arabic book said to have been written by Murtadi, son of Gaphiphe. The translator, born 1623, was physician to the Duc d'Orleans. Murtadi may be identified with a Shaikh Murtada-'d Din who died at Cairo in 1202. In bringing his Gebir from Bœtic Spain Landor ignored all that was said about him by Murtadi or other Arabic writers. The most notable allusion to the invader of Egypt is to be found in Yakut al-Hamawi's Geographical Dictionary where Ibn Ufair is quoted as having said that Jubair al-Mutafiki (Jubair of the cities of the plain) was the man who first built Alexandria. Mr. C. A. Storey, Librarian at the India Office, to whom special thanks are due for evidence proving Jubair's identity with Landor's hero, gives in Arabic what Yakut said on the subject:

وقال ابن عُفَيْر ان اول من بنى الاسكندرية جُبَيْر المؤتفكى

That this Jubair, *alias* Gebir, was prince or leader of Hyksos invaders seems not unlikely, but he cannot have come from Iberia. Queen Charoba's mother is said to have been a friend of Abraham's wife, Sarah. The name means in Arabic a carob bean, an emblem of Constancy. As regards Jubair there can be no doubt that Vattier, whose transliteration is often strangely incorrect, was wrong in reading the name as Gebir. The alchemist Gebir, praised by Roger Bacon and coupled by Ben Jonson with Raymond Lully and Paracelsus, was of course a very different person. Sidi Gebir el Ansari, whose name may be found in guide-books, as that given to a mosque and railway station near Alexandria, lived centuries after the age of Landor's Gebir.

Most of the following notes on *Gebir* are by Landor; a few have been added for the present edition. [W.]

GEBIR: BOOK I.

l. 12. As stated on p. 1 *n*. the 1831 and 1846 *edd.* of *Gebir* began here. In a MS. note given by Landor to Miss Kate Field he said the first four words should be: "Hear ye the fate". (*Atlantic Monthly*, 1866, p. 548.) [W.]

l. 15 *n*. Landor here rejects Gibbon's more accurate statement that the "familiar appellation of Gibraltar (*Gebel al Tarik*) describes the mountain of Tarik". *Roman Empire*, vi. 356. [W.]

ll. 43–4. Sidad . . . Gad.] See Sale's translation of the Koran, Chap. LXXXIX, and his notes. The fabled city of Iram, said to have been built by Sidad (Shaddat) in the desert near Aden, was confounded by Landor with Gadir, the name given by Phœnicians to the city they built in Spain, now known as Cadiz. Greeks called it Gadeira; Romans changed this to Gades. See Ford's *Handbook for Spain*. [W.]

l. 67. According to Forster (*Landor: a Biography*, i. 84 *n*.), Landor held that Sir Walter Scott had imitated this passage in his description of Richard Cœur de Lion's hound. But it was Sir Kenneth's hound, not Richard's, who "thrust his long rough countenance into the hand of his master" (*Talisman*, Chap. 7). [W.]

l. 100. Therefor . . . 'tis untold.*] the footnote, only in 1803, reads:

* Of the words "*Therefor*" and "*Wherefor*" some apology is requisite for deviating from the received orthography—tho' I could quote the authority of Milton. It appears to me just as absurd (or even more so for the reasons I shall give presently) to write "*therefore*" and "*wherefore*", as it would be to write "*whereofe*" and "*whereine*". *Fore* must ever be a long syllable; how then is it to be managed in the words above? "*Fore*", if it existed any where, would be the comparison [? *mispr. for* comparative] of "*first*": but it exists only in the compound "*before*". Is it not strange to see two compound words, of which the latter half of each is so precisely similar, so utterly different in their origin, at least in this latter half? As *first* is a superlative which has neither a positive nor a comparative, so another word may be remarked which is itself a positive, and from the structure of our language, can have no regular comparative or superlative. I mean the word *free*. We have seen both in prose and poetry, *freer* and *freest*, and we have received them always as dissyllables. But these vowels cannot be disjoined. *Freer* cannot exist, in obedience to the genius of our language, nor *freest* as an adjective: tho' in the second person singular of the verb *free*, it may be used both in prose and poetry, observing that it can be no other than a monosyllable. Now I find myself, tho' I came upon it unaware, on the subject of orthography, I shall add a few words more, in which however I am not concerned. I must ask why *preceed* and *exceed* are spelt differently in their termination from *recede*, and why they are not both spelt after the manner of the latter? I would also ask why we are so barbarously absurd as to continue the present mode of writing *height*. I know very well the origin of it: I know

NOTES

that it was in contradistinction to the passive participle or passive preterite, as we sometimes find it, *hight* (called). But as this preterite or participle is out of use, why may not the substantive and adjective, hight and high, acknowledge an unadulterated relationship? Can any thing be so absurd as to write *simile,* and to call it an English word? It would be really an English word, and would not *stand alone,* as it does at present, if it were written *simily.* I have thrown out these few hints that some man of learning may remove the anomalies of our language by attending to its analogies. But nothing can be done without consulting Milton: his words excel in orthography those of any other writer. If some are overloaded with consonants, we must attribute it to the stubborness of the Press. [L.]

l. 127. *edd.* 1803, 1831 have footnote which reads:

* It must be remembered that [It . . . that *om. 1831*] along [. Along *1831*] the Mediterranean coasts the tides are sensible of hardly any variation. But the [The *1831*] coasts of Egypt are so flat, particularly the most fertile parts, and [so flat, and *1831*] the water so very nearly [so nearly *1831*] on a level with them, ['em, *1831*] that Tamar may be supposed to fancy it arising from spring-tide. Those who have ever from a low and even country looked upon the sea, will have observed that the sea [that it *1831*] seemed higher than the ground where they stood. [L.]

l. 148. long shells explored *] Footnote, only in 1803, reads:

I make no apology for the comparison. The *Scuttle-shell,* tho' the name be inharmonious and harsh, so as not to be admissible in poetry, is of an elegant form and of a brilliant whiteness. [L.] *The application of a remedy not unlike that here referred to is described in* " Unexplored Baluchistan ", *by E. A. Floyer, 1882.* [W.]

l. 156. dove-color'd wave]. Landor told Forster that he had hesitated in determining whether the mantle or the girdle was to be dove-coloured; his doubts having arisen on recollecting that in Lucretius Roman ladies wear a vest of this kind. *thalassina vestis, &c. (De Nat. Deorum.* iv. 1123.) [W.]

l. 170. . . . shells of pearly hue*.] Footnote, only in 1859 ed., reads:

* W. Wordsworth borrowed this shell, and filled it to overflowing for the refreshment of the wayfarers in his " Excursion." The Lord of a Manor may wink at small encroachments on the common, but the Steward must note them in his book. [L.] See Wordsworth, " *Excursion* ", iv. 1130 *ff.* and Landor's " Satire on Satirists ". [W.]

l. 226. Footnote, only in 1803, reads:

* " *Gone down the tide.*" By some strange blunder it was printed " gone down *to* the tide ". No errors are so fatal as those which give a meaning, but give an improper one. If the *nymph* had merely gone *to* the tide, the narration of *Tamar* in all probability would not have ended—but she went *down* the tide, and consequently disappeared. Added to which, I dare not take such a liberty with a verse, even though the word should be useful and proper. The farthest that I have ventured, is, where the fastidious reader might make an elision, if he chose, in verse 190, " *If*

struggle and equal strength, &c". But I believe I shall meet with no critic who will condemn this license. [L.]

GEBIR: BOOK III.

1. 40 Gods thought otherwise.*] Footnote, only in 1803, reads:

* Let not this be considered as an imitation of the verse "*Diis aliter visum*". [*Æneid*, ii. 428.] There is no great merit in quoting old quotations, however apposite, and I am of opinion that this singular passage has generally been misunderstood. Among all the fooleries which men have combined in their ideas of a deity, can there be a greater than that the gods and mortals have a separate sense of right and wrong? Were it really the case, religious men would become daily less zealous, and the life of the wicked be but a game of chance; for, the virtues of the one party might not stand for virtues; nor the vices of the other be marked for vices. There was never a doctrine more calculated to make the generality of men despond, and to keep them dependent on the δογματοῦργοι. [L.] He may have invented this word: cf. θαυματοῦργος. [W.]

1. 118. Footnote, only in 1803, reads:

* "That radient robe" of light; "unseam'd and undefiled", unbroken in its texture and pure in its essence. This is a personification of an oriental cast, in which the stars are represented as crowding round their monarch, the sun, and as receiving from him those marks of favor, which inferior princes receive from their Sovereign. The Symphony of the stars is so common a theme of the poets, that I shall say no more of it; their "short repose" is in consequence of the nearest attraction to the more powerful body. "And with slow pace return."

> Tum vero quo cuique magis curvatus eundo
> Vertitur interior devexo tramite gyrus,
> Et præceps rota vergit, eo magis impetis auctu
> *Præteriit, vacuumque fugâ eluctatur in œquor.*
> *Lentus ibi ascensu labor et cunctantior actus*
> *Objecitur, donec jam largior orbita vastum*
> *Retulerit errorem.*—[L.]

[Landor also quoted these verses in *Gebirus*, 1803, saying: "*Hæc longe meleoribus, quam nostri sunt, exponamus.*" But he did not name the author.—W.]

ll. 184–222. [Forster thought it would be easy to recognize, among Gebir's ancestors, the wretch with white eyebrows (l. 184) as George III; the giant next him (l. 201) as William III; another wretch, who "sold his people to a rival king" (l. 215) as Charles II; and one whose spectral body showed space between purple and crown (l. 223) as Charles I (see Forster's *Landor: a Biography*, i. 91). Lest it might seem strange that the white eyebrowed spectre should shriek beneath a sword engine-hung (l. 187) Forster explained that, by pretending the whole passage referred not to George III but to Louis XVI, Landor may have hoped to escape a prosecution. A State prosecution was never even threatened, but Leigh Hunt composed an imaginary indictment (see *Examiner*, May 11, 1833) in which Lord Waldegrave and the author of *Gebir* were charged with defamatory libel of their late sovereign, while Horace Walpole and John Murray were accused of slandering Frederick, Prince of Wales.—W.]

347

NOTES

l. 44. drank *] Footnote, only in 1803, reads:

> * "Charoba, tho' indeed she never drank
> The liquid pearl, *or twined the nodding crown*, &c."

These verses allude to the history of Cleopatra. The first anecdote is well known: the second is less often mentioned, and perhaps less authentic. Antony was afraid of poison. Cleopatra, to prove the injustice of his suspicions, and the ease with which the poison might be administered, if such had been her intention, shook it, from the crown of flowers upon her head, into a goblet of wine which she had tasted the moment before, and which she instantly presented to Antony. Before he had raised it to his lips, she repressed him, she told him every thing, and established his confidence for ever. [L.]

l. 145. with simulated smile, constrain'd*]. Footnote, only in 1803, reads:

* This will be unintelligible to those who have never had an opportunity of observing the effect of the most powerful passions on the countenance; to those in particular who have never seen extreme sorrow aroused at the idea of ingratitude or injustice: the lips assume a strongly marked smile. The lips are the indicators of the temper only where there is genius and beauty, and never in brutes or brutal men, except when the whole frame is agitated by some *evil* passion. [L.]

l. 223. be with you peace" *] Footnote, only in 1803, reads:

* Such has been precisely the eastern salutation for several hundred and even thousand years, and amongst several millions of people. The word "*peace*" is mentioned first by the person who salutes, and last by the person saluted. Perhaps the original reason is, that in nations where hostilities were common, and almost perpetual, amongst innumerable tribes, it was requisite for men to declare, immediately, explicitly, at the very first motion, the very first breath, with what intentions and sentiments they met. This true principle of natural address, and in certain instances of genuine oratory, could not escape the notice of so accurate an observer as Livy. Above the flourishes of idle eloquence, he always puts the proper word in its proper place. For example. "*Sextus Tarquinius* sum: *ferrum* in manu est: *moriere*, si emiseris vocem." I need not remark how, in addressing a woman, he first appeals to her vanity, then to her fears; first announces his rank, secondly his resolution, but the most important words invariably take the precedence. I doubt whether any other writers would have chosen a similar speech for Tarquin; more so, whether any would have been contented with so little; most of all, whether any would have done so well. Shakespear is the only one that ever knew so intimately or ever described so accurately the variations of the human character. But *Livy* is *always* great. [L.]

l. 151. Footnote, only in 1803, reads:

* "*Unborn the maid*, &c." The story of the maid of Corinth is too celebrated for repetition. Drawing the lines of her lover's face against the wall, I have represented her as equally fearful of drawing them amiss,

and of being discovered by his awakening. [L.] See Pliny, *Hist. Nat.*
xxxv. 12. for the legend about the daughter of Dibutates the Corinthian
potter. [W.]

1. 173. Etna rose to view.*] Footnote, only in 1803, reads:

* This when applied to Etna will not appear too hyperbolical for poetry.
Virgil has said the like of a river. G. iii. 223.

> "Non scopuli rupesque cavæ aut objecta retardant
> "Flumina, correptosque undâ torquentia *montes.*" [L.]

[The reference should be to *Georgics,* iii. 253–4. For *aut* read *atque.*—W.]

1. 193. Footnote, only in 1803, reads:

* "A mortal man above all mortal praise." Bonaparte might have
been so, and in the beginning of his career it was argued that he would
be. But unhappily he thinks, that to produce great changes, is to perform great actions: to annihilate antient freedom and to substitute new,
to give republics a monarchical government, and the provinces of
monarchs a republican one; in short, to overthrow by violence all the
institutions, and to tear from the heart all the social habits of men, has
been the tenor of his politics to the present hour. [L.]

1. 292. triumphs that proceed.*] Footnote, only in 1803, reads:

* The following verses, which in themselves are not perhaps worse
than any others in the poem, were at first omitted; that too much might
not be said on one subject, and that the just proportions of the book
might be preserved.

> "If Glory call ye, turn to Mercy's side,
> Ye sons of Gaul, for Glory waits ye there.
> Pale Monarchy flies past! her Asian vase,
> Graven with tigers linked before her car,
> And riot Loves, and Satyrs, crown'd with flowers,
> Round which whole nations reel'd away from Truth—
> Flaw'd with the spear, and on the sands reverst,
> Spills the slow poison that consumed the brave.
> Now, Youth exult! now, harass'd Age, repose!
> Yours are the rural Sports, unchill'd by Fear,
> Yours, Plenty, Peace, and Liberty, that loves
> The household gods, and late unsheaths the sword.
> Round every cottage, and thro' every wild,
> For you the vine her purple wreath suspends,
> The glaucous olive bears the cold for you.
> Lo! while Garumna dances in the shade, &c." [L.]

GEBIR: BOOK VII.

ll. 249–52. [Writing to Southey, October 31, 1799, Charles Lamb said:
"I have seen Gebor (*sic*)! Gebor aptly so denominated from Geborish,
quasi Gibberish. But Gebor hath some lucid intervals. I remember
darkly one beautiful simile veiled in uncouth phrases about the youngest
daughter of the Ark." The quotation from Landor follows. Various and
conflicting accounts are given of the women admitted to Noah's ark.
According to Vattier's translation of Murtadi (see above, p. 344), Philemon,
an Egyptian priest, and his daughter were among those who found safety

349

therein. After the deluge the daughter is said to have married Misraim, Shem's grandson. "Jewish fancy", Sir James Frazer says, "tricked out the story of the flood with many new and often extravagant details," such as the curious episode of Fortune and the Lady Misfortune. (See *Folklore in the Old Testament*, i. 143 ff.) (W.)]

POST-SCRIPT TO *GEBIR*

LANDOR'S "Post-script to *Gebir* with remarks on some critics" was one of the pieces in verse or prose which in 1800, after getting them printed with other matter at Warwick, he decided not to publish. Forster in *Landor: a Biography* (1869) gave extracts from the Post-script amounting to about a tenth of the whole. Fragments of it were used in imaginary conversations. Now for the first time it is published in full. The source, with in some cases the context, of quotations is now given within brackets, and a few notes are added. In other respects the "Post-script" appears in much the same form it had when leaving Mr. Sharpe's press at its author's native town. The main text, taken from two mutilated copies of the 1800 volume preserved in the Forster Collection at South Kensington, is as follows: [W.]

Ego potius tranquillè vivere desidero quàm ab adversariis victorias et tropæa reportare. *Linnæus ad Gronovium.*

GEBIR in different quarters has been differently received. I allude not to those loyal critics, who, recently mounted on their city-war-horse, having borrowed the portly boots and refurbished the full-bottomed perukes of the ancient French chevaliers, are foremost to oppose the return of that traitor, whom, while he was amongst them, Englishmen called Freedom, but now they have expelled him, Anarchy: since, the very first *Reviews* of this Association were instituted, not merely for parade but for hostility: not for exercise, correctness, and precision, so adventurous and impetuous were these conscripts, but for actual and immediate battle. The *Critical* and *Monthly*, as being of the old establishment, are those on which at present I would fix attention. In respect to *Gebir*, the one perhaps is conducted by a partial, but certainly by a masterly, hand.[1] It objects, and indeed with reason, to a temporary and local obscurity, which I have not been able, or I have not been willing, or I have not been bold enough, to remove: but never on the whole, since it's first institution, has a poem been more warmly praised. The other's account is short: containing one quotation and two mis-statements. "That the poem was nothing more than the version of an Arabic tale; and that the author, not content with borrowing the expressions, had made the most awkward attempts to imitate the phraseology of Milton."[2]

The Review[3] is not before me. I believe I have softened, but I have not perverted, nor have I deteriorated his style. No man would make or meditate so rash indefensible an attack, unless he were certain that, if not already stationed there, he could speedily drop into obscurity. I repeat to him in answer, what I before asserted in my preface, that, so far from a *translation*, there is not a single sentence, nor a single senti-

---

[1] [Southey reviewed *Gebir* in *The Critical Review*, September, 1799.—W.]
[2] [*The Monthly Review*, 1800, vol. xxx, p. 206.—W.]
[3] Review [=Reviewer, *and in one copy so corrected.*—W.]

ment, in common with the tale. Some characters are drawn more at large, some are brought out more prominent, and several are added. I have not changed the scene, which would have distorted the piece, but every line of appropriate description, and every shade of peculiar manners, is originally and entirely my own.

Now, whether this gentleman has or has not read the poem, whether he has or has not read the romance, his account is equally false and equally malicious. For the romance is in english, therefor he could have read it; the poem is in english, and therefor he could have compared it. There is no disgrace in omitting to read them: the disgrace is, either in pretending to have done what he had not done, or in assuming a part which he was incompetent to support. But there *is* a disgrace in omitting to read Milton; there is a disgrace in forgetting him. The critic has not perused or not remembered him: it would be impossible, if he had, that he should accuse me of borrowing his expressions. I challenge him to produce them. If indeed I *had* borrowed them, so little should I have realized by the dangerous and wild speculation, that I might have composed a better poem and not have been a better poet. But I feared to break open, for the supply of my games or for the maintenance of my veteran heroes, the sacred treasury of the great republican. Although I might enjoy, not indeed the extorted, but the unguarded praise of an enemy, if my vanity could stoop so low and could live on so little,—of an enemy who, throughout so long a journey, and after so many speeches, and those on such various occasions, pertinaciously took me for Milton— I will add, for the information of my young opponent, what a more careful man would conceal, but what in his present distress will relieve him greatly, that this, which amongst the vulgar and thoughtless might currently pass for praise, is really none at all. For, the language of *Paradise Lost* ought not to be the language of *Gebir*. There should be the softened air of remote antiquity, not the severe air of unapproachable sanctity. I devoutly offer up my incence at the shrine of Milton. Woe betide the intruder that would steal it's jewels! It requires no miracle to detect the sacrilege. The crime will be found it's punishment. The venerable saints, and still more holy personages, of Rapheal or Michael-Angelo, might as consistently be placed among the Bacchanals and Satyrs, bestriding the goats and bearing the vases of Poussin, as the resemblance of that poem, or any of it's component parts, could be introduced in mine.

I have avoided high-sounding words. I have attempted to throw back the gross materials, and to bring the figures forward. I knew beforehand the blame that I should incur. I knew that people would cry out "your burden was so light, we could hardly hear you breathe, pray where is your merit". For, there are few who seem thoroughly acquainted with this plain and simple truth, that it is easier to elevate the empty than to support the full. I also knew the *body* of my wine, and that years must pass over it, before it would reach it's relish. Some will think me intoxicated, and most will misconstrue my good-nature, if I invite the Reviewer, or any other friend that he will introduce,—but himself the most earnestly, as I suspect from his manner that he *poetizes*—to an amicable trial of skill.—I will subject myself to any penalty, either of writing or of ceasing to write, if the author, who criticizes with the flightiness of a poet, will assume that character at once, and, taking in series my twenty worst verses, write better an equal number, in the period of twenty years.

NOTES

I shall be rejoiced if he will open to me any poem of my contemporaries, of my English contemporaries I mean, and point out three pages more spirited, I will venture to add more classical than the three least happy and least accurate in Gebir.

In challenging a comparison the discriminating will remark, that more expertness is used than bravery. They will certainly acquit me of presumption, altogether, and judge from the character of the person thus addressed, that the champion opposed to me will not be the stoutest or most dexterous, but the heaviest or most shewy, and will readily agree that I have little cause to tremble, when probably I shall find in array against me the *Sovereign* of Mr. Pybus, or a work no less patriotic, the labor of a worthy clergyman, and in praise of better things,—to wit— *bank-notes and strong-beer.*[1]

Many will think that I should have suppressed what I have said; but let them recollect that, amongst those ancient poets who contended for the public prize, each must not only have formed the same determination, (for defects are not usually compared with defects, but are generally contrasted with beauties) but have actually engaged, and that too more openly and personally, in a still more strenuous competition. If my rights had not been refused me, I should not have asserted my claims. Rambling by the side of the sea, or resting on the top of a mountain, and interlining with verses the letters of my friends, I sometimes thought how a Grecian would have written, but never what methods he would take to compass popularity. The nearer I approached him, tho' distant still, the more was I delighted. I may add,

> O belle agli occhi miei tende *latine*!
> Aura spira di [da] voi che mi ricrea,
> E mi conforta piu piu [pur che] m'avvicine.
> Tasso, *Gierru. liberata* [vi. 104.].

Several of these sketches were obliterated, still more laid aside and lost; various ideas I permitted to pass away, unwilling to disturb, by the slightest action, the dreams of reposing fancy. So little was I anxious to publish my rhapsodies, that I never sate down in the house, an hour at once, for the purpose of composition. Instead of making, or inviting, courtship, I declared with how little I should rest contented. Far from soliciting the attention of those who are passing by, *Gebir* is confined, I believe, to the shop of one bookseller, and I never heard that he had even made his appearance at the window. I understand not the management of these matters, but I find that the writing of a book is the least that an author has to do. My experience has not been great; and the caution which it has taught me lies entirely on the other side of publication. Before I was twenty years of age I had imprudently sent into the world a volume,[2] of which I was soon ashamed. It every-where met with as much commendation as was proper, and generally more. For, tho' the structure was feeble, the lines were fluent: the rhymes shewed habitual ease, and the personifications fashionable taste. I suffered any of my heroes, the greater part of whom were of a gentle kind, to look on one

---

[1] ["The Sovereign", a poem addressed by Charles Small Pybus, M.P., to the Emperor Paul, and "The Hop-Garden", by Luke Booker, LL.D., were noticed in *The Monthly Review*.—W.]

[2] *The Poems of Walter Savage Landor*, London, 1795. [W.]

HEROIC POEMS

side thro' the eye of Pity, on the other thro' that of Love; and it was with great delight, for I could not foresee the consequences, that I heard them speak or sing with the lips of soft Persuasion. So early in life, I had not discovered the error into which we were drawn by the Wartons.[1] I was then in raptures with what I now despise. I am far from the expectation, or the hope, that these deciduous shoots will be supported by the ivy of my maturer years. But, without any boast of prudence, I have hung up a motley and paultry skin for my puppies in their snarling playfulness to pull at, that they may not tear in pieces a better and costlier one on which I desire to rest.

After all, I do not wonder that they barked at *Gebir*—he came disguised and in tatters. Still there was nothing to authorize the impertinence with which the publication was treated by the Monthly Reviewer. These are not the faults which he complains of; tho' these might, without his consciousness, have first occasioned his ill-humour. I pity his want of abilities, and I pardon his excess of insolence. The merit is by no means small of a critic who speaks with modesty. For, his time being chiefly occupied, at first, in works fundamentally critical, at least if we suppose him desirous to *learn* before he is ambitious to *teach*, he thinks when he has attained their expressions and brevity, he has attained their solidity and profoundness. He must surely be above what he measures, else how can he measure with exactness? He must be greater, *ex officio*, than the person he brings before him; else how can he stigmatize with censure, or even dismiss with praise?

These illusions are indeed so pleasant that to part with them voluntarily is deserving of great applause. In many so strong is the fascination as not to have been broken even by personal attempts at original composition: not tho' the author has grasped even the isolated works of sublime imagination: tho' sinking thro' the dearth of conception, or lost in the deserts of enquiry: tho' pursued by the aggravating hisses, and assailed by the intolerable stings, of obloquy, scorn, and contempt. It is enough if he can enclose in his flimsy web, what, confident as he naturally is, he would be hopeless of reaching in it's flight. Such is the production of these miserable insects, *a month in generating, a moment in existence*. Miserable do I call them! alas, for the wise and virtuous, alas, for human nature! Tho' Justice, in descending on the world again, has given it a partial revolution, so that some who were in sunshine are in shade—some of the highest and most prominent—yet, when I cast my eyes immediately around me, and can discern what passes both in public and in private, I find too often that those are the least miserable who occasion the most misery. For, when any one has done an injury, the power, that enabled him to do it comes back upon the mind, and fills it with such a complacency, as smooths away all the contrition that the action of this injury would have left. And little power is requisite to work much mischief.[2]

Flies and reviewers fill their bellies while they irritate; both of them are easily crushed, but neither of them easily caught. They lead pleasant lives in their season. The authors who can come into a share of a monthly

[1] Wartons [Thomas Warton (*ob.* 1745), and his sons, Thomas Warton, author of *History of English Poetry*, and Joseph Warton, editor of Pope's Works.—W.]

[2] [Here in 1800 was printed, perhaps owing to an error of the press, an "Ode on Power", for which see p. 364.—W.]

publication, are happy as play-wrights who manage a theatre, or as debtors who purchase a seat in our excellent house of Commons.

> They in what shape they choose,
> Dilated or condensed, bright or obscure,
> Can execute their airy purposes,
> And works of love or enmity full-fill.
>
> [Milton, *Par. L.*, i. 428 seq.]

They hunt over domains more extensive than their own, trample down fences which they cannot *clear*, strip off the buds and tear away the branches, of all the most promising young trees that happen to grow in their road, plow up the lawns, muddy the waters, and when they return benighted home again, carouse on reciprocal flattery. Men of genius, on the contrary, may be compared to those druidical monuments, stately and solitary, reared amidst barrenness, exposed to all weather, unimpaired, unaltered, which a child perhaps may move, but which not a giant can take down.

I should rest awhile here, if my sole or even principal object were chastisement or correction. But I intend to give advice, and I hope instruction. It is possible too that I may present an opportunity of making some reprisals. For, having overthrown the works of an enemy, and offered him battle on *my* ground, I now venture forth and offer it on *his*. Let him detect any error of judgment, or any corruption of taste, in plans and observations entirely new, as mine are, and I will forgive him the blunders which he has committed, for the most part rather thro' stupidity than haste, and without the excuse of novelty.

It is the custom of such people, and a very convenient one it is, to speak in general language: it saves them much trouble, and gives them much importance. In passing sentence they are chancellors at once, they would become mere barristers by examination and enquiry. It has been observed, I think, that almost every writer has taken up some word or other which he cherishes with peculiar fondness. The word "*considerable*"* is the favourite here: it is the stoutest ally of ignorance and indifference, and is the most insurmountable enemy of acuteness and precision. "*This volume possesses considerable merit.*" Such decisions have I often witnessed on productions the most strongly marked—decisions not very improper, tho' rather too favorable, for poems like *Leonidas*,[1] &c.—where the faults are rare and the beauties faint, but where is an even tenor of language, by courtesy and common acception held poetic, and an equal dilation of appropriate thoughts, hardly anywhere trivial and no-where exquisite. But in works of stamp and character, would it not improve the public taste much more, if in general a few short passages were selected, and the defects and excellencies pointed out. Somewhat should be allowed rather above desert than under it, unless the boon be withheld to check the first prancings of presumption, wantonly and dangerously pushing on, ungoaded by injury or severity.

---

* "*Considerable*".—Perhaps it never occurred so often in the same space as in the first twenty pages of the "Life of Mary Wollstonecraft"—not seldomer, I believe, than seventeen or eighteen times—This I wonder at, extremely, as few writers are by habit and course of study less vague and indefinite than Godwin. [L.] William Godwin's "Memoirs" of Mary Wollstonecraft were published in 1798. [W.]

---

[1] ["Leonidas: a Poem", by Richard Glover, 1770.—W.]

354

HEROIC POEMS

But particularly should evidence and instances be adduced where accusations of plagiarism are preferred. Plagiarism, imitation, and allusion, three shades, that soften from blackness into beauty, are, by the glaring eye of the malevolent, blended into one. For the instruction of the learner, lines should be drawn between them by the dispassionate critic.

I shall exemplify my idea in passages which, I apprehend, have not hitherto been remarked, from two poets the most regular and accurate. In comparison with others, they seem greater than they really are: their lustre is clear and pure, but borrowed and reflected. Such are Racine and Pope. Opening a translation of Montaigne, I found, within few pages, two sentiments which the latter, I think, has taken and used. They are both quotations: but as they come so near together, and as Pope was a reader of modern more than of ancient literature, I am of opinion that he is indebted for them exclusively of Montaigne.

Why may not the goose say thus. "All the parts of the universe I have an interest in: the earth serves me to walk upon, the sun to light me &c. is it not man that treats, lodges, and serves me." B 2, ch. 12. [Montaigne, *Essays, Apology for Raimonde de Sebonde.*]

> Seas roll to waft me, Suns to light me, rise,
> My footstool earth—
>
> [Pope, *Essay on Man,* i. 139, 140.]
>
> * * * * * * * * *
>
> While man exclaims, "see all things for my use,"
> "See man for mine," replies a pamper'd goose.
>
> [Ibid., iii, 45, 46.]

Now, the former part of this quotation being set apart from the remainder, and differently applied, is rather in favor of my opinion than against it.

"The extremities of our perquisition all terminate in a mist, where, as it is in charts, all that is beyond the coasts of known countries is represented to be taken up with marshes, impenetrable forests, deserts, and places uninhabitable."
[Montaigne, *Essays, Apology for Raimonde de Sebonde.*]

The verses that correspond with this I feel a strong conviction are in Pope,[1] but I have looked for them in vain: however, that I may do no injustice to our poet, as in the course of my argument it will appear that I am little inclined to do, I shall pass over this, which has fallen of itself, and examine only the former charge. We have seen that taking the thoughts, and even the expressions, he has divided and disposed them in a manner quite different from the original. Now, the man who steals a bag of peas, and scatters them in his garden, is no less a thief than if he kept them in the bag and hid them in his chamber; but the criminal laws, and* those of which we are speaking, are widely different in this particular. A theft which comes under the cognisance of the former is not excused nor palliated by the use to which the thing stolen is converted: in the latter, you may steal wherever you find it convenient, —on subscribing to these condictions. First, that the property stolen be not the principal and most conspicuous part of your composition: and secondly,

---

* The law of plagiarism is somewhat on the Spartan model. You are punished not because you *steal*, but because you are detected, thro' want of spirit and address, in carrying off your booty. [L.]

---

[1] [*He presently found a parallel in Swift, see below*, p. 365.—W.]

NOTES

as others are to enjoy it, and not the mere carrier, that it loose nothing of it's weight or of it's polish by the conveyance. Nothing is more polished than the style of Strada.[1] Let us see.

"Neque enim ulli patientius reprehenduntur quam qui maximé laudari merentur."
[Faminianus Strada, *Prolusiones*, Oxon., 1745, p. 170.]

Here Pope, who comes again as a plagiary, makes atonement for it by his terseness.

"Those best can bear reproof who merit praise."
[Pope, *Essay on Criticism*, l. 583.]

I beg pardon for one more quotation; I shall instance in this a poet seldom read, tho' of a vigorous mind and lively imagination.

When needs he must, yet faintly then, he praises,
Somewhat the deed, but more the means, he raises,
So marreth what he makes, and praising most dispraises.
Personification of Envy, by Phineas Fletcher. ["Purple Island", vii. 66.]

It is unnecessary to retrace the celebrated character which Pope has drawn of Addison, or to hesitate, as we shall feel inclined to do, in the deliberation, whether it most excels in height of colouring or in accuracy of design. But it may be questioned whether he could have succeeded in so nice a resemblance unless he had applied the colors which he found prepared by Fletcher. The figure drawn by Fletcher does him credit; but leaves him little higher, we see, and little more noticed, than he would have been without it: while, assisted by these lines, the character drawn by Pope—tho' Horace is more insinuating, and Persius more important, who sometimes rivals even Virgil himself in the dignity of expression and sublimity of sentiment—is enough to rank him above any other satirist in ancient or modern times. Indeed, thro' the whole of this department, he adds the observation of Donne to the vivacity of Ariosto, and gives to the sword of Juvenal the point of Boileau.

I have not exceeded here the bounds that I proposed to myself, since it became me to shew that my animadversions on Pope, arose not from any malignity, but purely from a wish to enlighten my critic by elucidating my argument.

Let us now examine Racine, and that not in places where it is indifferent whether he has borrowed or otherwise, but in the two most admirable passages of all his works.

Je crains Dieu, cher Abner, et je n'ai [n'ai point] d'autre crainte.
[Racine, *Athalie*, Act I. sc. i.]

This very celebrated verse is taken from Godeau.[2]

Qui cherche vraiment Dieu, dans lui seul se repose.
Et qui craint vraiment Dieu, ne craint rien autre chose.
[A. Godeau, *Poesies Chrestiennes*, Paris, 1660-3.]

Et lave dans le sang le fer ensanglanté.
[Racine, *Britannicus*, Act. IV, Sc. iii.]

[1] [Landor cannot have noticed that the words attributed to Strada, professor of Rhetoric at Rome, were quoted from Pliny the younger, *Epistolæ*, vii. 20.—W.]
[2] [The same parallel in a verse by Antoine Godeau, bishop of Grasse and Vence, was again noticed in Landor's *Commentary on Memoirs of C. J. Fox*, ed. 1907, p. 166, and in the imaginary conversation between himself and the Abbé Delille.—W.]

HEROIC POEMS

This lies on the boundaries of plagiarism, but belongs to imitation; for, the scene and action (and consequently some of the principal words) are varied. I shall present the counterpart in the language of Mr. Potter.

> Wide thro' the *house* a tide of blood
> Flows where a former tide had flowed.
>
> Eschylus. *Chœphorœ.* Ep. 2 [l. 636, Potter's translation].

I could produce from the Tragedies of Racine, many more verses in the same predicament. Indeed it may be said of him, that, wherever you trace the steps of genius you loose the vestige of originality; for, wherever he is great, he is great by the existence of others. Those who have borrowed the most have always been treated the best: whether it be, that men are gratified by their own ingenuity in finding out what they imagine is hidden from their neighbours, and the good humour resulting from it expands itself all around and easily remounts to it's source; or, by indulging malignity in the discovery of any thing which lessens the merits of their superiors, they feel a quiet composure and plenary satisfaction.

In France and Germany, men of talents are received with cordiality by their brethren—In England, if their brethren look upon them, it is with grudging eye; as upon those no otherwise connected with them than to share their fortune. There it is thought that *genius* and *wit* enhance the national glory—in England, the acquisition of *sugar* and *slaves*. There, performances of literary merit find their utmost value: more than their sterling *weight* is taken into consideration; an addition is made for *fashion*. And, if we look a century back we shall find that in our own country, too, poetry in particular, while it was current, rose marvellously above it's level. In contemporary authors we still read the praises, of Parnell, of Mallet, of Ambrose Philips, and of many others, inferior even to those; and Johnson has written the *lives* of several, whose productions would hardly gain admittance in the corner of a provincial news-paper. The biographer himself, who, whatever may have been his taste, is too weighty to be easily reprehended, seems often to rest with the greatest complacency on poets the most inelegant and feeble. One would think that, in his estimation, Collins and Gray are no higher than Addison and Pomfret.

Mentioning our celebrated Essayist, it must be observed, I mention him not in that character; tho' even there, where indeed he is perfectly *at home*, I am more disposed to commend the cleanliness of his dishes than the flavour of his meat. His success, like that of most men, is the result of keeping *within* the scope of his abilities. He had wit, yet he never could have been a Molière; and he was penetrating in enquiry and skillful in argument, yet he never could have been a Beccarria.[1] He is cool and dispassionate: he is therefor a good observer and a bad poet. There is something, it must be acknowledged, inexpressibly charming in the manner of his narration: there is the slyness of Cupid, and the sweetness of the Graces. This sweetness, in the affairs of a public life, was turned to win the hearts of the rich and profligate; and this slyness, in the affairs of a private one, to undermine the rising reputation of his friends, and to hoard up treasures of wealth, which Ambition, pursuing him into his family, forbade him to enjoy.

[1] [Marchese Cesare Beccaria-Bonesana (d. 1794), whose book *Del delitto et pene* flew triumphantly, Lecky says, over Europe. (*Rationalism in Europe*, i. 363.)—W.]

NOTES

While Boileau[1] was attacking, in Quinault and others, men of more lively fancy than his own, Pope was very well contented to place himself lower than Addison.

> "The French and we still change; but, here 's the curse,
> They change for better and we change for worse."
>
> Dryden, *Prol[ogue] to Span[ish] Friar*.

The poets of that country, *now*, support the imbecility of each other by mutual embraces: we, on the contrary, waste our little strength in personal animosities.

In looking over the page I have finished, I find there several *proper names* with which my critical pupil may at present be unacquainted. The reading, and afterwards giving an account, of them, may serve as a task during his next monthly vacation. For his further improvement, I shall take him on a short excursion: but, if we happen to find any other young critics *out of bounds*, I must advise him beforehand rather to attend my trial of them, than to assume my powers, or exercise my mode of punishing. I hope to deter others from error, by the outcry, which undoubtedly will be raised, of chastized temerity; and for the sake of examination, I seize upon the two that attempt to push foremost in the paths of criticism. One,[2] whether from pride or modesty, takes the greatest pains to conceal the evidence of the religion in which he was educated. In the account of his life, which he is reported to have written, no mention is made whatever of the faith which he is said to have abjured: he there descends, as the name, it is observed, announces, from an *Italian* family. He is one of the children of Israel, nevertheless, as is also announced by the name D'Israeli. I mark this circumstance not by way of reproach, for in the number of my acquaintances there is none more valuable, there is not one more lively, more inquiring, more regular, there is not one more virtuous, more beneficent, more liberal, more tender in heart or more true in friendship, than my friend Mocatta[3]— he also is a Jew—and because I see no important differences in religions if they produce the same effects—I merely bring it as a contrast, in this respect, to the other critic.[4]

The other, who is backward in giving his name, declares himself, at almost every movement, a gentleman and a *christian*. The christian seems *abyssinian*: the gentleman *gasconades*. Such, in effect, is the fierce "Pursuer of Literature". In consideration of his quality, his papers shall be observed first. If any one of these shall be found sufficient to

[1] [Among the writers attacked by Boileau in his Satires were Philippe Quinault, (*ob.* 1688), Jean Chapelain, the Abbé Cotin, and Georges de Scudéry.—W.]

[2] [The one was Isaac D'Israeli, whose early writings Landor was about to criticize with ruthless severity. Nearly forty years later the author of *Curiosities of Literature*, &c. expressed in a letter to Landor a high admiration of his writings. "I have been", he said, "your constant reader . . . All that you have written has been masterly." There is reason to suspect that Mr. D'Israeli never read the "Post-script to Gebir".—W.]

[3] [Mr. Isaac Mocatta, to whom Landor showed proof sheets of the "Post-script", urged him not to publish it and, in a letter dated December 5, 1800, thanked him for having complied with this request. In the following July Landor learnt that Mocatta was dead.—W.]

[4] [The other critic was the anonymous author of "Pursuits of Literature, a satirical poem", published in instalments 1794–7 and not generally known till later to have been written by Thomas James Mathias.—W.]

358

HEROIC POEMS

condemn him, *capitally*, the trial, of course, will cease. Godwin, in "*The walk of a man of talents, and of a man without talents, from Temple-bar to Hyde-Park-corner*," [1] had said of the former, that "he consults by the aid of *memory* the books he has read, &c." To which the Critic has, with malice, not indeed much aforethought, replied, that "a man of talents never *reads* in the streets". Now Godwin had inserted the word *memory* to make it impossible, as he had reason to think, for any one to stumble into this mistake. This alone is sufficient to shew the validity of such a man's censure, and the acuteness of his *judgement*; another is requisite to set in a proper light the object of his applause, and to estimate the delicacy of his taste. His language is,

"Bion or Moschus have never exceeded these lines, I think they have never equalled them." [*Pursuits of Literature*], p. 147, 6 Ed.

> Ἁ χάρις εὐγενέων, χάρις ἢ βασιληΐδος ἀρχᾶς,
> Δῶρα τύχας, χρυσᾶς Ἀφροδίτας καλὰ τὰ δῶρα,
> Πάνθ᾽ ἅμα ταῦτα τέθνακε, καὶ ἦνθεν μόρσιμον ἆμαρ,
> Ἡρώων κλέ᾽ ὅλωλε, καὶ ὤχετο ξυνὸν ἐς Ἀΐδαν.[2]

Here* there is not a single verse, not a single expression, not a single word, that merits the slightest approbation. Let us analize the whole. The word χάρις, which has a most extensive signification, serves decently well for "*the boast*" of heraldry "*the pomp*" of power.

But there is a distinction in the english which in the translation is lost. This however I shall not insist upon, weightily and with stress, being of opinion that the word *pomp* in the original is, at least, as applicable to *heraldry* as to *power*; but I am also of opinion that neither of these words is adequately represented in the Greek. Why not *a* after the second χάρις as well as after the first?

The first δῶρα without a particle, and the next with one, on the strength, I presume, of it's adjective, are awkward in the extreme. The syllable ας, occurring three times, without any necessity, and without the intention of giving any force, I am certain that Bion or Moschus would have waved. Greek poets are so fond of this epithet χρυσεα, that I should be sorry to take it away from them, but I shall say that any one would have preferred

> Καλὰ τὰ δῶρα τύχας, Ἀφροδίτας καλὰ τὰ δῶρα.

Should critics object that καλά is more applicable to the δῶρα Ἀφροδίτας than to the δῶρα τύχας, I should be inclined not only to question it, and, according to it's enlarged acceptation, to defend the elegance of each expression, but to reply that χρυσᾶς seems here to lie on the waste, and

---

* *Venus Aurea* and *Venus aversa* are put in contradistinction; because the front alone, in the Grecian statues, and that not universally, was gilded; the back of the head displaying to advantage no such decoration. The wealthier brides in Greece, even still, as travellers inform us, gild their faces on the day of marriage. [L.]

---

[1] [William Godwin's essay so entitled was included in *The Enquirer, or Reflections on Education, Manners and Literature*, 1797. It was harshly dealt with in notes to "Pursuits of Literature", dialogue iv.—W.]

[2] [From the translation, by William Cook, Cambridge Professor of Greek, of Gray's "Elegy". His rendering of this quatrain and the extravagance of Mathias's praise of it were the subject of comments by De Quincey not less scathing than Landor's. (See De Quincey, *Works*, 1863, xi. 100.)—W.]

to be common both to Ἀφροδίτας and τύχας. *In the third line three theta's with a tau between them*—what a sound!

But what shall we say of this pompous eulogium on verses, the first of which is *indistinct*; the second *monotonous*; half of the third a wretched *expletive*; half of the fourth the *same*, with the addition of one false quantity. So much for the versification.

> Οὔτε φυτῶν τοσσῆνον, ὅσον περὶ πλέγματι γαθεῖ.
> [Theocritus, *Idyl* i. 54.]

A verse of Theocritus which the Editor has thus translated, "*Vel (nec) fructus vineæ tantum quantum opere suo delectatur*"—but which may be construed less paraphrastically for the Pursuer—"he is not so much pleased with the *stamina* as with the *composition*" of the verses. For we shall find on comparing them with the original, in Gray, that they present a very *faint* idea of *his* meaning, and substitute no very brilliant one of his own.

> The boast of heraldry, the pomp of power,
> And all that beauty, all that wealth e'er gave,
> Await alike th' inevitable hour.—
> The paths of Glory lead but to the grave!

The grand reflection in the fourth line, after the unusual and solemn pause in the third—ὅλωλε indeed! If we were to hear any thing of the "*heroes*", we should have heard of them in their proper place, above. They are entirely out of their sphere in the room of this awful close, of this general grand reflection. Perhaps the whole province of translation has never produced so starveling a scion from so vigorous a root.*

I have done with the *Pursuer,* and I open *Vaurien*[1]—a word which may serve both for the title of the hero and for the character of the book. To avoid all appearance of fastidiousness, I shall not object to such affected words as *senility* &c.—nor to *who* instead of *whom, he* instead of *him, drove* instead of *driven,* &c. Emily the heroine of the Romance, we are informed, "could give no satisfactory reason why she should prefer perfumes to ordure." [*Vaurien,* ii. 22.] She uses this expression to elucidate a matter of choice; and a most elegant one it is, in the mouth of a young lady. It unites, indeed, the lively remark of Vespasian, much heightened and far more striking, divested of its positiveness, with all the

* I beg to add one observation more, as I may not have again so good an opportunity. Dr. Johnson says, "the four stanzas beginning ' *Yet even these bones*', &c., are to me original: I have never seen the notions in any other place." [Johnson, *Lives of the Poets.*] Now the *notions* are in Swift, "With regard to fame there is in most people a reluctance and unwillingness to be forgotten. We observe even among the vulgar how fond they are of an inscription over their grave."
—A passage in Swift which is deserving of remembrance, since it is a passage in which he is amiable. I lament not so much this oversight, as that so little praise is awarded to a poem, which is not only an honor to our language, but which, as competitors with the moderns of other countries, or even with the ancients, we should select the first; and which, had the author not listened to an injudicious friend, who was vain enough to imagine he had made a grand discovery in shewing that, instead of *Stanzas,* it might be called an *Elegy,* and caused to be admitted in the room of a proper close, a wretched thing called an epitaph, destroying by this the unity of the piece, would have been the most perfect, as it is the most generally engaging, of poetical compositions. [L.]

---

[1] *Vaurien, or sketches of the times*; in another ed. *Vaurien, a satirical novel,* by Isaac D'Israeli, 1797. [W.]

dispassionate suspence of the natural historian, who indulges his nightly meditations, and pursues his acute research, in the philosophical city of Edinburgh. We see how a lady who is brought before us as a model of delicacy acquits herself. The author also makes a man whom he holds up to our ridicule, speak justly and sensibly in favor of the Jews. Let it pass. But I will not admit that "*every government must be good which is supportable*" ([*Vaurien*,] p. 282, v. 2). For every thing must be supportable, which has been, and may indefinitely be, supported. Now, the Turkish, the Moorish, and Irish governments—but, one of them is past. "*Like Virgil, as your Addison says, the fellow tosses his dung about him with some effect.*" Addison's is nonsense, and so is this, but this is not Addison's. Virgil, tossing the dung about with some effect, would be doing no more than any common farmer; for, whether tossed by *him* or by Virgil, we must naturally suppose that the dung would have some *effect*.

> [And oft, in Persian bowers (as evening falls)]
> "*On Turkish platforms, in Tartarean halls.*"
> ["Poetical Essay" in "Romances", by Isaac D'Israeli, 1799, ll. 91–2.]

Tartarean is, or ought to be, exclusively the adjective of *Tartarus*. *Tartar* is used both as substantive and adjective: it is properly the latter; for, when we say a Tartar, the substantive *man* is understood, unless preceded by some other substantive; as, "that horse is a *tartar*,"—which plainly shews that we assume a kind of licence when we use it absolutely as a substantive. At all events, ought not *Tartarus* to have an adjective of it's own.

> "*Profound their seas, and deep their pearl-beds rise.*"
> [Ibid., l. 155.]

Who has ever heard of any thing *rising deep*?

> *He meets his peers, and blames the loitering way*
> *Making such little speed since yesterday.*
> [Ibid., l.] 183.

When he had reason, apparently, to blame them for going so far before him; they having journeyed ten days which seemed to him only as one.

> The light waves [oars] dash the cool lake of Cashmere.
> *   *   *   *   *   *   *   *   *   *
> [A thousand youths, a thousand damsels pair]
> *Who by their true loves' black eyes sweetly swear.*
> D'Israeli, *Mejnoun and Leila*, ll. 19–22.]

Here are long syllables where should be short. In strong and vigorous verses the *fore-feet* may sometimes be a little impeded, but, if *time* be our concern, we would rid the hinder quarters, as much as possible of incumbrance. The words "*cool lake*" and "*black eyes*," pronounced as they must be, if any respect be had to the rythm, produce a most ludicrous effect.

> "[The full moon hung over the tent . . .] Nothing moved but the gliding shadows."
> [Ibid., p.] 71.

What made the shadows glide then?--I am so fatigued with transcribing, tho' indeed I have transcribed very few comparatively of the passages I had marked, they generally being false grammar, that I shall only advise Mr. D'. to correct at least the latter of these faults, before he passes sentence in so flippant a manner on men of superior genius.

NOTES

"*Our hero*," and "*our lovers*" are terms which should never be employed in any impassioned description or in any serious narrative. They destroy at one breath the most brilliant enchantments of fiction. The author attributes to a boy and girl* the invention of the arts, and most of them are discovered in the space of a very few hours. There never was a greater absurdity, either in Spanish poetry or Flemish painting: and yet this is the author to whom the "*Monk*" appears to have been planned by a *child*. It is probable that my opinion of the "*Monk*," respecting it's faults, is nearly the same as it's Author's. But there are passages both of surprising beauty and exquisite design. I abominate ghosts and goblins, yet there is something in "*Alonzo the Brave*"[1] that not only disarms one of frowns but seduces one into terrors: and as to the "*Exile*",† we have not a poet left amongst us who has hitherto shewn it's equal.

Far different from such a pure and animated composition are those I have just reviewed. With the finery and affectation there is also in the

---

* But tho' a boy and girl could invent all the arts, in as little time as is requisite to exhibit a puppet-shew, yet Anacreon could not compose his own poems. These were the works, Mr. D. ['Israeli] insinuates, of the Editor—whom he familiarly calls Henry Stephens [*Mejnoun and Leila*, p. 148 *n*.]. Here let me inform this gentleman that, tho' Scholars have sometimes taken this liberty, it is not allowed to other *folks*. He might as well call Cicero *Vetch*, and Fabius Maximus *Broad Bean*. Either Henri Etienne, which was his name, or Henricus Stephanus, as he wrote it in latin, is the proper term. We cannot suppose that, coming over to England, he would have called himself Henry Stephens. The same advice, a little varied, must be given to another writer. Why should *Des Cartes* be still *Cartesius* in an english page? Why should the reverend Gentleman make an apology for inventing the words *philosophist* and *philosophism*; when the apology was made and the words invented, in french, at least, more than a century ago. If any were requisite, it would be on the score of redundancing, since *sophis* and *sophism* serve equally well. [L.]

[In "The Lovers, or Origin of the fine arts", included in Isaac D'Israeli's "Romances' (1797), Amarillis traces her lover's shadow, and there is a note referring to the story of the Corinthian maid in Pliny's "Natural History". The "reverend gentleman" who apologised for inventing words may have been the Rev. Henry Kett, quoted in O.E.D., s.v. *philosophism*.—W.]

† Yet the "Exile" has it's faults. The metre, so admirably well chosen,—for our ordinary elegiac is rather solemn than plaintive,—is not equally well maintained. The usual and expected variation of cadence, from *eleven* syllables in the first to *ten* in the second line, is broken twice or thrice. The word "*hour*", sometimes a dissyllable in Shakespear, is singularly unfortunate, being used in this manner by the vulgar. "*Spires*" is drawn out so, too. It would have been better if the metre had been infringed at once, than partially defended by unskillful custom. "*Bowers, towers*, are monosyllables in verse, But a sound, which, in the middle of a line, may be deemed too feeble to support itself, may however be found sufficient at the close. The Italians, whose ear is so accurate, have not only admitted this fact, but admitted it as a principle. In "*mio, desio*" &c. that which any-where else has the power of simply one syllable, at the conclusion forms *invariably* two.

I have ventured, on this consideration, to place the name "Amphyllion" at the conclusion of a verse [*Phocœans*, l. 387], and am not without hope that it will make a good defence. I thought that I was doing it but justice, in conferring on it rank and power neither more nor less in an english iambic than it would indisputably claim in it's native greek. Added to which I was countenanced and supported by a modern versification, in numbers and discipline conformable to our own. [L.]

---

[1] ["Alonzo the Brave" and "The Exile" were among the poetry in Matthew Lewis's novel of *The Monk*.—W.]

language of this author[1] the coarseness and vulgarity of a prostitute. The warmer descriptions, in which he is fond of indulging, are gross and heavy. You are not permitted to remain at a distance, where the fancy may pry securely, but instead of the soft indistinct indescribable ideas, the various and evanescent shades,—which lest your breath should scatter, you breathe softly, timidly,—you are dragged reluctantly forward, you must examine the very pulse and panting, the very sweat and pores, of passion. The shew-man's glass is held close before your eye; the *catalogue of Sundries* is commenced; and attention, which staggers, is excited and held up by perpetual jerks of flippancy. In this exhibition, his hero and heroine learn a notable lesson from a pair of swans, which, tho' simple in itself, is made intricate and perplexing by the peculiarity of the preceptors, and, to be rendered practically instructive, requires a new arrangement. But the author is determined to lose no opportunity of imitating and amplifying. A couple of tame rabbits would have attended him at home on reasonable terms, and have instructed his pupils just as well, yet he could not refrain from going out of his way and consulting the sacred swans. Sacred I call them; for none can ever have been more so than those under the genius of Buffon. The poet of France, who neither says too little nor too much, and says every thing better than any other could say, should have protected them from this unseasonable intrusion. Compare the description of the natural historian with that of the Romance writer. Compare the poetry of the latter with that of Mr. Lewis. Instead of a whole that is graceful and compact, and cloathed in simple words, but elegant, free, and flowing, we have here an ill-concocted mass, which has gathered in it's formation some glittering pebbles, only to increase it's unevenness and throw sufficient light on it's deformity. The abrupt transposition and whimsical arrangement of extracts often beautiful, reminds me of a certain old gentleman who cut into pieces two or three fine mirrors for the purpose of panneling a water-closet. I shall conclude with one short observation: that, the thoughts of other men which are taken and expressed on the spot, are very different from those which have lain sometime, and by degrees been mellowed in the memory. They are rather, for the most part, contortions than combinations. If Genius be absent, it is only the maturity of time that can give form and facility.

[1] [Meaning Isaac D'Israeli, to whose *Romances*, 1799, Landor again refers. In that of "Lycidas and Amaryllis" Buffon's description of the swan is quoted in a note.—W.]

[END OF THE POST-SCRIPT TO *GEBIR*]

The main subject matter of Landor's "Post-script to Gebir" ends here. Beneath the passage given on pp. 353–354 from "work much mischief" to "exposed to all" was printed with a brief introduction "Ode on Power". Since this would seem to have no direct bearing on the context it is now printed separately, being as follows: [W.]

ODE ON POWER

Those who in "*Poems from the Arabic and Persian*" have found me so faithful a translator, will be pleased, I hope, with a version of an ancient Greek Dithyrambic. [L.]

"Power discharges the mulct which Remorse should pay. Men look towards Power, and already have made atonement. In every shape, in

NOTES

every mode and color, Power is before them whether they sleep or wake. Even at the feasts of Love he sits as sovereign. He enters; you cannot behold him—but harken! the music sounds! sing ye! sing in harmony. He is seated and is not discovered. He departs, and the lamps are extinguished. Tho' the guests, and even the master, are ignorant of it—perhaps many months and years,—it is Power who has given the last and highest, the most permanent and yet most intoxicating, gratification. Yes! wretched mortals, every other ceases when predominance declines. In your outward habits and gross experience, Power is the associate of Violence and Fear. Pardon me, great Gods, if I utter the forbidden!—It is Power, at whose feet, in secret, Love is prostrate: it is Power at whose absence he incessantly repines. It is Power whose mysterious name, tho' suppliant, he dares not pronounce; for he believes it would shake his bright abodes, and subvert their most deep foundations. When Power departs from Love, Love transforms himself and vanishes. But when Power departs from Hate, she retains her form, she exalts her stature, she exasperates her features: the object of her violence still is nigh, but still is beyond her reach. Dragging the chains of Fate, and mocked by Phrenzy, in the wild rotation of imaginary pursuit she makes no progress. Again she darts forward; shall she never seize her prey? Better have been held eternally in the irons which she has loosened, than struggle with so much labor, so much pain, to the utmost (and alas, impassible) boundaries that separate earth from heaven. Ye Gods! that inhabit those regions, and govern these, hold, I beseech ye, that demon from my house. And ah! my beautiful Atthis, ah! never depart from my side. Tho', by bathing so many hours of spring in the fountain of the Graces, I ever am chilled and torpid, or faint and feverish—thirsty from draughts too sweet, and blinded with excess—yet I adjure thee, Atthis, by Pan and all the Goddesses—go not away, tho I slumber! A kiss from another on thy lips, dear Atthis, would cover with briars the resting-place of my soul. It might flutter for ever round, but could alight no more. On thy lips, it would utterly efface all the pleasures, that Love, in those exquisite tablets, holds out to Memory: nor could the waters of Lethé, sprinkled over my temples by heroines the daughters of Gods, whether by Antiopé, or by Helen, or by the tender-hearted mother of Perseus,—nor could poppies from the gardens of Persephoné, poppies, the gales of which are among the blessings of Elysium—in a hundred years of wandering, do away that one kiss. Alas! nor the cup of Hebé; twined around with amaranths, and bright with immortality. Son of Latona, thou art happiest of all the Immortals, not that thou knowest song or that thou knowest fate, or indeed that arrayed in transcendant glory thou guidest the jewel'd car of day; but that amidst the very heights of heaven, in the pure serenity of thy unrivalled course, thou feelest, and thy ambrosial steeds feel too, the gentle agitation of thy ruling rein. It is this that sheds soft light; the rest is impetuosity and heat. O may I also, suspended, as I have been, on the wings of exstacy, feel under my panting bosom, as I descend, the buoyant conciousness of deep security."

[END OF THE ODE ON POWER]

HEROIC POEMS

[ADDENDA TO POST-SCRIPT]

[Among the *Addenda* in the volume containing *Post-script to Gebir* is the following correction of an error on p. 355.—W.]

This volume has pretty well escaped the errors of the press: but the author thinks it unfair to overlook some passages which may be less satisfactory to the reader. Tho' the copies have long been printed off, he determined that they should not be given to the public till he had solved that question in particular which relates to the second quotation from Montaigne [p. 13]. The beautiful idea which it exhibits, he feels a satisfaction in not having insisted on as a mark of Pope's imitation. It is, however, to be found in an author, he will not say whose works have been printed and bound up with (for that alone could create no confusion) but whose works are read and compared with, and whose studies and opinions, affectations and antipathies, are very much the same with Pope's. It is in Swift.[1]

> So Geographers in Afric maps
> With savage pictures fill their gaps;
> And o'er unhabitable downs
> Place elephants for want of towns. [L.]
>
> [Swift, *Poetry: a Rhapsody.*]

[Of another *Note* at the end of the 1800 volume the greater part was reproduced in the 1803 edition of *Gebir*, and the two first paragraphs are all that need be given here. They are as follows:—W.]

RESIDING many miles from the town where *Gebir* was printed, and without the advantage of an established post, the Author was unable to superintend the press. In consequence of this, the errata, marked and unmarked, are numerous. Besides, the Preface sent was incomplete. Another more correct was blotted: hence the mistake. But the greatest fault was the result of his own irresolution. In Book 7 the following lines were written—not without alterations since—but at the moment of sending them to the Printer, when the Author was leaving the country, the boldness of personification made him drop them. They have left an abruptness, much heightened by two typographical errors.

"Against colonization in peopled countries. It's success mere chance. All nature is favorable to equality. Dissuades from repletion. Abhors a void." [L.]

[The above passage within " " differs but slightly from the beginning of the *Argument* prefixed to Book VII of *Gebir*, 1803 (see above, p. 48). The remainder of the 1800 *Note* consists of twenty-nine lines of verse. Of these the first six = *ll.* 8–13 in Book VII, *Gebir*, 1803, and had appeared in the 1798 *ed.* The remaining twenty-three lines were rejected in 1798 but inserted with one notable variant in the 1803 *ed.*; where = *ll.* 14–36 (see above, pp. 48–49). In *l.* 18, instead of "stream far off", the 1800 *Note* has "distant stream".—W.]

---

[1] [Landor, in his second imaginary conversation between Johnson and Horne Tooke, pointed out that the original of Swift's simile is to be found in Plutarch's life of Theseus, *ad init.*—W.]

[END OF ADDENDA TO POST-SCRIPT]

P. 56. CRYSAOR. A passage in Diodorus (iv. 156) was the only conceivable source found by Sir Sidney Colvin for such a myth as Landor had in mind when composing this poem. It is just as likely, however, to

NOTES

have been suggested by the account Apollodorus Atheniensis gave of the Chrysaor who with Pegasus sprang from Medusa's blood when Perseus beheaded her. The same Chrysaor became the father, Apollodorus said, of Geryon whose cattle were carried off by Hercules. Landor when he read Justin at Oxford may have noted his statement: "*saltus vero Tartessiorum in quibus Titanas bellum adverus deos gessisse proditur*", and have taken something from each of the three authors named. For other references see W. Bradley's *Early Poems of W. S. Landor.* Writing to Landor in 1824 Wordsworth said that, some years before, he had been struck by this "piece on the war of the Titans", but whether Landor's Crysaor is a Titan is open to doubt. In l. 89 he is described as last of the race of earth-born giants. Some of the ancients failed to distinguish between giants and Titans, and Landor may have done the same. [W.]

l. 41. The following note in the 1802 ed. was not reprinted:

* V. 41. *Henceforth let merchants value him, not kings.* It may seem contradictory that merchants should be mentioned here, when in verse 166 it is expressly said

> "Not ever had the veil-hung pine outspread
> O'er Tethys *then* her wandering leafless shade."

But foreign merchants are not necessarily understood. Those who cannot disengage the idea of slave-merchants from the Europeans in Guinea, may still recollect that there were some native ones in that country antecedent to our own, and that the princes themselves sold their prisoners to any of the neighbouring tribes. It does not require the practice of navigation to make or sell slaves. The petty princes of Hesse and Hanover have within our own memory committed this outrage on humanity, like their brethren the petty princes of Negroland; with this one difference—that the former calculated how much more valuable the cargo would be to the taskmaster if employed in the ruin and slaughter of those whom he had rendered his enemies, than in merely tilling the earth like the African, and therefor set a greater price on the service of a few years, because the service was *summary*, than their brethren in Negroland usually do on a gentler and less degrading one for life.

This poem describes a period when the insolence of tyranny and the sufferings of mankind were at the utmost. They could not be so without slavery; and slavery could not generally exist without some sort of barter. Merchants then were necessary. It appears that Crysaor, wicked as he is represented, had no personal share in it's propagation. He encouraged it. But, a Sovereign who is powerful enough, either by the fears or affection of his people, to abolish from amongst them this inhuman traffic, and who makes not one effort, uses not one persuasion, for the purpose, deserves the execration which followed, and the punishment which overtook Crysaor. Every man, instead of waiting with awe for some preternatural blow, should think *himself* a particle of those elements which Providence has decreed to crush so abominable a monster. [L.]

P. 62. FROM "THE PHOCÆANS". In the 1802 ed. the following introduction was prefixed to the first fragment of the poem:

The Phocæans were a nation of Ionia, who founded several cities, in

HEROIC POEMS

Italy, in Sicily, in Corsica, and in Gaul. Their war with a prince of the latter country, where they afterwards built Marseilles, is the main subject of this poem. The circumstances described in the following extracts are historically true. On leaving Phocæa, which Harpagus, the general of Cyrus, was besieging, and who, afraid of driving them to despair, is said to have connived at their departure, they threw into the sea a mass of burning iron, and swore that, until it should float, inextinguished, on the surface, they would never return. Their bravery in the cause of liberty, they thought, would entitle them to the protection of the Grecian states. But, what they in vain expected from their allies, was afforded them at the court of Arganthonius in Spain. In their voyage to Gaul they were attacked by Carthaginians, whom, tho' unequal in number of ships, they totally defeated. This gives the poem its first important movement; but as there is no allusion to it here, it is sufficient just to mention it. The whole of their history, that is extant, may be comprised in a very few lines. I shall be able to blend with it some actions [*so in errata*] of other nations, with which tho' they were relatively, they were not immediately concerned. These actions will promote the catastrophe, and heighten the interest [*so in errata*], of the poem. But, I have not perfected my plan. It even is possible that the greater part of the *first* extract may be rejected. This, instead of a reason for witholding it, is a very sufficient one, with me, for it's insertion. The celebrated historian of the *decline and fall of the Roman Empire* has informed us how many times he recommenced that work, before he acquired the *key and tone* most proper for his performance; and we all recollect the story of a painter, no less celebrated, who exhibited one of his pictures for the express and sole purpose that the public might mark it's defects. For my part, I wish to ascertain not merely whether the poetry be good, but whether it be wanted—whether so much of the Iberian affairs be proper in this place, on any condition? For the *second* I make no apology. Unless as an extract from an unpublished poem, it requires from me less solicitude than any thing else that I have ever written. The remainder I shall not continue, till I can visit the country where the scene is laid: since, for works of this nature, not poetry alone, but chorography too is requisite. [L.]

It should be clear from the above introduction that, although the adventures of the Phocæans in Gaul were to be the "main subject" of Landor's projected poem, these are not dealt with in the 1802 "extracts". Referring, however, to what was then in print Sir Sidney Colvin said that it "tells of the founding of the colony of Massilia by emigrants of that [the Phocæan] race". Mr. Bradley[1] has pointed out that it does not do so; nor is there any evidence that the "main subject" was ever handled in Landor's verse. In "Pericles and Aspasia" there is a narrative in prose of adventures of the Phocæans, including the foundation of Massilia, but not their sojourn in Spain. Herodotus is cited as an authority and it was from him, rather than from Justin, that Landor got most of the material used in his poem. [W.]

P. 91. GUNLAUG AND HELGA. In Landor's Preface to "Simonidea" 1806, he said: "The Story of Gunlaug he [the reader] must have found in Mr. Herbert's translations from the Icelandic, a work which it is impossible

---

[1] *Early Poems of W. S. Landor*, by William Bradley, 1914.

to read without improving the taste and warming the imagination." In a note appended to a metrical translation in "Select Icelandic Poetry", 1804, the Hon. and Rev. William Herbert gave "a brief account of the history of Rafen and Gunlaug, one of the most entertaining old Icelandic works", and from this Landor took most of his material. For the episode of Hialmar and Ingebiorg—Landor's Ingebiorn (*ll.* 95–130)—see Herbert's translation in the same volume from "Hervarar Saga", and his note on the song of Asbiorn the Proud from Orms Storolfsonar Saga for the allusion (*ll.* 396 *ff.*) to that hero's fight with a Jotun. Gunlaug and Rafen are said to have met at Upsala (*l.* 155) during the reign, A.D. 993–1024, of Olaf, King of Sweden.

P. 91. *l.* 1. Sophia. [This lady was the eldest daughter of John Venour of Wellesbourne whose wife was a sister of Dr. Walter Landor, the poet's father. Married in 1790 to John Shuckburgh, it was to her that the earliest of Landor's English poems was addressed. See "To a lady lately married", reprinted in *Appendix* from the volume published in 1795. Mrs. Shuckburgh died a widow in 1848. W.]

Major variants from 1806 text are given below:

Between ll. 80–1 of 1806 text 1831, 1846 edd. insert 32 ll. as below:

> Mosses he knew of every race,
> And brought them from their hiding-place,
> And mingled every sweet-soul'd plant
> On mountain-top, or meadow slant,
> And checker'd (while they flowered) her room
> With purple thyme and yellow broom.
>   There is a creature, dear to heaven,
> Tiny and weak, to whom is given
> To enjoy the world while suns are bright
> And shut grim winter from its sight . .   10
> Tamest of hearts that beat on wilds,
> Tamer and tenderer than a child's . .
> The dormouse . . this he loved and taught
> (Docile it is the day it 's caught,
> And fond of music, voice or string)
> To stand before and hear her sing,
> Or lie within her palm half-closed,
> Until another's interposed,
> And claim'd the alcove wherin [wherein *1846*] it lay,
> Or held it with divided sway.   20
>   All living things are ministers
> To him whose hand attunes the spheres
> And guides a thousand worlds, and binds
> (Work for ten godheads!) female minds.
> I know not half the thoughts that rose,
> Like tender plants neath vernal snows,
> In Helga's breast, and, if I knew,
> I would draw forth but very few.
> Yet, when the prayers were duly said
> And rightly blest the marriage-bed,   30
> She doubted not that Heaven would give
> To her as pretty things as live.

HEROIC POEMS

l. 91. *1806 has footnote, om. 1831, 1846:*

"*Blissis bar.*"—I am forced to adopt here the oldest and best manner of spelling. In future I shall employ it without force. It is impossible, that one **s** following another should *make* a separate syllable, though it might be the *sign* of one. Such contractions are not less absurd than those ridiculed by Dean Swift, and yet they are common in our poets.

Between ll. 274–5 *of 1806 text 1831, 1846 edd. insert 12 ll. as below:*

> Pray'd not to issue forth so soon,
> But eat and drink and sleep till noon;
> And mention'd other valiant lords
> Who dozed thus long upon their swords,
> Yet ne'er had suffer'd gash nor prick,
> Nor bruise, unless from hazel-stick.
> He was persuaded; for his brain
> Floated in firy [fiery *1846*] floods of pain,
> From hopes, three long long years afloat,
> Now, by one evil turn, remote.   10
> He was persuaded; for he knew
> Whose was of all true hearts most true.

l. 398. *In footnote 1831 has after* fabulous. *the following addition:*

In the north at all times have existed men of enormous stature. We ourselves have seen them from Ireland; our fathers have seen them, our children will see them. That the number was much greater formerly cannot be doubted; but it must always have been very disproportionate to that of ordinary men. These would fear them, lie in ambush for them, persecute them, and, whenever they could do it with advantage, combat them, until, where their numbers once were formidable, not a single one remained. Where they were fewer, as they were in Ireland, their alliance would rather be sought against a common enemy, and they would be objects more of curiosity than of terror. In peaceful times their stature and strength would, after a few generations, diminish from inactivity; and mothers at last would produce creatures of nearly or quite the common size; yet occasionally one resembling the old stock would reappear.

P. 103. CORYTHOS. This poem was first written in Latin and so published with title "Corythus sive mors Paredis atque Ænones" (*sic*) in "Idyllia Quinque", 1815. No ancient writer seems to have told the story exactly as Landor does, but almost every detail and allusion in "Corythos" might have been taken from one or other of various extracts in Bayle, *s.v.* Œnone. Though Landor had most likely read Œnone's letter to Paris in Ovid's *Heroides* when at Rugby, the reply of Paris "as feigned by Sabinus" may have been unknown to him till he found in the great Dictionary a quotation from it coupling Xanthos and Simoeis (*cf.* "Corythos", *ll.* 55–6). Œnone's skill in prophecy (see "Corythos", *ll.* 13 *ff.*) is described by Bayle with a reference to Apollodorus. The account of her death given by Quintus Celeber and quoted by Bayle differs widely from the statements of better known authorities but is nearly the same as Landor's; and this with other evidence may warrant the belief that here as elsewhere Landor owed much to Bayle.

The English version on pp. 103 *ff.* was recast and so published in three

NOTES

parts—the third part with a new title—in 1859. This later text is given below. Parts I–II, reproducing the substance of *ll.* 1–331 and 335–423 of 1847 text, are as follows:

CORYTHOS.

[FIRST PART.]

ŒNONE had been weeping, but the blast
Bitterly cold had dried her tears, for high
Upon the mountain stood she, where the grass
Was short and dry, and where the fir-tree cones
Roll'd as the whirlwind rusht along the down.
Thence she beheld the walls and temples doom'd
So soon to fall, and view'd her husband's roof,
(Hers he was once, altho another's now)
And call'd their Corythos from out the wood.
  "Go," said she, "go, my child! there is at Troy   10
One who, without thy mother, may love *thee.*
Thy father lives . . alas! lives unaware
How few before him lie his destined days:
For now from Lemnos Philoctetes comes
And brings with him the deadly shafts bequeath'd
By Hercules, wherewith, the Fates have sung,
Paris must perish and the city fall.
Hated thou wilt not be by her he loves,
Altho no child she ever bore to him
And thou art mine, if thou canst but delay   20
The hour foredoom'd: he may remember days
Of other times, and how serene they were,
Days when the poplar on its bark retain'd
Two names inscribed by him, and when invoked
Was Xanthos to bear witness to his vow.
When his lost son hath saved him, and he knows
He may not be ungrateful, but become
The kinder father for unkindness past."
  She mingled kisses with o'erflowing tears,
Embraced him, then consigned him . . not at once . .   30
To Agelaos: he was oft recall'd,
And urged with admonitions fresh and fresh
To keep as distant as was possible
From wave sail-whitened and insidious shore,
And every spot where Argive rampires rose.
  Downward, thro crags and briars they wend their way.
Fixt to the place, she heard not long the shout
Of Corythos, nor outcry of shrill birds
He pelted, whooping; then she turn'd around
Toward her mountain home, and thus exclaim'd . .   40
  "Mountains and woods, the birthplace of my child,
I see ye yet! he, dearer to my eyes,
Is lost to them! Paris, once gone, return'd
No more to me! alas! nor love remains
Nor pledge of love! not only have I lost
Him who might bring again to me past hours

370

By countenance, by mien, by sound of laugh,
By words persuasive, when presaging fear
Darkened my brow, that cause was none for grief,
I have lost here . . how little if success   50
Follow the loss! . . all solace, all support!
All things beside are just the same around.
Xanthos and Simöis tremble at the touch
Of early morning; then approaches me
Tenedos, one unbroken mass distinct,
And sidelong surges overleap the cliffs.
I am changed nothing; nothing can I change:
Such is the life of Nymphs; it must not cease,
Nor must the comeliness of youth decay.
   Wretched! what look I back on? that frail gift   60
And fugitive, which others grasp, I mourn.
   Œnone! O Œnone! beauteous once
He thought thee; he whom thou wilt ever hold
Beauteous and dear, now sees thee like the snow
That lost its colour in a southern gale.
   How easy is it to snap off the bud
Of tender life, and sow upon a breast
Laid open ineradicable cares!
How soon droops youth when faith, that propt it, fails!
How often in her anguish would the maid   70
Recall irrevocable hours, and grieve
Most for the man whose future grief she sees!
   Asteropè, my sister! happy thou
In him who loves but one! canst thou believe
That Æsacos and Paris are cognate?
But him the mild Arisbè bore; and him,
Born of a furious River, Hecuba.
   I envy not alone the happier wed,
But even the wretched who avoid the light,
The unmarried too whose parents turn'd aside   80
Their nuptial torch, and widows o'er whose beds
Black wreaths are drooping; for the pang that death
Inflicts, time may, tho time alone, assuage.
   Where Nile besprinkles from his lotus-cup
The nuptial floor; where sacred Ganges rolls
Alike inscrutable his vaster stream,
If Memnon's mother sheds ambrosial tears
Before the sun arises; if, ye maids
Of ocean, in the refuge of your caves
Ye daily hear your Thetis wail her loss,   90
Shunning wise Glaucos, deaf to Triton's shell,
To Doris, and the Nymphs that wait around;
If maids and matrons wail'd o'er Hector's corse,
Mangled, and stretcht upon a tardy bier,
Hector was stil Andromache's, as when
He drave before him the Achaian host,
As when he tost his infant to his crest
And laught that Hector's child could ever fear.

What fault, ye Gods, was mine, unless to love
And be deserted, and to pass my nights 100
Among the haunts of beasts, where wolves and bears
Break my first slumber, and my last, with howls,
And the winds roar incessant from above?
Perhaps the Gods hereafter may look down
With gentler eyes, nor deem my fault so great.
Howe'er it be, may Corythos be blest
With other days, with better than pursuit
Of stag, or net thrown over birds when driven
By cold and hunger to scant oats unhous'd . .
O may they grant him happier, and forbid 110
That children suffer when their sires transgress.'
  Meanwhile the youth was stopping near the walls,
And stood there wondering that e'en those, so vast,
So lofty, had resisted such a host
Under so many tents on all sides round.
"But where is that old figtree? where the scene
Of Hector and Achilles face to face?
Where that of Venus when she drew the cloud
Around my father to preserve his life?"
  Such were his questions, siezing the guide's hand, 120
Hurrying him onward, and entreating him
Forthwith to lead him into Troy itself,
Even into Priam's house. Thus Agelaos
Represses him.
             "Thy mother's sole command
Was *Onward! strait to Helena's abode.*"
  An aged man, who heard the two converse,
Stopt them.
           "O Dardan" cried the impatient boy,
"Say where dwells Helena?"
                        With sterner voice
"Go," said the Dardan, "the destroyer's court
To all is open . . there it lies: pass on." 130
The youth threw instantly both arms around
The old man's neck, and, "Blessed" he exclaim'd,
"Blessed, to whom my mother's injuries
Are hateful! It is virtue so to hate
The wicked Spartan. Here none other house
Than Priam's will I enter, where with his
Abides my father, where Andromachè
Prostrate on earth bemoans her husband slain,
While that bold wanton, fearing neither Pan
Nor Zeus, with busy needle works, I ween, 140
For other temples golden tapestries,
Or twitches the shrill harp with nail of Sphynx."
  Many, as they were speaking, past them by.
One woman, pausing, askt them if the ships
Could be discern'd from Ida whence they came,

99 , ye . . . was] *so in corrigenda,* was ever *in text.*   117 face . . . face]helm to
helm *MS. emendation.*

And whether favorable were the winds
For their departure: to the eld she spake,
But gazed upon the youth: he saw her cheeks
Redden and pale: his guide too, not unmoved,
Thought, if in Ilion be such beauty, who   150
Would turn a glance elsewhere, tho all the Gods
And all the Goddesses might promise more?
Now saw the youth, nor had he seen til now,
The maidens following her; their vests succinct,
Their hair close-braided; faultless all in form,
All modest in demeanour. Not so fast
The motion of his heart when rusht the boar
Into his toils, and knotty cornel spear
Whiz'd as it struck the bristles, and the tusks
Rattled with knashing rage thro boiling blood.   160
   Whither were going they, she gently askt.
"To where Assaracos and Ilos dwelt,"
Replied the elder, "where dwells Paris now."
Then she, "The way is safer shown by us,
And sooner will ye find him when he leaves
The citadel. At early dawn he heard
A clamour from the coast; and soon a skiff
Was seen: an old man landed; one alone
Came with him; 'twas Odysseus; more behind.
Soon roam'd the sailors, culling on the coast   170
Bay and verbena; soon was every prow
Glimmering with these unhoped-for signs of peace."
   Shaking his head, the Idæan answered thus.
"'Twas surely Philoctetes who arrived.
The arms he bears were those of Heracles,
And now the bow of Nessos, and the shafts
Infected by the Hydra, come against
The falling city of Laomedon."
   Struck by the words she heard, the more she wisht
To hear, the quicker went she on, and bade   180
Her damsels hasten too: she did look back,
Yet hasten'd. The Idæan strangers moved
Tardily now thro crowds who stood before
The house of Hector: there they stood; there came
Widows and maids and matrons, carrying
Honey (the outraged Manes to appease)
And children on their shoulders, who lookt up,
Stretching their eyes, stretching their bodies out
To see their equal-aged Astyanax.
The older and the younger wept alike   190
At the morn silence: all things were laid waste
Around the roof-tree of their hero's house.
   The palace now they reach where Paris dwelt;
They wonder at the wide and lofty dome,

149 Redden and] First red, then *MS. emendation.*
Mœnia Dardanides nuper nova fecerat Ilus.—W.]
Hercules *in text.*   162 Ilos [*cf.* Ovid, *Fasti.* vi. 419,
   175 Heraclesl] *so in corrigenda,*

The polisht columns and the brazen forms
Of heroes and of Gods, and marble steps,
And valves resounding at the gates unbarr'd.
They enter them. What ivory! and what gold!
What breathing images depicted there!
Dædalos had enricht the Cretan king   200
With divers; and his daughter when she fled
With Theseus, who had slain the Minotaur,
Brought part away within his hollow ship;
And these were Helena's: a scient hand
Drew her, the fairest, foremost into light
Among the girls she danced with, while the Gods
Of heaven and ocean gazed on her alone.
Above them sate the Sire of all, and nigh
She who on Cypros landed from her shell;
Curl'd conchs less bright the round-eyes Tritons blew. 210
      Helena sent for Paris: what had said
The shepherd she related, but one fact
Repressing . . who the mother of the boy,
And whom the boy resembled. Such was once
Paris, the guest of Sparta; but ten years
Had cull'd and carried off the flower of youth.
      She thought not in these moments of his flight
Inglorious from the spear of Diomed,
Of nearer peril thought she; he, reclined
Upon his purple couch, her fear controll'd.   220
      "No Philoctetes is arrived, afar
Sits he, alone upon the Lesbian rock,
Heavy with mortal wound; a wing drives off
The beasts from worrying their expected prey,
Often he waves it o'er his weary head
Lest vulture settle on it, often sees
The brazen breast of eagle close above,
Too weak his voice to scare it off, too weak
His groans, tho louder. Thinkest he who bore
All this from faithless friend, who sits athirst,   230
Ahungered, on the beach, who bends his ear
Down to the earth and hears the pulse of oars
Fainter and fainter, and the seaman's song
Lively as ever, and while he bemoans
His wasting and immedicable wound . .
What can Lernæan arrow do against us?
Grant, if that far-famed bowman limp across
The heavy sands crisp with Achaian gore,
Year after year, in flakes not washt away,
Where lies our danger? He but comes to find   240
Broken the chariot that had drag'd along
Hector, the blackened pyre where Ajax lies,
The corslet of Patroclos. Lo, O Troy!
Those mighty hands that threaten now thy fall!
Now is the time for us to turn our backs,
To leave our heritage, to leave the fane

Of Pallas, fane inviolate till now,
The roofs that Neptune helpt her to erect,
And over which Apollo, shining forth
And shouting and exhorting, bent his bow.   250
An old man bears an older on his back,
Odysseus Philoctetes. Aye, 'tis time,
My Helena, our footsteps to retrace
Toward Mycænai: let us bear away
Our household Gods, by former wars unmoved . .
Carry thou the Palladion in thy breast
That trembles so with pious fear, and bring
Gifts to Diana on Taygetos!
The rampire of the Achaians is o'erthrown;
The Myrmidons are scattered; every tent   260
Lies open . . that is little . . for, behold!
A lame man wins the race and grasps the prize!
While dark invidious Heré exercised
Her hatred on her judge, and arm'd the son
Of Tydeus, and while Ajax rear'd his shield
Covered with seven bull-hides, and Nereid-born
The proud Æmonian shook Aetion's towers,
Thy fears, even then, I might, in jest, rebuke.
On me no prowess have the Gods bestow'd?
No Venus, no Apollo, favored *me!*"   270
   Her failing spirits with derisive glee
And fondness he refresht: her anxious thoughts
Followed, and upon Corythos they dwelt.
Often he met her eyes, nor shun'd they his,
For, royal as she was and born of Zeus,
She was compassionate, and bow'd her head
To share her smiles and griefs with those below.
All in her sight were level, for she stood
High above all within the seagirt world.
At last she questioned Corythos what brought   280
His early footsteps thro such dangerous ways,
And from abode so peaceable and safe.
At once he told her why he came: she held
Her hand to Corythos: he stood ashamed
Not to have hated her: he lookt, he sigh'd,
He hung upon her words . . what gentle words!
How chaste her countenance.
                         "What open brows
The brave and beauteous ever have!" thought she,
"But even the hardiest, when above their heads
Death is impending, shudder at the sight   290
Of barrows on the sands and bones exposed
And whitening in the wind, and cypresses
From Ida waiting for dissever'd friends."

267 Æmonian] *sc.* Achilles.   284 Corythos . . . stood] *so in corrigenda,* him:
now first was he *in text.*   285 lookt . . . sigh'd] *so in corrigenda,* looks, he sighs *in
text.*   286 hung] *so in corrigenda,* hangs *in text.*   288 thought] *so in corrigenda,*
said *in text.*

NOTES

CORYTHOS.

[SECOND PART.]

HELENA long had pondered, at what hour
To charm her Paris with the novel sight
Of such a son, so like him.
                Seldom bears
A beauteous mother beauteous progeny,
Nor fathers often see such semblances
As Corythos to his. To mortal man
Rarely the Gods grant the same blessing twice;
They smile at incense, nor give ear to prayer.
With this regretful thought her mind recurs
To one so infantine, one left behind   10
At morning, from the breast she just had warm'd.
"Will no one ever tell me what thou art,
Hermionè! how grows thy destined spouse
Orestes."
          Now invade her other cares
How to retain her Paris . . oft she wisht
She had a boy like Corythos . . at least
Hers she would make him by all tenderness,
Atoning, if atonement there could be,
For what his mother by her crime sustain'd . .
But was it not decreed so from above?   20
She argued . . and remorse was thus appeas'd.
  Then Agelaos call'd she, and besought.
"Perform, O Agelaos, my request.
  Two youths have been entrusted to thy care,
Paris and Corythos: one care is mine.
Already hast thou seen the torch extinct
That threatened Troy, and strong as be thy wish
Again to press thy earlier pupil's hand,
Be not thou overhasty: let a son
Receive a father's blessing quite alone."   30
Then he. "Not different were the wise commands
His mother gave me. Should I see the man
I left a child, he might not recognise
Old Agelaos in these wrinkled cheeks,
These temples sprinkled now with hoary hair,
These limbs now slow, this voice and spirit weak;
Nor haply would the prince be overjoyed
To know his servant had outrun his lord
In virtue's path: my help the royal heir
Wants not; but Corythos may want it, him   40
Never until death parts us will I leave."
  Revolving in her mind a thousand schemes,
She now decided that her guest should come
Before his father when the harp and wine
Open the breast, and the first lamps were lit
To show the dauntless unsuspicious youth;

376

She oftentimes had thought of it before,
And now the day was come.
               The Trojans turn'd
Again to strains of intermitted glee,
Not unafraid, however, of reproof   50
Tho mild; the times had so debased the lyre,
And for heroic deeds of better men,
It tinkled now, in city and in camp,
With little else than weak lasciviousness,
Until its strings were stifled with applause.
Helena heard not such complacently;
Adultress as she was, she had not lost
The early bloom of Spartan modesty.
   Around the chamber shone the images
Of boys and maidens robed in vest succinct,   60
And holding burnisht lamps, whence incence wreath'd
Its heavy cloud whitened with cedar oil,
And under them the purple seats gleam'd forth,
And over was the residence of Gods,
And nectar-bearing youth, in light serene.
   Helena, now impatient of delay,
Looks often out the portal's tissued folds
Heavy with fringe of interwoven gold,
And often stops when even Paris speaks,
Listening, but not to Paris as before,   70
And, once or twice, half springing from her seat.
   Now enters Corythos: the splendors round
Amaze him, and one image strikes him dumb,
His lofty sire's: he would advance, but awe
Withholds him: he can only fix his gaze
On Helena.
            When Paris first percieves
A stranger, of fresh age and ardent mien,
Advance, then hesitate, and then retreat
Disturb'd and trembling, voiceless, motionless,
Nameless, and without call or office there,   80
And when he sees the purple robe he wears,
Woven by Helena in former days,
Perhaps too for the man she since had loved,
A thousand furies rush into his breast,
He tears it off, he hurls it on the ground,
He strikes with rapid sword, the face, the neck,
The bosom, of his child, and with his heel
Stamps on the hands in vain to heaven uprais'd,
And hears, infuriate wretch! but bubbling blood,
And one loud female shriek .. *Thy child! thy child!*   90

NOTES

CORYTHOS.

[THIRD PART.]

[In the 1859 *ed*. Parts I–II are printed in sequence, but Part III—
reproducing the substance of ll. 424–652 of the 1847 text—is separated
from Part II by other pieces. It is given below properly placed:]

DEATH OF PARIS AND ŒNONE.

CLOSED had the darkened day of Corythos.
  When Agelaos heard the first report,
Curses he uttered on the stepmother,
Fewer on Paris by her spells enthrall'd,
For in the man he now but saw the child,
Ingenuous, unsuspicious. He resolved
To hasten back to Ida, praying death
To come and intercept him on the way.
What tale to tell Œnone! and what thanks
From parent at a prosperous son's return,   10
Anxiously hoped for after many years,
Last gift of wife deserted, now deprived
Of him whose voice, whose gesture, day and night
Brought the beloved betrayer back again
Into her closing and unclosing eyes,
And sometimes with her child upon the knee
Of her who knew him not, nor cared to know.
Grief and indignant virtue wrung her breast
When she repeated to the fond old man
Such intermingled and such transcient joys;   20
But when she met him on his sad return
Ida was hateful in her eyes, for there
Love bore such bitter and such deadly fruit.
  When Paris knew the truth, on cheek supine
And cold a thousand kisses he imprest,
Weeping and wailing; he would expiate
(If expiation there might ever be)
The murderous deed: he built up high a pyre
Of fragrant cedar, and in broken voice
Call'd on the name, a name he knew so late.   30
"O Corythos! my son! my son!" he cried,
And smote his breast and turn'd his eyes away;
Grief wrencht him back, grief that impell'd him on,
But soon return'd he, resolute to catch
The fleeting ashes and o'ertake the winds;
So from the brittle brands he swept away
The whiter ashes, placed them in their urn,
And went back slowly, often went alone
In the still night beneath the stars that shed
Light on a turf not solid yet, above   40
The priceless treasure there deposited.
Achaians, wandering on the shore, observ'd
His movements thither, Laertiades,
Epeos, and that hero last arrived,
Pæantios, catching the cool air with gasps.

378

There rose the foss before them: they advanced
From the Sigæan side thro copse and brake
Along the winding dell of darker shade,
Awaiting Paris.
            Under a loose string
Rattles a quiver; and invisibly   50
Hath flown an arrow, and a shout succedes;
No voices answer it. One listens, groans,
Calls for his foe; but calls not any God's
Or any mortal's aid; he raves, and rests
Upon his elbow. Back thro the soft sands
They from their ambush hasten, for no shield,
No helmet had they taken, no defence.
Below his knee the arrow has transfixt
The pulp, and hindered all pursuit; in vain
Strove he to tear it out; his vigorous arm   60
Could only break the arrow; blood flow'd hot
Where he would wrench it.
               All night thro, he roll'd
His heavy eyes; he saw the lamps succede
Each other in the city far below,
He saw them in succession dim and die.
In the fresh morn, when iron light awakes
The gentle cattle from their brief repose,
His menials issue thro the nearer fields
And graves adjacent to explore their lord,
And lastly (where perchance he might be found)   70
Nearer the pointed barrow of his son.
Thither ran forward that true-hearted race
Which cheers the early morn, and shakes the frost
From stiffened herbs, which lies before the gate
Alike of rich and poor, but faithful most
To the forsaken and afflicted, came
And howl'd and croucht and lickt their master's face,
And now unchided mixt their breath with his.
   When man's last day is come, how clear are all
The former ones! Now appear manifest   80
Neglected Gods, now Sparta's Furies rise,
Now flames the fatal torch of Hecuba
Portended at his birth, but deem'd extinct
Until that arrow sped across the tombs
Of heroes, by a hand unseen, involves
In flame and smoke the loftiest tower of Troy.
Such were the thoughts that vanisht like a mist,
And thee, Œnone, thee alone he sees,
He sees thee under where the grot was strown
With the last winter leaves, a couch for each,   90
Sees thee betrotht, deserted, desolate,
Childless . . how lately not so! what avail
The promises of Gods? false! false as mine!
  "Seek out, ye trusty men, seek out," said he,
"The Nymph Œnone: tell her that I lie

NOTES

Wounded to death: tell her that I implore
Her pardon, not her aid."

               They, when they reacht
High up the hill the woodland's last recess,
And saw her habitation, saw the door
Closed, and advancing heard deep groans, which brought   100
Even to the sill her favorite doe and stag
Springing before them with defiant breasts,
They paus'd; they entered; few and slow the words
They brought with them, the last they heard him speak.
Briefly she answered with her face aside.
  "I could not save my child; one who could save
Would not."
           Thick sobs succeded.
                     Twas not long
Ere down the narrow and steep path are heard
The pebbles rattling under peasants' feet,
Whose faces the dense shrubs at every side   110
Smite as they carry on his bier the man
Who thinks his journey long; 'twas long to him
Wounded so grievously, to him about
To close his waning day, before his eyes
Might rest on hers and mix with hers his tears.
How shall he meet her?
                Where the rocks were clear
Of ivy, more than once the trace is seen
Of name or verse, the hunter's idle score
Indifferent to pursue the chase; and where
There was a leveler and wider track   120
He might remember, if indeed he cared
For such remembrances, the scene of games
At quoit or cestus closed by dance and feast.
He drew both hands before his face, and wept,
And those who carried him, and found him faint
And weary, placed their burden on the ground,
And with averted faces they wept too.
  Œnone came not out; her feet were fixt
Upon the threshold at the opened door,
Her head turn'd inward that her tears might fall   130
Unseen by stranger; but not long unseen
By Paris: he was in his youth's domains,
He view'd his earliest home, his earliest loves,
And heard again his earliest sighs, and hers.
  "After how many and what years!" he cried,
"Return I, O Œnone! thus to thee!"
  She answered not; no anger, no reproach;
For, hours before, she prayed the Eumenides
That they would, as befits the just, avenge
The murder of her Corythos; she prayed   140
That she might never have the power to help
The cruel father in the hour of need.
A voice now tells her from her inmost heart,

Voice never, to the listener, indistinct,
It is not granted to so wild a prayer.
Weary of light and life, again she prayed.
  "Grant me, O Zeus! what thou alone canst grant.
Is death too great a boon? too much for me,
A wretched Nymph, to ask? bestow it now."
  When she had spoken, on the left was heard   150
Thunder, and there shone flame from sky serene;
Now on her child and father of her child
Equally sad and tender were her thoughts;
She saw them both in one, and wept the more.
Heedless and heartless wretch she call'd herself,
But her whole life, now most, those words belied.
  Paris had heard the words, "Those words were mine
Could I have uttered them: wounds make men weak,
Shame makes them weaker: neither knowest thou,
Pure soul! one fit for immortality!   160
Let us, Œnone, shouldst thou ever die,
Be here united, here is room for both . .
Both did I say? and not for one beside!
Oh! will his ashes ever rest near mine?"
To these few words he added these few more.
"Restrain, Œnone, those heartrending sobs!"
His he could not restrain, nor deeper groans,
Yet struggled to console her. "Are not these
Our true espousals? Many may have loved
But few have died together!" Then she shriekt   170
"Let me die first, O husband! Hear my prayer
Tho the Gods have not heard it! one embrace!
Paris is mine at last; eternally
Paris is mine.
                  Oh do not thou, my child,
Shun or disdain amid the Shades below
Those who now die, and would have died for thee!
  The gift of Venus I have often mourn'd,
With this one consolation, that my grief
Could not increase: such consolation lasts
No longer: punishment far less severe   180
Could Heré or could Pallas have decreed
Than Venus on this Ida, where she won
A prize so fatal, and to more than me."
  The maidens of the mountain came and rais'd
Her drooping head, and drew from tepid springs
The water of her grot, and, from above,
Cedar and pine of tender spray, and call'd
Her father Cebren: he came forth, and fill'd
After due sacrifice the larger space
That was remaining of the recent urn.   190
  Paris had given his faithful friends command,
Whether the Fates might call him soon or late,
That, if were found some ashes on his breast,
Those to the bones they covered be restored.

NOTES

P. 119. THE LAST OF ULYSSES. According to a legend known to Plutarch (*Quæst. Græc.*, xiv) Ulysses, after slaying Penelope's suitors, went to Italy. He had been banished, it was said, by the decree of Neoptolemus, to whom the kinsmen of the suitors had appealed for justice. Theopompus, a writer of less repute, states that Ulysses went to Etruria, took up his abode at a place identified with the later Cortona, and died there in his old age. In the story more often told, instead of going to Italy he ended his days in Ithaca, dying from a wound inflicted accidentally by Telegonus, his son by Circe. (See Apollodorus, *Epitome*, vii. 34 *ff.*, and Sir James Frazer's notes thereon.) Landor, however, either expanding Plutarch's legend or having met with yet another variant, brings the hero to Argyripa, the city founded in southern Italy by Diomed (see *Æneid*, xi. 246), where he is received by his former brother-in-arms and is presently joined by Penelope. Then Telegonus comes to Argyripa and the scene of the encounter of father and son with its fatal consequence is thus transferred from the Greek island to an Italian city the ruins of which may still be seen near Foggia.

Professor Gilbert Murray suggests that, with the myth in what is left of the *Telegonia* and also found in *Odysseus Acanthoplex*, fragment of a play by Sophocles, Landor combined some legend of the wanderings of Ulysses in Etruria, Tarentum, and elsewhere. Professor C. Foligno, to whose erudition Oxford scholarship also owes much, notes that during the Middle Ages many stories were told about Trojan exiles and Greek adventurers in ancient Italy. Failing a definite clue, however, to what was in Landor's mind, his account of the death of Ulysses might be accepted as not less an invention of the poet who wrote it than the beautiful story in Dante's *Inferno* (xxvi. 106 *ff.*) of the seafaring which took the hero past the Pillars of Hercules to perish in the Atlantic.

P. 131. *l.* 22. To the Shepherd Aglauros Landor gives a name better known as that of a woman, turned into stone by Mercury. (See Ovid, *Met.* ii. 737, Sir J. Frazer's note to Pausanias, *Library*, iii. xiv, and Dante, *Purg.* xiv. 39.) By some writers she was called Agraulos= 'Αγρος αὐλή, but on two Greek vases the inscription has Aglauros.

P. 148. CATILLUS AND SALIA. The passage in Plutarch's *Moralia* which suggested the theme of this poem was thus rendered in Goodwin's translation:

"Anius, a king of the Tuscans, had a delicate, handsome daughter, whose name was Salia, and he took great care to keep her a virgin. But Cathetus, a man of quality, seeing her sporting herself, fell passionately in love with her, and carried her away to Rome. The father made after her, and when he saw there was no catching of her, he threw himself into a river that from him took the name of Anio."

Landor in his poem seems to have combined two legends, that of Latinus and his daughter Lavinia (see *Æneid*, vii. 46 *ff.*), and the story of the Etruscan King Anius told by Plutarch, who called Salia's lover Cathetus. See also Bayle's *Dictionary*, *s.v.*, Amphiaraus, Tibur, &c., from which many of Landor's allusions may have been taken.

The following list of places mentioned in *Catillus and Salia*, and marked on the accompanying sketch-map, may help in tracing the route followed by the fugitive lovers. Open numbers give the lines in the 1847 edition of the poem; those within [ ] to the 1859 edition.

It was not till some five years after he had published the Latin—which was the earliest—version of his poem that Landor visited this part of Italy. In an unpublished letter to his sister Ellen, written at Florence in March, 1826, he told her about his recent, and first, journey to Rome and back. In general, he said, the road was as uninteresting as any upon earth except only in the vicinity of Bolsena; but there was nothing under the sun so lovely as the vicinity of Narni and Terni. He had not yet, perhaps, got so far as Tivoli, or seen the Albunean lake and the floating islands. Joseph Addison, on his way to Tivoli, saw the lake with its floating islands and described it as one of the most extraordinary natural curiosities about Rome. Thomas Gray spoke of Aquæ Albulæ as "a vile little brook that stinks like a fury". Both ancient and later writers, however, have at times failed to distinguish between the name of Albula (white water) and that of the Sibyl, Albunea, whose tomb was near Tivoli. But Aquæ Albulæ seems properly to include the Albunean lake (Lago delle Isole Natanti) and two or three smaller ones.

The revised version of Catillus and Salia published in 1859 and reprinted 1876 is given below.

CATILLUS AND SALIA.

AGAINST the lintel of Voltumna's fane,
Which from the Cyminus surveys the lake
And grove of ancient oaks, Catillus left
His spear; his steed stood panting, and afraid
Sometimes of sight obscure, sometimes of sound
Strange to him, of wild beast or falling bark
Blackened by fire, and even of witherd leaves
Whirld by the wind above his bridle-bit.
　　"Voltumna," cried the youth, "do not reject
My vow to Salia; she despiseth not,　　　　　　　　　　10
Nor doth her father, love so pure as mine;
But there are oracles which both believe
Are obstacles against the nuptial torch.

3 Catillus] *mispr.* Coresus *in text, here corrected.*

Goddess! thou knowest what the Powers above
Threaten, for from thy fane the threats procede,
Thine be it all such sorrow to dispell!
Amphiaräus could, not long ago,
Have taught me what impended; with him went
His art, alas! he with his car of fire
Sunk near Ismenos.

               Ancient bards have sung   20
That the king's house and king himself must fall,
And that his daughter, when she weds, will bring
Destruction on them both. Her braver heart
Sees thro the oracles, at first obscure,
Nor fears to love me; should not I abide
The fate of arms, whatever it may be?
I would not they should part us; I would now
And ever be with her, altho the Gods
So will that we must pass the Stygian pool
Or, what is worse, roam thro the stranger's land.   30
O Salia! be thou mine a single day,
Another's never, nor a banisht man's."
A hollow murmur moves the forest heads,
The temple gloams, and from the inner shrine
A voice is heard, "Unhappy daughter! sprung
Of parent more unhappy, thus forewarnd
Of coming woe." The voices ceast . . the groves
Afar resounded when the portal closed.
Silence more awful followed, thro the sky
And lofty wood and solitary fane;   40
If any bird winged over, in that bird
He saw not whence might come an augury
To solace his torn heart; among dense shade
Some there might be; but over all the lake
He heard no sound, no swan was visible,
For shining afar off they floated high,
Or smooth'd their wings upon the swelling wave.
  Now he thro shady fields of trelliced vine
Waving o'er-head, and thin-leaved olives hied.
Twas evening; on the earth he threw himself,   50
Hoping some dream might waft away his dread.
Sharp was the radiance of the stars above,
And all the sky seemed moving in a course
It never yet had moved in; what he heard
Beneath the roof of Anius, and within
The temple of Voltumna, now returnd,
And what seemd there so difficult, he felt
Plain to expound and easy to achieve.
  The daughter and the father he resolves
To save forthwith; he snatches up the rein,   60
Leaps on his charger, and ere breaks the dawn
Reaches the city-gate: few sentries stood
Before or near it, long enjoying peace.
Well might the troop have known their youthful friend,

Broad-chested, of high brow, of lustrous eye,
Familiar speech, large heart and liberal hand,
And prompt on horse or foot with Argive spear.
Fast went he to the mansion of the king.
Beneath the gateway Periphas he meets,
Seizes his hand, "I haste to Salia,"   70
Cries he, "Voltumna threatens mortal woe,
Woe which her father never can avert.
Piety may be blind, love open-eyed
Is ever on the watch: I bring with me
The Goddesses own words, words now confirmed
By surest omens, even by my dreams."
 Unhappy Salia had already past.
She early every morning sacrificed
To Dian in the little fane anear
The city-gate: the hero's threatening steed 80
Neighd, and the palace-archway sounded loud
From frequent tramps of his impatient hoof.
It was the hour when each expiring lamp
Crackled beneath, now showing, hiding now,
The chain it hung by; when the hind prepared
To throw upon the slowly rising ox
His wooden collar, slow himself, morose
With broken sleep; along the lower sky
Reddened a long thin line of light that showd
But indistinctly the divided fields. 90
Catillus meets his Salia, "Fly," cries he,
"Fly while tis possible; the Gods have given
Sure omens; now distrust them never more."
He lifts her, ere she answers, on the steed,
Leaps on it after, spurs with rapid heel
The flank, and off they fly. "Now tremble not,
My Salia, there was room and time for fear
When flight was difficult and hope unsure.
Dian, to bless thy pious vow, had given
What now Voltumna gives; fallacious dream 100
Came never from her fane. Feel, Salia, feel
How quiet, without snort and without shy,
Moves under us the generous beast we ride!
Is then my arm too tight around thy waist?
I will relax this bondage . . and stil sigh!
Weary thou must be; we will here dismount
And leave behind us the brave beast to rest
Under the roof-tree of that cottage near,
We will reward him for his oaten bread,
And for the skiff he idly lies along." 110
 Large was the recompence; the pair imbarkt;
The hind stood wondering, "*Are they then some Gods?*"
Muttered he to himself.
     The little sail
Catillus hoisted, hoisted leisurely,

   108 cottage near] cottager *MS. emendation.*

That he might turn it whatsoever breeze
Haply should rise, but more that he might sit
On the same thwart, and near enough to screen
The face of Salia from the level sun,
And any gazers from the banks they pass.
Catillus listened; and whatever voice   120
Came to his ear, he shuddered at, but most
Dreaded lest Fescennine loose song reach hers.
Cautious he was of meeting the approach
Of the Volsinians; he would then avoid
The flowery fields that Farfar's rills refresh,
And those too where, when Sirius flames above,
Himella guides her little stream away.
Therefor he wisely wore a coarse attire,
Unrecognized, and seem'd a stranger hind
Returning to his kin at even-tide.   130
His crest and spear beneath dense rushes lay.
Long was the way by land, by water long,
Nor would he, if he could, say what remaind
To travel yet. "Thou seest with how mild light
Hesper advances, now oscillating
Alone upon the water; how befriends us
The pale and tender sky; earth, water, heaven,
Conspire to help us." Sleepless, nor inclined
To slumber, both form dreams: supreme the bliss
Soon to be theirs, if but one touch inflames   140
Each thrilling fiber with such high delight.
   Never be wise, ye youths; be credulous;
Happiness rests upon credulity.
Why should I, were it possible, relate
In what discourses hour succeded hour,
How calm the woods, how rich the cultured fields,
Or in how many places they could spend
Their lives most willingly, or why recount
The girlish fears when any sudden swell
A hands-breadth high rose up against the skiff,   150
Or lower bough and slender toucht her cheek?
Catillus too was not without his fears;
Whether some silent woman crept along
The river side, expecting the return
Of tardy husband, or burst suddenly
The light from cottage near, or fisherman
Crownd the black corks along his net with flames.
All night their watery way do they pursue.
At dawn Catillus willingly was borne
On where the stream grew lighter; to the right   160
He left those seven hills, of name unknown,
Where dwelt Evander: upon one had stood
A fortress built by Saturn, opposite
Had Janus rais'd one; both were now decayed;

135 now oscillating] *so in* errata, oscillating now *in text;* now *wrongly om. 1876.*
136 water; how] *so in* errata, water; look up, how *in text.*

Catillus wondered how such mighty piles
Could ever perish. He had soon arrived
Upon the borders of his native home.
He took the maiden's hand; he prest her chin,
Raising it up to cheer her, and he said,
"Tis lawful now to visit those abrupt   170
And shattered rocks, that headlong stream, that cave
Resounding with the voices of the Nymphs:
Here is thy domicile, thy country here,
And here the last of all thy cares shall rest.
Preserv'd by thee thy sire, thy faith preserv'd,
Anius will not regret that thou hast shown
Obedience to the Gods, and given to him
A son who will not shame him by the choice.
Think, who will envy us our rural life?
What savage mortal carry thee away?   180
Thy father's kingdom who will dare invade?
We have our own, let every other rest!
Now peace be with the Sabines.* May thy sire
Enjoy it long, unanxious and secure!
Instead of realm for dower, instead of gates
With soldiers for their bars, be thou content
With the deep wood where never Mars was heard
Above the Tiber ere he leaps and foams,
Or doze where under willowy banks obscure
Pareusius gently winds his gleamy wave.   190
Look! what a distance we have left behind!
How the fields narrow which we thought so vast!
How the sun reaches down the city-wall
Even to the base, and glows with yellower light."
Wherat her eyes she raises, but not yet
To his; the ancient city she surveys
Dimly thro tears, "Live, O my father! live,
Be comforted, be happy! If Voltumna
Commands it, never let thy love for me
Obstruct our pious duties: let me live   200
Amid the solid darkness of these woods,
Or see nought else than that mysterious lake †
Which other than its own shades wrap in gloom,
Enough for me if thee I leave at rest."
   Catillus heard the pious wish, and said,
"Behold that rest at last by thee secured!
However might Voltumna have desired
One so devout and duteous to retain,
She bade thee go, for she had heard thy prayer.
Now art thou mine indeed, now lawfully   210
And safely love and liberty are ours;
No deities oppose us: here is home."

---

* Plutarc reckons as Sabines the Volsinians. The nations of Italy often changed their boundaries. [L.]

† Small ilands composed of weeds float upon the lake. [L.]

He raises up his helm; it lights the copse
With splendour; soon the rural youth come down
With oxen reeking from laborious plough,
And war-horse after his long rest from toil.
Yet, slower with all these auxiliaries
The hours moved on than when the oar at eve
Was thrown upon the thwart, and when the winds
Had their own will.
      Catillus would not land   220
Near bare and open downs; he knew a path
Safer and pleasanter, where soft and cool
About the hazles rose high grass oer moss.
"But, Salia! one step farther . . let us on,
And we shall view from that so short ascent
Our own domains, our Tibur."
        They had reacht
The summit: thence what sees she opposite?
Only the wavy willows bend their heads
Below her, only higher elms oershade
The darker herbage, and their trailing vines   230
Which pat and pat again the passant stream.
What sees she then, fastening immovably
Her eyes upon one object? why so pale?
Her father! at first sight of him her limbs
Stiffen to stone.
      He from across exclaims,
"Stay thee, O wretched girl! whom wouldst thou fly?"
  She wrencht her feet from where they stood, and flew
Faster at every word, but slower seem'd
Her flight to her at every step she took.
Doubtful it was to those upon the walls   240
Whether she drew the youth along, his spear
Holding as now she did in mortal dread,
Or whether he was guiding, to assure
Her footsteps; she was foremost of the two
Where the road was not wide enough for both,
He where the incumbent rock was hard to climb.
Indignant Anius watches them mount up,
Watches them enter thro the city-gate
Amid loud trumpets and applause as loud.
He raged not, waild not, but both hands comprest   250
His burning brow. How bitter must be grief
That such sweet scenes one moment fail to lull!
Fixt stood he just above the cave profound
Whence flows Pareusius, but the torrent's roar
He heard not; saw not the white dust of spray
Return above it over mead and wood,
Wherein are many birds that raise the throat,
Pouring a song inaudible, and more
That fly the eternal thunder; for their nests
Were not built there, nor there their loves inspired.   260

   235 exclaims] exclames *MS. emendation*

388

Others protect their brood with cowering wing
Or flit around to bring them food, unscared.
  "The world as ever let Injustice rule,
Let men and Gods look on and little heed,
Let violence overturn the bust, and spill
The treasured ashes, yet above the tomb
Sits holy Grief, and watchful Muse warns off
Oblivion.
                Why, O Powers above! from lands
The fairest on the earth, why should complaint
Rise up from mortal to your blest abode?   270
Why from a father's breast, from Anius?
Who offered ever gifts more cheerfully
Before your altars, or with purer hands?"
Anius smote his breast, and gaspt and groand,
  "Piety! where now find it! She deserts
Her parent, conscious as she can but be
Of ills impending: kind, religious, chaste,
All ever thought her; so she was to all,
Alas! that I alone could not deserve
To be, as faithless stranger is, beloved!"   280
A pause ensued, and then with bitter scorn,
  "Now learn I what a daughter's duty is!
O partner of my sorrows and my joys,
Whose sole contention throughout life was which
Should be the fonder parent of the two,
If Libitina had prolonged thy days
How wouldst thou mourn such contest! I have since
Assumed thy place: when any little pain
Befell her, light as may be, could I rest?
Could I away from her bedside?"
                                He dasht   290
The tear from off his burning cheek, and cried
In agony and desperate, "Go then; sieze
The nuptial torch, and sing endearing song,
As once at home; let down the saffron veil . .
And be thy child, if child thou have, like thee.
If other rites thou hast omitted all,
If without dower, such dower as king should give
With daughter, if it shames thee not to run
Hither and thither over foren lands,
The fault is mine, thy father's: that one fault   300
I now will expiate; I can yet afford
One victim." At these words, there where the rocks
Protrude above the channel they burst through,
Headlong he cast himself from crag to crag;
And then rose reddened the resurgent spray.
The deed is unforgotten, and the stream
Is now calld Anio since that fatal hour.

NOTES

SECTION II. DRAMAS AND DRAMATIC SCENES

P. 161. COUNT JULIAN. The historical framework on which, with added fiction, the plot of *Count Julian* is constructed might be outlined almost in the words of Gibbon. He relates how in A.D. 709 Muza ibn Nusair, the Khalif's governor in Mauritania, after being repulsed before the walls of Ceuta by the courage and vigilance of Julian, general of the Goths, received a message from the Christian chief soliciting the disgraceful honour of introducing Moslem arms into the heart of Spain. If we inquire, says Gibbon, the cause of this treachery Spaniards repeat the popular story of Julian's daughter, seduced or ravished by her sovereign —Landor's King Roderigo; of a father who sacrificed his religion and country to the thirst for revenge. Gibbon goes on to describe the first invasion under Tarik; and Roderigo's defeat, flight, and death. Muza, with a larger host, is made to arrive in A.D. 712. Landor brings him from Africa before that date, confuses Tarif with Tarik, calls Julian's daughter Covilla instead of Florinda or La Cava, and prolongs, as Southey does, Roderigo's life. Gibbon, Southey, and Landor alike ignore the statement of some Arabic writers that Count Julian was neither Spaniard nor Goth, but a Berber chief, Ilyan the Nazarene, lord of Ceuta and a vassal of the Gothic king. According to another tradition, perhaps unknown to Landor, Roderigo's wife Egilona was a Moorish princess who, voyaging in a ship wrecked off the Spanish coast, was cast ashore, and after being persuaded or forced to become a Christian presently found favour in the eyes of a Christian ruler. (See Calvert's *Toledo, &c.*)

Writing to Lady Melbourne in April 1813, Byron referred to "a Mr. Landor's tragedy the reputation of which I was obliged to bear". The late Sir John Murray, who edited this and other correspondence between Byron and her ladyship, supposed that the tragedy was Robert Landor's *Count Arezzo*. On being told, however, that *Count Arezzo* was not published till 1824, and that it must have been *Count Julian* which was attributed to Byron, Sir John readily admitted his error.

In *Landor: a Biography* Forster gave two passages from the first draft of *Count Julian* which were sent to Southey in 1810. In these the variants from the 1812 *ed.* are shown below:

ACT V, SCENE 4.

219 = 1 *in 1810 draft.*   weep . . . more] will not weep *1810.*   exultation] joy and pride *1810.*
220 Sway] Soften me *1810.*   : are . . . both]. (*Pause.*) *Are* they *1810.*
221 Aye] Yes *1810.*   *ll.* 223–4 *not in 1810.*   225 My] O *1810.*

For ll. 232–59 *1810 substitutes four lines:*

> Of soul, the wheel that racks the heart, is heard,
> Nature, amidst her solitudes, recoils
> At the dread sound, nor knows what she repeats.
> The cities swell with it. The villager

260 Sweetens] Honeys *1810.*   children's] infants' *1810.*

[To Southey, who was puzzled by this line, Landor wrote: "The villager sweetened his children's lessons by giving them a story of fallen pride. This is the meaning."]

390

DRAMAS AND DRAMATIC SCENES

For ll. 261–358 *1810 substitutes five lines:*

The element we breathe will scatter it.
The ministers of heaven, presiding o'er them,
Breathe it! And none dares dream where it arose.
From prisons and from dungeons mortals hear
Expiring truth, nor curse repentant crime

ACT V, SCENE 5.

1 Speak] Pause *1810.*   2 hopes] hope *1810.*   3 tho'] though *1810.*
ll. 4–16 *not in 1810.*   *l.* 19 *not in 1810.*   20 Yes] O *1810.*
24 *after* thee *1810 has:*

—for I see again
My native land, and cover it with woe.

ll. 25–33 *not in 1810.*

P. 225. INES DE CASTRO AT CINTRA. To an imaginary conversation "Ines de Castro, Don Pedro and Doña Blanca", published in 1828, Landor appended the following note:

This is not the true history of Ines, who was murdered some time after.

Character is the business of the Dialogue: chronology must be contented to yield a little, in distant ages and countries. The adventures of Ines supply two fine subjects for tragedy. The first, when king Alphonso had resolved to murder her at Coimbra, and desisted from the resolution on seeing her beauty, and that of her children: the second, when the assassination was accomplishing. La Mothe * and others have composed a drama on Ines, and her story is the most interesting part in the *Lusiad* of Camoens. This distinguished and admirable poet was not felicitous in the development of character; which, whatever may be talked and repeated on the beautiful and the sublime, is the best and most arduous part of poetry. It is this which gives to Homer a large portion of his glory; it is this which sustains us half-stifled in the Socratic school of Euripides; and it is this which, even with a third of the poetry, would have elevated Shakespear immeasurably above all.

A portion of the 1828 conversation was in blank verse. In 1831 the metrical portion was recast, seven out of 28 ll. being omitted; the prose was turned into verse; and the whole, with variants and additions, brought more into accord with accepted history. In 1846 another scene was added. The 1828 conversation had ended with the murder of Ines, then represented as taking place when Pedro in defiance of Queen Blanca's threats would not forswear his love for Ines and marry Constantia. Historians, on the other hand, relate that in 1341, yielding to parental pressure, he did marry Constantia, who died four years later after giving birth to a son; that he and Ines were secretly married in 1354; and that she was murdered in 1355.

CHARACTERS.

Ines de Castro. Daughter of Don Pedro Fernandez de Castro "the Warrior".

Pedro. Son of Alfonso IV., "the Proud", King of Portugal; succeeded to the throne on his father's death in 1357, and died 1367.

Constantia. Daughter of Don Juan Manuel, Duke of Peñafiel; married Pedro 1341 and died 1345.

* *Inès de Castro,* tragedy by A. H. de La Motte, was produced at the Théâtre Français in 1723. [W.]

391

NOTES

Queen Blanca. By some authorities called Beatrix or Brites, Wife of King Alfonso IV. Mariana says she was a sister of Ferdinand IV of Castile and, when eight years old, was married to Alfonso before his accession to the throne. In 1828 Landor made her speak of Constantia, before that lady's marriage to Pedro, as her own daughter. The same relationship is implied more than once in the 1831 version; but Landor may have forgotten to correct these errors.

King Alfonso. See above. A speaker in Act III, interpolated 1846. Succeeded his father, Denis, in 1325.

P. 236. *ll.* 372–415. The metrical passage in the imaginary conversation, 1828, consists of 28 lines recurring with variants in 1831, and seven lines then omitted. In 1831 the recurring lines appear in order shown below:

1828 lines	1831 lines		1828 lines	1831 lines
1– 6	= 392–397		23–24	= 412–413
7–17	= 401–411		26–28	= 414–416
19–22	= 372–375		33–34	= 384–385

l. 17 *(1828)* = 411 *(1831) after* loved *1828 has, and 1831 omits:*

> Queen.   Sir, loose that hand . .
> *Ines.* And . . yes . . love too . . but only love not Ines

l. 24 *(1828)* = 413 *(1831) after* beauteousness *1828 has, and 1831 omits:*

> Where am I! in whose presence! . . but we part . .

l. 28 *(1828)* = 416 *(1831) after* before me *1828 has, and 1831 omits:*

> Again must I command you? loose that hand, sir;
> No transports here, no palm to breast or cross,
> Unless for grace and pardon; and methinks
> These things are best alone, or with the priest.

l. 34 *(1828)* = 385 *(1831) after* alone *1828 has, and 1831 omits:*

> Give me my hand. Oh! make me take it back.

Other variants are noted on pp. 236, 237. The rest of the 1828 conversation is in prose.

P. 242. INES DE CASTRO AT COIMBRA. *l.* 256 (= *Act V, l. 202 in 1846 ed.*). *After* Heaven. *1846 has 35 ll. of which all but the first were printed with minor variants in* ADDITIONS *1831, but could not be inserted in the present text, the directions given being ambiguous. The 1831* ADDITION, *with later variants, is given below:*

> [Queen.]   (*To* PEDRO *aside.*)
> Thou art perhaps more obstinate than she.
> I have my doubts . . rainy-eyed girls see double . .
> Toss on two pillows, and drop tears on each . .
> I would say nothing more . . I may be wrong,
> But other names than Pedro may have crept
> Among the curtains in Don Pedro's house.
> *Ines.* O may they ever! glorious names! Blest saints
> Of Paradise! have ye not watcht my sleep?

For stage direction and l. 1 1846 substitutes:

> Blanca. Heaven gives wide views, very wide views, to many

Have ye not given me thoughts of him, and hopes,
And visions, when I prayed you to protect   10
Him and his children, and that gracious queen
Who sees me not aright thro love of him,
Wishing him loftier aims and brighter joys.
   Queen. My doubts now darken: do not thine at this
Evasion?
   Pedro. O my Ines! sure the Blest
Are the more blest to share thy love with me,
And I to share it, as I do, with them.
   Queen. How the man raves! no stain, no spot in her!
Immaculate! beware! repeat the word
With those unholy lips, call her that name   20
Which only one of mortal race had ever . .
   Pedro. Lady! that one was meek no less than pure.
   Queen. So am I too, who suffer all this wrong,
This violence, this scoffing, this deceit,
From one like her, false, loathsome, dull, low-born,
Others know all; I know not half, nor would.
   Pedro. Hot lolling tongues bespatter fairest names
With foulest slurs: black shows not upon black.
   Queen. Well! let us hope! all may be right at last.
There are bad minds, Don Pedro, in the world,   30
As you must have observed.
   Pedro.   A glimpse or two.
   Queen. I did then wisely when I warned you both,
Tho 'tis a thankless office, as most are
Where we consume our days in doing good.

                               (*To* INES.)

Yet little as thou hast deserved of me, &c. &c.

    The heading prefixed in 1831 to this ADDITION indicates that it was
then meant to follow l. 221 of the present text, while the indicatory line
at the end corresponds to l. 240. Landor may have intended but forgot
to make room for the new passage by cancelling ll. 222–39, and when
revising the scene for the 1846 ed. have decided to retain those lines and
insert the ADDITION further on.

    P. 253. IPPOLITO DI ESTE. When Longmans declined in 1811 to publish
"Count Julian", Landor threw the MS. of another tragedy into the fire.
Two scenes of what he at first called "Ferrante and Giulio" were rescued
from the flames and, with emendations now impossible to detect, were
included under the title "Ippolito di Este" in "Gebir, Count Julian and
other poems", 1831. The plot appears to have been taken from Sis-
mondi's *Histoire des républiques italiennes*, but for some unknown reason
Landor represented Ferrante and not Giulio as Rosalba's favoured lover
and victim of Ippolito's hatred. According to E. A. Gardner (see his
Dukes and Poets in Ferrara) the lady called by Landor Rosalba was
Angela Borgia, a cousin of the more famous Lucrezia.

Between ll. 17–18 1846 inserts one line:
                 Alike to me art thou immaculate.
Stage direction after l. 34 om. 1846, 1876.   35 Yet . . . me]=*l. 240, 1831 ed.*

NOTES

P. 275. Two Dramatic Scenes. Scene II. Referring to the headline
" . . . in Epping Forest" Count D'Orsay wrote to Landor: "I think that
Henry the Eighth was at Richmond-on-the-Hill when Ann Boleyn was
beheaded. They say that he saw the flag which was erected in London
as soon as her head fell."

P. 279. Andrea of Hungary. Writing to Forster in the autumn of
1838 Landor told him that, having on the previous Saturday sent for
Mrs. Jameson's *Female Sovereigns*, he began, after Sunday tea, a drama;
and that by Monday morning above 170 verses were written. Within
a fortnight *Andrea of Hungary*, the first part of what presently became a
trilogy, was completed. *Giovanna of Naples*, the second part, was turned
out with the same celerity and, in 1839, both dramas were published in
one volume. *Fra Rupert*, the third part, followed in 1840.

"A horrible confounder of historic facts", as he himself admitted,
Landor paid little heed to dates and details given in Mrs. Jameson's
sketch of his heroine, in an anonymous work on which this was mainly
founded, or in other books he had read. According to the best authorities
(see *Joanna of Naples* and *Robert the Wise*, by St. Clair Baddeley)
Giovanna and Andrea, betrothed in childhood, were duly married in
1342; the bride's grandfather, King Robert, died January 19, 1343;
Giovanna was crowned in August, 1344; Andrea was murdered September 18, 1345. Landor's *Andrea of Hungary* opens in hour after the marriage ceremony. In Act II Giovanna speaks of the crown having been
placed on her brow. In Act V Andrea is styled "the bridegroom";
Giovanna is "our gracious queen espoused today"; and the drama ends
that very night with the murder of the bridegroom. Thus events to
which historians allot a good three years are in the drama supposed all
to occur during the space of less than twenty-four hours.

There is, however, one possible explanation of such deviation from
facts. The manuscript of *Andrea* was sent to Forster piecemeal to arrange
and, if he thought fit, to condense. He may have put the scenes in wrong
order and left out passages that would make the chronology less perplexing.

The table on the opposite page is based mainly on the genealogies given
by Mr. St. Clair Baddeley in *Queen Joanna I of Naples* (1893), and *Robert
the Wise and his heirs* (1897). It shows the relationship of most of the
chief persons in the trilogy. "Maria of Sicily", Boccaccio's "Fiammetta",
who does not appear in this pedigree, was King Robert's natural daughter
and is therefore wrongly described in the lists of characters as Giovanna's
half-sister.

DRAMAS AND DRAMATIC SCENES

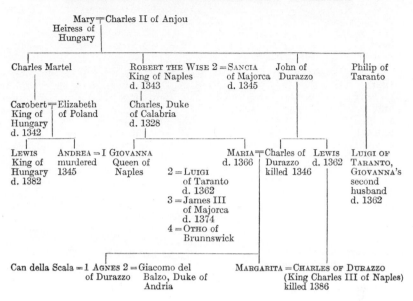

Mary⊤Charles II of Anjou
Heiress of
Hungary

Charles Martel

ROBERT THE WISE 2 = SANCIA   John of   Philip of
King of Naples   of Majorca Durazzo   Taranto
d. 1343   d. 1345

Carobert⊤Elizabeth   Charles, Duke
King of │ of Poland   of Calabria
Hungary │   d. 1328
d. 1342 │

LEWIS   ANDREA ⇒ I GIOVANNA   MARIA⊤Charles of LEWIS   LUIGI OF
King of   murdered Queen of   d. 1366 │ Durazzo d. 1362 TARANTO,
Hungary   1345   Naples   2 = LUIGI   killed 1346   GIOVANNA'S
d. 1382   of Taranto   second
d. 1362   husband
3 = James III   d. 1362
of Majorca
d. 1374
4 = OTHO of
Brunnswick

Can della Scala = 1 AGNES 2 = Giacomo del   MARGARITA = CHARLES OF DURAZZO
of Durazzo   Balzo, Duke of   (King Charles III of Naples)
Andria   killed 1386